CONTENTS

1 a traditional Tuscan stew

2 aerial view over Lucca

3 San Gimignano tower

4 Chianti's black rooster wine logo

5 Piazza del Campo, Siena

6 narrow road in the Val d'Orcia

DISCOVER
FLORENCE & BEYOND

Florence, the birthplace of the Renaissance, inspires with its orderly streets lined with yellow façades, its famous Renaissance art, and its romantic bridge crossing the Arno river. Justly famous for its glorious past, its invigorating present is just as enticing. As you explore,

let curiosity be your guide. Pedal a bike along the Arno, sip espresso at the counter of a coffee bar, and pause with the locals for a Negroni during *aperitivo* hour. Immerse yourself in the modern city, and its liveliness, diversity, and traditions may surprise you.

Florence gets most of the attention, but there's more to Tuscany than one stunning city, from Siena's shell-shaped square to Lucca's sturdy ramparts, to the soft, gentle hills that Romantic poets described as the entrance to heaven. Grapevines and olive trees line winding roads, where every town, it seems, is worthy of a detour. There are ancient pilgrim paths to tread and old roads that

beckon to be explored on a bicycle or Vespa. And when it comes to food, Tuscany can't be beat. Portions are generous, flavors are robust, and there's certainly no shortage of red wine to choose from.

More than just a gorgeous landscape, Tuscany is the birthplace of thousands of ideas that changed art and architecture forever. This is where Brunelleschi solved the 15th century's greatest engineering puzzle; where da Vinci contemplated flight; where Michelangelo worked magic with marble; and where Galileo contemplated the heavens. Once you've experienced Florence and Tuscany for yourself, you, too, may never see the world the same way again.

MY FAVORITE EXPERIENCES

1 Climbing to the top of the **Duomo** for views across Florence (page 41).

2 Savoring **Tuscan flavors**, from *pappa al Pomodoro* to surprising tripe sandwiches (page 74).

3 Enjoying Negroni cocktails during *aperitivo* **hour** (page 88).

>>>

4 Gazing at works by Leonardo da Vinci, Michelangelo, and Botticelli inside the **Uffizi** (page 51).

5 Waking up in a countryside *agriturismo* (page 120 and 232).

>>>

6 Hiking ancient pilgrim paths through pristine Tuscan countryside (page 196).

>>>

7 Getting up close and personal with **Michelangelo's *David*,** the world's most famous statue, at the Accademia in Florence (page 53).

8 **Exploring Tuscany on two wheels,** bicycle or Vespa (page 162).

9 **Tasting local wines** in Chianti and the hill towns of Tuscany (page 22).

EXPLORE
FLORENCE & BEYOND

Three days is enough time to get a good introduction to Florence. From there, there's no shortage of single and multi-day trips outside the city. Key considerations (in addition to your interests) are time and mode of transportation. **Pistoia**, **Lucca**, and **Pisa** can all be quickly reached by train and make good individual day destinations, or can be combined into longer excursions. **Siena** is also reachable by rail and a feasible day trip. **Volterra**, **San Gimignano**, **Chianti**, and the **Hill Towns** south of Siena are not accessible by train, so driving is the most convenient option for exploring these parts of Tuscany.

view of Florence

BEST OF FLORENCE

Three days will allow you to visit a number of Florence's major sights, get a taste of Tuscan cuisine, and take a bus out to Fiesole for sunset views of the city. Visit www.firenzeturismo.it to make reservations for the Accademia and Uffizi before arriving to the city. Reserving a table at Fiesole's La Reggia degli Etruschi at the end of this itinerary is also recommended.

DAY 1

Explore Florence's historic center on your first full day. (For a more detailed itinerary, see Florence on Day 1, page 36).

- See the *David,* climb to the top of the **Duomo,** and enjoy art at **Museo Nazionale del Bargello,** a tranquil alternative to the Uffizi.

- End your day sampling **Tuscan cuisine** at one of the *osteria* (restaurants) lining **Borgo la Croce.**

DAY 2

Spend day two exploring the Oltrarno neighborhood south of Florence's historic center. (For a more detailed itinerary, see Florence on Day 2, page 36).

- Hike to **Basilica San Miniato al Monte** for great views of Florence, visit local craft workshops below, and taste a tripe sandwich for lunch.

- Check out *Adam and Eve* inside the **Brancacci Chapel.**

- Get *aperitivo* started with a Negroni cocktail from one of the bars in **Piazza Santo Spirito.**

Ponte Vecchio, Florence

LUGGAGE STORAGE

If you're setting off on multiday trips from Florence, you may want to leave unneeded luggage in storage at the train station. **Luggage Storage** (Via dell'Albero 22, www.stowyourbags.com) is a private company that charges €14 a day for a standard size locker.

DAY 3

Experience Florence like a local (page 37) or continue sight-seeing, with a side trip out to Fie-sole for views over Florence.

- Get to the **Uffizi** early, before it gets crowded, and cross the **Ponte Vecchio** for fun (or to browse jewelry shops with a loved one).

- Walk up to **Museo San Marco** and see where monks lived, including one who was burned at the stake in Piazza della Signoria.

- In the afternoon, ride bus 7 (20 minutes) up to **Fiesole** and take a look at the town's Roman **amphitheater**. Enjoy the view outside **Convento di San Francisco,** the convent, and get a table on the terrace at **Reggia degli Etruschi** for dinner with a view.

PISTOIA-LUCCA-PISA

There's a lot more to Tuscany than Florence, and these three cities provide plenty of cultural and artistic perspective on the region. They also give cyclists a chance to get beyond city limits and explore aqueducts, riversides, and natural parks. Reserve your ticket for the Leaning Tower of Pisa 1-20 days in advance at www.opapisa.it.

All three of these cities are accessed by rail, making this itinerary possible without a car. Pack light, since you won't have a place to stow items when you're exploring Pisa en route to Lucca. (You can leave extra luggage in storage at the train station in Florence.)

DAY 1: FLORENCE TO PISTOIA AND LUCCA

- From Florence, catch an early train (30-50 minutes) to **Pistoia**. Trains depart Florence's Santa Maria Novella station hourly. No reservations are necessary; just get a ticket and go.

- The train will drop you off just a 15-minute walk from the historic center. Climb the **Campanile** bell tower, then enjoy a traditional

medieval bell tower and gothic Saint John Baptistry in Pistoia

aerial view of the Cathedral of Pisa in Italy

lunch at **Locanda del Capitano del Popolo.**

- Head back to the station and buy a ticket to **Lucca** (45-60 minutes). Settle into your hotel, then rent a hike and ride around the city's ramparts, or ride the 4-kilometer (one-way) **Parco del Nottolini** trail next to the old aqueduct.

- Have dinner at **Gigi Trattoria** in Lucca before turning in for the night.

Piazza dell'Anfiteatro, Lucca

DAY 2: LUCCA TO PISA

- In the morning, take a leisurely stroll down the elegant streets of Lucca. Discover **Piazza dell'Anfiteatro,** the cutest square in Tuscany.

- Have lunch at Lucca's **Trattoria Canuleia** in a garden away from the tourist traps.

- Get on the next train to **Pisa** (30 minutes), and don't be late for your appointment to climb the famous **Leaning Tower.** You get 30 minutes at the top.

- At dusk, walk the city's narrow ramparts, **Mura di Pisa,** for a view of the city from above.

- Follow the sound of students gathering socially in the squares around Borgo Stretto and get a taste of Pisa's **nightlife** yourself. Drinking in the streets is a summertime ritual for many locals.

17

DAY 3: PISA BACK TO FLORENCE

- Rent a bike and **cycle around the city's walls.**

- Circle back for another look at the **Piazza dei Miracoli** (Square of Miracles) and have lunch at **Osteria Rossini** in a quieter square away from the masses. Board the next train back to Florence (50-70 minutes).

CHIANTI-SAN GIMIGNANO-SIENA

Tuscany owes much of its legendary status to these three destinations. This rural itinerary (best enjoyed by car) gets better around every curve. There's endless wine, magnificent vineyards surrounded by idyllic landscapes, and gastronomic treats waiting in each romantic town along the way. Make advance reservations for Castello di Verrazzano winery.

DAY 1: FLORENCE TO CASTELLINA IN CHIANTI AND RADDA IN CHIANTI

- Head out early from Florence on the **SR222 south** to Chianti.

- Stop at **Castello di Verrazzano** (reservations required), an historic winery, then continue driving to Castellina.

- After arriving in Castellina, park your car, then order *pici* pasta at an *osteria* in town, like romantic **Ristorante Sotto le Volte**, located under medieval vaulted passageways.

San Gimignano skyline

TRAVEL LIKE A LOCAL

If you want to experience Florence and the surrounding countryside like a local, you have to think less about monuments and museums and more about simple pleasures like lunch, conversation, and *aperitivo*. Traveling like them also means respecting culture. You may have to kiss someone on the cheek, resist leaving a tip (anything more than €5 labels you as a tourist), and get up the nerve to taste a tripe sandwich, but trying new things is fun and why you came to Florence in the first place.

- **Take a pre-dinner stroll.** Much of Florence's center is pedestrianized, and the pre-dinner stroll is a ritual that takes place along Borgo la Croce, San Frediano, and the Arno. When locals tire they linger on benches or church steps, where conversations go on until the late hours.

- **Ride a bike.** Florentines ride bicycles everywhere, and cycling is a green way to get around the city and surrounding countryside. Renting or using the city's bikeshare program is easy and once you get a handle of the local disdain of breaks you'll be ready to explore destinations like Fiesole, where mountain bike enthusiasts converge on weekends.

- **Take a long lunch.** Sitting down for lunch is a Tuscan tradition. Adapt to the pace, unless it's extremely slow, in which case, feel free to get as angry as the locals do.

- **Skip the S&P.** The Italian philosophy is that food is served the way it's meant to be eaten, so you won't find salt, pepper, olive oil, or Parmesan on tables.

- **Order espresso at the counter.** It's not only cheaper than sitting at a table; it's the local way.

- **Use local water fountains.** Water here is free, and refilling containers is a green way to travel.

- **Avoid spending money in tourist areas.** Turn a corner and find better deals on everything, from snacks and drinks to souvenirs.

- **Take a break.** Nothing important happens on weekdays between 2pm and 4pm, when many stores close and most Tuscans remain indoors. It's also when locals take their summertime naps and awake refreshed, ready to start the day all over again.

- Visit **Rocca,** the town's fortress, before departing for Radda, 13 kilometers (8mi) east along the SR429 regional road.

- After arriving in Radda, **rent a Vespa** from Tuscany Scooter Rental and explore the Tuscan countryside.

- Spend the night at **Podere Terreno** *agriturismo* and wake up with a wonderful view.

DAY 2: RADDA TO SAN GIMIGNANO AND SIENA

- Have breakfast at the *agriturismo*, then hit the road towards San Gimignago, 45 kilometers (28mi) west back along the SR429 and onto the SP51. The drive takes about an hour.

- Park in one of the town's lots (€2/ hour) and climb **Casa Campatelli,** one of the last remaining tower houses in San Gimignano.

WHERE TO GO FROM FLORENCE

Destination	Why Go	How To Get There from Florence	How Long to Stay
Fiesole	hikes; sunset views over Florence	Bus (20 minutes); walking (60-90 minutes)	half a day
Pistoia	mini version of Florence (without the crowds) halfway between Florence and Lucca	Train (30-50 minutes)	half a day
Lucca	Renaissance ramparts and city cycling	Train (1.5-2 hours)	1-2 days
Pisa	Leaning Tower; beach access	Train (1 hour)	1 day
San Gimignano	tower houses; wine; atmosphere	Car (1 hour)	1-2 days
Volterra	shopping; Etruscan artifacts; hill-town atmosphere	Car (1.5 hours)	1-2 days
Chianti	wine-tasting	Car (45 minutes to Greve, the region's gateway)	1-3 days
Siena	stunning town with famous square; gateway to Tuscan Hill Towns	Train (1.5 hours)	2 days
Tuscan Hill Towns	wineries; monasteries; tranquility	Car (2 hours to Montalcino)	1-3 days

- Circle the city's **ring walls** on foot, and visit **Palagetto** winery, a 10-minute walk from town.

- Set off for **Siena,** 42 kilometers (26mi) south along the Firenze-Siena highway, and park for the night.

- Visit the **Duomo,** which is second to none in terms of craftsmanship and beauty, then climb **Torre del Mangia** for sunset views.

- Spend the evening at a small *enoteca* making friends and falling in love with Tuscan food.

DAY 3: SIENA TO PANZANO, AND BACK TO FLORENCE

- Sample local pastries at **Pasticceria Bini** outside the center of town, then wander Sienna's Renaissance streets around **Piazza del Campo,** and enjoy some souvenir shopping on **Via di Città.**

- Return towards Florence by driving north on the SR222 road. After about an hour, make a rest stop in Panzano for the local steak specialty at **Officina della Bistecca.**

- Make it back to Florence in time for *aperitivo.*

SIENA AND TUSCAN HILL TOWNS

Siena is a cultural dynamo filled with Renaissance monuments that are second to none. It's also an ideal starting point for exploring the stunning hill towns and magnificent wineries south of the city. For this itinerary, take a train to Siena, then rent a car there to explore the hill towns to the south.

EXPLORE

DAY 1: FLORENCE TO SIENA

- Take the train from Florence to Siena (90 minutes), and spend a day (or two, if you have the time) exploring the city. For the best ways to spend your time in Siena, see page 247.

DAYS 2-3: SIENA TO MONTALCINO AND PIENZA; PIENZA TO MONTEPULCIANO

- Rent a car in Siena's train station at **Siena Rent,** then begin your drive south to the hill towns. For a detailed two-day itinerary of this region, see page 264. Highlights include **tastings at local wineries** and **wine cellars, sunset views** across Tuscany, and a half-day **cycling tour** with panoramic views.

Montepulciano at sunset

WINE TASTING IN TUSCANY

You can learn a lot about wine in Florence, but there's something raw and earthy about drinking it at the source. There are two ways to do this: Join a wine tour and follow a preordained path (page 217) or set out on your own, which is the adventurous option. The best areas to explore are **Chianti** and the **Tuscan Hill Towns** of Montalcino, Pienza, and Montepulciano.

Chianti's famous Sangiovese grapes

TASTING AT WINERIES

Almost as soon as you leave the Florence city limits, you'll see signs pointing to wineries. Dozens are clustered around the SR222 in Chianti, between Florence and Siena, and it's impossible not to stumble on one. South of Siena, dozens of vineyards are located within sight of Montalcino, Pienza, and Montepulciano. A few can be reached on foot from nearby towns and many more are within a short drive. The majority of Tuscan wineries are equipped with tasting rooms where you can sample and purchase wine. Many also offer organized tours, and some provide dining and accommodation facilities.

Wineries are often family owned, without dedicated hospitality staff, so it's useful to call ahead and reserve tours rather than just showing up. Simple tastings are often free, while more elaborate cellar visits have a fee of around €10-25, depending on length and the quality and number of wines to be sampled.

After visiting a winery it's always tempting to buy. If you decide to ship a case or two home, make sure all transport and duty fees are included up front or you could face some expensive surprises later.

If you're driving, remember that the legal blood alcohol limit in Italy is 0.5, which is lower than in the US and UK (both 0.8). Most wineries are just a short taxi ride—or, in some cases, a short walk—from the nearest town.

TASTING AT WINE BARS AND CELLARS

Another way to taste local wines is to swing by an *enoteca* (wine bar) in any of the towns in Chianti or those south of Siena. The good thing about wine bars is, unlike restaurants that close after lunch, they remain open and you can pop in whenever you like for a glass of wine, *taglieri* (cheese and cold cut platter), and often more substantial first course dishes. Most are causal, and you'll be given a warm welcome whether or not you can tell a Chianti from a Chianti Classico.

The Tuscan Hill Town of Montepulciano has an especially high concentration of *cantinas* (wine cellars), where wine from local vineyards is served. You can visit a number of these in town. Tastings are inexpensive, and there's often a shop onsite where bottles can be purchased.

BEFORE YOU GO

WHEN TO GO

Florence is one of the most visited cities in the world. Deciding when to go will have a significant impact on your experience.

SUMMER

Summer sees a dramatic increase in arrivals, with July and August the apex of the tourist season. Airlines and hotels take advantage of demand to raise their rates, and temperatures rise to sweltering. Avoid these months if you can. If you can't, book ahead and purchase sightseeing passes like the Firenzecard (Florence) and combination tickets in smaller towns to speed entry to monuments. The majority of Italians take their vacations in August, which means many small businesses close and it can feel like tourists outnumber locals.

One advantage of arriving in summer is how many events are planned in Florence and throughout Tuscany. The cultural calendar is full of outdoor concerts, festivals, and street fairs that make a visit even more animated than usual.

SPRING AND FALL

Late spring and early fall are ideal times to visit. May and September are especially pleasant. Not only are there fewer visitors but temperatures are mild, daylight is long, and precipitation low. Hotels charge midseason

farmhouse in the Val d'Orcia

rates and locals are engaged in their usual routines. Autumn is also harvest season, when food-related *sagra* (festivals) are held and newly picked grapes transformed into wine, making September-October the most interesting season to visit wineries in the Tuscan Hill Towns. Cantina Aperta (Open Cantina, last Sun. in May) is the best time for wine lovers in Chianti. This is when wineries open their doors and let anyone sample their wines.

WINTER

November and December are the rainiest months and can be very cold in Florence. Christmas and New Year festivities attract a wave of visitors over the holidays, as do *Carnevale* and Easter. Apart from the holiday season, accommodation and airfare

Christmas in Florence

are more affordable in winter and accessing popular sights like the Uffizi in January takes minutes rather than hours.

GETTING THERE

Florence's airport, Aeroporto di Firenze-Peretola (FLR, Via del Termine 11, tel. 055/30615, www. aeroporto.firenze.it), has no direct flights from anywhere outside Europe. There are regularly scheduled flights to and from London, Birmingham, Edinburgh, and other UK destinations with British Airways (www. britishairways.com), City Jet (www. cityjet.com), and Vueling (www. vueling.com). A new runway and renovated arrivals hall are projected to open in 2020 with the aim of developing intercontinental routes.

Tuscany's busiest airport is Aeroporto di Pisa-San Giusto, an hour from Florence by bus, train, or car. There are few direct flights from North America, and none from Australia, New Zealand, or South Africa to Pisa but many connecting flights via other European cities. Ryanair (www.ryanair.com), Easyjet (www.easyjet.com), and British Airways (www.britishairways.com) operate daily direct flights from London.

WHAT YOU NEED TO KNOW

Currency: Euro (€)
Conversion rate: €1=$1.14 USD; €1=£0.88GBP
Entry Requirements: E.U. citizens can travel visa-free to Italy with a valid identity card or passport. The U.K.'s exit from the EU may affect travelers from Britain. Travelers from the United States, Canada, Australia, and New Zealand do not need a visa for visits of less than 90 days, but a passport is required. For travelers from South Africa, a visa is required. There is a fee, and the application process takes two weeks.
Emergency number: 118
Time Zone: GMT+1
Electrical system: 220-volt system. (Plugs have two round prongs.)
Opening hours: Small businesses often close between 1-3pm. Many shops close on Sundays and restaurants and museums are not usually open on Mondays.

BUDGETING

Espresso: €1
Beer: €3 (small), €5 (large)
Glass of wine: €3-5
Sandwich: €3-5
Lunch or dinner: €25-35 per person
Hotel: €90-150 d
Agriturismo: €80-120 d
Wine tour: €15-30 per person
Bike rental: €3-5 per hour, €15 per day
Car rental: €70-100 per day for a mid-size vehicle
Gasoline/petrol: €1.90 per liter (€1.75 per liter for diesel)
Parking: €1 per hour
One-way train fare: €5-10 from Florence to cities such as Pistoia, Lucca, Pisa, and Siena

GETTING AROUND

TRAVELING BETWEEN TOWNS

Train is the most convenient way of reaching cities near Florence such as Pistoia, Lucca, Pisa, and Siena. Reservations are not required and there are dozens of daily departures to each of the destinations, which can be reached in under 2 hours. Tickets are cheap and stations are located near the historic centers.

Chianti and the Hill Towns to the south have no rail connections and often require long bus rides. A car is convenient for visiting these out-of-the-way towns, especially since many are small and can be explored in a couple of hours. Wineries and many sights are located beyond town walls, which makes cars very useful. Another fun option is renting a scooter from Florence, although this is best for exploring Chianti as long journeys on two wheels are uncomfortable and slow.

GETTING AROUND EACH CITY

Once you've arrived at your destination the chances of requiring a car or

Volterra

public transportation is low as even the biggest city of Florence can be navigated on foot. Bikes are also immensely popular with residents across the region and rental shops are easy to find in Lucca, Pisa, and even in smaller towns.

WHAT TO PACK

Beware of overpacking, especially if you're visiting several destinations and will be unpacking and repacking frequently. It's probably best to leave expensive watches and jewelry at home. Also, email yourself any important credit card codes or customer service numbers as backup in case you lose your wallet.

Luggage: A wheeled suitcase makes getting around airports and to hotels easier. Backpacks or handbags are good for daily excursions and should have zippers to dissuade pickpockets. A money belt can be useful for storing cash and valuables.

Paperwork: You'll need your passport and a driver's license if you plan on renting a moped or car. An international permit is not required but can prevent confusion with local authorities. ID is also usually required when borrowing audio and video guides at museums.

Clothing, shoes, and accessories: Select comfortable clothes that can be mixed and matched. Layers are important in spring and fall when mornings are chilly and temperatures vary throughout the day. Formal clothes may be necessary if you plan on any fine dining or clubbing. Remember that knees and shoulders must be covered when entering religious buildings. Sunglasses are essential during the summer, especially if you'll be doing any driving, and hats are useful. You'll probably do a lot of walking, so bring at least two comfortable pairs of shoes.

crossing the Ponte di Mezzo bridge in Pisa

Toiletries and medication: A high-SPF sunscreen is vital during summer. If you take medication, make sure to bring enough and have a copy of your prescription in case you need a refill. If you forget something, pharmacies in Italy are useful for replacing lost toiletries or picking up aspirin. Most hotels provide hair dryers, but if you're staying in a B&B or a hostel you may want to pack one. It should be adaptable to Italy's 220 voltage. Hand sanitizer is useful for removing bacteria while on the go.

Electronics: Voltage is 220 volts in Italy and plugs have two round prongs. Electronic devices that need recharging call for an adapter, which all U.S., U.K., and non-EU travelers will require. Simple U.S.-to-European travel adapters are available for under $10 at electronic stores and double that at airports. They're harder to find in Italy but many hotels supply them to guests free of charge. An extra memory card is useful for digital photographers and a portable battery charger can prevent phones and other devices from going dark.

Binoculars are helpful for observing church façades and Tuscan landscapes.

DAILY REMINDERS

Many sights (monasteries in particular) are only open mornings, while others close for lunch or on **Mondays.**

Museums outside of Florence tend to have **seasonal hours,** closing a little earlier from November to March. Check opening times in advance to avoid disappointment.

Ticket offices stop selling tickets an hour before closing and metal detectors or some other form of security is common at entrances in Florence. Traveling light is advisable but cloakrooms and lockers are often available.

SIGHTSEEING PASSES

There are a few sightseeing passes to consider in Florence. Smaller towns may offer combination tickets, which are covered in each chapter.

The **Firenzecard** (€72, www.firenzecard.it) is the most comprehensive pass available and a convenient way to visit the city. It is valid 72 hours and allows priority access to 72 monuments and museums, including the Duomo, major churches, gardens, towers, and the Uffizi. Just look for the Firenzecard sign and have your card ready to be scanned at each sight. It also provides Wi-Fi access. Even on a two-day visit it can be worth the investment, especially in summer when tourism is at its peak and you can skip long lines waiting to enter the Ufizzi.

Piazza del Duomo is the religious heart of Florence and contains six of the city's most popular sights: the Cattedrale di Santa Maria del Fiore, Cupola di Brunelleschi, Campanile di Giotto, Battistero, Cripta, and Museo dell'Opera. All six attractions can be accessed with **Il Grande Museo del Duomo Card** (€18) available online or from the **ticket office** (Piazza San Giovanni 7, tel. 055/230-2885, www.museumflorence.com, daily 8:15am-6:30pm) opposite the northern entrance of the baptistery. If you purchase the Duomo Card at the ticket office you may want to pick it up the day before to save time. Once you've entered the first monument you have 24 hours to visit the others and aren't allowed into the same monument twice. You'll also need to reserve a 30-minute time slot for visiting the cupola. Waiting until the last minute to do so in July or August may reduce your options. The Duomo Card is a good bet if you're not planning on visiting any museums or only have a short time in the city. A **combined ticket** (www.uffizi.it/en/tickets, €38)

KEY RESERVATIONS

IN FLORENCE

It's easy to spend more time waiting in line than actually visiting the iconic monuments of Florence. It's therefore vital to make reservations for the sights you intend to visit, or purchase a **Firenzecard**, which provides quick entry. Advance reservations for many sights, including the **Accademia** and **Uffizi**, can be made on the city's official website www.firenzeturismo.it. Visitor numbers to the **campanile** bell tower and **cupola** are limited to avoid overcrowding on the panoramic terraces, and access to the latter is by designated time slots booked online or at the ticket office.

OUTSIDE FLORENCE

The **Leaning Tower of Pisa** must also be reserved at least one day in advance and the half-hour slots fill up fast in summer. Most **wine tours** should be booked ahead of time, although many wineries provide on-the-spot **tastings** during opening hours. Reservations also ensure getting a table at popular restaurants and bikes or Vespas at small rental shops with a limited number of vehicles.

Piazza del Duomo

is also available for visiting the Uffizi, Palazzo Pitti, and Boboli gardens. It's valid three days, can be purchased online or directly at the Uffizi ticket office, and allows speedier entry.

The **Firenzecard+** (€7) is a transportation card that provides single access to the city's bus and tram lines for 72 hours once activated. It also offers 10-15 percent discounts to selected restaurants, shops, and touristic services. Accompanied minors travel free of charge on Florence's public transportation network.

FLORENCE

Firenze, as locals call their city, has a justified marble chip on its shoulder. After all, this was the cradle of the Renaissance, where civilization was given an injection of creativity after centuries of artistic stagnation.

Visiting Florence means walking the same streets that Dante Alighieri, Leonardo da Vinci, Machiavelli, Galileo Galilei, and many of history's most influential writers, artists, and thinkers once walked. Today, the Ponte Vecchio still stands, and the Uffizi remains the place to go for art. On the other side of town, Michelangelo's

HIGHLIGHTS

✪ **DUOMO:** Rising above the city is a monumental reminder of the Renaissance. Climb inside the dome to see how its unique structure defies gravity (page 41).

✪ **BARGELLO NATIONAL MUSEUM:** One of the least crowded museums in Florence offers a look at Donatello's *David*, ancient military hardware, and the city's first police headquarters (page 48).

✪ **UFFIZI GALLERY:** What started as the private collection of the Medici family is now accessible to all. Discover how Florentine artists added a realistic dimension to art and transformed painting forever (page 51).

✪ **ACCADEMIA:** It takes a special kind of genius to make marble life-like. Michelangelo's statue of *David* lives up to its reputation and is even more impressive in person (page 53).

✪ **HIKING TO BASILICA SAN MINIATO AL MONTE:** This church marks the highest point in Florence and provides undisturbed views of the skyline. Take the quiet back route up the hillside to avoid the crowds (page 67).

✪ **GELATO:** There are 136 *gelaterie* (gelato shops) in Florence. Sample as many as possible to find a favorite (page 80).

✪ **ITALIAN COFFEE:** Coffee is taken very seriously in Florence, and the city's contribution to espresso-making helped define caffeine history (page 84).

✪ *APERITIVO* **BARS:** Never skip *aperitivo* (happy hour). Order a local Negroni cocktail accompanied by light snacks and make a relaxed transition from afternoon to evening (page 88).

David waits to be examined, and Brunelleschi's majestic dome is never far from view.

Museums and basilicas aren't the only attractions. Florence gradually seduces with its clean, well-ordered streets and pleasant yellow façades. Beauty is everywhere in this city. Many old towers and lavish homes as well as large portions of the defensive walls are still standing. There are secluded monasteries and chapels to explore, where a little curiosity leads to unexpected discoveries. The city hasn't lost its creative touch, either (although the Renaissance will always be a hard act to follow). Artisans pound away on the backstreets of the Oltrarno neighborhood, and the wallets sold along Via de' Tornabuoni are hard to resist.

Discovering Florence also means getting to know its inhabitants. Florentines may be more reserved than their Roman cousins, but they are always ready to talk about their city and remain as devoted to it as the Medici family, Florence's famed patrons of the arts. Their pride is visible in workshops, markets, and squares where young and old congregate daily. It can be heard on summer nights when music echoes down the streets on both sides of the Arno, and tasted at the *trattorie* faithfully serving traditional *pappa al pomodoro* and *ribollita*. Experiencing this side of Florence is a lot easier than getting into the Uffizi—and equally satisfying.

HISTORY

Florence's history is a long one, and it involves the usual suspects. There were once Etruscans here, preceded by Iron Age tribes. The settlement along the Arno was one of the only ones in the region on flat terrain. It provided a natural funnel for traffic coming down from the nearby mountains to the north. The sea was also close, and the Mediterranean opened up markets for wool merchants and other trades that brought wealth to the town. With wealth came leisure and with leisure came art. The town's craftsmen became the best in the world, and fine jewelers still line the Ponte Vecchio. It was only a small jump from creating beautiful ornaments to creating beautiful sculptures, frescoes, and eventually entire buildings.

The greatest geniuses of Italy—Giotto, Dante, Machiavelli, Brunelleschi, Michelangelo, Donatello, Raphael, and so on—resided in or had some connection with Florence. With minds like these and a wealthy political class, the result was explosive. They didn't call it the Renaissance then; to them, revitalizing the Western world was simply business as usual.

Orientation

The historic center of Florence is compact and flat, making walking or cycling the best way of getting around the city. The only time you may want to consider hopping a bus or hailing a taxi is on the climb to San Miniato al Monte, which is the steepest part of the city.

Florence's historic center, or *centro storico,* is relatively small. Located north of the Arno, it is split into four neighborhoods (Duomo, Santa Maria Novella, San Marco, and Santa Croce). This is where the Romans originally founded the city, influential families like the Medici built imposing *palazzi,* and many Florentines still live and work today. The Duomo, visible from nearly every angle of the city, makes getting lost difficult. The Arno River also helps navigation and creates a distinct divide.

There are a handful of bridges that connect the two sides of the city, but Ponte Vecchio is by far the most recognizable. The bridge is crowded with visitors en route to or from Palazzo Pitti and is a convenient way to discover the city's lesser-known neighborhoods.

DUOMO AND AROUND

Most of Florence's major sights, including the Uffizi and Palazzo Vecchio, are located around the Duomo. There is a constant flow of visitors in this neighborhood at the heart of the historic center that's lined with tall buildings and impressive stone façades. Piazza della Repubblica,

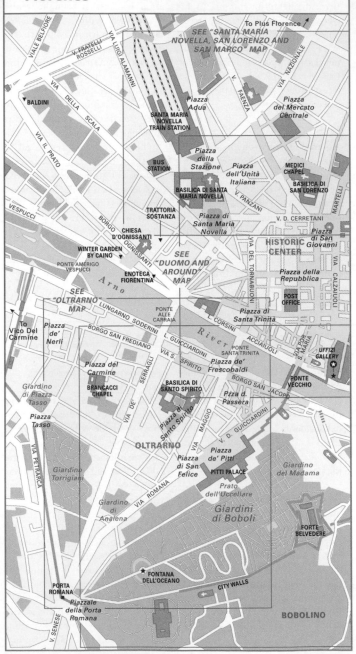

Florence

SEE "SANTA MARIA
NOVELLA, SAN LORENZO AND
SAN MARCO" MAP

To Plus Florence

VIALE BELFIORE

V. FRATELLI
ROSSELLI

VIA LUIGI ALAMANNI

V. FAENZA

VIA NAZIONALE

VIA DELLA SCALA

BALDINI

Piazza
Adua

Piazza
del Mercato
Centrale

VIA IL PRATO

SANTA MARIA
NOVELLA
TRAIN STATION

VESPUCCI

BORGO D'OGNISSANTI

BUS
STATION

Piazza
della
Stazione

Piazza
dell'Unità
Italiana

MEDICI
CHAPEL

BASILICA DI
SAN LORENZO

V. PANZANI

MARTELLI

BASILICA DI SANTA
MARIA NOVELLA

TRATTORIA
SOSTANZA

Piazza di
Santa Maria
Novella

V. D. CERETANI

CHIESA
D'OGNISSANTI

Piazza
di San
Giovanni

HISTORIC
CENTER

WINTER GARDEN
BY CAINO

SEE
"DUOMO AND
AROUND"
MAP

VIA DEL TORNABUONI

VIA CALZAIUOLI

PONTE AMERIGO
VESPUCCI

ENOTECA
FIORENTINA

Arno

SEE
"OLTRARNO"
MAP

LUNGARNO SODERINI

Piazza della
Repubblica

POST
OFFICE

PONTE
ALLE
CARRAIA

L. CORSINI

Piazza di
Santa Trinità

To
Vico Del
Carmine

Piazza
de' Nerli

BORGO SAN FREDIANO

L. GUICCIARDINI

River

ACCIAIUOLI

PONTE
SANTA TRINITA

VIA S. SPIRITO

Piazza de'
Frescobaldi

L. CORSINI

VIA POR S. MARIA

UFFIZI
GALLERY

Piazza del
Carmine

BRANCACCI
CHAPEL

VIA DE' SERRAGLI

BASILICA DI
SANTO SPIRITO

BORGO SAN JACOPO

PONTE
VECCHIO

Piazza di
Santo Spirito

Pzza d.
Passera

Giardino
di Piazza
Tasso

Piazza
Tasso

OLTRARNO

VIA MAGGIO

V. D. GUICCIARDINI

VIA PETRARCA

Piazza
di San
Felice

Piazza
de' Pitti

PITTI PALACE

Giardino
del Madama

Giardino
Torrigiani

VIA ROMANA

Prato
dell'Uccellare

Giardino
di
Analena

Giardini
di Boboli

FORTE
BELVEDERE

PORTA
ROMANA

FONTANA
DELL'OCEANO

CITY WALLS

Piazzale
della Porta
Romana

V. SENESE

BOBOLINO

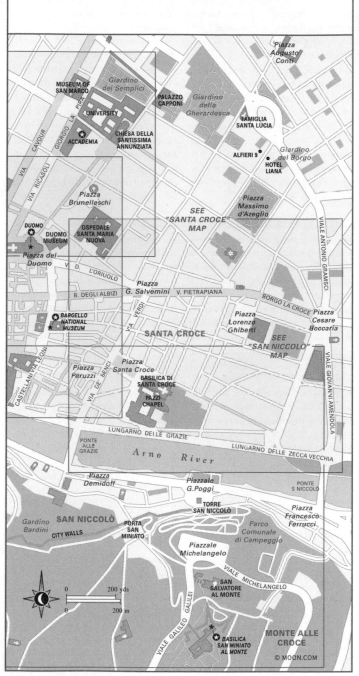

Piazza
Augusto
Conti

MUSEUM OF
SAN MARCO

Giardino
dei Semplici

PALAZZO
CAPPONI

Giardino
della
Gherardesca

UNIVERSITY

FAMIGLIA
SANTA LUCIA

CHIESA DELLA
SANTISSIMA
ANNUNZIATA

★ ACCADEMIA

Giardino
del Borgo

ALFIERI 9

HOTEL
LIANA

VIA CAVOUR

VIA RICASOLI

GIORGIO LA PIRA

Piazza
Brunelleschi

SEE
"SANTA CROCE"
MAP

Piazza
Massimo
d'Azeglio

DUOMO
★ DUOMO
MUSEUM

OSPEDALE
SANTA MARIA
NUOVA

VIALE ANTONIO GRAMSCI

Piazza del
Duomo

V. D. L'ORIUOLO

B. DEGLI ALBIZI

Piazza
G. Salvemini   V. PIETRAPIANA

BORGO LA CROCE

Piazza
Cesare
Boccaria

★ BARGELLO
NATIONAL
MUSEUM

V.A VERDI

Piazza
Lorenzo
Ghiberti

SANTA CROCE

SEE
"SAN NICCOLÒ"
MAP

CASTELLANI LEONI

Piazza
Peruzzi

VIA DE' BENCI

Piazza
Santa Croce

BASILICA DI
SANTA CROCE

PAZZI
CHAPEL

VIALE GIOVANNI AMENDOLA

LUNGARNO DELLE GRAZIE

PONTE
ALLE
GRAZIE

LUNGARNO DELLE ZECCA VECCHIA

Arno River

Piazza
Demidoff

Piazzale
G. Poggi

PONTE
S NICCOLÒ

TORRE
SAN NICCOLÒ

Piazza
Francesco
Ferrucci

Gardino
Bardini

SAN NICCOLÒ

CITY WALLS

PORTA
SAN
MINIATO

Parco
Comunale
di Campeggio

Piazzale
Michelangelo

VIALE MICHELANGELO

0   200 yds

0   200 m

SAN
SALVATORE
AL MONTE

VIALE GALILEO GALILEI

★ BASILICA
SAN MINIATO
AL MONTE

MONTE ALLE
CROCE

© MOON.COM

with its cafés and merry-go-round, is the geographical center and the largest open space where the Roman Forum and later the Jewish Ghetto once stood. Much of the Duomo area is pedestrian, making it easy to browse the elegant shops and covered market where leather belts, wallets, and bags are displayed daily and tourists rub the nose of a bronze boar for good luck. Many of the city's most expensive hotels are located here and summer concerts are regularly scheduled in Piazza della Signoria.

SANTA MARIA NOVELLA

Santa Maria Novella lies on the western side of the historic center and is the first neighborhood most visitors enter. The main train station, bus depot, and tram terminal are located here and it's busy throughout the day. The main attraction is the Basilica di Santa Maria Novella with its secluded monastery and smaller churches like Chiesa di Ognissanti where Boticelli is buried and you can get a glimpse of a stunning *Last Supper* fresco. Buildings are less grand than those near the Duomo to the east, shops cater to locals, and simple *trattorie* are likely to be filled with residents rather than tourists. Being near the train station means there are many hotels, hostels, and *pensione,* although these tend to fall into the lower price categories and offer few amenities other than a comfortable bed and a convenient location. Further west along the banks of the Arno lies Parco Ciascine, the city's largest park.

SAN LORENZO
AND SAN MARCO

San Lorenzo is south of San Marco and centered around the church of the same name that's surrounded by vibrant food and leather markets. Mercato Centrale, the city's largest covered market, is full of vegetable stands, gourmet shops, and historic eateries where tripe sandwiches and other local delicacies are prepared daily. The streets outside are lined with hundreds of leather kiosks and sellers from all over the world. There are plenty of restaurants in the area, and the second floor of the market is a popular food court. It's not all chaos and commerce in San Marco or San Lorenzo: The farther north you walk the more residential and quieter things get.

San Marco forms a triangle north of the Duomo that was once delimitated on two sides by the old city walls and is now bordered by wide avenues built at the end of the 19th century when the city outgrew its medieval limits. This is where Florence's most famous family, the Medici, lived, prayed, and are buried. It's also where the statue of *David* was moved when the town's leaders decided it was too valuable to leave outside and the streets around Galleria dell'Accademia are often jammed with visitors waiting to view Michelangelo's colossal work.

SANTA CROCE

Santa Croce is one of the liveliest and best-preserved sections of the city. It forms the eastern end of the historic center and is full of maze-like medieval alleys, bars attracting foreign drinkers, cheap eateries, and long pedestrian streets like Borgo la Croce where locals take their evening stroll. Life goes on here with little concern for the monuments only minutes away, and university students gather in the small squares or inside the city's second-largest covered market where Trattoria da

Rocco has been satisfying stomachs for over three decades. Michelangelo is buried nearby inside **Basilica Santa Croce,** and you can visit the house he left to his nephew a few blocks away at **Casa Buonari** or discover what a Renaissance residence looked like at the **Horne Museum**. Continue east to reach the city's historic soccer stadium or cross the Ponte alle Grazie and discover another side of Florence.

OLTRARNO

When the Romans founded Florence they set up camp along the flat northern banks of the river and that decision forever influenced the city. Oltrarno, on the southern bank, means "beyond the Arno," and includes the Santo Spirito and **San Niccolò** neighborhoods. Both developed later than the historic center, and

thus are noticeably quieter areas that often get overlooked. The neighborhood can be reached on foot from the historic center by way of the Ponte alle Grazie, Ponte Vecchio, or Ponte Santa Trinita bridges. The main attractions are **Palazzo Pitti** and the hillside views from **Piazzale Michelangelo** and **San Miniato al Monte.** The village-like atmosphere is ideal for seeking refuge from the masses, browsing for antiques, and enjoying Florentine street food. Here you can wander past medieval walls, up deserted paths overlooking olive groves, and through ornate gardens that remain pleasantly cool during the summer. Down below, in squares like **Piazza Santo Spirito** and the neighborhood's principle thoroughfare of **Borgo San Frediano,** are bars and restaurants that fill up with locals until the late hours.

view of Florence from Piazzale Michelangelo

Itinerary Ideas

FLORENCE ON DAY 1

Spend your first day exploring Florence's historic center. Visit www.
firenzeturismo.it to make reservations for the Accademia and Uffizi before
arriving to the city.

1 Fortify with a coffee and breakfast fare at **Ditta Artigianale,** located
near the Duomo.

2 Head to **Galleria dell'Accademia** before the crowds arrive to admire
Michelangelo's larger-than-life *David.*

3 From the Accademia, it's a short stroll to the **Duomo.** Visit the inside
of the church for free.

4 If the line to the top of the Duomo is too long (it can be over an hour
in the summer), get an equally good view of the city a few blocks south
at **Palazzo Vecchio,** where things are generally quieter. The inside of the
city's most illustrious civic building also provides a vivid idea of how the
Renaissance elite once lived.

5 Visit the **Mercato Centrale,** Florence's biggest and most animated
neighborhood market where Florentines go every day to purchase fresh produce and socialize. Order a tripe sandwich from Narbone or head upstairs
to the second-floor food court.

6 Getting into the Uffizi can be tough, even with reservations. The
Museo Nazionale del Bargello is a tranquil alternative. There are far
fewer visitors here, and you can admire sculptures by Michelangelo and
Donatello nearly alone.

7 Walk to **Basilica di Santa Croce** nearby, where Michelangelo is buried.
Afterward, stop for an espresso break or find a *gelateria* and take your cone
for a tour without consulting a map. The best discoveries are serendipitous,
and Florence's side streets are a destination unto themselves.

8 Join the evening procession of locals down **Borgo la Croce** and begin
browsing the menus along the way. Choose a restaurant with outdoor seating and order a Florentine T-bone cooked to perfection.

FLORENCE ON DAY 2

Spend day two exploring the less-crowded Oltrarno on the southern side of
the Arno River.

1   Head up the hillside to **Basilica San Miniato al Monte** along the grassy path and under the pine groves. You'll discover the city's bucolic side and get a great view across the Arno River.

2   After exploring the ancient basilica and paying homage to the author of *Pinocchio* buried in the adjacent cemetery, head back down and follow the medieval walls toward **Forte Belvedere** and the **Boboli** gardens, overlooking the city.

3   Keep walking until you reach **Palazzo Pitti.** It includes several museums and could take all day to visit, so you're better off focusing on just one like the Royal Apartments rather than rushing through them all.

4   The streets nearby are full of workshops and craftspeople creating one-of-a-kind souvenirs. **Il Papiro** is the place to purchase marbled paper and learn how it is made.

5   Whenever you're hungry walk down Borgo San Frediano. There are dozens of appetizing eateries along this popular street but the most typical option is **Il Trippaio di San Frediano,** where you can sit at an outdoor counter and sample tripe or beef sandwiches.

6   After lunch, head around the corner to the **Cappella Brancacci,** where you'll see Adam and Eve before and after eating the apple. (The audioguide provides all the background you need on this famous fresco.)

7   Take an *aperitivo* break with a Negroni cocktail from any of the bars lining **Piazza Santo Spirito.**

8   Disappear into the side streets of the Oltrarno for dinner. Sample local specialties like *pappa al pomodoro* or *bistecca al Fiorentina* accompanied by a carafe of house wine. Choose a *trattoria* with outdoor tables like **Osteria Antica Mescita** and observe Florentine street life while you eat.

FLORENCE LIKE A LOCAL

Florentines have been to the Duomo and the Uffizi by the time they've finished elementary school and spend their days very differently than visitors do. If you want to live like them, you have to forget about monuments and museums and start to think about simple pleasures like lunch and relaxation.

1   Start with an espresso at **Caffe degli Artigiani,** a no-thrills Oltrarno neighborhood bar where you can make some small talk with the bartender. *Buon giorno* (good morning), *tutto bene?* (everything ok?), and *bella giornata* (nice day) will all do.

2   Walk out of the little square and follow Via Toscanella toward **Piazza Santo Spirito.** Even though you saw it yesterday, it's worth a morning visit

Florence Itinerary Ideas

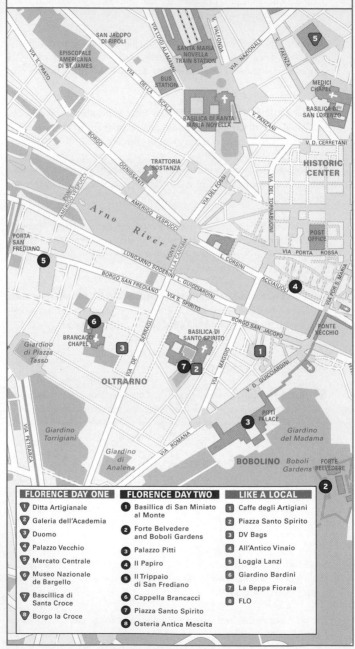

FLORENCE DAY ONE	FLORENCE DAY TWO	LIKE A LOCAL
1 Ditta Artigianale	1 Basillica di San Miniato al Monte	1 Caffe degli Artigiani
2 Galeria dell'Academia	2 Forte Belvedere and Boboli Gardens	2 Piazza Santo Spirito
3 Duomo	3 Palazzo Pitti	3 DV Bags
4 Palazzo Vecchio	4 Il Papiro	4 All'Antico Vinaio
5 Mercato Centrale	5 Il Trippaio di San Frediano	5 Loggia Lanzi
6 Museo Nazionale de Bargello	6 Cappella Brancacci	6 Giardino Bardini
7 Bascillica di Santa Croce	7 Piazza Santo Spirito	7 La Beppa Fioraia
8 Borgo la Croce	8 Osteria Antica Mescita	8 FLO

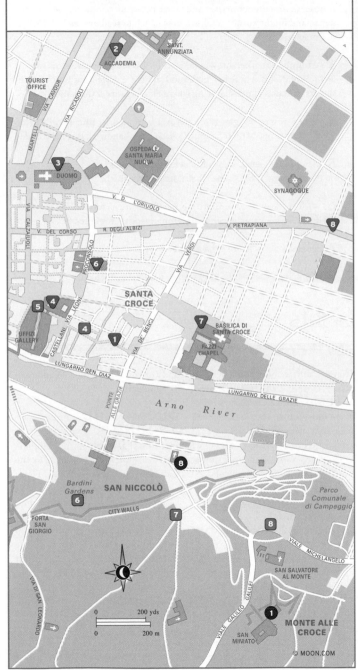

to observe the outdoor market and grab a newspaper or magazine from the newsstand on the corner. Sit down on a bench to read or watch the action in the square.

3 Around the corner, browse for leather at **DV Bags** or womens wear at Hello Wonderful. These neighborhood shops are perfect for watching designers in action and discovering where Florentines get their style.

4 When you're hungry, cross the Arno and get in line at **All'Antico Vinaio.** Order one of their famous €5 *schiacciata* sandwiches at the counter.

5 After lunch, head over to the nearby **Loggia Lanzi,** where you can sit on the steps and listen to the musicians playing nearby.

6 Visit the *loggia* in the **Giardino Bardini** gardens for another coffee or get *aperitivo* hour started with a Negroni or spritz from the bar.

7 Have dinner *al fresco* at **La Beppa Fioraia.**

8 If you have the energy, head over to **FLO** for a nightcap.

Sights

Florence's three most popular sights (**Galleria dell'Accademia, Duomo,** and **Uffizi**) are nearly always inundated with visitors. To avoid long lines, make advance reservations, or consider a Firenzecard. There's a lot more to Florence, however, and many other wonderful museums, monuments, and gardens are surprisingly empty. Make it a point to seek these out if you have the time and energy.

Museum staff all have passed rigorous state exams and are passionate and knowledgeable about where they work. Don't hesitate to ask questions even if you don't speak Italian. You can also learn a lot from the audio and app guides available at many sights. These are inexpensive, easy to use, and very informative, especially if you didn't attend (or don't remember) catechism and are unversed in the Old and New Testaments.

DUOMO AND AROUND

Piazza del Duomo is the religious heart of Florence and home to the Cattedrale di Santa Maria del Fiore, Cupola di Brunelleschi, Campanile di Giotto, Battistero, Cripta, and Museo dell'Opera. Visiting requires patience and stamina. Those determined to do it all may want to start with the **Battistero,** which opens the earliest and is the oldest of the bunch. You can then continue to the top of the dome before going inside the **Cattedrale** (also called the **Duomo**) and exploring the **Cripta.** The bell tower is open the latest. You can end a visit there or at the **Museo dell'Opera,** which was completely renovated in 2015 and is vital for understanding how Brunelleschi constructed the cupola. It also contains many works of art that have been removed from the other buildings for safekeeping. The **Cupola** and **Campanile** involve climbing hundreds of steps. You may want to choose one or the other, as the views from the top are fairly similar.

✪ DUOMO
(Santa Maria del Fiore)

Piazza del Duomo, Mon.-Sat. 10am-5pm, Sun. 1:30pm-4:45pm, free

Florence was undergoing significant change at the end of the 13th century. The churches of Santa Maria Novella and Santa Croce were completed, an outer ring wall protecting the city was erected, and the newly built Palazzo Vecchio towered over the center. The ancient cathedral in Piazza del Duomo, however, was decrepit in comparison, and leading citizens decided to build a bigger and better cathedral to express Florence's new ambitions.

Work began on Santa Maria del Fiore, or Duomo for short, in 1296 and took nearly six hundred years to complete. Today, many consider the Duomo the finest church in Italy. The cupola, or dome, may look like a simple matter of bricks, but it presented a huge dilemma, as the traditional methods of construction would not work for a dome this size. In 1417, self-taught architect Filippo Brunelleschi won a competition to design the dome. His ingenious design, which relied on a double shell and eight ribs bound together by horizontal rings—without scaffolding—led to the completion of the dome in a mere 16 years and transformed architecture forever. It can be seen from nearly everywhere

the Duomo, also known as Santa Maria del Fiore

41

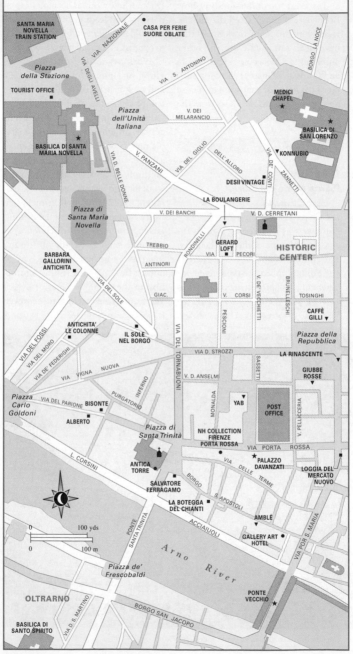

Duomo and Around

SANTA MARIA
NOVELLA
TRAIN STATION

CASA PER FERIE
SUORE OBLATE

BORGO LA NOCE

VIA NAZIONALE

VIA S. ANTONINO

Piazza
della Stazione

TOURIST OFFICE

MEDICI
CHAPEL

VIA DEGLI AVELLI

Piazza
dell'Unità
Italiana

V. DEI
MELARANCIO

BASÍLICA DI
SAN LORENZO

KONNUBIO

BASÍLICA DI SANTA
MARIA NOVELLA

V. PANZANI

V. DEL GIGLIO

DELL'ALLORO

VIA DE' CONTI

VIA DE'
ZANNETTI

DESII VINTAGE

LA BOULANGERIE

V. D. CERRETANI

Piazza di
Santa Maria
Novella

V. DEI BANCHI

VIA D. BELLE DONNE

TREBBIO

RONDINELLI

GERARD
LOFT

VIA
PECORI

HISTORIC
CENTER

BARBARA
GALLORINI
ANTICHITA

ANTINORI

VIA DEL SOLE

GIAC.

V. CORSI

V. DE' VECCHIETTI

BRUNELLESCHI

TOSINGHI

CAFFÈ
GILLI

ANTICHITA'
LE COLONNE

VIA DEL FOSSI

VIA DEL MORO

VIA DE' FEDERIGHI

IL SOLE
NEL BORGO

PESCIONI

VIA DEL TORNABUONI

Piazza della
Repubblica

VIA D. STROZZI

LA RINASCENTE

VIA VIGNA NUOVA

V. D. ANSELMI

SASSETTI

GIUBBE
ROSSE

PURGATORIO

INFERNO

Piazza
Carlo
Goldoni

VIA DEL PARIONE

BISONTE

MONALDA

YAB

POST
OFFICE

V. PELLICCERIA

ALBERTO

L. CORSINI

Piazza di
Santa Trinità

NH COLLECTION
FIRENZE
PORTA ROSSA

VIA PORTA ROSSA

ANTICA
TORRE

SALVATORE
FERRAGAMO

VIA
DELLE
TERME

PALAZZO
DAVANZATI

LOGGIA DEL
MERCATO
NUOVO

BORGO S. APOSTOLI

LA BOTEGA
DEL CHIANTI

AMBLÉ

PONTE SANTA TRINITÀ

ACCIAIUOLI

GALLERY ART
HOTEL

VIA POR S. MARIA

0   100 yds

0   100 m

Arno River

Piazza de'
Frescobaldi

PONTE
VECCHIO

OLTRARNO

BASÍLICA DI
SANTO SPIRITO

VIA D. S. MARTINO

BORGO SAN JACOPO

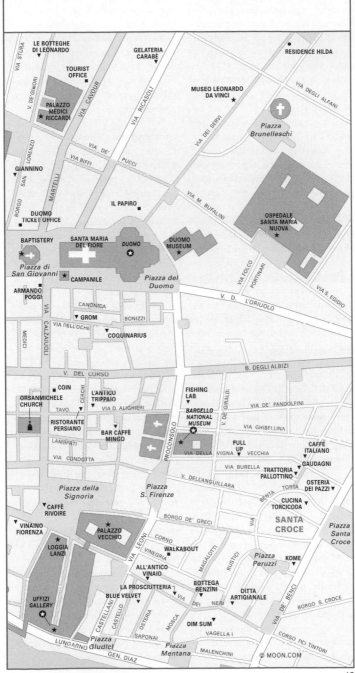

in the city and far beyond. The cathedral itself is spectacular at night, when floodlights illuminate the decorative carvings and sculptures that aren't always visible during the day.

Inside, the Duomo appears even bigger, and can easily hold 3,000 worshippers. The nave is 148 feet (45 meters) high and over a football field and a half long. The interior is austere, reflecting the Renaissance preference for geometrical harmony over decoration. The dome reveals itself as you approach the altar. Standing underneath, you can feel its immensity. The 38,750 square miles (3,600 square meters) of frescoes illustrating the *Universal Judgment* seem to lead toward the heavens.

The **Cripta** (Mon.-Sat. 10am-5pm, Duomo Card €18 or Firenzecard) is down a set of marble stairs on the south side of the cathedral. This crypt is the oldest part of the church, with some walls dating back to the city's Roman origins. Mosaic floors are still intact and embedded with the Latin names of the individuals who financed construction. There are also many gravestones, including the tomb of Brunelleschi. The vast, well-lit complex is an incredible sight and one of Florence's unique spots.

One-hour **tours** (Mon.-Sat., 10:30am-11:30pm, €30) of the Duomo and rooftop terrace are available daily except Sundays from 10:30am to 11:30am. Vespers and Gregorian chants are sung on Sundays at 10:30am and 5:15pm. Around the corner is the dusty **workshop** (Via dello Studio 3) dedicated to maintaining the hundreds of carvings and sculptures inside and outside the church. You can have a glimpse of the modern stonemasons carrying on ancient traditions or take the 90-minute **craft** tour (www.museumflorence.com, Mon., Wed., Fri. noon-1:30pm, €30) to learn how medieval tools are still used to keep the past in perfect condition. Both tours are conducted in English, must be booked online, and include entry to the dome, bell tower, and museum.

Climbing the Cupola

Climbing to the **Cupola** (Mon.-Sat. 8:30am-7pm, Sun. 1pm-4pm, Duomo Card €18 or Firenzecard) is one of the most popular activities in Florence, though it's a much harder climb than either the campanile or Palazzo Vecchio, with fewer places to rest. The payoff includes a close-up view of the mosaics inside the cupola, plus one of the best views of Florence from the outdoor terrace.

The entrance to the cupola is on the northern side of the Duomo and there's a long line most of the day. The climb starts with a set of tightly winding spiral staircases followed by a flat section. From here, a narrow staircase winds between the inner and outer shells that make up the dome. This method of construction, conceived by Brunellesci, is considered a great engineering innovation. It takes about twelve minutes without stopping to climb all 463 steps, and if you haven't exercised in a while you'll feel it. The reward is a 360 view over Florence. There are benches and four sets of strategically placed binoculars (€1) for getting a close-up of the city and hillsides.

Be careful going down: Falls are frequent, and the descent may make you dizzy. Hold on to the handrails and if you're taller than the Renaissance average keep your head down to avoid bumping it. Near the exit is a display of wooden tools used to build the cupola and a touch-screen kiosk where visitors can leave their digital autograph.

Remember to book your visit to the Cupola in advance. You can do that online when you buy the Duomo Card or at the ticket office. Reservations are scheduled for 30-minute time slots and it's wise to show up ten minutes early. Once you're in line make sure the people in front of you have reserved the same slot and if they haven't, politely move ahead to the right group.

CAMPANILE

The Campanile (Piazza del Duomo, daily 8:15am-7pm, Duomo Card €18 or Firenzecard) is one of the unique features of the Florentine skyline and arguably the most beautiful bell tower in Italy. It's also one of the only towers not directly connected to a church, which was partly due to the independent nature of Florence during the Renaissance. Getting to the top is easier than ascending the cupola, and there's often a line of tourists ready to climb its 414 steps.

The tower measures 279 feet (85 meters) in height and is only 50 feet (15 meters) wide. It's also called Giotto's Tower in reference to the artist who initiated work on it in 1337. He died three years later, and it was up to Andrea Pisano and Francesco Talenti to complete the job. They fitted the tower with its polychrome marble similar to the Duomo and added scores of sculptures illustrating the Old Testament and the *Redemption of Man*. Many pieces have been moved to the Museo dell'Opera to avoid damage by the elements. Completed in 1359, the Campanile remains one of the finest examples of Gothic architecture in the city.

The best chance of finding fewer visitors is when it opens or an hour before closing. This is one of the most accessible climbs in Florence and there are several intermediary platforms to rest and admire increasingly better views of the Duomo and city. Passageways are less hazardous than the cupola but visitors going up and down must squeeze by each other, making the journey occasionally tricky. Protective fencing surrounds the upper terrace and there are two sets of binoculars (€1) for a close-up look at the city. The Campanile is a working bell tower and rings throughout the day.

BAPTISTERY
(Battistero)

Piazza del Duomo, Mon.-Fri. 8:15am-10:15am and 11:15am-6:30pm, Sat. 8:15am-6:30pm, Sun. 8:15am-10:15am and 11:15am-7:30pm, Duomo Card €18 or Firenzecard

The green-and-white marble Battistero was built around the 6th or 7th century. This is where citizens were baptized, and it was one of the most revered buildings in Florence. Making it look good was a matter of civic as well as religious pride. The

Campanile

original wooden doors were eventually replaced with bronze doors that have been a major attraction ever since.

Andrea Pisano cast the first of the three sets of doors, which now face south, in 1336, and recount the life of John the Baptist. Lorenzo Ghiberti won the competition to design the next set of doors, and spent 21 years working on them. The project would cost millions in today's currency. His doors are located on the north entrance of the baptistery and tell the life of Christ in 28 panels read from left to right starting at the bottom.

The city liked the result so much they commissioned Ghiberti to create a third set. This one took him 27 years to complete and became known as the *Porta del Paradiso,* or **Gates of Paradise,** a dazzling achievement that marked the beginning of the Renaissance. The *Gates of Paradise* were severely damaged during flooding in 1966 and underwent restoration that was completed in 2012. During their absence, a replica—a great work in its own right—was created and has remained at the Battistero. The original set is now on display inside **Museo dell'Opera del Duomo.** If you're interested in understanding the significance behind each panel of the *Gates of Paradise*, download the app (€3) from the baptistery website.

The Baptistery is the oldest of the five monuments on the Duomo tour and the one to start with if you prefer doing things chronologically. Inside there's a lot to look at, including the gold mosaic ceiling depicting the *Last Judgment* and hypnotically intricate floor tilings. Both are original and were created at the dawn of the Renaissance when craftsmen began expanding the possibilities of art and architecture. You'll also find the only

pope buried in Florence, John XXIII. Donatello and Michelozzo built the tomb, and the Latin epitaph ruffled a few feathers back in Rome. There are several rows of wooden benches on one side of the octagon-shaped building where mass is said and visitors sit to admire the surroundings. Lines vary throughout the day from long to nearly none and several sections have been undergoing restoration since 2018.

Lorenzo Ghiberti's Baptistery doors

DUOMO MUSEUM (Museo dell'Opera)

Via della Canonica 1, tel. 055/230-2885, Mon.-Sat. 9am-7pm, Sun. 9am-1:30pm, Duomo Card €18 or Firenzecard

The Museo dell'Opera, located directly behind the Duomo, is essential for understanding how the cathedral was built and is an excellent place to start or finish a visit to the area. Throughout construction of the adjacent monuments it was used as a repository and workplace. It's where Brunelleschi confronted the day-to-day challenges of building the cupola and contains the large wooden model he used as a basis for construction. It's also where Michelangelo sculpted *David* and has a terrace with a great view of the Duomo.

Once the cathedral was completed the building was transformed into a museum focused entirely on preservation and the safekeeping of over 750 works of art. It reopened in 2015 and now covers 64,583 square feet (6,000 square meters) over three floors. Exhibits include many of the original relics and artwork from the baptistery, cathedral, crypt, and bell tower. The *Gates of Paradise,* the famed doors Ghiberti created for the Battistero, have a befitting place behind an immense glass case.

Once you're clear follow the suggested itinerary projected onto the floor or use the museum map. The first stop is an enormous hall housing the baptistery doors along with sculptures by Donatello and Arnoldo di Cambio. Many of these are set in their original positions on a faux cathedral façade that lines one side of the enormous space.

Around the corner stands one of Florence's greatest treasures: Michelangelo sculpted several versions of *La Pieta* over his lifetime and although this one is not as famous as the work he created in Rome, it is noteworthy because of the artist's self-portrait in the scene, which was intended for his tombstone. Unfortunately the marble was of poor quality, which explains why Jesus is missing a leg, and Michelangelo destroyed parts of the unfinished work in anger. The sculpture survived thanks to his devoted assistants and still ranks among Michelango's best.

There are more interesting artifacts on the upper floors and a sunny roof terrace with benches from which to gaze upon the Duomo. It's a good angle to notice that the decoration of the base supporting the dome is unfinished. There are two explanations, both of which may be true. The first is that the elaborate balcony was simply too heavy to be completed and the second that Michelangelo, who was not chosen for the job, ridiculed the work one day by comparing it to a cricket's cage (*gabbia di grillo*), which is what it is still called today.

Construction didn't always go well and the circular marble plaque in the street outside marks the spot where the first gold ball crowning the Duomo fell. There's a nice gift shop on the ground floor with a variety of unique gifts, the majority of which are made in Italy, and a café at the museum entrance.

ORSANMICHELE CHURCH (Chiesa Orsanmichele)

Via dell'Arte della Lana, tel. 055/238-8606, daily 10am-5pm, free

Chiesa Orsanmichele is a massive three-story church *palazzo* that looks more like a wealthy merchant's house than a place of worship. It began as a grain warehouse and the ground floor was later transformed into a church after sightings of the Virgin Mary. The site was destroyed and rebuilt several times, and in 1336 the city decided to erect a building that would serve both religious and civic functions. The ground floor became a place to worship the Virgin Mary, while the upper floors were set aside for grain storage.

The government encouraged the guilds to decorate the exterior of the building, which occupied a place of special prominence between the Duomo and Palazzo Vecchio. Fourteen niches were created along the north and south sides. Over decades, these were filled with sculptures that led to an artistic evolution that fueled the Renaissance. No two niches are the same, and competition between the guilds meant that the most talented artists in the city were commissioned to contribute.

Donatello created two of the finest statues. The Guild of Armor and Sword Makers hired him to represent San Giorgio, while the linen workers requested a portrait of San Marco. The resulting sculptures mark a rediscovery of classical forms of beauty. The statues have been replaced with copies that still have a powerful presence, while Donatello's San Giorgio now resides in the Museo Bargello.

The church on the ground floor is devoted to the Virgin Mary and dominated by Andrea Orcagna's tabernacle. He spent 10 years perfecting his marble bas-relief of *The Death of the Virgin* and *Assumption*. On the opposite wall is Bernardo Daddi's *Virgin and Child*, in which baby Jesus tenderly touches his mother's cheek while angels look on. The museum (Mon. 10am-5pm) is accessed from here. Inside, you can view many of the original sculptures that appeared in the niches around the outside of the church.

PALAZZO DAVANZATI

Via Porta Rossa 13, tel. 055/238-8610,
Mon.-Fri. 8:15am-1:50pm and Sat.-Sun.
1:15pm-6:30pm, €6 or Firenzecard

To get an idea of how wealthy medieval Florentines lived, visit Palazzo Davanzati. The Davanzati were a family of lace merchants who ran their business on the first floor (where a small gift shop and ticket desk are now located) and lived on the upper floors. The difference between medieval and Renaissance-era *palazzi* is evident from the greater height of the

building and its cramped courtyard and wooden staircase, which is humble by Medici standards. They did, however, have an internal well, good plumbing, and en suite bathrooms that can be seen as you tour the well-preserved living quarters refurbished with period antiques. The third and fourth floors where the second banquet hall, kitchen, and medieval graffiti are located are accessible by tour only at 10am, 11am, and noon for a maximum of 25 visitors.

✪ BARGELLO NATIONAL MUSEUM
(Museo Nazionale del Bargello)

Via del Proconsolo 4, tel. 055/238-8606,
daily 8:15am-6pm, €9 or Firenzecard

While some of Florence's museums and monuments are besieged by tourists, the Bargello is often deserted. This is where you'll find Donatello's *David,* which preceded Michelangelo's version. Although it's overshadowed by the latter, Donatello's *David* marks an important moment in the early Renaissance. Donatello accompanied Brunelleschi to Rome and played an essential role in the rediscovery of classical art. His sculpture was the first cast in bronze since the fall of ancient Rome and inspired an entire generation of artists.

The building itself is a holdover from the Middle Ages and was the first public office in the city. It was the headquarters of the chief of police (known as the *Bargello*) and used as a prison for centuries. Torture and executions were conducted in the courtyard as punishment for offenses that would be classified as misdemeanors today. The death penalty was abolished and the gallows destroyed in 1786, making Tuscany one of the first states to ban capital punishment.

Donatello's bronze statue of *David* at the Bargello

The immense rooms overlooking the courtyard are nearly as interesting as the art within the museum. On the ground floor are a number of marble and bronze sculptures and several works by Michelangelo. The great hall one flight up contains Donatello's *David* and the bronze door panels Ghiberti and Brunelleschi submitted for the Baptistery competition. A little further on is the chapel with faded frescoes where prisoners were given their last rites. On the upper floor is a fine collection of antique armor and weapons including swords, crossbows, lances, and early firearms.

PIAZZA DELLA SIGNORIA

Piazza della Signoria's asymmetrical shape has a lot to do with the buildings and towers that were torn down by the Guelphs in the mid-13th century to make sure their enemies never recovered. The resulting square became the administrative center of the city and is home to Palazzo Vecchio, Loggia Lanzi, and many fine statues and monuments. It's where Florentines gathered to defend the city, prisoners were executed, and public celebrations are still held today.

In the center of the *piazza* is the round plaque marking the spot where Savonarola was hanged and burned at the stake. Nearby, there's a bronze statue of Cosimo I on horseback and a marble Neptune that exalts the seafaring glories of the city. The *piazza* is one of the great urban spaces in Florence. It fills up with visitors during the day and is used to stage concerts on summer nights.

Chiasso dei Baroncelli, adjacent to Loggia Lanzi, is closer to an alley than a street and the perfect escape from the crowds in the square. If you walk to the end, turn right, and continue through the intersection along Borgo Santi Apostoli, you'll arrive at Piazza Santa Trinità where street musicians perform throughout the day and night.

LOGGIA LANZI

The triple-arched Loggia Lanzi (free) is the imposing structure next to Palazzo Vecchio on the southern side of Piazza della Signoria. A *loggia* is an open-air building popular in the Renaissance that generally functioned as a market or meeting place. This one was completed in 1382 and was used to shelter government officials during ceremonies. When the Republic fell in 1530 artists were allowed to use the covered space as a workshop. Today it's a public gallery with statues from different periods; the only two placed in the *loggia* during the Renaissance were Giambologna's *Rape of the Sabine Woman* and Cellini's *Perseus*. The latter portrays the Greek hero holding Medusa's head and was an attempt to outdo Michelangelo's *David* standing nearby. It may not have succeeded, but the 12-foot bronze statue remains impressive. The number of visitors allowed to enter the *loggia* is limited, but turnaround time is quick, and sculptures are clearly visible from the *piazza*.

PALAZZO VECCHIO

Piazza della Signoria, tel. 055/276-8325, museum Oct.-Mar. Fri.-Wed. 9am-7pm, Thurs. 9am-2pm, Apr.-Sept. Fri.-Wed. 9am-11pm, Thurs. 9am-2pm, tower Oct.-Mar. Fri.-Wed. 10am-5pm, Thurs. 10am-2pm, Apr.-Sept. Fri.-Wed. 9am-9pm, Thurs. 9am-2pm, €10 for single sights, €14-18 combined ticket options or Firenzecard

The Duomo may get more attention, but the decision to build the cathedral and countless other decisions that shaped the city were made at Palazzo Vecchio. This *palazzo* served as a political and administrative hub where magistrates lived and nobles, dignitaries, and citizens gathered. The exterior looks impregnable, which is exactly what Arnolfo di Cambio intended when he began construction in 1298. Walls are made of rough-cut stone and rise high above the square. The 308-foot (94-meter) tower is even more impressive.

Palazzo Vecchio can be entered from the gateway next to the statue of David. The ticket office is located off the internal courtyard designed by Michelozzo and decorated with a graceful fountain. Even if you don't intend to visit the *palazzo* it's worth a peek inside the courtyard and at the Roman remains underground, both of which are free. Take the stairs inside the ticket office and follow the walkway overlooking the massive brickwork. The courtyard is the best example of Roman architecture in the city and it provides an idea of what lies below street level.

The lower floors include residential quarters and reception halls that were the home of Cosimo I and other members of the Medici family when they rose to power. The grandest of these is the **Salone dei Cinquecento**, which has a high frescoed ceiling and two walls covered with gigantic paintings illustrating Florence's military successes. Michelangelo and Leonardo da Vinci were originally commissioned to undertake this project but neither ever completed the task. Had they done so the *salone* would be one of the unique artistic sights in Italy. Nonetheless it remains impressive, especially when viewed from the balcony on the third floor.

Palazzo Vecchio

The route to the **tower** starts at the staircase near the front entrance. The number of visitors within the tower is limited, so you may encounter a short wait after a few flights. On the way up, you'll pass a small prison cell known ironically as the *alberghetto,* or little hotel, where Savonarola and other illustrious prisoners were detained. Farther along, you can circumnavigate two terraces that offer the best panoramas from the tower. These are where soldiers once kept watch over the city. At the very top, views are obstructed by high ramparts except for a ledge where visitors take turns photographing the Duomo. Lookouts once observed the countryside from here and rang the bells that hung in the wooden structure above if they spotted enemies approaching. A friendly attendant is always present and happy to answer questions. The tower is closed whenever it rains and is off-limits to children under six.

There are evening **tours** (€4) of the tower during the summer and **tablet guides** (€5) to the *palazzo*.

TOP EXPERIENCE

✪ UFFIZI GALLERY
(Galleria degli Uffizi)

Piazzale degli Uffizi 6, tel. 055/294-883, www.uffizi.it, Tues.-Sun. 8:15am-6:50pm, €20, €38 combined ticket or Firenzecard

Galleria degli Uffizi is the mother of all museums and what started out as a pastime for the Medici family eventually became one of the greatest collections of art in the world. This grand 16th-century building stretches from Palazzo Vecchio to the Arno River. Inside are many of the world's finest paintings, from 13th-century religious frescoes to Renaissance masterpieces by the likes of Giotto, Beato Angelico, Botticelli, Mantegna, Leonardo, Raphael, Michelangelo, and Caravaggio. It's a match for any museum, and its relatively small dimensions make it possible to visit in a morning or afternoon.

You can pick up a map of the museum and an **audio guide** (€6 single/€10 double), which is essential for understanding the paintings to come, at the information desk. The gallery itself begins on the third floor, where 35 rooms are organized around two enormous wings. Tourists huddle in front of the pearls of the collection, such as Botticelli's *Birth of Venus,* on display in room 10. The floor below contains a permanent collection as

Uffizi Gallery

well as a number of temporary exhibition spaces. Dutch painters are housed in rooms 53 to 55, while works by Caravaggio hang in room 90.

Outside, artists and street vendors fill the long rectangular courtyard, while hundreds of visitors line up underneath the portico entrance. The shorter line is for reserved tickets (which can be picked up at the office on the opposite side) and Firenzecard holders. The longer one is for everyone else. If you take photos inside, turn the flash off. Selfie sticks are prohibited, as are umbrellas, large bags, and food. On the top floor is a cafeteria where you can have an espresso or light snack and sit on the spacious terrace with a view of Palazzo della Signoria.

The museum shop holds hundreds of volumes of art and history, including many titles in English. Several more rooms are filled with posters, gadgets, and clothing, and funnily enough, there's a small post office near the museum exit where travelers can send a postcard (€3) or purchase stamps.

SANTA MARIA NOVELLA

BASILICA DI SANTA MARIA NOVELLA

Piazza Santa Maria Novella 18, tel. 055/219-257, www.smn.it, Oct.-Mar. Mon.-Thurs. 9am-5:30pm, Fri. 11am-5:30pm, Sat. 9am-5:30pm, Sun. 1pm-5:30pm, Apr.-Sept. Mon.-Thurs. 9am-7pm, Fri. 11am-7pm, Sat. 9am-5:30pm, Sun. 1pm-5:30pm, €8 or Firenzecard

Basilica di Santa Maria Novella lies opposite the train station and is often ignored by travelers. The basilica is called *novella* (new) because it was built over a smaller church by Dominican monks, who completed the structure in 1360. The recently remodeled *piazza* out front provides the

Basilica di Santa Maria Novella

best view of the green-and-white marble façade begun in the Middle Ages and completed in the Renaissance.

The basilica consists of a monumental church, a half-dozen chapels, and several cloisters. There's rarely a line to enter, and impressive artwork throughout. The most striking artifacts are the large wooden crucifix by Giotto hanging above the altar, a small fresco by Botticelli near the entrance, and *The Trinity* by Masaccio that's one of the earliest examples of perspective in painting.

frescoes inside Basilica di Santa Maria Novella

The **Chiostro Verde** (Green Cloister) is down a short flight of steps on the left side of the church. It's named after the green pigment used in the frescoes lining the walls that vividly illustrate stories of sinners and saints. Farther down is the **refectory** where monks ate meals and restored artworks. Hanging on the wall is a painting of the Last Supper, and below are glass cases containing religious garments.

Mass is held daily in the **Capella della Pura** chapel at 7:30am and 7pm in July and August and 7:30am and 6pm the rest of the year. Sunday mass is at 10:30am and 7am during the former and 10:30am, noon, and 6pm

during the latter. Services (in Italian) last 45 minutes.

CHIESA D'OGNISSANTI

Borgo Ognissanti 42, tel. 055/239-8700, Mon.-Fri. 7:15am-noon and 4-8pm, Sat.-Sun. 9am-1pm and 4-8pm

Many religious orders were active in Florence, and Ognissanti was founded by the Umiliati in the 12th century and later used by the Franciscans, who were responsible for the Baroque makeover of the façade. Being one of the most prestigious orders meant they could afford the best artists of the day and Giotto, Botticelli, and Ghirandaio all contributed to the interior. Many paintings were moved to the Uffizi but what remains, such as Ghirlandaio's *Last Supper* in the adjacent monestary and Botticelli's *Saint Agostine*, are impressive. The latter artist is buried inside and it's common to find notes of admiration and flowers near his tomb. The Vespucci family chapel is located along the right nave and is where famed navigator Amerigo once prayed.

SAN LORENZO AND SAN MARCO

TOP EXPERIENCE

✪ ACCADEMIA (Galleria dell'Accademia)

Via Ricasoli 58-60, tel. 055/238-8609, www.galleriaaccademiafirenze.beniculturali. it, Tues.-Sun. 8:15am-6:50pm, €8 or Firenzecard, €4 online reservation fee

If you're looking for *David*, you'll find him inside the Galleria dell'Accademia. Michelangelo sculpted the masterpiece from an enormous piece of secondhand marble that had frustrated lesser artists. David was a popular subject and, like Donatello's version, this one is naked.

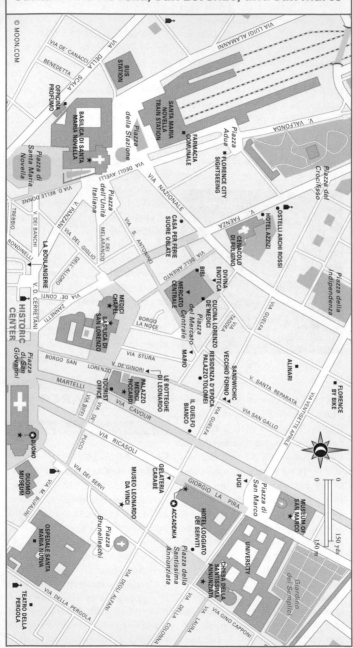

Santa Maria Novella, San Lorenzo, and San Marco

© MOON.COM

Michalangelo's *David* in the Accademia

The line for unreserved ticket holders to get into the Galleria dell'Accademia often stretches around the corner, and the wait can be over an hour during the summer. The reserved ticket and Firenzecard line is slightly shorter, but still requires patience. Only 600 are allowed inside at any one time. A good strategy for avoiding crowds is to arrive early.

Michelangelo, however, chose to capture the tense moments prior to the struggle with Goliath. The face is not relaxed but reveals the kind of apprehension you'd expect before facing a giant. The statue gets an entire room to itself and is easily visible regardless of the number of visitors. Remember to walk around the statue and observe what many consider *David's* finest asset.

The museum would be worth visiting even if it didn't contain Michelangelo's masterpiece, though the unique collection of medieval paintings, half-completed sculptures, Florentine art from the 12th to 15th centuries, and some surprises are often overlooked. Other works by Michelangelo include four unfinished sculptures that were ordered for the tomb of Pope Julius II but remained embedded in stone. The effect is eerie and inspired future generations of sculptors to adopt this *nonfinite* technique. The music room contains more than 50 antique instruments including a Stradivari violin and the oldest upright piano in the world.

MUSEUM OF SAN MARCO
(Museo di San Marco)
Piazza San Marco 3, tel. 055/238-8608, Mon.-Fri. 8:15am-1:50pm, Sat. 8:15am-4:20pm, €4 or Firenzecard

The Dominican monastery that houses Museo di San Marco is a hidden gem just moments from the Galleria dell'Accademia but with only a fraction of the visitors. Inside you'll find frescoes by Beato Angelico, the city's first public library, and one and a half depictions of the Last Supper. This is also where the fanatical monk Girolamo Savonarola preached and resided. The completed *Cenacolo,* as the Last Supper is called in Italian, is by Ghiberti and notable for the vivid colors and the disciples' detailed expressions.

Upstairs, you'll find the 44 cells where monks lived. Each contains a fresco of Jesus in various states of crucifixion. San Domenico is also present and recognizable by the star above his head, while the order's first martyr (San Pietro di Verona) is usually depicted as bleeding. Beato Angelico oversaw the painting of the frescoes and worked on those closest to the entrance himself. Museum attendants on duty are happy to answer questions and share their insight with visitors. The library is on the same floor and is where the monks studied. The delicately colonnaded space was built

MISSION MICHELANGELO: FLORENCE

Florence produced many geniuses during the late Middle Ages and Renaissance but none acquired as much fame in life and after as Michelangelo. He left an unmistakable mark on the city that can still be seen today. Although some of his greatest works require standing in line for hours, others are far more accessible and can be visited in a morning or afternoon.

Casa Buonarotti houses Michelangelo's first serious attempts at sculpture, created when he was barely out of his teens. Some of the artist's architectural models and drawings are also on display.

Michelangelo found refuge in **Basilica di Santo Spirito** after the death of his benefactor Lorenzo the Magnificent. The young artist was allowed to dissect cadavers in the church hospital, a task that played an instrumental part in his growth as an artist. He paid the monks back for their hospitality by sculpting a wooden crucifix in 1493 that still hangs in the basilica. It's a realistic and human portrayal of Christ that hints of the sculptures to come.

After the Medici were exiled in 1494 Michelangelo journeyed to Rome, *where* he carved the *Pieta di San Pietro* and *Bacco*. These sculptures are the first signs of a mature artist at the height of his talents. They were eventually returned to Florence and now reside in the **Museo Bargello.** The museum also contains other works from the same period, and comparing one with the other reveals a subtle evolution in style.

Upon returning to Florence in 1501 Michelangelo created some of his most famous masterpieces including the statue of David. The **Galleria dell'Accademia** also contains his sensual uncompleted statues, in which rough chisel marks can still be seen and the figures appear trapped in stone. Getting into the gallery is a challenge, as it is at the **Uffizi** where Michelangelo's first painting, *Tondo Doni,* is on display in room 35. It's a colorful portrayal of the Holy Family and the only one of his paintings in Florence.

Two members of the Medici family served as pope between 1515 and 1534, and during that time they commissioned Michelangelo to design and decorate the **Cappelle Medici** (Piazza di Madonna degli Aldobrandini 6, tel. 055/238-8602, daily 8:15am-6pm, €6) chapel. It's perhaps his most complete work, in which he demonstrated talent both as an architect and as a sculptor. He created two tombs on which muscular statues lounge and a symmetrical interior that was different from how chapels were designed to look at the time.

Michelangelo's final sculpture was created in Rome and later moved to Florence, where it now resides inside **Museo dell Opera del Duomo.** The life-size figures are noteworthy for the expression of grief on their faces and the self-portrait of the artist in the center. Michelangelo intended it for his tomb but didn't complete it in time, and the city commissioned another artist to decorate his final resting place inside **Basilica di Santa Croce.**

during the Renaissance and contains hand-decorated manuscripts, some of which are now on display.

Downstairs, the fresco cycle along the cloister recounts the youth, conversion, and religious life of San Marco and begins diagonally from the entrance. It illustrates how Florence looked and how locals dressed and acted during the 11th century. Beato Angelico painted the spaces above the doorways, all of which hint at the rooms beyond. The "Half Supper" is located in the refectory where monks ate. It isn't the highest quality but remains interesting for its realistic portrayal of the monks who inhabited the monastery. The monk standing on the far left dressed entirely in white financed the work. Anyone who joined the brotherhood was required to give up their worldly wealth and applied any riches they had to the beautification and improvement of the monastery.

BASILICA DI SAN LORENZO

Piazza di San Lorenzo 9, tel. 055/216-634, Mon.-Sat. 10am-6pm, €7

Before the Duomo was completed, the Basilica di San Lorenzo was the most important place of worship in Florence and the Medici family church. It's recognizable from the unfinished brick exterior and a simple gray interior designed by Brunelleschi, Michelozzo, Michelangelo, and Donatello. Visitors enter through the cloister that was a common feature of many Florentine churches, and this one is characterized by a rare second-floor loggia with slender ionic columns. The adjacent underground museum is where Cosimo Medici is buried within the foundations of the building near his friend Donatello. Cosimo's offspring had a library built next door where 11,000 manuscripts are stored. The 16th-century **Biblioteca Medicea Laurenziana** (Mon.-Fri. 9:30am-1:30pm, €3) was the work of Michelangelo and the only structure he entirely built from scratch. There are frequent exhibitions but photography is not allowed and the church is closed to non-worshippers during mass.

MEDICI CHAPEL
(Cappelle Medici)

Piazza di Madonna degli Aldobrandini 6, tel. 055/238-8602, daily 8:15am-1:50pm, closed 2nd and 4th Sun. and 1st, 3rd and 5th Mon. of every month, €8, audio guide available

Cappelle Medici is the final resting place of the members of the Medici dynasty. The chapel inside San Basilica di San Lorenzo was the family's parish church and a short walk from their residence on Via Cavour. The complex consists of an Old and New Sacristy built by Brunelleschi and Michelangelo. The latter is notable for its scale and the muscular statues lounging on the monumental tombs. The main octagonal chapel is covered in precious marble and rises to a towering 194 feet (59 meters). The family members are not actually resting inside the stone tombs; their remains are instead within the walls of the crypt at the entrance of the museum. Restoration of the chapel's interior and exterior are ongoing, and scaffolding is not an uncommon sight.

PALAZZO MEDICI RICCARDI

Via Camillo Cavour 3, tel. 055/276-0340, Thurs.-Tues. 8:30am-7pm, €7 or Firenzecard

The Medici family combined wealth and political power in a way that was unprecedented and unequaled in Florence. Letting other families know their social status was not only a matter of pride but it ensured their place in Florentine society. They wanted the biggest villa on the block and set a new standard in architecture building it. Their massive 15th-century villa may look austere on the outside but the inner courtyard and living quarters were full of Renaissance comforts. The most notable of these is the **Cappella dei Magi** chapel decorated with a fresco depicting different generations of the Medici dressed in their Sunday best. The house was later sold to the Riccardi clan, who made their own additions including the **Galleria degli Specchi**, or mirror gallery, where foreign dignitaries were entertained and lavish parties organized. Outside in the small garden is a collection of Greek and Roman statues that Michelangelo and other local artists studied for inspiration.

Last Supper fresco inside Museo di San Marco

Over the centuries, artists have illustrated hundreds of episodes from the Bible—and one of the favorite images is the *Cenacolo* or *Last Supper*. Monasteries and convents frequently commissioned Middle Ages and Renaissance artists to paint this iconic scene. The basic scene is nearly always the same: Jesus sits in the center of a long table, with followers seated on either side. John is to the left and often hunched over in near sleep. Each figure sports a halo, except Judah, who is usually seated across the table from the other figures and portrayed with a dark beard. Everything else including the background, expressions, and the food itself were up to the artist, many of whom specialized in painting this single scene.

Florence counts over 50 versions of the Last Supper, and tracking a few down is a rewarding venture that costs next to nothing. Searching for *Last Suppers* requires a little planning, as many of the monasteries where they're located are only open mornings on certain days. The ones listed below are all within walking distance of one another and can be covered in a couple of hours:

Cenacolo di Ognissanti (Borgo Ognissanti 42, tel. 055/294-883, Mon. and Sat. 9am-1pm, free) stands near the Arno facing an elegant *piazza*. The *Last Supper*,

CHIESA DELLA SANTISSIMA ANNUNZIATA

Piazza Santissima Annunziata, tel. 055/266-181, daily 7:30am-12:30pm and 4-6:30pm, weekday mass every hour on the hour 7am-noon and 6pm

It's easy to walk past Santissima Annunziata without a second look on your way to the Duomo but you'd be missing one of the most elaborate interiors of the city. Inside is lined with over a dozen chapels on both sides of the central aisle and each of these belonged to noble families responsible for their decoration. Competition and one-upmanship led to some pretty extraordinary paintings, all of which show the influence of Renaissance tastes. The small archway in the right corner was the private entrance of the Medici, who preferred to enter unseen by ordinary citizens. The *piazza* outside is one of the most harmonious in Florence and hasn't changed since Brunelleschi designed the delicate porticoes that distinguish this quiet square.

completed by Domenico Ghirlandaio in 1488, covers the far wall in the refectory where monks gathered for meals. Ghirlandaio was an expert in the genre and completed several others around the city with the help of his brother and assistants. This one is notable for the detailed expressions and use of perspective. The artist sketched a rough draft that hangs on the side wall. Comparing the two makes for some interesting speculation about John. Botticelli is buried in the adjacent church.

Head north toward the train station to reach the **Cenacolo di Fuligno** (Via Faenza 40, tel. 055/280-391, Sat. and Sun. 10am-1pm, free). Pietro Perugino worked three years on the *fresco* and completed the work in 1496. It was severely damaged during the great flood of 1966 and underwent a long period of restoration that was completed in 1990. The apostles in this portrayal are hungry and all those to the left of Jesus are busy enjoying their food. The landscape above them is visible through the columns of an imaginary *palazzo* that adds depth to the scene.

Walk up Via Nazionale and take a left on Via Ventisette Aprile to reach **Cenacolo di Sant'Apollonia** (Via XXVII Aprile 1, tel. 055/238-8607, daily 8:15am-1:50pm, free). This was once the biggest convent in the city, but there's a good chance you'll be the only one observing the painting Andrea del Castagno completed in 1450. He imagined the scene taking place inside a finely decorated room with a long table and many geometric patterns. Judah is notable for his dark features and there's less interaction and more contemplation among the diners. Castagno painted each apostle's name (in Latin) near his feet.

Down the street inside **Museo di San Marco** (Piazza San Marco 3, tel. 055/238-8608, Mon.-Fri. 8:15am-1:50pm, Sat -Sun. 8:15am-4.50pm, closed 1st, 3rd, 5th Sun. and 2nd, 4th Mon. every month, €4) is another *Cenacolo* designed by Ghirlandaio and completed with the help of his brother in 1480. The background, tablecloth, and perspective are very similar to his earlier work; however, the colors are more vivid here and the artist took the liberty of adding a cat. Today the painting shares a room with a small bookshop.

Seeing several *Last Suppers* in a single day requires getting up early, but if closing is still an hour off and you have the energy, walk east toward the city's second train station and **Cenacolo di Andrea del Sarto** (Via di S. Salvi 16, Tues.-Sun. 8:15am-1:50pm, free). This one is the most recent of the bunch—it was completed in 1527—and is quite animated, with apostles on their feet in heated discussion. They haven't earned their halos yet and John is wide awake while Judah on the far right of the fresco doesn't look so villainous. One of the figures above the main scene is said to be a self-portrait of the artist.

Afterward you can walk back to the center along the Arno or search for your own supper in a neighborhood *trattoria*.

MUSEO LEONARDO DA VINCI
Via dei Servi 66/68R, tel. 055/282-966,
www.mostredileonardo.com, daily
10am-7pm, €7

Inside this museum, you'll learn about the life of the multitalented artist and inventor and discover many of his creations. Dozens of wooden machines are on display in full or close-to-full scale. Best of all, most of the models are fully functional and meant to be touched. There are civil as well as military inventions, including the predecesor of the modern tank, da Vinci's famous flying machines, and warships, and a section dedicated to the research and anatomy work he conducted with 3-D explanations. The museum has obvious kid appeal but adults will find the feats of engineering creativity equally appealing.

SANTA CROCE
BASILICA DI SANTA CROCE
Piazza Basilica di Santa Croce 16, tel.
055/246-6105, www.santacroceopera.it,
Mon.-Sat. 9:30am-5pm, Sun. 2pm-5pm,
€8 or Firenzecard, tablet guide €5

Basilica di Santa Croce lies on the eastern edge of the Historic Center in

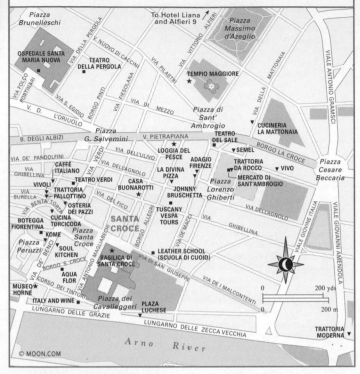

Santa Croce

a working-class district (also called Santa Croce) that once housed tanneries and leather workshops. The Franciscan monastery was enlarged in the late 13th century and the façade was completed centuries later in 1863.

Basilica di Santa Croce

The basilica is designed in a Latin cross plan with three naves, a number of side chapels, and a vast wooden ceiling. The style is predominantly Gothic with frescoes by Renaissance artists who set the early standards of Western art. None of these is more influential than Giotto, who decorated two chapels. His use of space and the positioning of figures influenced generations of Florentine artists and significantly impacted the Renaissance painting that would follow.

Santa Croce is the final resting place of Michelangelo, Machiavelli, and Galileo Galilei, all of whom are buried inside. Dante would be lying next to them had he not been banished from Florence; the city later made amends by installing a statue of the poet on the steps outside. Funerary monuments dedicated to the city's all-time greats are located along the walls. A passage, opposite the basilica entrance, leads to the peaceful 14th-century cloister and **Pazzi Chapel** designed by Brunelleschi. The architect died before work was completed, and the façade has remained unfinished.

The basilica is the city's most visited church after the Duomo and lines form early. A tour app is available for download, but you're better off asking the friendly volunteers who wait inside the church and organize free impromptu-guided tours.

Worshippers can enter Monday through Saturday from 7:30am until 6:45pm from a separate entrance and are not required to wait in line or purchase tickets. Just inform attendants of your intentions and remain within the designated prayer areas on the left side of the nave. Mass is celebrated Monday through Saturday at 6pm and on Sunday at 11am, noon, and 6pm.

CASA BUONAROTTI

Via Ghibellina 70, tel. 055/241-752,
Wed.-Mon. 10am-5pm, €7 or Firenzecard

Michelangelo's last name was Buonarotti but he didn't live in Casa Buonarotti, which was built by his nephew and transformed into a museum after the extinction of the family line. Today it houses Michelangelo's first serious attempts at sculpture, created when he was barely out of his teens. *Battaglia dei Centauri* and *Madonna della Scala* may not compete with his later work, but they do show clear signs of potential. In those early years Michelangelo used a bas-relief technique that requires chiseling away at a marble background and is best viewed from the front. Some of

the artist's architectural models and drawings are also on display, along with personal belongings such as Michelangelo's shoes, which indicate he had very small feet.

MUSEO HORNE

Via dei Benci 6, tel. 055/244-661,
Thurs.-Tues. 10am-2pm, €7 or Firenzecard

This small villa, the former home of 19th-century English art critic Herbert Percy Horne, contains 14th-16th-century art that provides an idea about how upper-class Renaissance families once lived. The museum is off the radar and usually deserted, which means you're likely to be alone with the guardians who know the house well and are eager to show visitors around. Highlights incude a painting by Giotto that Horne purchased for £9.

TEMPIO MAGGIORE

Via Luigi Carlo Farini 4, tel. 055/245-252,
www.firenzebraica.it, Sun.-Thurs.
10am-10:30pm and Fri. 10am-5pm, €7
or Firenzecard

Unlike Rome and Venice, where the old Jewish ghettoes have remained standing, the neighborhood in Florence where Jews were once confined was demolished, but you can learn about the city's Jewish past and understand what the ghetto was like inside the Tempio Maggiore, or Great Synagogue. It's the second largest synagogue in Italy and the culmination of centuries of Jewish activity in Florence.

Construction began in 1871 a short way from the historic center and the façade's pink-and-white stone is meant to recall those found in Jerusalem. The style is Arabesque and the inscriptions in Hebrew recount the Ten Commandments.

Inside there's a museum with

Ponte Vecchio

models of the old ghetto and a gallery overlooking the main worshipping hall. The altar and dome are similar to Christian interiors, as is the organ that occasionally gets played. Service is held every Friday evening and anyone can attend, although security is tight and the entrance to the synagogue is under permanent guard.

LOGGIA DEL PESCE
Piazza dei Ciompi, 24/7, free
This elegant covered market consists of 20 arches supporting a long rectangular roof that once housed the fish market in the center of the city. It was inaugurated in 1568 and designed by Vasari. The structure was later moved to its present location to make way for Piazza della Rebublicca and no longer has anything to do with fish, although the plaques above the arches hint at its former purpose. The surrounding square has been closed since 2018 for restoration and the nearby streets are favored by Florentines out for their evening strolls.

OLTRARNO
PONTE VECCHIO
There are many bridges in Florence but Ponte Vecchio is the one everyone wants to cross. It's the oldest in the city and has spanned the Arno since 1342. What makes it special are the workshops built on both sides of the bridge by butchers who once plied their trade here and discarded waste in the gaps at the center (where tourists now line up to take pictures of the river). Above the eastern side of the bridge runs the corridor that connects the Uffizi and Palazzo Pitti. It was completed in less than five months and used by Cosimo I de Medici to avoid the chaos down below. A few years later in 1593 the butchers were ordered to leave and replaced with jewelers who didn't smell as bad. During World War II, Ponte Vecchio was the only bridge in Florence that was not destroyed by the retreating German army.

For most of the day and night, Ponte Vecchio is filled with pedestrians half admiring the storefronts and

Oltrarno

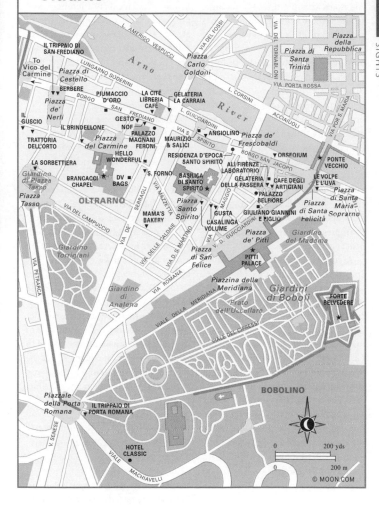

L. AMERIGO VESPUCCI
VIA DEL FOSSI
VIA DEL TORNABUONI
Piazza della Repubblica
IL TRIPPAIO DI SAN FREDIANO
Piazza Carlo Goldoni
Piazza di Santa Trinità
To Vico del Carmine
Piazza di Cestello
LUNGARNO SODERINI
Arno
River
VIA PORTA ROSSA
BERBERE
BORGO SAN FREDIANO
PIUMACCIO D'ORO
LA CITÉ LIBRERIA CAFÉ
GELATERIA LA CARRAIA
L. CORSINI
ACCIAIUOLI
VIA POR S. MARIA
Piazza de' Nerli
IL GUSCIO
GESTO
L. GUICCIARDINI
IL BRINDELLONE
NOF
VIA S. SPIRITO
ANGIOLINO
Piazza de' Frescobaldi
TRATTORIA DELL'ORTO
PALAZZO MAGNANI FERONI
Piazza del Carmine
MAURIZIO & SALICI
RESIDENZA D'EPOCA SANTO SPIRITO
BORGO SAN JACOPO
ORSEQUM
PONTE VECCHIO
HELLO WONDERFUL
LA SORBETTIERA
S. FORNO
ALI FIRENZE LABORATORIO
LE VOLPE E L'UVA
Giardino di Piazza Tasso
BRANCACCI CHAPEL
DV BAGS
BASILICA DI SANTO SPIRITO
GELATERIA DELLA PASSERA
CAFE DEGLI ARTIGIANI
PALAZZO BELFIORE
Piazza di Santa Maria Soprarno
Piazza Tasso
OLTRARNO
VIA MAZZETTA
VIA DEL CAMPUCCIO
VIA SERRAGLI
Piazza Santo Spirito
GUSTA
GIULIANO GIANNINI E FIGLIO
Piazza di Santa Felicità
MAMA'S BAKERY
CASALINGA
VOLUME
VIA V. D. GUICCIARDINI
Giardino del Madana
Giardino Torrigiani
VIA DE' MARTIRI
VIA DELLE CALDAIE
VIA D. S. MARTINO
Piazza di San Felice
Piazza de' Pitti
PITTI PALACE
Giardini di Boboli
VIA PETRARCA
Giardino di Analena
VIA ROMANA
VIALE DELLA MERIDIANA
Piazzina della Meridiana
Prato dell'Uccellare
FORTE BELVEDERE
VIALE DEI CIPRESSI
BOBOLINO
Piazzale della Porta Romana
IL TRIPPAIO DI PORTA ROMANA
V. SENESE
VIALE MACHIAVELLI
HOTEL CLASSIC

0   200 yds
0   200 m

© MOON.COM

in no hurry to get to the other side. The bridge is best viewed from the streets running along the Arno and the neighboring bridges, which attract less attention. People gather on **Ponte Santa Trinità,** 150 yards downriver, to watch the setting sun transform the pastel-colored shops of the Ponte Vecchio. **Ponte Alle Grazie** on the opposite side is farther away and provides a better view in the morning. Both bridges lead to lesser-known parts of Oltrarno.

BASILICA DI SANTO SPIRITO

Piazza Santo Spirito 30, tel. 055/210-030, www.basilicasantospirito.it, Thurs.-Fri. 10am-12:30pm and 4pm-6pm, free

Basilica di Santo Spirito is one of only two basilicas in Oltrarno. From the outside it looks a little like the Alamo, with a plain façade facing a modest tree-lined *piazza* that hosts a daily market in the morning and gets lively at night. It was founded by Augustan monks in 1250, but a devastating fire led to the hiring of Brunelleschi to work on the reconstruction. Rebuilding and expanding the church was so costly that the monks were forced to give up one of their daily meals until work was completed. The famed architect died a few years after construction started, but many of his plans were carried out, including the cupola and strict geometric proportions that give the interior an impressive harmony. Daily mass is held at 5:30pm.

A small museum (Piazza Santo Spirito 29, tel. 055/287-043, Mon.-Sun. only 10am-4pm, €4) to the left of the basilica was once part of the medieval convent and now contains a collection of religious artifacts and the remains of Andrea Orcagna's enormous *Last Supper* fresco. The apostles have disappeared but Jesus remains high above on a crucifix surrounded by angels. The room itself is full of Gothic fittings and is a stark contrast to the Renaissance concepts employed inside the church. There are daily masses at 9am, 10:30am, 6pm, and 9pm, with confession in English on Thursdays from 5pm to 6pm.

BRANCACCI CHAPEL
(Cappella Brancacci)
Piazza del Carmine 14, tel. 055/238-2195, Mon. and Wed.-Fri. 10am-5pm, Sat.-Sun. 1pm-5pm, €6 or Firenzecard

Santa Maria del Carmine was founded by a group of Pisan monks in 1268. The inside was nearly completely destroyed by a fire in 1771, but the Cappella Brancacci survived. This chapel was commissioned by Felici Brancacci, a wealthy merchant and politician, and recounts the life of St. Peter. The frescoes were the result of three successive artists including Masaccio and Filippo Lippi, who completed the chapel in 1480. The new interior is one of the few examples of Roman baroque in the city.

The most striking of the frescoes depict Adam and Eve before and after giving in to temptation, represented by a snake with a female head. Their body language and complexions are completely transformed. A keen observer might also notice the belly buttons on the first couple. Some speculate it was an oversight by the artist, as both Adam and Eve were created by God and would not have needed an umbilical cord.

Only 30 people are allowed in the chapel at a time, but lines are short, even in summer. The chapel is just beyond the bookshop on the far side of the cloister. If you're not well versed in the Bible pick up the tablet (€3) at the shop. It's easy to use and makes sense of the fresco cycle one image at a time.

PITTI PALACE
(Palazzo Pitti)
Piazza Pitti 1, tel. 055/294-883, Tues.-Sun. 8:15am-6:50pm, €16, €38 combo ticket or Firenzecard, audio guide €6

Palazzo Pitti, the largest palace in Florence, can easily take a half day to fully explore. It was built in the 14th century for a wealthy banker (Luca Pitti) who wanted to show off his power and flattened a neighborhood to get his wish. His fortunes turned, and before the *palazzo* was completed it fell into the hands of his archrival, Cosimo I de Medici. Today, the palace contains two art galleries, several museums, a costume collection, the royal apartments, and an 11-acre garden. Sights are divided into two itineraries with separate tickets.

Galleria Palatina originated as the personal collection of the Medici and covers the entire first floor. Paintings hang as the last residents of the *palazzo* left them, with little concern for chronology. The haphazard display is refreshing, and the gallery labels read like a who's who of the art world. Works by Botticelli, Tiziano, Perugino, and Veronese fill 11 finely decorated salons. The entire collection owes its existence to Anna Maria Ludovica, who was the last Medici heir and bequeathed her family's treasures to the city in 1737 on the condition they would never be divided, sold, or taken from the city.

The Royal Apartments provide further insight into the family's taste for luxury. The Dukes of Lorraine, who were later residents and lived in the *palazzo* until the 19th century, ordered the neoclassical redesign. They liked their decor ostentatious, and the climax is the plush throne room where visitors were received and tourists now gather. If you aren't suffering from artistic overload visit the Galleria d'Arte Moderna (tel. 055/238-8616, Tues.-Sun. 8:15am-6:50pm) on the second floor. This gallery opened in 1924 and is dedicated to Italian painters between the late 18th century and World War I.

The second itinerary starts on the opposite wing at the Museo degli Argenti, which the Medici used as their summer apartments. The museum displays glassware and carpets, as well as fine jewelry cherished by the family. This option also includes the Galleria dei Costume, which is worth visiting if you have an interest in 19th-century womens wear and ancient

fashions. The real reason to get this ticket is for the Giardini Boboli (daily Nov.-Feb. 8:15am-4:30pm, Mar. and Oct. 8:15am-5:30pm, Apr.-May and Sept. 8:15am-6:30, June-Aug. 8:15am-7:30pm, closed first and last Mon. every month, €10, €38 combo ticket or Firenzecard) gardens that come into full bloom in late spring and provide a tranquil escape from the city. There are four entrances to the gardens, which are free on the first Sunday of every month.

Special half-price tickets to Palazzo Pitti are available when purchased before 8:59am and used prior to 9:25am.

FORTE BELVEDERE

Via di San Leonardo 1, tel. 055/27681, Tues.-Sun. 10:30am-6:30pm, €3

Forte Belvedere lies on the hill above the Boboli Gardens and provides one of the best views of the city. This fortress is a little harder to reach than Piazzale Michelangelo, whose convenient parking makes it a mandatory stop for busloads of camera-happy tourists, but offers a closer perspective of the city. If you aren't planning on visiting Lucca or any of the other fortified towns in Tuscany, Belvedere's star-shaped ramparts are also an excellent primer in military architecture. The fortress was built at the end of the 16th century and served as insurance for the Medici, who were wary of attacks from outside the city and rebellions from within. It was also a reliable place to stash their treasure. Today you can walk around the upper and lower terraces, which often host summer art exhibitions.

The fort has two entrances. It can be reached directly from the northeastern exit of the Boboli Gardens or through the main entrance near the medieval walls, which also flank the

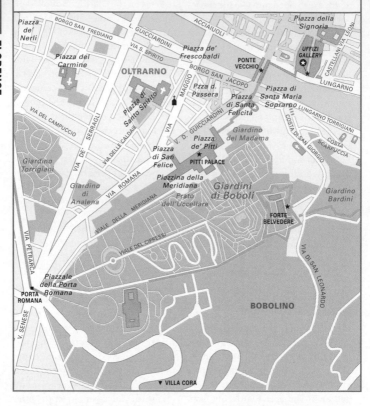

San Niccolò

(Map labels:)

Piazza de' Nerli — BORGO SAN FREDIANO — L. GUICCIARDINI — ACCIAIUOLI — Piazza della Signoria

VIA S. SPIRITO — Piazza de' Frescobaldi — PONTE VECCHIO — UFFIZI GALLERY — CASTELLANI — VIA LEONI

Piazza del Carmine — OLTRARNO — BORGO SAN JACOPO — LUNGARNO

VIA DEL CAMPUCCIO — Piazza di Santo Spirito — VIA MAGGIO — Pzza d. Passera — Piazza di Santa Maria Soprarno — LUNGARNO TORRIGIANI

VIA DELLE CALDAIE — VIA V. D. GUICCIARDINI — Piazza di Santa Felicita — COSTA DI SAN GIORGIO — COSTA SCARPUCCIA

Giardino Torrigiani — Piazza de' Pitti — Giardino del Madama — PITTI PALACE

Giardino di Analena — Piazza di San Felice — Piazzina della Meridiana — Giardini di Boboli — Giardino Bardini

VIA ROMANA — VIALE DELLA MERIDIANA — Prato dell'Uccellare — FORTE BELVEDERE

VIA PETRARCA — VIALE DEL CIPRESSI — VIA DI SAN LEONARDO

Piazzale della Porta Romana — PORTA ROMANA — BOBOLINO

V. SENESE — ▼ VILLA CORA

nearby Giardino Bardini. Hours may vary according to the exhibitions taking place.

SAN NICCOLÒ
PIAZZALE MICHELANGELO

Piazzale Michelangelo is Florence's most famous observation point and a mandatory stop for many tourists. It was built during the city's brief stint as capital of Italy and sits on a hillside from where most of Florence is visible. You can arrive by car or bus (line 12) but most people climb up from the San Niccolò neighborhood. If you choose to walk you can take the pedestrian walkway past the rose garden or the

winding monumental steps that begin from Piazza Giuseppe Poggi. In the center of the square stands a bronze copy of Michelangelo's *David*. There are several other copies of his work nearby. The elegant neoclassical *loggia* across the street was meant to house a Michelangelo museum, but the project was never completed and it has since become a restaurant and café serving local specialties.

The 1870s was a period of urban restructuring in Florence. Along with the *piazza*, tree-lined avenues leading to the square were created. Two of these, Viale Galileo and Michelangelo, wind through

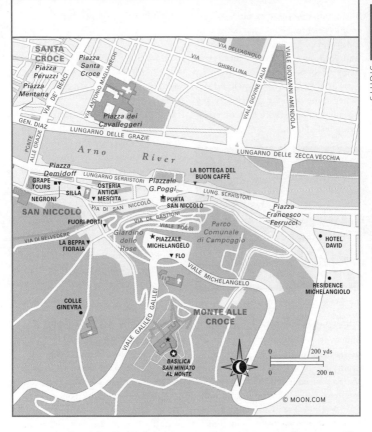

the countryside and offer further glimpses of the city.

✪ BASILICA SAN MINIATO AL MONTE

Via delle Porte Sante 34, tel. 055/234-2731, Mon.-Sat. 9:30am-1pm and 3pm-7pm and Sun. 8:15-7pm, free

The hilltop church of Basilica San Miniato al Monte is one of the oldest Romanesque churches in the city and was dedicated to the first Christian martyr of Florence. It's rarely crowded and the cool interior provides relief on hot summer days. There are three levels connected by marble steps; each is decorated in the green-and-white marble common to the region. The walls are covered with ancient frescoes of saints. An audio booth near the entrance sheds light on the origins of the building.

From the wide gravel terrace in front of the church you can admire the entire city. Unlike at Piazzale Michelangelo, the view is unspoiled by tour groups and street vendors hawking selfie sticks. Look upon the Duomo and rooftops of the city while sampling sweets prepared by the Benedictine monks in the adjacent monastic shop (tel. 055/234-2731, daily 10am-12:15pm and 4pm-6pm) or explore the **cemetery,** where the author of *Pinocchio* is buried. The monks celebrate Eucharist daily with Latin and Gregorian chants at 7:15am and 5:45pm (5:30pm on Sundays). They also provide hospitality to devout travelers who must follow Benedictine curfews and rituals. It's not a hotel but a search for God and a tiring test of faith.

Basilica San Miniato al Monte

Getting to San Miniato is a small endeavor. Although the church can be reached by bus 12 or 13, the most gratifying approach is hiking up along Via San Niccolò and through the old medieval gate. Take the second right onto Via dell'Erta Canina and continue a short way to the path on the left that leads uphill. It's also called Erta Canina, but you'll know you're in the right place if there's grass growing in between the rough paving stones and no one's in sight.

As you climb, you'll pass olive groves and cottages that appear more suited to a village than the city spreading out below. At the end of the narrow road you can turn left onto Viale Galileo or cross the avenue and continue up the improvised steps through a glade of pines until you come to the fortifications hastily constructed by Michelangelo during a siege of the city. The dirt path eventually disappears;

follow the walls in either direction and you'll reach the basilica.

PORTA SAN NICCOLÒ

Via dei Bastioni, tel. 055/276-8224, June-Oct., daily 4pm-8pm, €6 or Firenzecard

If you're climbing back down from San Miniato, it's hard to miss Porta San Niccolò, a tower that overlooks the Arno and once guarded the city. It's the only surviving tower to maintain its original height and is open to the public between July and September. Tours are conducted in Italian and English and depart on the hour. The 30-minute visit includes an explanation of Renaissance fortifications and a walk up the 160 steps to the terrace where you can get a riverside view of the city.

GREATER FLORENCE
MUSEO STIBBERT

Via Federico Stibbert 26, tel. 055/475-520, www.museostibbert.it, Fri.-Sun. 10am-6pm and Mon.-Wed. 10am-2pm, €8 or Firenzecard

Frederick Stibbert came from an Italo-English family with a military background and from an early age began collecting weapons. The collection is primarily formed of 16th-18th-century armor, hand-to-hand weapons, and firearms from Italy, France, Germany, and beyond. There are hundreds of items and dozens of suits of armor, many mounted on horses that were equally armored. Like cars today, armor was personalized as the owners saw fit to distinguish themselves and intimidate enemies. The collection is housed in a villa a short walk from the center. Otherwise, ride bus 4 from the train station through residential 19th-century neighborhoods and across the city's only canal.

Food

It's hard to have a bad meal in Florence. Food here is a tale of traditional rural recipes prepared generation after generation. Ingredients are simple and in harmony with the seasons. The city offers a variety of unique dishes, many of which hail from a humble era when ingredients were whatever was available. For the most part that meant grains, legumes, vegetables, and meat. Florentines use all of these. The city is also famous for T-bone steaks and soups.

Long before the word *restaurant* was invented Italians were heading to *trattorie* for good food at next-to-nothing prices. Some of the oldest date back hundreds of years and are often run by different generations of the same family in historically working-class neighborhoods. They're not fancy and barely romantic, but they are full of charm and where *pappa al pomodoro* and *bistecca alla fiorentina* taste the best.

DUOMO AND AROUND

There are hundreds of eateries in the *centro storico* in all categories and price ranges. The best and most authentic are nearly never located on major squares or thoroughfares that rely solely on the tourist trade. Good restaurants look as though they've been around for decades. Many have wonderful rustic interiors and good-natured staff who usually have time to share a word or a joke.

ITALIAN
Giannino in San Lorenzo
Via Borgo San Lorenzo 33-37r, tel. 055/239-9799, daily 11:30am-11:30pm, €12-20, pizza €7-9

Like many historic restaurants founded after World War II, Giannino in San Lorenzo has managed to survive thanks to a new generation of restaurateurs eager to keep old traditions alive. In this case Riccardo Bartoloni and his son are behind the renaissance. They serve great steaks, tripe in all its incarnations, and excellent pizza. There's something for everyone inside this venerable establishment where quality still matters.

Konnubio
Via dei Conti 8R, tel. 055/238-1189, daily 7:30am-11:30pm, €14-16

Konnubio is proof that Florentine dining isn't only about traditional dishes served within rustic interiors. This cosmopolitan restaurant around the corner from Basilica San Lorenzo could easily be located in New York or Paris. The restaurant's four attractive rooms are decorated in contemporary style with wood-and-metallic furniture that is beyond cool. Tuscan, international, and vegan dishes are served nonstop from breakfast to dinner. Plate appearance matters as much as the ingredients selected.

SEAFOOD
Fishing Lab
Via del Proconsolo 16r, tel. 055/240-618, daily 11am-12am, €10-€14

This lively restaurant in a vibrant frescoed location has great décor and

❂ **TRATTORIA SOSTANZA:** This modest eatery serves Florentine classics in 1950s-era surroundings (page 73).

❂ **CUCINA TORCICODA:** It's restaurant, *osteria*, *pizzeria*—and wholly original (page 78).

❂ **MERCATO CENTRALE:** Browse the ingredients at this lively market—the center of Florentine food scene since 1872—before settling in at its second-floor food court (page 73).

❂ **ALL'ANTICO VINAIO:** Tourists and locals line up for mammoth sandwiches stuffed with local cold cuts. Don't worry; the line moves fast (page 71)!

❂ **OSTERIA ANTICA MESCITA:** Enjoy down-to-earth dishes at affordable prices en route to admire the views from the hillside of San Miniato (page 86).

❂ **LA BOTTEGA DEL BUON CAFFÈ:** This Michelin-rated restaurant facing the Arno makes dishes that are close to art—at an accessible price (page 86).

❂ **VECCHIO FORNO:** Good-smelling Tuscan bread and pastries are baked in the oven out back at this cute corner bakery (page 75).

❂ **GELATERIA DELLA PASSERA:** Enjoy the creamiest gelato in the city on the lovely little square facing this tiny shop (page 85).

a youthful staff who know their seafood. The menu includes raw, fried, and traditional options along with a street menu that can be ordered in half or full portions. Atmosphere is informal and service friendly and efficient.

INTERNATIONAL
Ristorante Persiano
Via dei Cerchi 25r, tel. 055/094-5695, daily 12:30-3:30pm and 7-11pm, €9-13

Dining possibilities have expanded exponentially in recent years thanks to places like Ristorante Persiano that have introduced new flavors to the city. This colorful eatery specializes in oriental flavors and the menu contains a mix of beef and chicken kebabs served with rice and yogurt, and exotic starters that provide a pleasant break from Italian food.

Dim Sum
Via dei Neri 37r, tel. 055/284-331, Tues.-Sun. noon-3pm and 7pm-11pm, €14-16

Dim Sum is a small, modern restaurant with a bright interior and an open kitchen where chefs prepare southern Chinese specialties. Diners are greeted with a cup of tea (which is continually refilled) and a menu that includes steamed appetizers, dumplings, and pot stickers, and vegetarian, noodle, and rice dishes. It fills up fast on weekends. Reservations can be useful.

SANDWICHES
The most reliable destination for thick sandwiches and generous platters of

All'Antico Vinaio

Bottega Renzini

Via dei Neri 45r, tel. 055/010-6070, daily 10am-8pm, €12

If the line at All'Antico Vinaio is too long, head down the street to Bottega Renzini. This 2017 entry to the Florentine fast-food scene offers more than local specialties and there's a little of nearly every Italian region inside. It's a gastronomic "best of" with an attractive interior and gourmet options.

La Prosciutteria

Via de'Neri 54r, tel. 055/265-4472, daily 11:30am-11pm, €8-10

La Prosciutteria specializes in Chianti wine and locally produced cold cuts and cheeses served on long wooden cutting boards. It's a fun place where friends meet to share a meal in relaxed company that spills out onto the sidewalk.

cold cuts and cheeses served with wine is **Via dei Neri.** It's one of the most mouthwatering streets in the city, with plenty of Florentine fast-food options to choose from.

✪ All'Antico Vinaio

Via dei Neri 65r, 74r-76r, tel. 055/238-2723, daily 10:30am-10pm, €5

The secret to a great sandwich is fresh bread and quality fillings, and All'Antico Vinaio has nailed both—which explains why the line outside their small shop is 20-30 deep most evenings. What people are waiting for is enormous slices of focaccia filled with cold cuts, cheese, and vegetables, for just €5. The *Schacciatela*, overflowing with prociutto ham, is the most popular, but you can also pick from a tempting selection that includes a vegetarian option. To avoid the rush arrive around 11am or 6pm. There are a few tables inside, but Florentines just sit on the curb of the pedestrian street outside. This local sandwich empire has grown and there are now three locations next door to each other.

Vinaino Fiorenza

Via Vacchereccia 13, tel. 055/265-5847, daily 9am-11pm, €3-6

The best thing about Vinaino Fiorenza is that you can find a dozen kinds of Italian sandwiches all crafted with the regional products that make them unique. There's *mozzarella di bufala* from Campania, *porchetto* from Lazio, *'nduja* sausage from Calabria, and much more. The glass case facing the street is filled with tempting options that can be eaten at one of the stools inside the small shop or in Piazza della Signoria down the block.

L'Antico Trippaio

Piazza dei Cimatori, daily 11am-9pm, €5

L'Antico Trippaio is a similar setup to I Trippaio Fiorentino, with the addition of photos identifying each of the sandwiches on offer. Hours sometimes vary but both generally open from lunch until dinner.

COFFEE

Florence's historic cafés are elegant institutions that have been in business for decades. They continue to serve regulars and curious visitors inside little-changed interiors where artists and literati of previous eras spent their days in animated discussion.

Giubbe Rosse

Piazza della Repubblica 13/14r, tel. 055/212-280, daily 8am-11pm, €2-5

The only place an aspiring 20th-century Florentine writer or painter would consider entering was Giubbe Rosse. Named after the red jackets still worn by the waitstaff, this tearoom was founded by two German brothers in 1896. It became famous a decade later as the principal hangout of Futurist artists. It's a mandatory stop for bibliophiles, and traces of the café's literary past are still evident.

Caffè Gilli

Piazza della Repubblica 39r, tel. 055/213-896, daily 7am-midnight, €2-5

On the other side of the *piazza* lies Caffè Gilli, with its elegant chandeliers and closely spaced round tables. The location and Liberty-style décor have changed little since the 1920s.

Caffè Rivoire

Piazza della Signoria 5, tel. 055/214-412, Tues.-Sun. 7:30am-9pm, €2-5

Caffè Rivoire is diagonally opposite Palazzo Vecchio and has been in business since 1872. Initially they only served chocolate, but coffee, tea, and pastries were soon added to the menu and attracted the cultural elite of the time. The shop still draws people who want to step into the past and enjoy a good view of the square. All that has changed are the topics of conversation and the prices—which are double or triple that of an average bar.

✪ Ditta Artigianale

Via dei Neri 32r, tel. 055/274-1541, Mon.-Thurs. 8am-10pm, Fri. 8am-midnight, Sat. 9:30am-midnight, Sun. 9:30am-10pm, €2-3

The key to great coffee is the bean. At Ditta Artigianale they choose theirs carefully and control every step in the blending process. The result is one of the best espressos in the city. You can also sip on tea, have a light lunch, or enjoy a predinner cocktail inside this hip coffee hangout adorned with repurposed and vintage furnishings.

✪ Amblé

Piazzetta dei Del Bene 7a, tel. 055/268-528, daily 10am-midnight, €3-5

Nothing matches at Amblé, but that's part of the charm of this coffee and fruit bar moments from the Ponte Vecchio. The other part is the feeling of stumbling upon a place that can only be found by accident. Friends and couples relax outside on brightly colored deck chairs, benches, and stools all partially shaded by an ancient wall.

Bar Caffè Mingo

Piazza San Martino 1r, tel. 055/215-646, daily 8am-8:30pm

Bar Caffè Mingo is stuck in time on a little square that has nothing very special about it except its refusal to change. Sit outside on the metal chairs away from the sun and watch the pedestrians pass. It doesn't feel like the center of Florence, but it's around the corner from everything and is a good caffeine refuge.

GELATO
GROM

Via del Campanile, 2, tel. 055/216-158, daily 10am-midnight

Not all chains are necessarily bad and Grom is the proof. This popular gelateria has made a global name for itself based on quality and original flavors. Prices are higher than average but for €4 you get an overflowing cone with creamy classics or fruity sorbets around the corner from the Duomo.

SANTA MARIA NOVELLA
TUSCAN
✪ Trattoria Sostanza

Via Porcellana 25r, tel. 055/212-691, Mon.-Sat. 12:30pm-2pm and 7:30pm-9:45pm, €8-10

Trattoria Sostanza is on an anonymous street you'd probably avoid unless you were hungry. It has the character that comes from decades of preparing the same dishes a dozen times a day. No attempt is made at reinventing traditional recipes and no one seems to care. The daily handwritten menu includes pasta, soup, *Trippa alla Fiorentina, bistecca alla fiorentina*, and side orders of beans.

Baldini

Via il Prato 96r, tel. 055/287-663, Mon.-Fri. noon-2:30pm and 7:30pm-10pm, €14-16

Baldini may seem like a long way to walk for a meal but it's actually still within the old city walls and only minutes from the train station. It's hard to get more traditional than this. The fundamental ingredients are bread, olive oil, grilled meat, and wine. In addition, you'll find Tuscan classics like *tagliatelle* with wild boar, *ribollita,* and tripe. The desserts are homemade daily and fish is only served on Fridays.

COFFEE
La Boulangerie

Via de'Rondinelli 24r, tel. 055/281-658, daily 7am-8pm, €5

La Boulangerie is a good place to take a break from sightseeing or shopping. It's an instant respite from the busy street outside and serves coffee, fresh-squeezed orange juice, pastries, and a variety of tempting baguette sandwiches. Take a seat at the long wooden counter or grab a stool near the front and observe the world walking by.

SAN LORENZO AND SAN MARCO
TUSCAN
Mario

Via Rosina 2r, tel. 055/218-550, Mon.-Sat. 12:30pm-3:30pm, €10-12, cash only

The word has been out about Mario since 1957, and this compact *trattoria* is nearly always busy with young and old seated close together eating whatever the daily menu has on offer. It's always delicious and the long, tiled dining room is nearly always full. Chefs prepare a steady stream of *ribollita* and roast chicken for eager customers drinking carafes of house wine. It's a good place to try *bistecca alla fiorentina* that's perfectly tender and always served rare. Reservations aren't accepted, but they'll take your name and seat you when a space opens up. Seating is often communal, which means there's a high probability of meeting people.

✪ Mercato Centrale

Piazza del Mercato Centrale, tel. 055/239-9798, daily 8am-midnight, €12-14

If you can't decide between pizza, pasta, or a T-bone steak, the food emporium on the second floor of the recently restored Mercato Centrale is the solution. It contains over 20 quality

TUSCAN CUISINE

ribollita

In a country known for food, Tuscany is recognized by Italians as one of the best regions in which to eat. Meals don't have to be formal, and simple dishes are very often the best. Besides conventional *trattorie* where you can sample local cuisine, the city has a long tradition of street food. Here are some tips for tasting Florence's most authentic dishes:

AT THE *TRATTORIA*

Nearly every Florentine *trattoria* has *ribollita* and *pappa al pomodoro* stews on their menu. Both are vegetarian friendly and highly filling. Fortunately, you can order a half portion (*mezza porzione*) of either and sample both.

- **Antipasti:** Appetizers, which are a delicious way to begin any meal. Choices include **crostini** along with local cold cuts and cheeses, often served in wine bars on wooden platters and accompanied by honey and olives. Central Italy is a great producer of **prosciutto** and other hams. The local variety is slightly spicy.

- **Crostini:** A lighter version of *bruschetta* that consists of grilled unsalted bread topped with oil, chopped tomatoes, or *fegato* (ground chicken liver similar to paté).

eateries that can satisfy multiple cravings. It's a popular lunch and dinner spot where diners bring whatever they like back to the central eating areas or sit and watch dishes being prepared at the counters. Beer and wine have their own dedicated sections and local soccer fans gather to watch games on Sundays.

SANDWICHES
Sandwichic

*Via San Gallo 3, tel. 055/281-157,
Mon.-Thurs. 10am-11pm and Fri.-Sun.
10am-midnight, €5*

Sandwichic is housed inside a former haberdashery. *Panini* have replaced textiles and sewing machines, but thread and buttons are still on display.

- **Ribollita:** An authentic vegetarian stew, often made in winter when the black cabbage in the recipe is in season, though it can be found throughout the year with substitute vegetables.

- **Pappa al pomodoro:** A vegetarian, tomato-based stew that's perfect in summer. It's reminiscent of gazpacho although the bread used gives it a thicker texture.

- **Bistecca alla fiorentina:** A thick T-bone steak that is the most popular main course in Florence. It's cut from *Chianina* beef, a local cattle breed raised along the Tuscan coast and prized for its flavor. It's priced by the kilo. Don't bother asking for medium or well done: *Fiorentina* steaks are grilled for three minutes on either side and served alone on a plate close to rare. *Contorni* (sides) are ordered separately and generally consist of green beans (*fagioli*), broccoli, and zucchini. Roasted potatoes (*patate arrosto*) are also usually on offer.

- **Vino:** Wine! Tuscany is home to some of the finest vineyards in Italy. **Chianti** and **Barolo** are world-renowned. If you're not an expert, the **vino della casa** (house wine) of any decent restaurant is always drinkable. Order it by the glass or by quarter, half, or full carafe. Cold **vino bianco** (white wine) is popular in summer while **vino rosso** (red wine) usually accompanies meat and cheese dishes.

STREET EATS

The favorite fast-food ingredient in Florence is tripe (*trippa*), made from the inside of a cow's four stomachs (not intestines). This traditional ingredient is a holdover from the Middle Ages, when people didn't throw away just anything. Tripe in fact has great gastronomic possibilities and has generated a variety of dishes. Locals can point the way toward the best of the remaining stands that serve tripe. Favorites depend on tenderness of the meat, concentration of spices, and personality of the vendors.

- **Lampredotto:** Tripe simmered for hours with tomatoes, onions, and parsley. It's eaten as a stew accompanied by a green herb sauce or in a sandwich. Find it at mobile kiosks around the city and inside Mercato Centrale.

- **Trippa alla Fiorentina:** Tripe sautéed with vegetables, tomatoes, and Parmesan, then simmered until the liquid slowly evaporates. It's on many menus and a good introduction to tripe.

- **Schiacciata:** The Florentine version of *focaccia*, served at bakeries to make sandwiches or enjoyed straight up. It's a speedy and delicious snack that's thick and doughy, and often topped with grilled vegetables or stuffed with local cold cuts.

The three street chefs aren't trying to revolutionize the sandwich—they're just obsessed with using the best bread and local hams to make them. Wine is self-served for €1 a cup. Daily specials are written on the blackboard or fresh ingredients can be chosen to create an original sandwich.

BAKERIES
✪ Vecchio Forno

Via Guelfa 32, tel. 055/265-4069, Mon.-Sat. 7:30am-8pm, €3

Florentine bread lacks salt. According to legend this was due to a Pisan blockade and the inability to import the mineral for several years. The taste for unsalted loaves stuck and dozens of *forni* (bakeries) in the center are busy baking it every morning. Vecchio Forno is a small shop on a corner where locals come for typical *pan di ramerino,* sweet bread made with raisins and rosemary. Glass cases display tempting sandwiches, cakes, and tarts, and the shelves are filled with an assortment of Tuscan breads. You can take it to go or sit at one of the half-dozen stools and listen to local chatter.

Pugi

Piazza San Marco 9b, tel. 055/280-981, Mon.-Sat. 7:45am-8pm, €5

If you haven't tried *schiacciatta all'olio* (Tuscan focaccia), grab a number and get in line at Pugi. The *schiacciata* comes dabbed with olive oil and topped with zucchini, sliced potatoes, or red peppers or stuffed with *prosciutto* ham. When it's your turn just point and gesture to the friendly uniformed ladies behind the counter. They also have great desserts and seasonal specialties at Carnevale, Easter, and Christmas. There are several other locations around the city in case you develop a habit.

Garbo

Via Dino del Garbo 2, tel. 055/437-8740, Mon.-Fri. 7am-8pm, Sat.-Sun. 7:30am-1pm, €3-5

People obsessed with bread won't mind the long walk to Garbo, a neighborhood bakery run by Carlo Scorpio and his wife, Silvia. They can spend hours talking about flour and yeast. Everything here is made by hand using local ingredients and a grindstone Carlo claims is the secret to making great bread. You'll notice the difference from the smell wafting out of the ovens and the perfectly stacked loaves behind the counter. Every day is dedicated to a different flavor: If you arrive on a Saturday you can sample the *paillasse* (Florentine baguette) and dried fruit buns. They also create pastries and serve a light lunch menu that can be eaten there or taken away.

GELATO

Gelato prices start at around €2 for two scoops in a cup or cone. Each additional scoop is €0.50. Whipped cream is free but you may have to ask for *panna* in case it's forgotten.

Le Botteghe di Leonardo

Via de'Ginori 21r, tel. 055/933-7083, Tues.-Sun. 12:30pm-8:30pm, €3-5

Le Botteghe di Leonardo makes a great dark chocolate flavor, but if you ask Francesco what he suggests combining it with he won't give you a straight answer. Fortunately, he'll let you sample any flavor that catches your interest on the menu board. The gelato is kept in metal containers and out of sight. Once you've made a decision you can enjoy it on the chairs facing a *fresco.* This *gelateria* is part of a cooperative and there are several others around the city.

Gelateria Carabè

Via Ricasoli 60r, tel. 055/289-476, Tues.-Sun. 10am-7pm, €3-5

Gelateria Carabè takes the Sicilian approach to gelato, which explains the *granite* and *cannoli* that are also available. Watch the gelato being made while you wait and enjoy it on one of the benches inside or out. Every flavor is based on fresh ingredients, including almonds, hazelnuts, and pistachios imported from Sicily. There's even an olive oil and several gluten-free flavors. (Gelato is often gluten-free, but some shops use flour as a thickener, and flavors like tiramisu may contain wheat.)

SANTA CROCE

TUSCAN

Osteria Dei Pazzi

Via dei Lavatoi 1r, tel. 055/234-4880,
Tues.-Sun. 12:30pm-2:45pm and
7:30pm-10:45pm, €7-10

Osteria Dei Pazzi is an unassuming restaurant around the corner from Piazza Santa Croce. The sign above the entrance is vintage 1960s and little on the inside has changed since then. The food is typical Tuscan, and Italians occupy most of the tables under ceiling fans that keep the large dining room cool.

Trattoria Pallottino

Via Isola delle Stinche 1r, tel. 055/260-8887,
Tues.-Sun. 12:30pm-2:30pm and
7:30pm-10:30pm, €8-10

Trattoria Pallottino has been serving local Tuscan dishes since 1911. It's a good place to try *pappa al pomodoro* and *ribollita*. The narrow dining room is paved with cobblestones and lined with wooden tables and chairs that have been used by generations of diners. There's outdoor seating along the pedestrian street near Santa Croce. Daily specials are written on a blackboard near the entrance.

Trattoria da Rocco

Piazza Ghiberti, tel. 339/838-4555, daily
11am-3:30pm, €5-6

Locals and tourists have been coming to Trattoria da Rocco for 35 years for honest portions, Florentine specialties, and low prices. Firsts are €5, non-fish seconds €6, and sides of vegetables €4. The house wine, kept in straw-covered bottles, is priced by how much you drink, and desserts are all homemade. Booths at this small diner-like institution can be hard to come by and are often shared between hungry strangers. Service is fast and cheery.

Adagio Firenze

Via de' Macci 79r, tel. 055/051-7094,
Mon.-Sat. 11am-11pm, €14-16

The culinary concept behind this trendy bistro is to highlight a different Italian region every month and, depending when you arrive, you could enjoy pesto from Liguria or polenta from Alto Adige. They also feature a permanent menu of local favorites and delicious chocolate desserts.

Trattoria Moderna

Lungarno del Tempio 52, tel. 055/234-3693,
Mon.-Sat. 12:30-2:30pm and 7pm-midnight,
€12-16

Tuscan food isn't stuck in the past and chef Riccardo Serni likes experimenting with flavors from around the world. The best thing to do here is opt for one of the three tasting menus that start from €37 and provide a welcome introduction to Florentine fusion.

ITALIAN

Johnny Bruschetta

Via dei Macci 77r, tel. 055/247-8326, daily
12:30pm-3pm and 7:30pm-11pm, €8-12

Johnny Bruschetta is a fun place for beer and bruschetta near Mercato di San Ambrogio. They prepare 17 varieties of bruschetta that can be sampled on a 30-inch (76-centimeter) cutting board with two types, 50-inch (127-centimeter) board with three, and 80-inch (203-centimeter) board with four. It's a lot like a tapas bar, and tables fill up with friends sharing this fun finger food. They also serve cured meats and cheeses, a vegetarian option, and craft beer from the taps. The area is animated at night and a good place to start or spend an evening.

SEAFOOD
Vivo

*Largo Annigoni 9 A/B, tel. 333/182-4183,
Tues.-Sun. 12:30-2:30pm and 7:30-11:30pm,
€16-20*

Vivo is the latest restaurant in an up-and-coming *piazza* lined with tempting eateries. The open-plan dining room and contemporary atmosphere are a break from rustic interiors. Fish is the main attraction, and the fact that the menu changes based on the daily catch is a good sign.

SANDWICHES
Semel

*Piazza Lorenzo Ghiberti 44r, no tel.,
Mon.-Sat. 11:30am-2:30pm, €6-8*

Locals love this cozy snack spot and gather for lunch to drink wine and feast on gourmet sandwiches filled with anchovies, fennel, and other original ingredients enjoyed on the narrow wooden counter inside or on the sidewalk outside.

PIZZA

Pizza isn't native to Florence. It was introduced by Neapolitan expats and is thicker than the Roman version. Few restaurants are entirely devoted to pizza but it does appear on many menus.

✪ Cucina Torcicoda

*Via Torta 5r, tel. 055/265-4329, daily
noon-3pm and 7pm-11pm, €10-14*

In recent years Cucina Torcicoda has distinguished itself with its versatility: it's a restaurant, *osteria,* and *pizzeria* all in one. San Marzano tomatoes, Campania *mozzarella,* and Tuscan oil find their way into the daily pizza special and great *calzone.* All the ingredients from the menu can be purchased at the little gourmet shop in the back.

Caffè Italiano

*Via dell'Isola delle Stinche 11/13r, tel.
055/289-368, daily 12:30pm-3pm
and 7pm-11pm, €8*

Caffè Italiano has a wood-burning oven and is obsessed with using the best ingredients in traditional ways. That's probably why they only serve three types of pizza: *Margherita, Napoli,* and *Marinara.* The lack of variety hasn't stopped Vincenzo D'Anetra from building a loyal following that can make finding a table inside this delightful brick and wood-paneled *osteria* difficult.

La Divina Pizza

*Via Borgo Allegri 50r, tel. 055/234-7498,
Mon. 6:30pm-midnight, Tues.-Sat.
11:30am-3:30pm and 6:30pm-midnight,
€6-8*

Pizza enthusiasts who aren't interested in décor should visit La Divina Pizza. It's a *pizza al taglio* shop run by an enthusiastic father-and-son team. They pull out mouthwatering tins of pizza and *focaccia* throughout the day that are served by the cut to a steady stream of clients. Choose three or four kinds and eat them inside on a little wooden tray or ask for takeaway (*per portare via*) and enjoy your pizza in Piazza Santa Croce or along the river.

Cucineria la Mattonaia

*Via della Mattonaia 19r, tel. 055/386-0564,
daily 7:30pm-11:30pm, €9-12*

The atmosphere at Cucineria la Mattonaia is more refined than you'd expect for a *pizzeria,* but then again they also serve an extensive selection of meat and fish dishes. The pizza comes in over 20 varieties that include the classics as well as some originals topped with cheese and vegetables.

INTERNATIONAL

The influx of Japanese and Chinese tourists as well as a steady stream of North African and East Asian immigrants has led to a diversification of dining options in Florence over the past few decades. Today it's easy to find sushi and noodles in the center, and kebab shops and Indian takeaway along the streets north of Mercato Centrale where newcomers to the city tend to gather.

Kome

Via dei Benci 41, tel. 055/200-8009, Mon.-Sat. noon-3pm and 7pm-11pm, bento box lunch special €15

There are quite a few sushi restaurants in Florence, and Kome is one of the liveliest. Choose between the *kaitan* belt (€25-40) on the ground floor where experienced chefs keep the sushi, sashimi, and tempura plates coming, or head to the grill-it-yourself tables for Japanese barbecue (€40-60 for two). It's a lot of fun, but if all you're after is a shot of *sake* the downstairs lounge has a regular Wednesday happy hour that includes an extensive tasting menu.

STREET FOOD

The areas around Mercato Centrale and Mercato San Ambrogio are havens for street food. Several long-standing *trippaio* or **mobile tripe stands** still operate throughout the city, including **I Trippaio Fiorentino** and **L'Antico Trippaio**.

I Trippaio Fiorentino

Via Vincenzo Gioberti 133r, tel. 335/821-6880, daily 10am-7pm, €6

I Trippaio Fiorentino is recognizable by the metal stools surrounding a little van where Marco Bologesi has been preparing tripe sandwiches for over 20 years. It's usually surrounded by locals reading their newspapers and waiting for Marco to put the finishing touches on their order.

Gaudagni

Via Isola delle Stinche 20, tel. 055/239-8642, Mon.-Sat. 9am-7pm

Alimentari are small deli-like shops most visitors never enter. They carry food and drink supplies as well as freshly prepared sandwiches, pasta salads, and occasionally pizza. Gaudagni is a neighborhood stalwart around the corner from Santa Croce run by husband and wife Stefano and Stefania. They've seen the neighborhood change dramatically in the last 30 years and greet local customers like old friends. It's the perfect place to improvise a picnic or enjoy a cold beer outside in the little square. Drinks are reasonably priced and can be drunk openly—though Stefania does suggest moderation.

GELATO
Vivoli

Via dell'Isola delle Stinche 7r, tel. 055/292-334, Tues.-Sat. 7:30am-midnight, Sun. 9am-midnight, €3-5

Vivoli has maintained its quality since the 1930s. This is the old-school approach, with classic cream and fruit flavors and little concern about innovating or improving their English skills. Hazelnut, coffee, pear, and lemon are among the dozens of flavors available in a cone or cup at prices that may keep you coming back for more.

Carapina

Piazza Oberdan 2r, tel. 055/676-930, daily noon-10:30pm

Simone Bonini helped revolutionize gelato in Florence, and his Carapina was one of the first gelato shops to use

the many flavors of gelato

Gelato has been produced in Florence ever since the Medici developed a taste for the treat. Today there are over 136 *gelaterie* in the city and every Florentine has a favorite. The best have been around for generations, preparing their gelato and *sorbetto* on-site or close by using all-natural ingredients.

Gelato is just milk, sugar, and natural fruit and cacao flavors, but when those ingredients are fresh and combined with care something special happens. Understanding the difference between good and great gelato takes practice. A few basic guidelines for finding the best:

- **Avoid unnatural colors and showy displays.** If the color looks too bright or the gelato is displayed in gravity-defying mounds, artificial flavoring and preservatives may be to blame.

old-fashioned refrigerated containers (called *carapina*) where the product remains hidden inside cold metal vats. He's experimented with salty flavors and brought a gourmet approach to gelato. The *crema al Vin Santo* and *stracciatella* flavors are unbeatable. It's outside the center but worth the walk.

Dario Ceccarelli's

Via Capo di Mondo 40r, tel. 055/660-561, Mon.-Fri. 7:30am-7:30pm and Sat. 7:30am-noon, €3-4.5

Without *gelateria* written on the sign it would be easy to pass Dario Ceccarelli's small shop without a second thought. If you did you'd be missing one of the best old-fashioned gelato

joints in Florence. Dario uses the same machines he did a half century ago and you can taste the quality. The *Crema Antica* is made from a secret recipe and classics like *nocciola*, *noci*, *torrone*, and *stracciatella* are all served in this shop a short distance from the Historic Center.

OLTRARNO

There are fewer restaurants across the Arno. Most are small, rustic places serving traditional Tuscan food at affordable prices. There are some notable exceptions where Michelin-starred chefs create culinary masterpieces and *al fresco* dining includes views of olive trees and medieval walls. **Borgo San**

- **Start with the classics.** Start with the classics like chocolate, cream, and a wild card. Read labels next to each flavor carefully and remember the names of the ones you like.

- **Taste test.** Gelato clerks readily provide small samples on miniature plastic spoons.

- **Mind the line.** Unless you exert some authority inside a crowded *gelateria*, you may never place an order.

- **Go cone-less.** *Gelateria* always offer a choice between cup or cone. Purists advocate the former on grounds of taste.

- **Get the scoop(s).** Gelato is ordered in several different sizes that usually translate into two, three, and four scoops. Each scoop can be a different flavor. There's only one size of cone, while cups get progressively larger.

- **Enjoy *al fresco*.** Gelato is street food and best enjoyed while moving. It has an undeniable effect on the view, and walking through the streets of Florence with a gelato has a way of making even good days better.

Below are some of the best options for gelato in Florence:

- **Carapina:** Appealing to the adventurous palate, Carapina proves that gelato doesn't have to be sweet. Head here to discover the culinary potential of gelato (page 79).

- **Le Botteghe di Leonardo:** The secret here is the freshness: Milk comes from Trentino, the eggs are delivered daily, and all of the fruit is seasonal (page 76).

- **Vivoli:** Classic flavors from the oldest gelaterie in Florence. They know what they're doing and have been doing it longer than anybody else (page 79).

- **Gelateria della Passera:** Not only can you get a great cone here, but the small triangular piazza may just be the most scenic place to lick a cone of gelato. (page 85)

Frediano near the river is particularly rich in gastronomic options and is lined with dozens of inviting eateries. Neighborhood squares like **Piazza Santo Spirito** are also reliable destinations for those in search of authentic flavors. Here coffee, pasta, cocktails, and gelato can all be had within a short radius. Snack bars and restaurants near the Ponte Vecchio and Palazzo Pitti often cater exclusively to tourists and are best avoided.

TUSCAN
Casalinga

Via Michelozzi 9r, tel. 055/218-624, Mon.-Sat. 12:30pm-2:30pm and 7pm-10pm, €13-15

Casalinga has been serving lunch and dinner in the Oltrarno neighborhood since 1963. Nello and Oliviero have retired now, but their three children maintain the tradition inside this simple *trattoria* where waitstaff in red aprons dash from table to table delivering traditional favorites. The menu is quite dense and there are many possibilities for creating a memorable meal. One option is the mixed *crostini* plate, followed by minestrone soup and *bollito misto*. Ask the server about the daily special and leave room for the *torta della nonna*. If you can't arrive around opening time, make a reservation.

Il Brindellone

*Piazza Piattellina 10, tel. 055/217-879,
Tues.-Sun. 12:30pm-1:45pm and
7:30pm-9:45pm, €7-9*

If décor isn't essential and all you're after is Florentine classics, Il Brindellone is a good choice for lunch or dinner. This *trattoria* is popular with locals and there's jovial banter between the owner and regulars who come for the beef. They also prepare a very tasty *ribollita* and *pappa al pomodoro* that can easily feed two. Don't worry about reservations or dressing up.

Il Guscio

*Via dell'Orto 49a, tel. 055/224-421,
Mon.-Fri. noon-2:30pm and 7:30pm-11pm,
Sat. dinner only, €12-15*

Il Guscio is a friendly, informal restaurant where first courses arrive before you can begin nibbling on the bread, and seconds include *bistecca alla fiorentina* and seared tuna. Portions are enviable and prices honest. The wine cellar includes over 400 Tuscan bottles and you can order Chianti by the glass or carafe.

ITALIAN
Trattoria dell'Orto

*Via dell'Orto 35a, tel. 055/224-148,
Wed.-Mon. noon-3pm and 7:30pm-11:30pm,
€8-12*

Owner-chef Arturo Caminatti spends his mornings selecting ingredients from local meat and vegetable suppliers and the rest of the time in his kitchen at Trattoria dell'Orto. The result is mouthwatering plates of *crostini*, cold cuts, and chargrilled steaks that look as good as they taste. The bottles lining the movie set-like interior aren't only for show, and there's more in the vaulted cellar down below.

The garden is a lovely place to eat during the summer.

Angiolino

*Via di Santo Spirito 36r, tel. 055/239-8976,
daily 12:15pm-3:30pm and 7pm-11:30pm,
€10-14*

Angiolino is a historic *trattoria* run by three jubilant brothers, where Florentine families come for long Sunday lunches. Their menu includes handmade pasta, grilled meats, and specialty sandwiches such as lobster roll and roast beef club. Wine can be ordered by the bottle or glass, and the dark wood interior is perfect for escaping the heat outside.

Gesto

*Borgo San Frediano 27r, tel. 055/241-288,
daily 7pm-2am, €3-5 per plate*

Gesto is an ecofriendly eatery where menus are written on tables and orders are taken using small chalkboards that double as trays. Martina Luccatelli and her all-female staff have created a welcoming space that's artsy and comfortable. The food is tapas-style with some vegetarian twists that surprise the senses. Portions are small and the fish, meat, vegetable, and sweet plates are suited for a light dinner rather than a heavy feast.

PIZZA

Florence doesn't have the same pizza-making tradition as Rome, but there are still plenty of places where it can be found. Most common is the thin, soft-crust Neapolitan variety. You'll also find *pizza al taglio* shops offering freshly baked trays of pizza with various toppings. These are sold by the cut *(taglio)* and you can choose whatever dimensions you like.

Gusta

Via Maggio 46r, tel. 055/285-068,
Tues.-Sun. 11:30am-3:30pm and
7pm-11:30pm, €6-10

Gusta is one of the most popular pizzerias in the neighborhood, with a mix of university students, locals, and visitors vying for tables inside or out of this small and unpretentious establishment. Service is fast but friendly. Arrive early to avoid the rush or ask for takeaway and eat on the steps of Santo Spirito just a minute away.

Gusta

Berbere

Piazza de'Nerli 1, tel. 055/238-2946,
Mon.-Thurs. 7pm-midnight, Fri.-Sun.
12:30pm-2:30pm and 7pm-midnight, €7-11

Berbere is known as a slightly frenetic place where you can grab a stool at the marble counter and watch pizza being made or sit down in the back room for a little more intimacy. There's a choice of dough, original toppings, and thick crust that always gets sliced before being served to diners. The selection of regionally produced craft beer is worth tasting and the *piazza* outside becomes a popular hangout during the summer.

Vico del Carmine

Via Pisana 40r, tel. 055/233-6862,
Mon.-Sat. 7:30pm-midnight, Sun.
12:45pm-2:45pm and 7:30am-midnight,
€6-9

Vico del Carmine is a traditional Neapolitan *pizzeria* with a wood-fired oven that has satisfied several generations of stomachs. The family also prepares southern Italian specialties, fried *antipasti,* and homemade desserts. The rustic interior is decorated like a small shrine to Naples. Getting there is a pleasant walk through the old city gates and down Borgo S. Frediano where tempting stops await.

STREET FOOD
Il Trippaio di San Frediano

Piazza dei Nerli, no tel., Mon.-Sat.
10:30am-8:30pm, €5

Tripe has a long history in Florence and is served at market stalls and kiosks around the city. Il Trippaio di San Frediano is one of the oldest and a good place to begin a tripe tour. The menu includes the classic sandwich (€4) and gets progressively more intricate as vegetables, beans, and other meats are added. There's a row of stools inside or the takeaway option, which can get messy if you're not careful.

Il Trippaio di Porta Romana

Piazzale Porta Romana, no tel., Mon.-Sat.
9am-3pm, €5

Skipping Il Trippaio di Porta Romana is the gastronomic equivalent of missing out on the Duomo. Mario and Manola Albergucci set up their mobile kiosk just outside the medieval walls and have been serving tripe sandwiches there for decades. He's a former butcher and prepares *lampredotto* with passion while she dishes out sides of beans, artichokes, and whatever

⊗ ITALIAN COFFEE

Un cafè per favore…

Coffee wouldn't be the same without Florence. Not only were the Medici the first to import beans to Italy in the early 18th century, but two local brothers pioneered the modern coffee machine in the 1930s. Their patented horizontal boiler simplified coffee making and made the drink accessible to all.

Today, coffee is a daily ritual for thousands of Florentines who crowd into bars for their morning fix and often end their lunches with a cup. Most of them drink at the counter and there's hardly ever a wait. It's one of the cheapest pleasures in the city and rarely exceeds a euro, unless you sit down at a table or find yourself in front of Piazza della Signoria where the views increase the cost. Before placing an order consider the following options:

- **Caffè:** Espresso served black. This is the most popular way of drinking coffee in Italy. (Espresso has become so popular that when you order a *caffè* you automatically receive an espresso.) The espresso is served in a ceramic cup, unless *al vetro* is requested—in which case it will be poured into a shot glass.

- **Caffè Corto:** An espresso served short (*corto*), making it slightly stronger.

- **Caffè Lungo:** An espresso served long (*lungo*), making it slightly weaker.

- **Caffè Macchiato:** Espresso with a dash of steamed milk. (*Macchiato* means stained; the milk "stains" the *espresso*.)

- **Latte Macchiato:** The opposite of *caffè macchiato*—a glass of milk stained with a little coffee.

- **Cappuccino:** One of Italy's greatest exports. In Florence it's almost always ordered in the morning and often accompanied by a pastry. A cappuccino is served in a larger cup and is creamier than a caffè macchiato.

- **Marocchino:** A cross between a caffè *macchiato* and miniature *cappuccino* topped with cacao and served in a glass or ceramic cup.

- **Caffè Freddo:** Italians don't stop drinking coffee in summer, but they often order iced *espresso* when temperatures rise. It's served black, with milk, or topped with whipped cream.

- **Shakerato:** An espresso blended with crushed ice and served in a glass. It occasionally comes presweetened and presented in a martini glass.

- **Spremuta d'Arancia:** Not coffee, but fresh-squeezed orange juice. Most bars have sophisticated juicers and oranges are in season nearly all year long.

Below are some of the best coffee shops in Florence:

- **Amblé:** The perfect caffeine break, located near Ponte Vecchio but remote enough to feel out of the way (page 72).

- **Ditta Artigianale:** Coffee conoisseurs with locations on both sides of the Arno. This is where locals like to chill out (page 72).

- **Giubbe Rosse:** Old-school espresso house where Florence's artists have hung out for generations (page 72).

else is in season. Diners eat at portable counters set up underneath the trees. When you're done, take a stroll through the Boboli Gardens or up Viale Machiavelli to enjoy the view.

BAKERIES
S. Forno
Via Santa Monaca 3r, tel. 055/239-8580,
www.ilsantobevitore.com, daily
7:30am-7:30pm, €4

S. Forno is more than a bakery. At breakfast they offer a tempting assortment of breads, muffins, scones, and tarts. At lunch soups, salads, and freshly made sandwiches are accompanied by fruit juice, wine, or beer. Pull up a stool and eat underneath the barrel vaulting or head to Piazza Santo Spirito to enjoy an *al fresco* picnic. If you have a canine friend inquire about their homemade dog biscuits.

Mama's Bakery
Via della Chiesa 34r, tel. 055/219-214,
Mon.-Fri. 8am-5pm, Sun.-Sat. 9am-3pm, €5

Homesick? Make a beeline for Mama's Bakery, where Matt Reinecke and his wife, Christina, prepare bagels, American-inspired cookies, cupcakes, pies, and brownies that can cure any gastronomic nostalgia. Matt can also inspire anyone contemplating a full-time move to Italy. The California native launched the bakery in 2008 and has rarely been out of the kitchen since. Mama's is popular with expats and locals who have developed a taste for American flavors made with Italian ingredients.

GELATO
✪ Gelateria della Passera
Via Toscanella 15r, tel. 055/291-882,
Tues.-Sun. noon-11pm

Gelateria della Passera is a tiny shop facing a lovely little square. Flavors are made on the premises with fresh natural ingredients. A short line is always possible, as there's little space inside and some important decisions to make. Enjoy the flavors on one of the nearby benches where grandparents like to gather.

Gelateria La Carraia
Piazza Nazario Sauro 25r, tel. 055/280-695,
daily 11am-10:30pm

People come to Gelateria La Carraia for the chocolate and come back for all the other flavors. The cones here are nearly as tasty as the gelato and come in different colors, shapes, and varieties. This inviting parlor is located on a corner facing the two Arno bridges west of the Ponte Vecchio.

La Sorbettiera
Piazza Torquato Tasso 11r, tel. 055/512-0336,
Mon., Tues., Thurs. 12:30pm-9pm, Fri.-Sat.
12:30pm-10:30pm, Sun. 11am-1pm and
3:30pm-9pm

Over in Piazza Tasso, children play and locals pass the time on their cell phones. The only *gelateria* on the square is La Sorbettiera, where people have been getting gelato since 1934. There's less variety but what they do have is top-notch. A little counter faces the street and clients order from outside. Enjoy the gelato on a stool facing a neat line of parked mopeds or in the park.

COFFEE
There are coffee bars in most squares and a choice of three or four in Piazza Santo Spirito that all come with views of the church; the outdoor tables at Caffè Ricchi (daily 7am-11pm) are nice for sipping coffee or cocktails. Over in the triangular *piazzetta* where Via dello Sprone meets Via Toscanella, Caffè degli Artigiani (Via Dello

Sprone 16r, tel. 055/291-882, daily 8am-1am) serves coffee out of an intimate little bar that barely seats one. Fortunately, the *espresso* is good and there's outdoor seating around the corner.

There are several bars in Piazza Pitti facing the palace. Street traffic and the continual flow of tourists along the sidewalk make these less inviting regardless of the view. For a more relaxed and authentic afternoon coffee stick to the lesser-known streets and squares of the neighborhood.

La Cité Libreria Café

Borgo San Frediano 20r, tel. 055/210-387,
Mon.-Sat. 9am-2am and Sun. 3pm-2am,
€3-5

La Cité Libreria Café is part coffee shop, part bookshop, and both parts are very bohemian. The relaxed space close to the Arno is a cultural lounge that mixes good coffee with literature, music, and theater. Rest here for as long as you like browsing the books, using the free Wi-Fi, and discussing politics with staff.

Ditta Artigianale

Via dello Sprone 5r, tel. 055/045-7163,
Mon.-Fri. 8am-11pm and Sat.-Sun. 9am-11pm

If you start to crave coffee and a place to hang out, head to Ditta Artigianale. The mini caffeine chain has two locations in Florence. This one is the quieter option, populated with locals sipping cappuccino on stools and comfortable armchairs or having light lunches at the tables set on two levels. Baristas are friendly and there's a good chance of meeting expat bloggers like Georgette Jupe (aka the Girl in Florence), who's a regular here.

SAN NICCOLÒ
TUSCAN
✪ Osteria Antica Mescita

Via Borgo S. Jacopo 60r, tel. 055/234-2836,
daily noon-12:30am, €7-12

A number of restaurants and bars line the street leading toward Piazzale Michelangelo and San Miniato. Osteria Antica Mescita is one of the simplest. The outdoor tables are an excellent place to seek Tuscan nourishment before or after walking up to see the view. The menu consists of a half-dozen firsts and seconds, none of which exceeds €8 or has been translated into English (which is usually a good sign). If you're hungry, you can have a two-course meal for a very reasonable €12, which includes water. The house wine is more than satisfactory and served by the glass or carafe.

ITALIAN
✪ La Bottega del Buon Caffè

Lungarno Benvenuto Cellini 69r, tel.
055/553-5677, Mon. 7:30pm-10:30pm,
Tues.-Sat. 12:30pm-3pm and
7:30pm-10:30pm, €26-41

There are five Michelin-rated restaurants in Florence, but the elegant La Bottega del Buon Caffè is the only one facing the Arno. Here a team of young chefs diligently prepares dishes that look like they belong in a modern art museum. What each plate lacks in quantity it makes up for in flavor and creativity. The kitchen garden supplies vegetables; other ingredients, like venison, lamb, and pigeon are all locally sourced. The interior is simple but refined, with vaulted brick ceilings and comfortable chairs, and waitstaff anticipate every need. There's a memorable four-course tasting menu at lunch. Reservations are recommended.

La Beppa Fioraia

Via dell'Erta Canina 6r, tel. 055/234-7681,
www.labeppafioraia.it, daily
12:30pm-2:30pm and 7:30pm-11pm, €8-12

Make the second right just beyond the medieval gates and you'll stumble onto La Beppa Fioraia. This large restaurant with indoor and outdoor seating is popular with locals for the convenient parking and bohemian atmosphere. It's perfect for families; the large lawn facing an olive grove allows children to play while parents relax in the shade. The menu includes a variety of *tagliere*-tasting platters with different combinations of cheese, cold cuts, honeys, and fruits. Vegetarians are catered to and fresh bread is served with every meal by an enthusiastic staff.

outdoor dining at La Beppa Fioraia

Bars and Nightlife

In Florence, nightlife doesn't start at night. It begins in the lazy part of the afternoon when people stop thinking about work, and officially commences once an *aperitivo* is ordered. That leads to dinner and the opportunity to dine *al fresco* in another spot. Florence is a small and dynamic city, and you're bound to stumble upon music, dancing, or a lively, crowded square. Market workers dismantling their stalls along with the shutting of doors and the opening of others are all clues to the onset of nightlife. Most of the city's nightlife options are located near the Historic Center, with a few in the Oltrarno.

If you opt out in favor of a good night's rest, you wouldn't be alone. Most Florentines turn in early, and the city doesn't have a reputation for nightlife like Rome does. Still, there are enough young professionals, artists, *bon vivants*, university students, and curious travelers to provide a pleasant, relaxed energy at night.

Much of the time that energy isn't organized—it's just dozens of people watching the Ponte Vecchio at sunset or hanging out in a square. Any search for nightlife should include both sides of the Arno. **Piazza Santo Spirito** is a good destination whatever the time, and the bars and restaurants along **Borgo San Friediano** in Oltrarno are bustling from dinner until midnight. Other likely sources of nightlife are villas and parks where stages with live music pop up during the summer. It can also be generated by a single bar or kiosk where people crowd onto sidewalks and steps, transforming a street into an outdoor lounge.

APERITIVO HOUR

Florentines are social, so they love to sit down for an *aperitivo* (pre-dinner drink) with friends. The city even has its own cocktail invented nearly a century ago by Count Camillo Negroni. The drink, called a Negroni, consists of Campari, Vermouth, and gin. Today, cocktails are served with complimentary light snacks from 5pm onward at bars throughout Florence. There's an abundance of venues to choose from, but these are some of the best:

- **Winter Garden by Caino:** Sophisticated hotel bar with plenty of plush seating and old world décor (page 88).

- **Volume:** No-nonsense grunge bar with indoor and outdoor tables where locals start and end evenings (page 89).

- **Negroni:** Florentine institution famed for its namesake cocktail reputed to be the best (page 89).

- **Coquinarius:** Shrine to Tuscan wines made even better with plates of local cheeses and cured hams (page 90).

- **Le Volpe e L'Uva:** Out-of-the-way *enoteca* with a tremendous selection of Italian vintages available by the glass or bottle (page 90).

✪ APERITIVO BARS

SANTA MARIA NOVELLA

✪ Winter Garden by Caino

Piazza Ognissanti 1, tel. 055/2716-3770, daily 11am-11pm

The Winter Garden by Caino recently earned its first Michelin star and deserves it on the decoration alone; come to this hotel along the Arno for drinks and its great hall will provide an eyeful of architecture and elegance. The meticulous bar and buffet are well stocked and cozy living room-like niches await. A Bloody Mary prepared with the addition of *Grappa di Brunello* is the house cocktail.

SANTA CROCE

Plaza Luchese

Lungarno della Zecca Vecchia 38, tel. 055/26236, 9am-midnight

Many hotel bars have great views, and Plaza Luchese is no exception—but the **Empireo** bar inside this hotel also boasts a spectacular riverside terrace and swimming pool. From Monday to Thursday the *aperitivo* includes a meticulously prepared buffet with live music for a modest €14. On weekends there's an *a la carte* menu.

Soul Kitchen

Via de' Benci 34, tel. 055/263-9772, Mon.-Fri. 11am-2am and Sat.-Sun. 6pm-2am, €8-10

Soul Kitchen is located on a lively street near Piazza Santa Croce. There's an extensive hot and cold buffet set on two long tables that can easily substitute for dinner. Leather couches and brick walls provide the atmosphere, and the piano at the back is often played. If you can't decide on a cocktail let the bartenders surprise you.

OLTRARNO
✪ Volume
Piazza Santo Spirito 5r, tel. 055/238-1460, daily 8am-1am, €5-8

Don't bother asking them to turn down the music at Volume. They like things loud at this workshop-turned-bar where carpentry tools are still on display and none of the armchairs match. Bands often perform inside, though conversation is possible on the outdoor patio overlooking the square.

NoF
Borgo San Frediano 17-19r, tel. 333/614-5376, www.nofclub.it, Wed.-Mon. 7:30pm-2am; no cover

It's hard to walk by NoF and not notice musicians playing in the front window. Inside this dark, intimate club stripped back to the essentials, Lapo, the bartender, serves pints of Heineken in plastic cups (€5) to a young to middle-age crowd. Dancing isn't allowed but there's lots of listening and the music gets loud. Monday is dedicated to jazz, Wednesday indie, and Thursday tributes, and weekends feature rock bands singing in Italian or English.

SAN NICCOLÒ
✪ Negroni
Via dei Renai 17r, tel. 055/247-8853, daily 7:30am-1am, €7-10

Negroni is named after the city's favorite cocktail and the namesake is the obvious drink to order. The bar's been the backdrop for several films and was in the vanguard of the *aperitivo*

movement. Crowds spill out onto the small terrace and surrounding sidewalks during the summer, and getting the bartender's attention can be difficult. Ask for finger snacks (*stuzzichini per favore*) if they aren't served.

Villa Cora
Viale Machiavelli 18, tel. 055/228-790, Thurs.-Sat. 7pm-10pm, €20

Viale Machiavelli is an elegant tree-lined avenue that begins in Piazzale di Porta Romana and snakes its way up the Oltrarno hillside. There are many villas along the way but Villa Cora is where both Napoleon III's wife and conductor Claude Debussy chose to reside. There are several bars and restaurants inside this refined five-star hotel including a champagne bar, a bistro, and a poolside lounge. Fridays and Saturdays are devoted to enjoying cocktails, tapas, and live jazz.

WINE BARS
Tuscany produces good wine, and you'll taste proof of that at restaurants and bars around the city. But if you take wine seriously, visit an *enoteca*. These shops are entirely dedicated to grapes and stocked with thousands of bottles waiting to be uncorked. The varieties most commonly grown on the hillsides overlooking Florence are Sangiovese, Canaiolo, and Trebbiano. These are pressed to create Chianti, which is the world's favorite wine and tastes good with everything. If your palate craves something more sophisticated you're ready for Brunello.

If you can't decide, that's not a problem. *Enoteche* are run by people who love wine and love sharing their knowledge of wine. Wine rarely goes without food in Italy and *enoteche* are great for understanding how each vintage tastes when paired with meats, cheeses, and other staples of the Tuscan larder.

DUOMO AND AROUND
✪ Coquinarius

Via delle Oche 11r, tel. 055/230-2153, daily 12:30pm-3pm and 5:30pm-10:30pm, €10-15

You'll find a mix of loyal regulars and satisfied visitors underneath the arched ceilings of Coquinarius. Every wine has a tale and you're likely to hear it by the end of the night. This jovial *enoteca* with bare wood tables and chairs is just around the corner from the Duomo. It's full of character and serves deliciously simple dishes. Come even if you aren't hungry to enjoy a glass and read a book within a timeless setting.

SANTA MARIA NOVELLA
Enoteca Fiorentina

Borgo Ognissanti 25r, tel. 055/388-0177, Thurs.-Tues. 12:30pm-3pm and 7pm-10:30pm, Sun. dinner only, €6-10

They know wine at Enoteca Fiorentina and are continually learning more about a subject that never ceases to surprise. They take pleasure in the infinite possibilities and have a preference for biological vineyards in Tuscany. Jonathal (that's his real name) can advise you on single or mixed varietals and accompany them with an original appetizer.

SAN LORENZO AND SAN MARCO
Divina Enoteca

Via Panicale 19r, tel. 055/292-723, Tues.-Sun. 10:30am-8:30pm, €10-14

As you read this, Brunello, Chianti, and Montalcino are aging in the cellar below Divina Enoteca opposite the San Lorenzo market. What started as a deli serving fried cod has become a reliable address for sampling classic Tuscan vintages. To accompany a glass, choose from a *bruschetta, panini,* or mixed plates of cured meat served with bread. It's all eaten on a marble table where strangers frequently become friends.

OLTRARNO
✪ Le Volpe e L'Uva

Piazza dei Rossi 1r, tel. 055/239-8132, Mon.-Sat. 11am-9pm, €10

Minutes from the Ponte Vecchio, Le Volpe e L'Uva has been serving some of the city's hardest-to-find Italian and French wines for more than 20 years. They do it unpretentiously and with a passion that is contagious. The *stuzzichini* (appetizers) are simple but satisfying. Cheese plates served with honey and mustard and *crostone* topped with Asiago are set tantalizingly on a circular counter where wine is the favorite topic of conversation. Reservations are useful for getting a table outside.

Obseqium

Borgo San Jacopo 17, tel. 055/216-849, daily noon-10pm, €8

A good place to sample local Tuscan vintages is Obseqium. Choose a bottle or a glass and accompany it with *taglieri* (plates) of regional cured hams, cheese, and good Tuscan bread. The owners are happy to advise inside this bright two-room rustic shop lined with bottles. It's perfect for making conversation and educating one's palate.

SAN NICCOLÒ
Fuori Porti

Via del Monte alle Croci 10r, tel. 055/234-2483, daily noon-11:30pm, €12

The San Niccolò section of Oltrarno has a wonderful bohemian feel that remains unspoiled by tourism. It's a great place to drink wine, and the fact that Fuori Porti has wine glasses set on the tables is a good sign. In summer, you can sit on the large terrace and choose from over 500 labels the owners have personally selected from the region's smaller wineries. The *crostini* and *carpaccio* make wonderful appetizers and there's plenty on the menu if you suddenly gain an appetite.

FLO
Viale Michelangiolo 82, tel. 055/650-791
www.flofirenze.com, summer daily
7:30pm-4pm

The disco with the best view of the Duomo is undoubtedly FLO. It's an elegant locale that caters to locals and tourists in their 30s and 40s. Cover charges are rare and drinks cost around €10. Happy hour includes an extended buffet served at an outdoor bar. DJs and live performers play '80s and '90s revival, R&B, hip-hop, and house. The dance floor gets crowded on summer weekends, so you're better off reserving a table.

DISCOS

If you consider nightlife to mean clubbing, you may be disappointed by Florence's options. Although discos exist, the good ones where you can dance until dawn are few. Still, Florence has a high concentration of foreign exchange students, and it's possible to listen to contagious electronic music and dance among locals and visitors. Many clubs are registered as private associations and operate a membership system in which first-time visitors must register before entering. It's a fairly straightforward process that requires filling out a short form with your name, details, and signature. There's usually a small fee (€5-10), which entitles you to a membership card and complimentary drink. Clubs that don't use this system charge a slightly higher cover that rarely exceeds €20 and is often waived for female revelers.

DUOMO AND AROUND
Blue Velvet
Via Castello d'Altafronte 16r,
tel. 055/215-521, Tues., Thurs.-Sat.
11:30pm-4:30am, €10

Blue Velvet is a small disco lounge on a narrow side street close to the river. The front room is filled with people sitting on velvet sofas and mingling in the blue-lit interior. Dancing is through the back where DJs, accompanied by live performers on Thursdays, keep bodies moving until late.

Full Up
Via della Vigna Vecchia 23r,
tel. 055/293-006, Thurs.-Sat. 10:30pm-4am,
€10

For a dose of glamour in stylish underground surroundings head to Full Up. The door policy is lenient but there's usually a small entrance fee that includes a drink. It's popular with locals and visitors who regularly flock to the small dance floor and lounge areas inside.

Yab
Via dei Sassetti 5r, tel. 055/215-160, Mon.,
Wed.-Sat. 11:30pm-4am, €10

Most discos in the center are small and rather intimate. If you want big and brash try Yab. Here you'll find cube dancers, international DJs, and a main dance floor populated by a mixed crowd most nights of the week. There's a hip-hop evening on Mondays, Wednesdays are for students, and from Thursday to Saturday you can dine and dance. Yab operates a pay-as-you-leave scheme in which you are given a drink card as you enter. It has one prepaid drink that can be used at any of the bars and is stamped each time afterward. You pay when you leave and are charged €50 if you lose the card.

GREATER FLORENCE
Tenax
Via Pratese 46, tel. 055/308-160, www. tenax.org, Fri.-Sat. 10:30pm-4:30am
A location outside the center near the airport hasn't stopped Tenax from becoming one of Florence's most popular Saturday night destinations. It's a €6 taxi ride from the train station or you can use public transportation. Once you arrive you'll find several bars, lounges, a big stage, balconies, a VIP area, and lots of people. The club is ideal for live shows and international acts regularly turn up. Tenax Friday and Nobody's Perfect on Saturdays are the busiest nights, when resident and guest DJs take turns spinning the latest vinyl. Cover charges range from free to €10 for women and €10-€20 for men with one drink included. Door selection is likely on weekends and under 18s are not allowed.

Performing Arts

CONCERTS
Music isn't hidden away in Florence. It's played outside throughout the day by the violinist seated along a quiet street and the singer dressed in jeans belting out *arias* in Piazza Santa Trinita. Street musicians are common and a variety of instruments from accordions to flutes serenade pedestrians. Melodies reverberate off the stone walls in summer, and finding music only requires following your ears. Larger, organized concerts are held in the larger squares like Piazza della Signoria where orchestras perform from the Loggia Lanzi. Summer events are also staged in parks and historic villas around the city. There are musical festivals from May to September and many bars regularly feature live music nights or DJ sets. Florence is an occasional stop for international acts as well, and megaconcerts are held in the soccer stadium.

Squares, villas, and churches have concerts scheduled throughout the summer. The city's **youth orchestra** performs several times a week in Piazza della Signoria. They usually start in the late afternoon and impromptu audiences sit wherever they can.

THEATER AND OPERA
Teatro Verdi
Via Ghibellina 99, tel. 055/212-320, www. teatroverdionline.it, box office Mon.-Sat. 10am-1pm and 4pm-7pm, €15 and up
Teatro Verdi is one of the longest-operating theaters in the city. It has a classic red-velvet interior and six tiers of seating that soar above the stage. There's room for over a thousand spectators who come for the Tuscan regional orchestra, which performs a varied repertoire from October until May. Throughout the year the theater also hosts concerts, musicals, ballet, and plays.

Teatro della Pergola

Via della Pergola 12-32, tel. 055/076-3333,
www.teatrodellapergola.com, box office
Mon.-Sat. 9:30am-6:30pm, €18 and up

Teatro della Pergola is the oldest theater in Florence and the first to introduce box seats, which were owned by wealthy families. Some say the divisions in the three upper tiers were built to prevent bickering between rival clans. Only one is still privately owned and they all provide great views of the ornate chandeliered ceiling and gilded wooden interior, which looks like a wedding cake. Plays are the mainstay of the theater and some of the finest Italian actors regularly appear on the illustrious stage. If you can't make a show, come for a drink at the **Caffè** (Tues.-Sun. 10am-late) inside the grand entrance hall or enjoy the buffet *aperitivo* on performance nights from 7pm to 9pm.

Opera di Firenze

Piazza Vittorio Gui 1, tel. 055/200-1278,
www.operadifirenze.it, box office Mon.-Sat.
10am-6pm

The Opera di Firenze provides a stark architectural contrast to the rest of the city. Inaugurated in 2011, it's one of the only contemporary buildings in Florence. The modern interior is split into several levels. Classics like *Madame Butterfly* and *The Barber of Seville* are seasonal mainstays. Ticket prices range from €10 for the upper gallery to €80 for front-row seats. The opera house is located west of the center near Parco delle Cascine and can be reached via tram or on foot in less than 20 minutes from the train station.

Teatro del Sale

Via dei Macci 111r, tel. 055/200-1492, www.
teatrodelsale.com, Tues.-Sat. 9am-10:30pm
and Sun. 9am-2:30pm

Perhaps the most original theater in

a concert in Piazza della Signoria

Florence is Teatro del Sale, located in a 14th-century convent. It is a dinner theater operated in association with the Cibreo restaurant and serving dazzling dishes created by Fabio Picchi. The curtain rises in the early evening and performances range from classical, jazz, and blues to poetry readings and one-act plays. To enter this versatile locale, you'll need to become a member; it's a formality practiced by many clubs in the city and in this case only costs €5. Reservations are a good idea.

Festivals and Events

Florence has a rich and varied cultural calendar, but the most dramatic annual events are those related to religious holidays and feast days. Many involve re-creations with hundreds of participants in historical costume. It might appear like playacting for the sake of tourists, but these celebrations have ancient origins and are ingrained into Florentine consciousness. Although religious fervor has declined, thousands of locals are still passionate about these unique events and participate with pride.

Like many cities Florence has its own **changing of the guard ceremony** which dates back to 1529 when the city was under siege by Carlo V. The threat of attack is long gone but local members of the Corteo Storico (historic parade) keep the tradition alive on the first Sunday of every month in front of Palazzo Vecchio. Guards are accompanied by a contingent of musicians all dressed in detailed Renaissance costumes. The exchange of arms occurs at 9am, 10am, 11am, noon, and 1pm, and lasts around 15 minutes. It is cancelled in the event of rain.

SPRING

TASTE is a three-day gastronomic event held in early March in the newly renovated **Stazione Leopolda** (Viale Fratelli Rosselli 5, tel. 055/212-622, www.stazione-leopolda.com) arts center. There are over a hundred stands providing free samples of specialty items from all over Italy. Besides eating a lot of delicious ham and cheese it's an opportunity to speak directly with producers and understand how things are made. You can also purchase a glass near the entrance in order to sample the many wines. Complete your tour with a stop in the gourmet gift shop.

Easter isn't a formality in Florence; it's a highlight. Even if you aren't a fan of organized religion you can taste the treats and watch festivities like the **Scoppo del Carro** (Blowing Up of the Cart) on Easter morning. The tradition dates back to the Crusades when a local knight brought back three stones from Christ's tomb. The rocks were later used to light sparks that symbolized the renewal of life and brought fire to the hearths of the city's families. It was a big deal then and still fills Piazza del Duomo with thousands of onlookers. Festivities start with a historical parade at 10am that weaves through the center and arrives at the Duomo at 11am, where the archbishop lights an enormous cart piled high with fireworks.

Music takes center stage in May during **Maggio Musicale** (Teatro Comunale, Via Solferino 15, tel. 055/213-535, www.maggiofiorentino. com). The festival was created as a means of exploring creative movements of the past and proposes a new theme every year, such as Romanticism or the works of Rossini. The world's finest conductors, soloists, and singers perform contemporary interpretations. Tickets cost €15-120 and can be purchased at select newsstands in the center. The **Teatro Comunale** (Piazza Vittorio Gui 1, www.operadifirenze. it), which hosts the event, also presents ballet and opera.

SUMMER

The **Feast of San Giovanni** (June 24) celebrates one of the city's most loved individuals. Giovanni Battista was known for his teachings as well as his courageous and determined spirit. He was made patron saint of Florence in the 11th century, and June 24 has been his day ever since. Events are held throughout the day. At 8am, you can attend mass in the Baptistery or watch the long parade that sets off a half hour later from Via Folco Portinari. Participants in Renaissance-era dress move slowly through city streets until arriving in Piazza del Duomo. Honors are bestowed upon the deserving at Palazzo Vecchio in the afternoon and the Calcio Storico sporting event final is held at 5pm in Piazza Croce. The day ends with fireworks over the Arno (best viewed from the bridges and the Oltrarno hillside) at 10pm.

It may feel like most Florentines leave the city during the summer, but there are still enough left to celebrate the popular saint and protector **San Lorenzo** on August 10. At 10am a parade of people in Renaissance regalia heads from Palazzo di Parte Guelfa near Ponte Vecchio to Palazzo Vecchio; there the city banner is collected and brought to Basilica di San Lorenzo. Festivities continue from 9:30pm onward in Piazza San Lorenzo with a traditional feast of *pasta al pomodoro* and free watermelon. There's music and dancing, too.

FALL

Festa della Rificolona (Sept. 7) is a popular feast connected to harvest season, when farmers would make the journey to Florence to sell their goods and celebrate the birth of Mary. They carried lanterns held aloft on long sticks that remain an integral part of the celebration. Find them in Piazza Santissima Annunziata behind Galleria dell'Accademia alongside a traditional folk and food market. At night floating lanterns are lit in the San Niccolò neighborhood and drift slowly down the Arno.

Every guild has its day, and for winemakers it's the last Saturday of September. Since the 13th century this has been the time to bring new wine into town to be honored and blessed. The wine in question was Valdisieve, and today the **Carro Matto** (Crazy Cart) re-creates the winemakers' ingenious way of transporting 2,800 flasks in a single carriage. The event begins with an afternoon procession from Piazza del Duomo through the surrounding streets. It's a colorful parade of heralds, flag wavers, and trumpeters performing traditional pageantry. Later the cart is drawn to Piazza della Signoria where festivities continue and the wine flows freely.

WINTER

La Cavalcata dei Re Magi is held on Epiphany (Jan. 6th) and is celebrated with an elaborate parade. It begins at 2:15pm and is led by the wise men, who walk from Palazzo Pitti over Ponte Vecchio and through Piazza della Signoria to Piazza del Duomo. The most spectacular part is the 500 participants representing all walks of Renaissance society. There are soldiers, monks, farmers, aristocrats, and maidens bearing flags, playing drums, pulling carts, and doing everything the way it was done in 1417 when the tradition started.

You can tell Carnevale season has begun when calorie-intensive desserts begin appearing in pastry shop windows. Festivities last from late January until *martedi grasso* (Mardi Gras or Fat Tuesday). It was the traditional day of excess when peasants filled up on the foods they would give up for Lent (meat, eggs, and milk) and occurs 47 days before Easter. The favorite temptation is *Schiacciata Fiorentina,* a two-level sponge cake with a cream filling topped with powdered sugar and a pinch of cacao. But eating isn't the only festivity: The masked fun begins on the Thursday prior to Mardi Gras. The highlight is the parade on the following Tuesday when floats leave Piazza Ognisanti and weave their way around the city until they reach Piazza della Signoria. There's always an international element, with participants from Brazil, China, Mexico, and the United States. At the end a prize is awarded to the best costumes and a local children's choir performs. There are many other events around the city and younger travelers can wear their disguises to the Carnevale dei Bambini (Sat.-Sun. 2pm-6pm) in Piazza Ognissanti.

Shopping

Shopping in Florence ranges from international boutiques housed in Renaissance-era buildings to simple street markets. The city offers plenty of fashion products. After all, this is where Guccio Gucci was born, and where stylists from Ferragamo to Cavalli got their starts. The Historic Center is lined with luxury brands and smaller shops that attract the fashion conscious. For everyone else, there are outdoor leather markets lined with scores of stalls where bags and wallets come in countless variations. Clothes, antiques, leather, stationery, and ceramics can all be found in the city. Even if prices are marked, asking for a discount is common practice in Italy and often leads to savings.

Although many traditional shops have closed or moved outside the city, handmade still means something in Florence. It can involve preserving papermaking traditions or skillfully operating vintage printing machines. A walk along the smaller streets leads to workshops where craftspeople hammer wood, sand shelves, paint shutters, weld metal, and perform other skills that have been repeated for generations. For curious travelers, these shops are a great opportunity to learn.

Most of the city's commercial activity takes place in the Historic Center, so it's a good place to begin a shopping spree. Besides the megastores, the largest street and covered markets are located here and provide a lively experience that may require some bargaining. When negotiating, remember that if the asking price seems too high it probably is. There's also a good chance you may be approached on the street. Itinerant salespeople are less aggressive than in Rome; however, they usually offer the same selfie sticks, trinkets, and other gadgets of dubious quality. Unless you absolutely need a glow-in-the-dark rubber bracelet, save your money for something that's made in Florence.

DUOMO AND AROUND

FASHION AND CLOTHING

The area around **Piazza della Republic** is the fashion heart of Florence. Gucci, Prada, and many other designer labels are all located here. Luxury is concentrated around **Via de' Tornabuoni** and **Via della Vigna Nuova** and many flagship stores are housed within *pallazi* that would make any museum envious. The big names can be slightly intimidating, but entering does not necessarily lead to buying—and walking through the elegant interiors is a pleasure in itself. There are also many appealing lesser-known boutiques that are usually a great deal less expensive. If you happen to arrive in July or January, you'll also be in time to enjoy the sale season when merchandise is significantly discounted.

Salvatore Ferragamo

Piazza di Santa Trinita 5, tel. 055/292-123, daily 10am-7:30pm

Salvatore Ferragamo began making shoes in Hollywood before returning to Florence and setting up shop in **Palazzo Spini Feroni**. It's one of the largest buildings in the city and the ground floor is still used to display the fashion house's latest creations. The architecture is as interesting as the shoes, but if you have a fetish **Museo Ferragamo** (tel. 055/356-2846, www.ferragamo.com/museo, daily 10am-7:30pm, €6, free first Sunday of every month) contains hundreds of pairs from many different eras. An audio guide is available along with guided tours in English on the first Saturday of every month at 10am and 11am upon reservation (tel. 055/356-2466).

Desii Vintage

Via de Conti 17-21r, tel. 055/230-2817, Mon.-Sat. 10:30am-7:30pm

On a side street off Via de' Tornabuoni, somewhat less glamorous shops like Desii Vintage wait to be discovered. Desii is an original vision of menswear that combines old and new, hip and classic, into one wearable look. It's difficult to resist buying at least one shirt or sweater and making the rest of your wardrobe jealous.

Gerard Loft

Via dei Pecori, 36r, tel. 055/282-491, Mon. noon-7:30pm, Tues.-Sat. 10am-7:30pm, Sun. 2:30pm-7:30pm

Gerard Loft sells cool. The shop stocks men's, women's, and children's brands that are a couple of seasons ahead of fashion. Labels include Munich Vintage 55, Swear, N.D.C., and limited-edition lines. The store feels like a gallery where the clothes are the art. Prices are high but there are discounted items on the second floor.

STATIONERY

Il Papiro

Piazza del Duomo 24r, tel. 055/281-628, daily 10am-7pm

Florence's primary sustainer of the art of paper production is Il Papiro, which operates six shops in the

Historic Center and one over the river in Oltrarno (Via Guicciardini 47r, tel. 055/277-6351). These are like small temples devoted to stationery and the art of writing. If you still enjoy using a pen and sending letters or postcards this is a mandatory stop. Three of the shops provide demonstrations of how marbled paper is made. These occur spontaneously when stores aren't busy and shop assistants have the 15-20 minutes it takes to make a sheet of marbled paper. You can search for a colorful book cover, notepad, or card while you wait for your piece of craftsmanship to finish. Although a purchase isn't necessary, it is appreciated and is hard to resist in any case. Prices range, but there's stationery for every budget.

ANTIQUES
Barbara Gallorini Antichita
Piazza degli Ottaviani 9r, tel. 055/230-2608, daily 10am-7pm

Barbara Gallorini Antichita is crowded with interesting items. The owner believes that anything can become a collectible, and it shows in her shop, which is filled with jewelry, candelabra, frames, books, and sculptures from many different eras. Although prices are marked, don't hesitate to ask for a discount *(un sconto)* when wavering to purchase or not.

CERAMICS
Armando Poggi
Via dei Calzaiuoli 103, tel. 055/211-719, Mon.-Sat. 10am-7:30pm, Sun. 11am-7pm

Armando Poggi has been selling ceramics since the 1930s. The store has an array of elegant objects as well as platters, trays, vases, and pitchers for everyday purposes. They're used to dealing with international customers and ship everywhere in the world.

SOUVENIRS
La Botegga del Chianti
Borgo SS Apostoli 41r, tel. 055/283-410, Mon.-Fri. 8am-7pm, Sat. 9am-7pm

La Botegga del Chianti hasn't changed much since it opened in 1934. You'll find the same wooden spoons, olive oil, copper tins, and ceramics they've always sold. It may be a little dusty and crammed with an eclectic mix of Tuscan products, but you're bound to find an interesting gift.

MARKETS
Loggia del Mercato Nuovo
Piazza del Mercato Nuovo, intersection of Via Calimala and Via Porta Rossa

Loggia del Mercato Nuovo is one of the prettiest covered markets in the city and has been used for different commercial activities since it was completed in 1551. Where silk and straw hats were once sold, leather is now the trade of choice and a dozen or so kiosks set up shop every day from 9am until 6:30pm. Visit the *loggia* after the market has closed and see the *pietra dello scandalo,* a circular stone embedded in the center of the market where debtors were chained and beaten during the Renaissance. Also within the market is the bronze boar whose shiny nose locals and tourists rub for good luck.

DEPARTMENT STORES
There are a couple of department stores in the center. The two biggest are convenient for finding a wide selection of clothing for men, women, and children.

Coin
Via dei Calzaiuoli 56r, tel. 055/280-531, daily 10am-8pm

Coin is a mid-range chain between the Duomo and Palazzo Vecchio selling international brands in modern semi-anonymous surroundings. They also carry shoes, household goods, and children's toys.

La Rinascente

Piazza della Repubblica, tel. 055/219-113,
Mon.-Sat. 9am-9pm, Sun. 10:30am-8:30pm

The upscale alternative is La Rinascente in Piazza della Repubblica. Even if you're not interested in shopping you can take the elevator up to the rooftop terrace bar and get a great view of the Duomo.

SANTA MARIA NOVELLA

LEATHER

Bisonte

Via del Parione 31-33r, tel. 055/215-722

Everything is meticulously handmade at the Bisonte, where new collections are presented every year and exported all over the world.

PERFUME

Officina Profumo

Via della Scala 16, daily 9am-8pm

On the opposite side of town Officina Profumo is Florence's oldest pharmacy, dating back to when pharmacies sold mixed herbs and medicine was in its infancy. Locals don't understand what the fuss is about but the cavernous rooms attract a healthy number of visitors who come to sniff the neatly arranged essences, perfumes, and soaps. Many of the aromatic scents are created using centuries-old formulas. Helpful multilingual assistants can guide you through the vast assortment of cosmetic and holistic products.

STATIONERY

Alberto Cozzi

Via del Parione 35r, tel. 055/294-968,
Tues.-Sat. 9am-1pm and 2:30pm-7pm

The smell of paper is strong at Alberto Cozzi. It's all made by Alberto and his

La Botegga del Chianti

siblings in a small workshop dedicated to rebinding and restoring worn-out editions of old books along with creating new stationery of all kinds and colors. There's a second location over the river on Via Sant'Agostino 21.

ANTIQUES

Tuscany has always been a good source of antiques, and there's been a thriving trade in relics, artwork, furniture, and bric-a-brac since the Renaissance. Dozens of stores can be found along Via dei Fossi and Via del Moro. These vary from galleries with a limited number of fine pieces to small shops cluttered with collectibles.

Antichita' Le Colonne
Via del Moro 38, tel. 055/283-690, Mon.-Fri. 10am-7pm, Sat. 9am-6pm

Antichita' Le Colonne is a large shop filled with furniture and curiosities. Merchandise is randomly displayed between stone columns and not always easy to reach. The owners can date items and explain the use of some devices that haven't been operated for centuries.

CERAMICS

In Italy, pottery is a little like pasta—every region produces its own particular style. Historically, the town of Montelupo a short distance down the Arno supplied ceramics to Florence and became famous for its colorful style depicting floral and abstract patterns. Today, decorative and everyday pottery is still produced and sold.

Il Sole Nel Borgo
Via della Spada 30r, tel. 055/246-6495, Mon.-Sat. 3:30pm-7:30pm and Sat. 10:30am-7pm

The pottery inside Il Sole Nel Borgo is less traditional in design and has a

vibrant country feel that can brighten a meal. Colorful jugs, plates, and platters are hand painted by the two sisters running this shop, which doubles as a bistro where you can try drinking from the ceramics before you buy.

SAN LORENZO AND SAN MARCO
LEATHER

A good place to start searching for leather is the San Lorenzo street market that runs along Via dell'Ariento adjacent to the central market. It is open from early morning to early evening 365 days a year. The street is lined with small stands selling every type of leather product. Behind these are narrow shop fronts with even more leather to be examined.

There are many shops beyond the market that transform leather into stylish designer goods. If you're after shoes, Via dei Cerretani and Via Pellicceria near the Duomo are good streets to start the hunt.

BiBi
Via dell'Ariento 12r, tel. 055/230-2400, daily 9am-7pm

Maurizio arrived in Florence in 1970 from Iran to become an architect, but found himself in the leather trade. He opened BiBi several decades ago and has been a fixture of the San Lorenzo street market ever since. Outside his stall is lined with handbags, wallets, book covers, and key chains of every type. Inside of the narrow store next door you'll find jackets, belts, and larger accessories that cover the walls.

BOOKS

Bibliophiles and librarians will appreciate the amount of shelf space in the city. Anyone looking for secondhand editions and out-of-date manuscripts

San Lorenzo leather market

should browse the bookshops on **Via dei Servi** (Bartolini at 24-28r and Cornici Campani at 22r) or around the **Biblioteca Nazionale** (Piazza S. Ambrogio 2, Mon.-Fri. 8:15am-7pm and Sat. 8:15am-1:30pm). A large **Feltrinelli** (Piazza della Stazione 14, daily 7am-10pm) with a bar is located inside the train station and is a good place to pick up reading material. A second, less hectic location that's better for browsing is at Via de' Cerretani 40.

MARKETS
✪ Mercato Centrale

Piazza del Mercato Centrale/Via dell'Ariento, tel. 055/239-9798, daily 8am-noon, closed Sat. summer

Mercato Centrale is the largest covered food market in Florence and attracts as many local shoppers as curious visitors. Florentines huddle around the fruit, vegetable, meat, and fish stands while tourists take pictures and browse the cheese and wine shops. There are dozens of stalls selling dried as well as fresh foods, making it a good place to purchase ingredients for a picnic. Mornings are busy with greengrocers entertaining clients and sharing gossip. At one end of the ground floor are a number of stalls selling specialty dishes that can be eaten at the tables and counters that fill up at lunchtime. Head to **Narbone**, part of the market since it opened in 1872, where Stefano has been preparing beef and tripe sandwiches over half his life. Salt and pepper are the traditional condiments, and if there's room at the marble tables you can sit and watch the stream of visitors who come to this historic eatery. The food court on the second floor of the market is open daily 10am to midnight.

San Lorenzo Street Market

Piazza San Lorenzo and Via dell'Ariento, daily 8am-midnight

The San Lorenzo Street Market is a busy open-air market on the pedestrian streets immediately surrounding Mercato Centrale. There are hundreds of regulated stalls selling

T-shirts, jewelry, notebooks, and most of all, leather. It's a browser's paradise and the multicultural vendors aren't too pushy. Many operate stand-alone stores behind their stalls where you can find higher-quality products. Prices are pretty standardized throughout the market and relatively cheap, but haggling is not uncommon and feigning disinterest can save you money. It's open 365 days a year from early morning to late afternoon.

SANTA CROCE
LEATHER
Botegga Fiorentina
Borgo dei Greci 5, tel. 055/295-411, Mon.-Sat. 10am-7pm

Botegga Fiorentina near Piazza Santa Croce is a good destination for bags, and there are several other stores nearby offering original styles.

Leather School (Scuola di Cuolo)
Via S. Giuseppe 5r, tel. 055/244-533, www.scuoladelcuoio.com, daily 10am-6pm

Many leather bottegas were once located in the streets around Santa Croce, and the area remains a good place to hunt for bags. You can even visit the Scuola di Cuoio or Leather School to discover exactly how leather goods are made. Prices are slightly higher and products are on the classic side, but it doesn't get more authentic than this. They also provide 1-hour tours (10:30am and 2:30pm, €16) that recount the history of the school and demonstrate the production process. Anyone curious about leather can sign up for their courses or 3-hour or 6-hour workshops (Mon.-Fri., €110-€220, prices vary according to participants) where you'll learn how to make bookcovers, belts, or pouches from leather masters. Tours and workshops must be reserved in advance.

PERFUME
Perfume isn't often associated with Florence, but it should be. During the Renaissance, the art of making perfume prospered in Florence. The city might still be associated with perfume if Caterina de Medici hadn't embarked to Paris with her personal perfumer, who shared his savoir faire with an eager audience of noblemen and women. They enthusiastically adopted the habit of dousing themselves in scent and helped make France the center of production.

Aqua Flor
Borgo Santa Croce 6, tel. 055/234-3471, daily 10am-1pm and 2pm-7pm

They haven't forgotten how to make perfume in Florence, and a visit to Aqua Flor will dazzle the nose. Inside this elegant shop you can sniff hundreds of essences and choose one of the unique blends contained in beautiful bottles on which your initials can be engraved. If you're really serious, spend an afternoon with the house perfumer who will analyze the PH level of your skin and help create a personalized scent. It's expensive and the session must be reserved in advance but there's nothing like *eau de you*. Ready-to-wear scents start from €50 and a one-of-a-kind perfume costs €500.

MARKETS
Mercato di Sant'Ambrogio
Piazza L. Ghiberti, tel. 234-9550, Mon.-Sat. 7am-2pm

Mercato di Sant'Ambrogio is a smaller, livelier food market a few minutes north of Piazza Santa Croce. It hasn't been sanitized for tourists and locals make up the majority of shoppers. Outside it's a bazaar with a little of everything on display including seasonal fruit and vegetables. Inside is entirely dedicated to gastronomy, with stalls covering all food groups. If you're not looking for ingredients but just want to sit down and eat, **Trattoria da Rocca** (daily 11am-3pm) is the neighborhood institution. Arrive as close to noon as possible because booths fill up fast. The menu is as simple as the décor but soup and pasta dishes are substantial and priced to please.

Mercato delle Pulci
Mon.-Sat. 8am-7:30pm
The Mercato delle Pulci flea market has temporarily moved to Largo Pietro Annigoni while the historic location in Piazza dei Ciompi is restored. The rickety-looking shops have been replaced with tents where merchants sell an odd mix of antique toys, watches, vintage clothes, plates, 19th-century postcards, and well-worn doorknobs. The market has been operating since 1967 near the old covered fish market and should return there once asbestos is removed from the site.

OLTRARNO
In Oltrarno shopping takes on more intimate dimensions. Few if any fashion labels are located here and the area is home to smaller shops and studios devoted to objects of art, antiques, craft, and one-of-a-kind items.

CLOTHING
Hello Wonderful
Via Santa Monaca 2, no tel.,
daily 10:15am-7:30pm
Hello Wonderful was made possible thanks to a city initiative encouraging artisans to repopulate Florence. Viviana and Livia won the craft competition and have been designing, making, and selling women's clothing ever since, inside this small studio

boutique. It's an original-yet-wearable style made from rolls of local fabric discarded by the large fashion houses and sewn into attractive blouses, skirts, and dresses. Everything is handmade and they've got the sewing machines in the back to prove it.

Viviana at work inside Hello Wonderful

LEATHER
Production of leather goods in Florence has decreased dramatically over the last few decades and the workshops that were once common are getting harder to find. Those that do remain operate on a very small scale and produce everything on-site.

Ali Firenze Laboratorio
Via Toscanella 9r, tel. 055/217-025,
Mon.-Sat. 11am-5pm
At Ali Firenze Laboratorio, Alicia and Ivana cut and sew leather into handbags, key chains, and other accessories. Prices are reasonable and you can watch them at work inside their one-room studio.

DV Bags
Via D'Ardiglione 22, tel. 366/453-4867,
Mon.-Sat. 9:30am-1pm and 3:30pm-8pm
At DV Bags you're guaranteed to find one-of-a-kind leather accessories. Owner and artisan Dimitri Villoresi does all the designing and stitching

103

MADE IN FLORENCE

LEATHER

Leather has a long history in Florence, where the transformation of hide into articles of clothing, bags, and other items goes back centuries. Most leather is still made near Florence but production has moved to large industrial sites outside the city. That doesn't mean leather is cheap. Both the raw material and the skilled labor are costly.

Today there are countless shops selling goods and not all quality is the same. There are a couple of things every leather shopper should consider:

- **Label:** If the label is sewn on, it's a good sign. If it's glued on or the stitching is faulty, walk away

- **Location:** Outdoor stalls and markets meet the demands of millions of tourists looking for low-priced souvenirs, but the best leather products aren't found on the street. If you're serious about leather you need to shop indoors, where the finest handcrafted items are displayed.

- **Price:** A nice wallet should be around €20, a handbag €50, and a medium-sized carrying bag €100. Prices vary, and browsing is the best way to find a compromise between quality and cost. Whatever sounds too cheap probably is. The saying around here is that it's better to pay more once than less many times. It's a convincing argument.

MARBLED PAPER

Paper production has a long history in Florence, though the marble variety for which the city is famous didn't originate here. Turks had been using the technique long before the Florentines, who did have the good sense to begin creating their own. The skill was widely diffused throughout Europe; however, today only Florence continues to produce significant quantities.

The process is fairly simple. First, colors are added to a rectangular glass basin containing a little water. Next, they're delicately brushed into the characteristic marble pattern. Finally, a sheet of stock paper is placed on top. The paper absorbs the color and is removed and hung to dry. At that point it's only a matter of ten minutes before the piece is finished.

Il Papiro has a near monopoly on marbled paper, and there are a handful of shops around the city where you can purchase stationery and see how it's made. The branch at Via de' Tavolini 13r periodically demonstrates the process and allows customers to make their own colorful sheets. **Giuliano Giannini e Figlio** on the other side of the Arno has no intention of becoming a chain store—and that's a good thing for anyone who stops in and learns from the father-and-son team who are keeping the art of stationery making alive.

himself. He's been advocating the importance of craftsmanship for over a decade and after a few minutes in his workshop you'll know exactly what "made in Florence" means. Prices are higher than the leather markets on the other side of the river, but items are guaranteed to last decades and get better with age.

STATIONERY
Giuliano Giannini e Figlio

Piazza Pitti 37r, tel. 055/212-621, Mon.-Sat. 10am-7pm and Sun. 11am-6:30pm

Giuliano Giannini e Figlio is one of the oldest shops in Florence and has been selling stationery since 1856. There's a pleasant smell of paper and ink inside this unlikely shop near Palazzo Pitti. The inside is lined with shelves full of temptations for office or home, and workshops are organized by the fifth generation of the same family. Basic demonstrations last 30-40 minutes, but if you want to learn how to bind a book you should count on a couple of hours. Reservations are required and prices vary depending on the number of participants.

JEWELRY

Jewelry means one thing in Florence: **Ponte Vecchio.** The bridge is lined with dozens of stores selling rings, necklaces, bracelets, pendants, and earrings of all sorts. The downside of shopping here is that the bridge is jammed with visitors most of the day, and browsing can become a claustrophobic endeavor. Avoid the crowds by arriving early or late and enter the boutiques in order to examine gold, silver, diamonds, and gems undisturbed. If you don't like the look of merchandise at one shop, simply say *grazie* and pop into the next.

T. Ristori

Ponte Vecchio 1-3r, tel. 055/215-507,
Mon.-Sat. 9:30am-7:30pm

T. Ristori is an elegant and tasteful place to start shopping on Ponte Vecchio and carries well-known jewelry brands as well as their own handcrafted line. This is also a good opportunity to see the inside of a *bottega* and catch a glimpse of the Arno without being crushed by the people outside. The red staircase in the corner of the shop was built for Francesco I de' Medici and is the only direct access from the corridor above to the bridge.

ANTIQUES

There are a number of antique stores in Oltrarno. **Via Maggio** is the main

thoroughfare for serious antique hunters.

Maurizio & Salici

Via Santo Spirito 32r, 328/716-7049,
Mon.-Sat. 9am-7pm

Maurizio of Maurizio & Salici sells items you don't need but would like to own anyway. Don't call it shabby chic, or he'll remind you everything is antique down to the 1920s office plaques and late-19th-century gilded mirrors. Generally speaking, nothing here is more than two hundred years old. It all looks good on a coffee table, shelf, or mantle. Prices are not listed and there's some room for negotiation, but like every good dealer, Maurizio knows the value of everything he sells.

Piumaccio d'Oro

Borgo San Frediano 65r, tel. 055/239-8952,
Mon.-Fri. 8:30am-1pm and 2:30pm-7:30pm,
Sat. 9:30am-12:30pm and 3:30pm-7:30pm

The Malenotti family has operated Piumaccio d'Oro for more than 70 years. That's a lifetime of antique restoration and creation. The techniques practiced in the small workshop and displayed in the store result in one-of-a-kind tables, chests, chairs, and smaller objects found nowhere else.

Piazza Santo Spirito

MARKETS

There are fewer markets on this side of the river. Those that do etxist don't thrive off tourists, but instead attract locals who buy their fruits and vegetables and browse racks of cheap clothing, shoes, and household gadgets. The busiest is in **Piazza Santo Spirito** and is held Monday through Saturday from 8am until 2pm. It has a handful of stands hawking cheap womens wear, shoes of every kind, undergarments, and vegetables. The **Arti e Mestieri D'Oltrarno** arts and crafts market also takes place 7am-7pm in the square on the second Sunday of every month except July and August.

Recreation and Activities

PARKS AND GARDENS

Giardini di Boboli

Piazza Pitti 1, daily 8:15am-7:30pm summer and until 4:30pm winter, €10, €38 combo ticket or Firenzecard

It's easy to overdose on art in Florence. Fortunately, there are gardens like Giardini di Boboli where you can relax and give your eyes a rest. The garden was created for the Medici and blends an initial perfectly manicured section with a wilder natural park opened to the public in 1766. Even here art isn't entirely absent, and there are grottoes, fountains, and statues lining many of the alleys. Boboli Gardens are off-limits to cyclists and pickup soccer games. Visitors must keep off the grass, remain on the footpaths, and refrain from climbing trees. You can, however, bring food and drink into the garden and eat on the benches as long as you clean up after yourself.

Giardino Bardini

Costa San Giorgio 2 and Via dei Bardi 1r, tel. 055/2006-6206, www.bardinipeyron.it, Tues.-Sun. 10am-7pm, €11

Giardino Bardini is a fraction of the size of the Boboli Gardens and only a short distance away near Forte Belvedere. The advantage of this park is not only its manageable dimensions (divided into three distinctive areas), but also the wonderful gravel terrace overlooking the city. The villa at the entrance of the property was built in 1641 and was opened to the public in 1965. It contains two small museums and an exhibition space. Guided tours of the elaborate gardens can be reserved, and the coffee house within the *loggia* has a great view of the garden and city below.

Giardino delle Rose

Viale Giuseppe Poggi 2, tel. 055/234-2426, daily 9am-8pm, free

Giardino delle Rose is located off the stairs leading up to Piazzale Michelangelo and is a fragrant stop in late spring and early summer when more than 400 varieties of roses are in full bloom. Interspersed among the plants are metal sculptures, small fountains, and wooden benches with wonderful views.

Parco delle Cascine

Piazzale delle Cascine, www.parcodellecascine.comune.fi.it, free

Parco delle Cascine is Florence's largest park. It's located just west of the Historic Center along the Arno and can be easily reached by foot, tram, or bike. The latter is the best option for exploring the long paths that run through the park and lead past meadows, woods, and sporting complexes. On summer weekends it can be quite animated. It's a park where few tourists tread and locals come to cycle, run, or just stroll along the banks of the Arno. There's a pedestrian bridge over the Arno you can cross to explore the residential neighborhood of low-rise apartment blocks immersed in green, or ride along the dirt path overlooking the river. In summer, the former racetrack and amphitheater within the park are used for concerts and exhibitions.

CYCLING

Cycling is a safe and convenient way to explore Florence. Most of the city is flat and traffic is respectful of cyclists. There are bike racks in nearly every *piazza* and dedicated lanes along both sides of the Arno and along many streets. Rental prices for an hour or an entire day are reasonable and some bike shops offer tours. If you're serious about cycling and aren't just out for a leisurely ride around the Historic Center, head for the hills surrounding the city and discover the Tuscan countryside on two wheels.

The long paths in **Parco delle Cascine** are excellent for exploring by bicycle. **Viale Galileo** and **Michelangelo** near Piazzale Michelangelo both wind through the countryside and have bike lanes that fill up with local cyclists on weekends.

Florence By Bike

Via S. Zanobi 54r, tel. 055/488-992, www.florencebybike.it, Mon.-Sat. 9am-1pm and 3:30pm-7:30pm

Florence By Bike is close to the train station and provides city, mountain,

Giardini di Boboli

touring, and road bikes that can be rented for an hour, half day, full day, or multiple days. Prices depend on the model and a half day with a good Dutch-style city bike is €9 while a mountain bike is double that. All sizes are available and accessories like baskets and child seats are an additional €3. Helmets and locks are included in the rental price. Florence by Bike also offers tours in and around Florence.

There's also a **bike sharing** service in the city. Visitors can sign up online and download the app that allows you to find a bike and use it for however long or little you need. **Mobikes** (www.mobike.com) are orange and gray, and cost €0.50 every 30 minutes.

Travelers who prefer discovering Tuscany on their own can rent a bike and board any regional train with a bike symbol. There are special bike compartments for up to 15 vehicles that must be loaded and unloaded by the cyclists themselves. Tickets for transporting bikes are €4 one-way and valid 24 hours.

MOPEDS

Alinari

Via San Zanobi 40, tel. 055/280-500, www.alinarirental.com, Mon.-Sat. 9am-6:30pm and Sun. 9:30am-1:30pm

Alinari rents classic Dutch bikes and Honda SH 125 mopeds for €55 per day. Credit card and ID are required.

New Tuscany Scooter Rental

Via II Prato 50r, tel. 055/538-5045, www. vesparental.eu, Mar.-Nov. daily 9am-6pm

New Tuscany Scooter Rental has a small fleet of red 125cc Vespas (€60 per day) that are easy to drive. All you need is a regular license, and you'll be on your way. They provide the helmets, maps, and additional insurance if you're anxious about scrapes or dents.

BEACHES

Spiaggia sul Arno

Piazza Poggi, www.easylivingfirenze.it, May-Sept. daily 10am-1:30am

Florence is only 55 miles (90 kilometers) from the sea and many residents spend their weekends and holidays on the Tuscan coast—but if you can't make it to the beach, the beach can make it to you. Every summer the city organizes a riverside beach along the sandy southern bank of the Arno River east of Ponte alla Grazie bridge. Spiaggia sul Arno attracts families and hipsters looking to relax. During the day you can sip drinks at the kiosk bar, rent lounge chairs, or practice beach yoga; after the sun goes down on weekends musicians and DJs alternate rhythms.

SKIING

The slopes of **Abetone** (tel. 057/360-001, www.abetone.org) are 50 miles (85 kilometers) from Florence and have been a popular winter destination since **Albergo Excelsior** (Via Brennero 313, tel. 057/360-010, www.albergoexcelsior.info, €90 d) and **Albergo Regina** (Via Uccelliera 5, tel. 057/360-007, www.albergoregina.com, €85 d) opened in the early 1900s. There are four valleys full of trails that keep downhill racers and cross-country enthusiasts occupied. Snowboarders can enjoy the snow park equipped with a half pipe, moguls, and nine-foot (three-meter) jumps. The season officially opens on December 8 and artificial snow machines guarantee coverage whether nature cooperates or not. Renting equipment is convenient and accommodations plentiful if you decide to stay the night. **Copit** (tel. 055/21463, www.copitspa.it) operates daily bus service from Largo Alinari near Stazione SMN.

SPECTATOR SPORTS

CALCIO STORICO

According to popular belief the English invented soccer, but Florentines know that *Calcio Storico*, an early form of the game, originated here in the 16th century—which may explain why Italy has won four World Cups. It's a bruising game that combines elements of soccer and rugby and in which head butting, punching, and elbows are allowed. A competition is held every year between teams representing the four historic neighborhoods of the city and takes place in Piazza Santa Croce during the second and third weeks of June. Matches last 50 minutes and enthusiastic crowds fill the bleachers around the square. The final is played on June 24, the feast day of Florence's patron saint, and the winning team wins bragging rights and a free dinner. Tickets (www. boxol.it) are priced €21-52 and go on sale in May.

FOOTBALL

Fiorentina is the local soccer (*calcio*) team. They regularly finish in the top half of the Italian Serie A championship, although they haven't won a title in over four decades. They play at the **Artemio Franchi** (Viale Manfredo Fanti 4, tel. 055/503-011) stadium, which opened in 1931 and was remodeled to host matches during the 1990 World Cup. Capacity is 47,000 but games are rarely sold out unless one of the league's top teams is in town. Matches are usually played on Sunday afternoons. Tickets can be purchased directly at the stadium or the team shop on the second floor of the **Mercato Centrale** (Piazza del Central Mercato, daily 10am-6pm). Seating is relatively close to the action, and unlike in Rome there's no running track around the field. The side tribunes provide the best views, while the curves offer more atmosphere and are where you're likely to hear fans singing support for their squad. The stadium is about 1.5 miles (a couple of kilometers) northeast of the center and can be easily reached from Stazione Santa Maria Novella or Piazza San Marco via buses 7, 17, or 20.

TOURS

There are over 2,000 registered guides in Florence and dozens of agencies offering tours of the city and Tuscany region. These range from walking and cycling tours to Segway and Vespa outings. All tours recommended here are led by English speakers.

WALKING
Elisa Acciai

Tel. 339/626-2031, elisaacciai@libero.it

Elisa Acciai always dreamed of being a tour guide in her native city, and she's been doing it professionally for more than a decade. Her interest began on school trips when monotone guides put her classmates to sleep with a dull monologue of names and dates. She decided to take the opposite approach and brings her city to life with facts and insights that will transform your perspective on Florence. You can customize tours based on your interests (monuments, neighborhoods, markets, etc.) or let her surprise you. Tours are €60 per hour for groups of up to six and conducted in English.

CYCLING
Florence By Bike

Via S. Zanobi 54r, tel. 055/488-992,
www.florencebybike.it

Florence By Bike offers guided tours of various lengths inside and outside of Florence. The four-hour tour (€39 including rental) along the Arno and through Parco delle Cascine leaves at 3:30pm on weekdays and 9am on weekends. If you want to pedal even farther they organize 40-60 mile (60-100-kilometer) trips to Chianti, Siena, and other Tuscan destinations.

I Bike Tuscany

Via Belgio 4, tel. 335/812-0769, www.ibiketuscany.com, €145

I Bike Tuscany specializes in single-day and multiday rides outside the city. Destinations include Siena, Chianti, and San Gimignano. Groups leave every morning and follow scenic routes through the Tuscan countryside past olive groves, vineyards, and villages where riders stop for lunch and gelato. Experienced local guides conduct tours in English that include 27-speed hybrid bikes, transfers to starting points, tastings, helmets, and water.

VESPA

The Vespa is Italy's most famous scooter brand and a synonym for mobility. It's easy to ride even if you have little or no motoring experience and is a delightful way of exploring the countryside around Florence. All agencies require a valid driver's license and include insurance in the prices.

Walkabout

Via Vinegia 23r, tel. 055/264-5746, www.walkaboutflorence.com

Walkabout uses restored vintage Vespas to take small groups on four-hour tours outside the city. There are several stops along the way to admire the views and explore narrow roads past castles and villas. Lunch is eaten al fresco and includes prosciutto, cheese, and Chianti. Tours depart at 9am and 2:30pm all year long and cost

€110 for a single rider and €170 for two. Helmets with two-way radios are provided by the English-speaking guides.

Tuscany Vespa Tours

Via Ghibellina 34r, tel. 055/386-0253, www.tuscany-vespatours.com, Mar.-Nov.

For longer tours that go a little deeper into the region try Tuscany Vespa Tours. These depart at 10am and head south into Chianti for seven-hour visits of the area. Along the way there's a stop at a 12th-century castle with a wine cellar and olive oil-producing facilities. Once you've climbed the tower and enjoyed the view, it's back on the moped along winding country roads to a family-run *trattoria* where a traditional lunch is served. Total distance is 21 miles (35 kilometers) completed at a very leisurely pace. Drivers pay €120 and passengers €90.

BUS

Florence City Sightseeing

Tel. 055/290-451, www.firenze.city-sightseeing.it

Several companies offer bus tours. Florence City Sightseeing operates red double-decker buses with open tops along three different routes. Ride them all for 24 (€24), 48 (€28), or 72 (€33) hours. The starting point is Santa Maria Novella train station and a complete circuit lasts one or two hours with numerous stops where passengers are free to get on and off. Tickets can be purchased online or on board and include audio commentary in English. They also provide group-walking tours of the Uffizi and other monuments and discounted family rates are available.

HORSE-AND-BUGGY

Horse-and-buggy teams line the *piazza* around the Duomo waiting to pick up fares for a trot around the city. It can be a lovely way to discover Florence; just avoid the five o'clock rush hour, and negotiate the price prior to departure. A 30-minute ride usually costs around €80 and a buggy can seat up to four adults.

WINE
Grape Tours
Via dei Renai 19-23r, tel. 333/722-9716, www.tuscan-wine-tours.com, €25-€110 pp for groups of 3-8

Wine tours can seem expensive but the best provide a memorable day of discovery that's hard to replicate on your own. Grape Tours organize half- and full-day visits to local wineries that include a light lunch and vineyard visits. At each stop you'll meet vineyard owners and learn about what makes their vintage different. The quality of the soil, the amount of rain, and the type of containers used for storage all influence taste. You'll get to sample a number of bottles at each stop, and with the help of passionate guides you'll begin to distinguish the flavors of Chianti and other Tuscan wines. The more people on a tour the less it costs.

Italy and Wine
Corso dei Tintori 13, www.italyandwine.net, Mon.-Fri. 9am-6pm

Italy and Wine offers dozens of one-day private and group tours of the region. A typical day out includes a tasting at two wineries and a light lunch at an authentic *trattoria* along the way. Participants are picked up at their hotel and accompanied by a sommelier who can help all levels of drinkers distinguish between grape varieties and understand the subtleties of wine production. The big advantage Vittorio and his team have are the

relationships they've developed with vineyards over the years. Participants get more than a generic tour and tasting; they get an intimate, behind-the-scenes look at what it means to live and breathe wine every day. There are a number of itineraries to choose from and shared tours start from €140 per person; the cost of private tours varies according to the number of participants, which never exceeds eight.

CLASSES
COOKING
Mama Florence
Viale Petrarca 12, tel. 055/202-4012, www.mamaflorence.it, €110 and up

Mama Florence is a cooking school geared toward visitors who already know how to handle a knife. Classes are run by an all-star lineup of mostly female chefs, including Beatrice Segoni from the Convivium restaurant, who balance theory with practice inside a state-of-the-art kitchen. Once you've finished cooking you get to enjoy your effort with a good bottle of wine and the company of other gastronomic enthusiasts. Classes cover the classics like making homemade pasta and pizza and last around four hours, including time spent eating your creations.

Cucina Lorenzo de'Medici
Piazza del Mercato Centrale, tel. 334/304-0551, www.cucinaldm.com

Cucina Lorenzo de'Medici is located on the second floor of Mercato Centrale and has been spreading Italian culture for the last 40 years. The cooking school is equipped with 16 single workstations and all the utensils needed to complete any recipe as well as tablets for following chefs who are filmed as they cook. Lessons start from €65 while lunch or dinner with a chef is €38 and up. Classes last two hours and are based around menus of pizza, pasta, and desserts. All ingredients are top quality and positive feedback is provided from beginning to end.

Cucina Riciclona

Caffeteria delle Oblata, Via dell'Oriuolo 26, www.cucinariciclona.it, €50

The low-cost way to wear an apron and get your hands into dough is with Cucina Riciclona. The recipes proposed are fairly simple and half the fun is getting to know other participants who may or may not speak your language. There's a "less is more" philosophy going on here that favors simplicity and creativity. During classes participants work at their own station and will have something to show for their effort by the end. Courses are generally held 7:30pm-10:30pm for 3-5 participants and cover topics like pasta with unusual sauces, pizza with alternative flours, special-occasion desserts, and dining on leftovers.

ART

Studio D'Arte Toscanella

Via Toscanella 33r, 340/737-1239, www.studiotoscanella.com, €30 per hour

Why buy a painting from an artist in front of the Uffizi when you can create your own work of art? At Studio D'Arte Toscanella you can do just that. Lukas provides all the materials you need inside his small street-side studio where both beginners and veteran painters are welcome. Just let the city inspire you and put your impressions of Florence on the canvas. You can work for an hour or return to your easel for as many days as you like.

Accommodations

Florence has a range of accommodation options including hostels, *pensiones*, residences, B&Bs, apartments, hotels, and monasteries. There are many low-star hotels and residences clustered near Stazione Santa Maria Novella where tour groups tend to stay. That isn't always bad, especially on short visits, but the city is small enough to make getting to and from most accommodations easy. If arriving by car, check the availability of hotel parking and ask for the necessary permits in order to enter the ZTL (limited traffic zone).

The proximity of the Tuscan countryside makes *agriturismo* (farmhouse accommodation) feasible. This is especially pleasant during the summer on extended stays when you can spend the morning visiting the city and hot afternoons relaxing by a pool. *Residenza d'epoca* (period residences) are another interesting option. This category of accommodation is based on meticulous attention to historical detail as well as comfort.

There are generally two seasonal rates in Florence: high season extends throughout late spring, summer, and on major holidays and low season comprises the rest of the year. All accommodation types charge a daily city tax that's not included in the list price; it ranges €2-6 based on the category of accommodation.

Most hotels are located in the Historic Center but very few have

FAMILY-FRIENDLY FLORENCE

the carousel in Piazza della Repubblica

Florence has little traffic and plenty of churches, gardens, streets, parks, and gelato shops to explore.

- The city offers free **Family Tours** (www.familytour.it) for ages 6-13 that include a bag, dedicated app, and materials for discovering museums the fun way. There are several itineraries starting from **Museo di Palazzo Vecchio** (Piazza della Signoria, Oct.-Mar. daily 9am-6pm and Apr.-Sept. Fri.-Wed. 9am-11pm, Thurs. 9am-2pm, €10, kids under 18 free), **Istituto degli Innocenti** (Piazza SS Annunziata 12, Mon.-Sat. 9am-9pm), Museo Novecento, and the Archeological Museum in Fiesole. These treasure hunt-like activities are a journey for the hands, eyes, and imagination that bring the city to life. Museum entry is not included but most provide discounts or don't charge children.

- Toddlers can chase pigeons in the city's *piazze* or explore elaborate gardens like **Giardini Boboli** (Piazza Pitti 1, €10 adults, €5 kids) where they can race Mom or Dad to the next fountain.

- Younger children can ride the old-fashioned **merry-go-round** (€2) in Piazza della Repubblica or board a **horse and buggy.**

- Older kids and teens may enjoy getting on **bikes** and pedaling around the city or to **Parco delle Cascine** (Piazzale delle Cascine, free) where local families cool off in the Olympic-size pool.

- For budding scientists there's the **Museo di Storia Naturale** (Via Romana 17, tel. 055/275-6444, Jun.-Sept. Tues.-Sun. 10:30am-5:30pm, Oct.-May Tues.-Sun. 9:30am-4:30pm, €6 adults, €3 6-14 year olds, under 5 free), which is rarely crowded and home to an extensive and surprisingly detailed anatomy collection.

- **Markets** are enjoyable for all ages and a good place to put allowance money to use. And there's nothing like **gelato** to bring a family together.

- Temper tantrum? Head to the nearest **newsstand.** Most kiosks have several racks filled with small toys, collectibles, playing cards, and gadgets that offer instant distraction.

- Consider allowing **older teenagers** to spend a couple of hours on their own. Florence is one of the safest cities in Italy and exploring it alone is an experience they'll never forget.

over a hundred rooms. Residences and lower-end hotels are concentrated around Stazione Santa Maria Novella, especially on Via Nazionale. Large buildings are often shared between several establishments of which the plaques can be seen out front. Higher-end hotels are located close to major monuments and along the Arno where prices grow incrementally. Many of these are located within historic *palazzo* where only the furnishings have changed and guests can get an idea of how the Florentine elite once lived.

DUOMO AND AROUND

€300-400
NH Collection Firenze Porta Rossa

Via Porta Rossa 19, tel. 055/271-0911, www.nh-hotels.it, €200-350 s/d

Although part of a chain, the NH Collection Firenze Porta Rossa has plenty of character and all the quality you'd expect from a four-star hotel. Rooms range from standard to presidential and mix modern furnishings with original vaulted ceilings and 13th-century detailing. The multilingual personnel are friendly and an extensive buffet breakfast is served in an elegant dining hall.

Residence Hilda

Via dei Servi 40, tel. 055/288-021, www.residencehilda.com, €230-340 d

A stay at Residence Hilda gives you an idea of what it's like to live in Florence. The suites are all decorated in light tones with simple modern furniture. Each is equipped with a small kitchen and there's a food delivery service if you don't feel like choosing your own tomatoes. Robiglio downstairs is the perfect coffee bar to start the day. From here, all major sights are within walking distance.

✪ Antica Torre

Via Tornabuoni 1, tel. 055/265-8161, www.tornabuoni1.com, €250-350 d

A night at Antica Torre provides a feel for how the Medici once lived. This medieval tower house in the center of Florence was restored with comfort and authenticity in mind. All rooms and suites have original antique furnishings and are equipped with a minibar, air-conditioning, and Wi-Fi. The best reason to stay here, however, are the stunning views from two rooftop terraces where breakfast is served and guests spend summer evenings sipping Chianti.

Gallery Art Hotel

Vicolo dell'Oro 5, tel. 055/27-263, www.lungarnocollection.com, €280-340 d

If after a day of gazing upon the past you crave something trendy and modern, Gallery Art Hotel doesn't disappoint. From the sculptures attached to the façade to the dark and cozy hotel bar, nothing is farther from the Renaissance than this luxury hotel around the corner from the Ponte Vecchio. Fashion designer Ferragamo recently redesigned the well-proportioned interiors and offset the whiteness of the walls with elegant brown furnishings. Rooms on the upper floors have private terraces with spectacular views. The Fusion restaurant downstairs provides a delicious alternative to traditional Tuscan flavors.

✪ **ANTICA TORRE:** Live like a Medici at this medieval tower house with rooftop terraces and stunning views (page 114).

✪ **IL GUELFO BIANCO:** Soak in the genuine Tuscan hospitality at the best three-star option in Florence (page 116).

✪ **HOTEL LOGGIATO DEI SERVITI:** Travel back in time at this former monastery, located on one of Florence's most beautiful squares (page 116).

✪ **ALFIERI 9:** Cozy boutique hotel on the eastern edge of the Historic Center with comfortable classic, superior, and junior suite rooms (page 117).

✪ **MONTE OLIVETO:** Enjoy a warm welcome at this B&B tucked away in a charming neighborhood that most tourists never see (page 117).

✪ **RESIDENZA D'EPOCA SANTO SPIRITO:** Choose from ten rooms named after illustrious women at this lovingly restored 18th-century *palazzo* minutes from the Ponte Vecchio (page 117).

✪ **TORRE DI BELLOSGUARDO:** This *agriturismo* is a virtual Eden on the outskirts of Florence (page 120).

SANTA MARIA NOVELLA

UNDER €100
Ostelli Archi Rossi
Via Faenza 94r, tel. 055/290-804,
www.hostelarchirossi.com, €90 d, €28 for
bed in shared room

Ostelli Archi Rossi is a laid-back hostel around the corner from the train station that's popular with students, families, and solo travelers. There are simple private rooms with en suite baths as well as dorm-style rooms with bunk beds and lockers that sleep up to nine. Guests eat downstairs at the convivial shared tables where a cafeteria-style breakfast (7am-9:30am) with eggs and bacon is served. Dinner and bar service are also available, along with €8 walking tours that leave the hostel at 10am.

Casa Per Ferie Suore Oblate
Via Nazionale 8, tel. 055/239-8202,
www.oblatespiritosantofirenze.it, €58 d,
summer only

Once you enter the thick wooden doors of Casa Per Ferie Suore Oblate the noise of the city disappears. This accommodation run by Catholic nuns houses university students during the academic year and visitors during the summer. Rooms are simple, large, and clean. Doubles consist of two single beds and a private bathroom. Several of the nuns speak fluent English. An 11pm curfew is enforced, but that may seem reasonable after a day walking the streets of Florence.

€100-200
Hotel Azzizi
Via Faenza 56, tel. 055/213-806,
www.hotelazzi.com, €130-150 d

Many hotels near the train station survive on location rather than quality, but Hotel Azzizi benefits from both. This friendly three-star establishment on the edge of the Historic Center offers a handful of bright, recently renovated rooms with modern bathrooms. They all come with air-conditioning, Wi-Fi, and an abundant buffet breakfast served in the comfortable common area where guests can relax on the sunny balcony.

SAN LORENZO AND SAN MARCO
UNDER €100
Plus Florence

Via Santa Caterina d'Alessandra 15, tel. 055/628-6347, www.plushostels.com, €60 d, €16-20 shared

The hippest hostel in town is Plus Florence, which attracts a young and international crowd who often forget about sightseeing and remain frolicking by the pool or panoramic terrace and drinking sex-inspired cocktails (€6). Private and shared, mixed, and female-only rooms are clean and minimal in design. An all-you-can-eat breakfast is served in the restaurant lounge, which transforms into a disco at night.

€200-300
✪ Hotel Loggiato Dei Serviti

Piazza della Santissima Annunziata 3, tel. 055/289-592, www. loggiatodeiservitihotel.it, €180-220 d

Hotel Loggiato Dei Serviti is the quickest way to travel back in time. Located inside a former monastery, this historic residence is in one of the most beautiful squares of the city and underneath an ancient portico that monks once called home. The inside has changed very little and there's an antique atmosphere that history buffs and anyone fascinated by the past will

love. About the only concession to modernity is the Wi-Fi access and the armchairs scattered around the cozy sitting rooms.

✪ Il Guelfo Bianco

Via Cavour 29, tel. 055/288-330, www.ilguelfobianco.it, €180-225 d

Why Il Guelfo Bianco only has three stars is a mystery. The colorful hotel, located moments from Galleria dell'Accademia, provides instant hominess and effortless charm that more luxurious accommodations struggle to match. All the rooms, from singles to suites, have been tastefully restored to their Renaissance best with the addition of antique furnishings, modern art, minibars, and air-conditioning. A sweet and savory breakfast is served inside a bright breakfast room or outside in the private courtyard where staff are on the lookout for cups to refill with coffee. The front desk is on duty 24 hours a day and can make reservations at local museums or the adjacent hotel restaurant (daily noon-10pm).

€300-400
Residenza d'Epoca Palazzo Tolomei

Via de' Ginori 19, tel. 055/292-887, www.palazzotolomei.it, €220-320 d

Staying at Residenza d'Epoca Palazzo Tolomei is a little like staying inside a museum and would satisfy members of the Medici family: Rooms are spacious; ceilings high and frescoed; floors covered in terra-cotta, marble, and wood; and mirrors gilded. Waking up here is the perfect beginning to a day in Florence. An Italian breakfast can be enjoyed in your room or at a nearby bar.

SANTA CROCE

€100-200
Hotel Liana

Via Vittorio Alfieri 18, tel. 055/245-303, www.hotelliana.com, €120-150 s/d

Hotel Liana is a short walk from the Duomo in an elegant residential neighborhood near the botanical gardens. The 18th-century *palazzo* once housed the English consulate and has maintained an old-world atmosphere uncorrupted by bad taste. Each of the 24 rooms contains refined furnishings.

✪ Alfieri 9

Via Vittorio Alfieri 9, tel. 055/263-8121, www.alfieri9.it, €110-160 d

Alfieri 9 occupies the first floor of a residential building 15 minutes from the Duomo and makes a cozy base for anyone wanting to escape from tourists and experience another side of Florence. Rooms are stylish, clean, and comfortable. Each comes with LED TVs, air-conditioning, safe, and well-stocked minibars (water, soda, juice, beer, and prosecco). Breakfast is a highlight served with a myriad of homemade sweet and savory options that provide all the calories you need to climb the Campanile. The nearby park is perfect for taking a break from art and history.

OLTRARNO

There are considerably fewer accommodations on this quiet side of the river, but waking up here provides an opportunity to observe the everyday habits of residents as they go about their morning routines. Several luxury hotels cluster around the Ponte Vecchio but for the most part accommodations consist of comfortable B&Bs, residences, and low-star hotels.

€100-200
✪ Residenza d'Epoca Santo Spirito

Via Santo Spirito 6, tel. 331/669-8881, www.viasantospirito6.it, €90-€140 d

Residenza d'Epoca Santo Spirito is a historic residence with ten lovely rooms each named after a famous woman. All are elegantly furnished and conveniently equipped with kitchenettes, Wi-Fi, and air-conditioning. It's a tranquil place where guests relax in the courtyard garden or second-floor lounge with sofas and a fireplace. The residence is on one of the city's nicest street minutes from the Ponte Vecchio, Palazzo Pitti, and the unexplored sights of Oltrarno.

✪ Monte Oliveto

Via Domenico Burchiello 67, tel. 055/231-3484, www.bebmonteoliveto.it, €80-150 d

Monte Oliveto is a slightly off-the-beaten-track B&B near neighborhood restaurants and shops most tourists never see. Donatella provides a warm welcome along with a generous homemade breakfast that can be served in her private garden or the comfortable common area. The four guest rooms are bright and airy with views of the hillside or the quiet street out front.

Hotel Classic

Viale Machiavelli 25, tel. 055/229-351, www.classichotel.it, €125-170 s/d

It's easy to forget you're in a city once you enter Hotel Classic. Nature is all around this delightful villa. A continental breakfast is served in the vaulted dining room, garden, or in your room. Parking is available and the Ponte Vecchio is just 12 minutes away on foot.

€200-300
Palazzo Belfiore

*Via dei Velluti 8, tel. 055/264-415,
www.palazzobelfiore.it, €190-230 d*

The team at Palazzo Belfiore like sharing their city with travelers. They do that by welcoming guests to their 14th-century residence with real gusto and making loads of suggestions. Saying they care is an understatement, and if you don't already have a friend in Florence it will feel like you do the moment you arrive. The eight cozy apartments have terra-cotta floors, wood beams, plush sofas, and antique furnishings that can be used rather than admired. They all come with small cooking corners and good Wi-Fi connections.

Palazzo Magnani Feroni

*Borgo San Frediano 5, tel. 055/239-9544,
www.florencepalace.com, €220-270 d*

Palazzo Magnani Feroni takes spacious to new heights. Each of the suites has 20-foot-high ceilings and enough room for a good pillow fight. Bathrooms are decked out in precious marble and there are no hustlers in the billiard room downstairs. A rooftop terrace and bar provides postcard-perfect views.

SAN NICCOLÒ
€100-200
Hotel David

*Viale Michelangelo 1, tel. 055/681-1695
www.davidhotel.it, €90-125 s/d*

Antique furniture, wrought-iron beds, and parquet flooring are the hallmarks of Hotel David where all rooms are soundproof and equipped with shower and bath. Drinks from the minibar, international phone calls, and daily happy hour are free at this hotel 25 minutes from the train station by bus. Buffet breakfast is served in a nice garden retreat where guests gather on summer evenings.

Residence Michelangiolo

*Viale Michelangiolo 21, tel. 055/681-1748,
www.residencemichelangiolo.it, €90-120 d*

Residence Michelangiolo is in a quiet neighborhood along the Arno a short walk from the center. The attractive three-story villa is surrounded by a garden with outdoor seating and free parking. Rooms are bright and spacious with compact kitchenettes and real king-size beds that aren't just two twins pushed together. Reception staff are attentive and can reserve museum tickets or restaurants should the need arise.

Colle Ginevra

*Via dell'Erta Canina 50, tel. 055/245-197,
€100 d*

Colle Ginevra could probably do with a makeover, but the husband-and-wife hosts are so friendly and the views so good it really doesn't matter. This B&B on the hillside overlooking Florence is one of the most secluded in the city. It feels like a rural oasis. It's just a 15-minute walk uphill from the center (easy unless you're carrying lots of luggage). The large and peaceful garden looks out onto olive groves as well as the Duomo. Breakfast is waiting whatever time you get up. Consider taking a taxi if you're traveling with heavy luggage.

€200-300
Silla

*Via dei Renai 5, tel. 055/234-2888,
www.hotelsilla.it, €180-220 d*

The Silla isn't the most modern hotel in Florence but it is one of the friendliest. Everyone from the front desk to the kitchen staff go out of their way to help guests. If you need an electrical adapter, want to make restaurant reservations, or have any dietary concerns they'll resolve the matter quickly. Rooms are pleasantly decorated and those in the front have a view of the Arno. The streets nearby are filled with good restaurants and the center is only a short walk away.

GREATER FLORENCE
UNDER €100
Bed & Breakfast Rovezzano
Via Aretina 507, tel. 055/690-0023,
www.rovezzano.com, €70-90 s/d
Bed & Breakfast Rovezzano is located in a residential area a 10-minute stroll from the center. There's free parking and a swimming pool. Rooms are rustic, with thick shutters that block light.

Breakfast is served in a large common living room where fellow travelers gather in the evening.

€100-200
Casa Schlatter
Viale dei Mille 14, tel. 347/118-0215,
www.casaschlatter-Florence.com, €85-105 d
Casa Schlatter was the home of a 19th-century Swiss painter. His ancestors have transformed the house into an elegant B&B. There are three rooms with large en suite bathrooms and modern fittings. Alessandra, the great-granddaughter of the artist, is an excellent host and serves breakfast in the small garden or the bright communal area where guests can relax.

Information and Services

TOURIST INFORMATION
TOURIST INFORMATION CENTERS
There are three official tourist offices in the center and another at the airport. The office opposite the train station (Piazza Stazione 4, tel. 055/212-245, Mon.-Sat. 9am-7pm and Sun. 9am-2pm) is the busiest and best avoided. You'll find a friendly multilingual staff at the office on Via Camillo Cavour 1r (tel. 055/290-832, Mon.-Fri. 9am-1pm) and another located on Piazza San Giovanni (tel. 055/288-496, Mon.-Sat. 9am-7pm and Sun. 9am-2pm) near the Duomo. All offices provide maps and event calendars, as well as sell the Firenzecard museum and event pass.

HEALTH AND SAFETY
EMERGENCY NUMBERS
For medical emergencies, call 118 and an ambulance will be sent.

POLICE
Florence is a safe city and there's less chance of being targeted by pickpockets than in other cities. There are a number of state and municipal police stations in the center. The most centrally located is the **Polizia Municipale Zona Centrale** (Via delle Terme 2, tel. 055/328-3333). This is where to go to report a theft or criminal activity.

HOSPITALS AND PHARMACIES
Ospedale Santa Maria Nuova
Piazza Santa Maria Nuova 1,
tel. 055/69381, 24/7
Ospedale Santa Maria Nuova is a

AGRITURISMI NEAR FLORENCE

Agriturismi are working farms that also provide accommodations and encourage guests to take part in rural activities. There are hundreds throughout Tuscany that produce everything from artichokes to wine and provide urbanites with an opportunity to relax and understand how the food chain functions.

❂ TORRE DI BELLOSGUARDO

Via Roti Michelozzi 2, tel. 055/229-8145, www.torrebellosguardo.com, €285-350 d

You don't have to travel far from Florence to leave the crowds behind and immerse yourself in green fields, olive groves, or vineyards. Torre di Bellosguardo is barely ten minutes from the center by car yet a world away. This grand historic residence surrounded by lush gardens seems trapped in time and occupies a quintessential corner of Tuscany. The inside of the palatial estate is fit for a Medici and every antique-clad room hints of other eras and the city's fabulous past. On the grounds is a bountiful vegetable patch that supplies the kitchen, and owner Ana Franchetti can show guests how to transform seasonal ingredients into traditional local dishes. There are donkeys, ducks, and rabbits that are an instant hit with children, who can fill their days exploring the garden paths and diving into the pool overlooking the city.

CASALE GIUNCARELLI

Via di Baccano 4, tel. www.casalegiuncarelli.com, €140 d, 3-night minimum stay

Casale Giuncarelli is on a hillside about a 10-minute walk from Fiesole overlooking Florence. The rustic farmhouse contains five self-catering flats of different sizes, all with private entrances and access to a nice garden with barbecue area and pool. Furnishings keep in style with the house and are perfect for travelers who don't feel the need to sightsee in the city all day. Car is the most convenient way of reaching the bumpy dirt road leading to the property, which can be a little hard to find; you can also take a taxi. Daniela provides a warm welcome and the location is great for anyone with the time to discover Florence and the countryside.

FATTORIA MONTIGNANA

Via Montignana 4, San Casciano, Val di Pesa, tel. 055/807-0135, www.montignana.com, €100-160 s/d, 2-night minimum stay

There's no possibility of running out of wine at Fattoria Montignana. This family-owned winery 20 minutes south of Florence has been producing Chianti Classico for generations, and the vines are right outside the door. During a stay you can visit their cellars and sample as much of the latest vintages as you like. Accommodation is in one of 11 authentically restored apartments that can house from two to six guests. Outside there's a pool and plenty of countryside to explore on foot or by bike.

---

hospital located in the Historic Center just east of the Duomo. If you can't walk, call a taxi or take bus 1, 7, 11, 17, or 23. If you're staying in a hotel, notify the front desk; many accommodations are prepared to handle any medical issues that may arise. For general health questions call 05/527-581.

Hospital Pediatrico Meyer

Viale Gaetano Pieraccini 24, tel. 055/56621, www.meyer.it

Hospital Pediatrico Meyer is a couple of miles (a few kilometers) north of Florence and one of the most modern children's hospitals in Italy.

Farmacia Comunale

SMN Station, Piazza della Stazione 1,
tel. 055/216-761

There are dozens of pharmacies on both sides of the river. Locals can usually direct you to the nearest one. Farmacia Comunale inside the main train station is open 24 hours a day. You can also call 800/420-707 to find the nearest open pharmacy.

PUBLIC RESTROOMS

There are a half-dozen public toilets in the Historic Center and a couple in Oltrarno. They cost €1 to use but you can also walk into any bar and use the restrooms for free. Bars will also provide a glass of tap water to anyone in need of hydration in a hurry.

FOREIGN CONSULATES

The **U.S. Consulate** (Lungarno A. Vespucci 38, tel. 055/266-951) is open weekdays 9am-12:30pm and can assist travelers in a jam. Canadians in trouble should head to the **Canadian Consulate in Rome** (Via Zara 30, Rome, 06/854-441, Mon.-Fri. 8:30am-noon and 2pm-4pm) or the **Canadian Consulate in Milan** (Piazza Cavour 3, Milan, 02/6269-4238, Mon.-Fri. 9am-1pm). **Australia** (Via Antonio Bosio 5, Rome, tel. 06/852-721), **New Zealand** (Via Clitunno 44, Rome, tel. 06/853-7501, www.nzembassy.com), and **South Africa** (Via Tanaro 14, Rome, tel. 06/852-541, www.lnx.sudafrica.it) only have embassies in Rome.

LOST AND FOUND

If you lose something in Florence, you have a good chance of recovering it. Head to the **Ufficio Oggetti Smarriti** (Via Francesco Veracini 5, tel. 055/334-802, Mon., Wed., Fri. 9am-12:30pm and Tues., Thurs. 2:30pm-4pm) 20 minutes northwest of SMN station. They receive thousands of objects every year and it's worth checking with them before giving up all hope. It's better to go in person, as they may have difficulty understanding your English over the phone.

COMMUNICATIONS

WI-FI

The city of Florence has created more than 450 free indoor and outdoor Wi-Fi hotspots (info-wifi@comune.fi.it). Most of the center is now covered, along with public libraries and the tram line. However, there is a 2-hour/300 megabyte limit and the network can be difficult to access without a European smartphone account. Ensure coverage for 72 hours by purchasing the Firenzecard or visit any of the many bars and restaurants that offer free Wi-Fi. Most accommodations provide unlimited-access Internet, as do high-speed trains to and from the city.

NEWSPAPERS

Newspaper stands are getting harder to find in Florence but still operate in the larger squares like Piazza Santo Spirito and Piazza Pitti. They sell a variety of local, national, and international papers as well as **Firenze Spettacolo** (www.firenzespettacolo.it, €2), a monthly event guide to the city with a dedicated English section. The influx of foreign visitors means that many European dailies are available at the **Feltrinelli** (Piazza della Stazione, daily 7am-10pm) bookstore inside the train station.

Transportation

GETTING THERE

AIR

Aeroporto di Firenze-Peretola

FLR, Via del Termine 11, tel. 055/30615,
www.aeroporto.firenze.it

Aeroporto di Firenze-Peretola, also known as Amerigo Vespucci Airport, is located a couple of miles (a few kilometers) west of Florence. There are daily flights to and from major European and Italian cities including Rome's Fiumicino Airport. Most Alitalia (www.alitalia.com) flights land in Pisa.

Amerigo Vespucci Airport has no direct flights to North America, Australia, New Zealand, or South Africa. There are regularly scheduled flights to and from London, Birmingham, Edinburgh, and other UK destinations with British Airways (www.britishairways.com), City Jet (www.cityjet.com), and Vueling (www.vueling.com). A new runway and renovated arrivals hall are projected to open in 2020 with the aim of developing intercontinental routes. The airport suffers from a high percentage of cancellations due to fog and wind, and even minor inclement conditions cause delays.

Ataf/SITA (800/424-500, www.ataf.net) operates Volainbus (€6) shuttle buses that depart every 30 minutes from outside the arrivals terminal 5am-10:30pm and drop visitors off at Santa Maria Novella train station. A taxi ride to or from the center takes 15 minutes and costs €15-20.

Aeroporto di Pisa-San Giusto

Piazzale d'Ascanio 1, tel. 050/849-111,
www.pisa-airport.com

Tuscany's busiest airport is Aeroporto di Pisa-San Giusto, an hour from Florence by bus, train, or car. Sky Bus Lines Caronna (tel. 366/126-0651, www.caronnatour.com, €14) buses depart from outside the arrivals terminal six times a day between 10:15am and 8pm (Sun. 9am-8:20pm) and drop passengers off at Stazione Santa Maria Novella in Florence. The slightly longer option is to ride the PisaMover (www.pisa-mover.com, daily 6am-midnight, €2.70) bus that departs every 8 minutes from the airport to Pisa Centrale train station, and from there board a regional train (€8.40) to Florence SMN station. Combined tickets (€11.10) are available from the Information Office inside the arrivals hall. There are few direct flights from North America, and none from Australia, New Zealand, or South Africa to Pisa but many connecting flights via other European cities. Ryanair (www.ryanair.com), Easyjet (www.easyjet.com), and British Airways (www.britishairways.com) operate daily direct flights from London.

TRAIN

The easiest, most convenient way of getting to Florence is high-speed train to Stazione Santa Maria Novella, near the city center. Rail tickets can be purchased online through Italo (www.italo.it) or TrenItalia (www.trenitalia.it). Both operators provide frequent

Stazione Santa Maria Novella

daily service and multiple levels of comfort that make rail a great option.

From Rome: Trains are direct, and arrive in less than two hours from Termini and Tiburtina stations. One-way standard fares start from €19 with over 50 daily departures between 6am and 10:30pm. All passengers have access to Wi-Fi and outlets for charging electronic devices.

From Venice: The journey from Venezia Santa Lucia station takes just over two hours. One-way standard fares start from €19, with dozens of departures throughout the day.

CAR

Florence is roughly halfway between Rome and Venice. Driving is a viable option, although the cost of tolls and fuel as well as the challenge of finding parking in the city center can offset any benefits.

From Rome: The journey north from Rome along the A1 highway is direct and the 143 miles (230 kilometers) can be covered in less than three hours.

You'll need to get onto the **Grande Raccordo Annulare** ring road and take exit 10 toward Florence. There's a toll (€18.40) that's paid at the end of the trip and several rest stops along the way. The speed limit on Italian highways is 120kmp (75 mph) and there are a half-dozen speed traps that are indicated in advance. The single-lane **Cassia state road** (SS2) is the scenic alternative. It won't get you to Florence quickly but it does cross some remarkable Tuscan countryside. Once you've left Lazio and entered Tuscany, there are opportunities for panoramic lunch stops and interesting detours in Viterbo, Siena, or smaller hill towns along the way.

From Venice: Florence is 162 miles (260 kilometers, €22.90 toll) from Venice and the distance can be driven in under three hours. It's not as direct as the trip from Rome: You'll have to take the **A57, A13,** and **A1** highways. Fortunately, signage is clear and Firenze (Florence) is well indicated. During the final 20 miles

123

(32 kilometers) of the route, which cross the Apennine Mountains, drivers should be wary of tunnels, curves, and speed traps.

BUS

Bus is the cheapest and slowest way of getting to Florence. It's only an option if you enjoy cramped seating, dodgy toilets, and the din of strangers speaking on cell phones, and it doesn't provide significant savings. A number of companies operate the Rome-Florence and Venice-Florence routes, and depart from the train stations in those cities.

From Rome: Tickets start from €7 and the trip takes over three hours. There are a half-dozen companies that operate the route and nearly all depart from Tiburtina station. **Flixbus** (02/9475-9208 www.flixbus.it, daily 7am-10pm) is a low-cost operator with a modern fleet of buses. There are 15 daily departures (€13.90-€31.80) on weekdays between 7:55am and 11:30pm and slightly more on weekends. Onboard amenities include Wi-Fi, restrooms, plugs, and snacks. **Baltour** (0861/199-1900, www.baltour.it) provides a similar service with 7 daily departures (2am-11:35pm) and single tickets start from €15. They also offer a BaltourCard that allows unlimited travel on all routes for a week or more. The 7-day pass in high season is €125; a 15-day pass is €135. It's not a bad option if you prefer to improvise, but it's still a bus.

From Venice: Baltour (www.baltour.it) provides daily service from the Tronchetto bus terminal in Venice to Santa Maria Novella station in Florence. Journey time is four hours and fifteen minutes and one-way tickets start from €17.

GETTING AROUND

Addresses in Italy consist of street names followed by numbers. The system in Florence, however, is slightly different and distinguishes between residential and commercial properties. Black numbers are used for houses and red ones for shops and businesses. Most restaurants, therefore, will have an "r" (*rosso* means red) and may sometimes be out of chronological order. Via Garibaldi 50r, for instance, is not necessarily next to Via Garibaldi 48 and can be several doors or blocks away. If you can't find the address you're looking for, don't assume they've gone out of business. Just keep searching for the right letter.

Much of the center is pedestrianized and distances between monuments are short, and if your accommodation is located in the Historic Center or Oltrarno you won't need public transportation unless you want to visit Fiesole or Parco delle Cascine. That said, getting on a bus or tram from the train station and riding it to the end of the line is always fun. Florence has many lovely residential suburbs where tourists rarely tread and you can get a different perspective on the city.

BUS AND TRAM

Florence ATAF (www.ataf.net) operates a transit network that consists primarily of buses. The **C1, C2, C3,** and **D** buses crisscross the Historic Center and can be boarded at **Stazione Santa Maria Novella** (Piazza della Stazione, tel. 055/89-2021, daily 4:15am-1:30am), which is practically in the center of the city and is a major transportation hub. Scenic lines include the **Bus 7** between Stazione Santa Maria Novella, San Domenico, and Fiesole, and **Bus 12** or **13** from Stazione Santa Maria Novella to Piazzale Michelangelo. Two modern tram lines stop at the train station and connect the Historic Center with the southwestern outskirts (T1) of the city and the airport (T2). The T1 is fun to ride and provides an entirely different view of Florence. Work on a third line is scheduled to begin in 2020.

The second train station is **Stazione Campo di Marte** (Via Mannelli, daily 6:20am-9pm) northeast of Basilica di Santa Croce. It is accessible on the 12, 13, and 33 bus lines.

A single ticket (€1.20) is valid 90 minutes on buses or trams. Tickets can be purchased at the **Ataf Point** (www. ataf.net, Mon.-Sat. 6:45am-8pm), located at windows 8 and 9 inside Santa Maria Novella, and at many newsstands or tobacco shops around the city. They can also be purchased for €2 on board buses. Tickets are also available in discounted **Carta Agile** card of 10 (€10), 21 (€20), or 35 (€30) rides. Daily (€5), 3-day (€12), and 7-day (€18) travel cards are also available along with a **Daily Family** (€6) card valid 24 hours for up to four members of a family.

BICYCLE

Bikes are everywhere in Florence, and most of the Historic Center is flat and easy to pedal around. Most rental agencies offer one-hour or five-hour periods on standard city bikes. If you want a more challenging ride you can rent a mountain bike and head over the river to the hillsides above Oltrarno or make an entire day of it and climb up to Fiesole. There are bike paths stretching along both sides of the Arno but the center is often a free-for-all. Locals ride fast and the sound of bells warning distracted tourists to get out of the way is frequent.

Florence by Bike (Via S. Zanobi 54r, tel. 055/488-992, www. florencebybike.it, Mon.-Sat. 9am-1pm and 3:30pm-7:30pm) and **Tuscany Cycle** (Via Ghibellina, 133, tel. 055/289-681, www.tuscanycycle. com, daily 9am-7pm) are near the train station and carry a range of bikes for different rider needs. The former rents single-gear city bikes with hand brakes and rat trap pedals for €4 per hour or €15 for an entire day; the price includes a helmet and lock. Reservations are wise during the summer. Both shops also run cycling tours of the city and the surrounding countryside.

TAXI

Taxis aren't that useful in a city this small, but they are available from stands in Piazza Santa Maria Novella, Piazza della Repubblica, Piazza Ognissanti, and several other squares. They can also be summoned by calling **Taxi Firenze** (4390 or 4242) and are useful at night or if you want to reach Fiesole quickly without taking a bus. On weekdays fares start at €3.30 and increase €0.85 per kilometer. Weekends start from €5.30 and at night (10pm-6am) the initial charge is €6.60. There's also a €1 supplement for luggage and for a fourth passenger. A ride from the train station to Palazzo Pitti costs €11.60. To calculate the fare of a specific journey, visit www. taxifarefinder.com.

CAR

If entering Florence by car, keep in mind the city operates a **ZTL** (Limited Traffic Zone) in the Historic Center and beyond that's active weekdays 7:30am-8pm and Saturdays 7:30am-4pm (hours may change during the summer). The zone is clearly indicated and a map of the boundary is available from SAS (tel. 055/40401, www.serviziallastrada.it). The best thing to do if your hotel is located within the zone is contact them and obtain a waiver or park at one of the lots on the edge of the ZTL. Vehicles rented in Florence are not subject to ZTL restrictions.

Street parking is hard to find in Florence, and you can avoid the headache of searching for a spot by using one of 15 lots Firenze Parcheggi (tel. 055/5030-2209, www. firenzeparcheggi.it) manages around the city. Rates range between €1-3 per hour or €15-20 per day at their Stazione SMN, Mercato Centrale and Sant'Ambrogio garages. There are a number of private garages on both sides of the Arno and some hotels also provide parking.

Most major rental companies have locations at the airport and on Via Borgo Ognissanti minutes from the train station. Avis (Borgo Ognissanti 128, 05/213-629, www.avisautonoleggio.it, Mon.-Fri.

8am-6pm, Sat. 8am-4:30pm, Sun. 8am-1pm), Hertz (Via Borgo Ognissanti 137r, tel. 055/239-8205, www.hertz.it, daily 8am-7pm), and Europcar (Via Borgognissanti 53/55, tel. 055/290-438, www.europcar.it, Mon.-Fri. 8am-7pm, Sat. 8am-4pm, Sun. 8:30am-12:30pm) are all located here.

Car2Go (www.car2go.com) and Enjoy (enjoy.eni.com) car sharing offer over a hundred two- and four-passenger vehicles around Florence. They're permitted to enter the ZTL, exempt from street-parking fees, and can be used for however long or little you like. Costs are reasonable and based on a formula of time and mileage (15 minutes is €3.75 and an entire day €50). Registration is simple and done online. All you need is a passport, driver's license, international driving permit (available from AAA branch offices for $20, www.aaa.com), and credit card. It's a good alternative to traditional renting and a convenient way to set off on day trips with zero hassle.

FIESOLE

Fiesole (fee-AY-so-LAY) is a sleepy little town of 14,000 with ancient ruins, elegant villas, scenic walking routes, fabulous food, and impressive views over Florence. It was founded by Etruscans in the 4th century on a hill overlooking the Arno valley before Florence even existed, and was later expanded by the Romans who built an amphitheater, temple, and baths. Wealthy Renaissance families, led by the Medici, designed luxurious summer retreats with ornate gardens, and the Franciscan convent erected in

HIGHLIGHTS

✪ **ARCHEOLOGICAL AREA AND MUSEUM:** Fiesole's Etruscan and Roman past come alive inside the archeological park with an intact amphitheater and small museum displaying local relics (page 131).

✪ **CONVENTO DI SAN FRANCESCO:** It's a ten-minute hike up to this cozy medieval convent, which has the best birds-eye views of Florence (page 132).

✪ **WALKING AND HIKING ROUTES:** The journey from Florence doesn't have to end in Fiesole. There are scenic paths and narrow roads where few tourists tread, leading from Piazza Mino past olive groves and pretty villas (page 136).

the Middle Ages still houses a community of monks. Today the town is a popular getaway. Florentines spend summer evenings here, and visitors come to escape the city for a few hours and enjoy the views.

PLANNING YOUR TIME

Fiesole is a 20-minute uphill bus ride from Florence and an ideal interlude from the city. It's a great lunch or dinner destination with memorable sunsets. Mornings (when there are fewer

view from Fiesole

crowds) or late afternoons are the best times to visit. Note that if you arrive too late in the evening it's hard to find a place to eat, unless you've reserved in advance.

Most restaurants remain open on Sundays and close on Mondays. Sunday is when most Florentines head up to Fiesole for family lunches and collectors come to browse the antique and craft markets held twice a month.

ORIENTATION

It's nearly impossible to get lost in Fiesole. The tiny hill town north of Florence is centered around Piazza Mino da Fiesole from where the museum, monastery, and panoramic trails are easily reached on foot.

Itinerary Idea

ESSENTIAL FIESOLE

It's possible to see the best of Fiesole on an afternoon trip from Florence. Bring only what you'll need for the day and return to your hotel in Florence for the evening.

1 Ride bus 7 from Piazza San Marco in Florence to the end of the line in **Piazza Mino,** Fiesole's main square. It's a 20-minute trip out of the city and into beautiful countryside.

2 After you get off the bus, have a look around the pretty square and inside **Cattedrale di San Romolo.**

3 Walk through the town's ancient Etruscan and Roman ruins at the nearby **Archeological Area and Museum.**

4 Climb Via S. Francesco to **Convento di San Francesco.** The terrace and garden near the convent entrance provide the best views of Florence.

5 Make your way back down the hillside from Convento di San Francesco in time to enjoy dinner and a Tuscan sunset from the outdoor terrace at **La Reggia degli Etruschi.** Afterward head back to Florence on bus 7.

Fiesole

4 ★ CONVENTO DI
SAN FRANCESCO

3 ★ ARCHEOLOGICAL
AREA & MUSEUM

ESTATE
FIESOLANA

CATTEDRALE DI
SAN ROMOLO **2**

MUSEO
BANDINI

TOURIST
OFFICE
ℹ

VIA ZANOBI   PORTIGIANI

SP54

BAR FERRO
BATTUTO

JJ HILL

FIESOLEBIKE   PIAZZA MINO **1**

5 LA REGGIA
DEGLI ETRUSCHI

OSTERIA
IL PENTOLINO

VINADRO

PIZZERIA
DI FIESOLE

VILLA
GARDENS
TOURS

VIA VECCHIA FIESOLANA

0   50 yds

0   50 m

VILLA
MEDICI

ESSENTIAL FIESOLE

1 Piazza Mino

2 Cattedrale di San
Romolo

3 Archeological Area
and Museum

4 Convento di
San Francesco

5 La Reggia degli Etruschi

FIESOLE

VILLA
MEDICI

PIATTI E
FAGOTTI

SR65   SR302

SP54

FLORENCE

San Marco
Square

Train
Station

BUS TO
FISOLE

DUOMO

0   1 mi

0   1 km

© MOON.COM

Sights

PIAZZA MINO

Piazza Mino is a large square in the heart of Fiesole where most visitors begin or end a visit. **Cattedrale di San Romolo** is on one side, the town hall on the other, and a string of bars and restaurants line the rest. From the square, various streets lead to **Convento di San Francesco,** the **Archeological Area,** and **Monte Ceceri,** all of which are easily accessible on foot. You can enjoy a gelato in the shade here, join a cycling tour, or browse the popular Sunday market.

Cattedrale di San Romolo (Duomo)

Piazzetta del Cattedrale 1, tel. 055/59242, daily 7:30am-1pm and 3pm-6pm, free

Cattedrale di San Romolo, known simply as the Duomo to locals, was consecrated in 1028 and is a good example of Romanesque architecture. The exterior consists of light sandstone quarried from the hills outside of town and there's little ornamentation. The church was built on a strange angle so that its side faces Piazza Mino, and the entrance is around the corner in a small square opposite an oratory. Inside, there isn't much decoration other than the twin chapels behind the altar. Bishops are buried in the crypt below and the organ gets played every Sunday during mass (10:30am and noon). The bell tower was added two hundred years later and rebuilt in 1739. It rises 42 meters (about 138 feet) above town but is closed to the public.

✪ Archeological Area and Museum

Via Portigiani 1, tel. 055/596-1293, www.museidifiesole.it, Nov.- Feb. Wed.-Mon. 10am-3pm, Mar. and Oct. daily 10am-6pm, Apr.-Sept. daily 9am-7pm, €7 archeological area, €10 archeological area + museum, €12 combo ticket, or Firenzecard

The Archeological Area, located behind the Duomo, contains some of the best-preserved Roman monuments in the region. The area was the center of the ancient town, and an amphitheater was built here around the turn of the first century BC. There are nice views from the top tiers of the amphitheater, and the rest of the park contains remnants of a thermal bath, temple, and necropolis. Interactive tablets (ID

Roman amphitheater of Fiesole

Convento di San Francesco

required), included with the entry fee, explain how Romans heated their saunas and recount the history of Fiesole. It's a great place to ponder the past and is rarely crowded.

A small museum is located near the entrance to the archeological area. Bronze and ceramic relics are on display inside. The ground floor is dedicated to local finds, and upstairs you'll find sculptures and coins. **Guided tours** (tel. 055/596-1293, info.musei@ comune.fiesole.fi.it) of the museum and archeological site are available for €5. There's also a café and souvenir shop.

As you exit the archeological area, walk along **Via delle Mura Etrusche** for a close-up view of a massive wall **built by the Etruscans (Fiesole's first inhabitants)** that forms the southern end of the archeological area. The road extends several hundred meters next to the wall and you can touch the immense blocks that residents during the Middle Ages believed were built by giants.

Museo Bandini
Via Dupre 1, tel. 055/59118, www.museidifiesole.it, Mar.-Oct. Fri.-Sun. 9am-7pm, Nov.-Feb. Fri.-Sun. 10am-3pm, €5, €12 combo ticket or Firenzecard

Museo Bandini owes its existence to Angiolo Maria Bandini, who was a scholar and avid collector of antiquities. He was particularly interested in 12th-14th century art, and amassed religious paintings, iconography, and ceramics. This intimate museum provides insight into Tuscan medieval art that is arranged by type and origin.

✪ Convento di San Francesco
Via S. Francesco 13, tel. 055/59175, daily 8:30am-6:30pm, museum hours vary, free

The hilltop on the western edge of Fiesole has long had spiritual significance to locals. Ancient Etruscans built their acropolis here, and a small chapel (which still stands) was constructed during the Middle Ages. A community of monks later added two miniature cloisters and a refectory that's still used today. Several monastic cells can be visited, including one where a saint once slept. There's also a tiny museum with relics collected during missions to China and Egypt. Entry to the museum and convent are free, but you can leave an offering inside the church.

It's a short, steep climb (no more than 10 minutes) from Piazza Mino to the convent. At the top, visitors are rewarded with a stunning view of

Piazza Mino

Florence and the Apennine mountains in the distance. You can sit on a stone wall or admire the same view from a second terrace in the garden below.

Villa Medici

Via Frà Giovanni Angelico 2,
annamarchimazzini@gmail.com, Mon.-Fri.
9am-1pm, €15, reservations only

During the Renaissance, wealthy families who wanted a getaway from the city began to build elaborate second homes on the hillsides overlooking Florence. Villa Medici, designed by Leon Battista Alberta in 1451, set a new architectural standard and inspired many imitators. The UNESCO world heritage site is privately owned and inaccessible except on weekday mornings when visitors can access the **ornamental gardens**. These were restored and expanded in the early 20th century by British owners and offer pleasant views of the city. Reservations must be made in advance, but once inside, you can stroll along the gravel paths past trimmed hedges, potted lemon trees, and shaded pergola until closing time.

Food

For a small town, there are a lot of places to eat in Fiesole. The bars and restaurants lining Piazza Mino have shaded outdoor seating and attract the most tourists. That isn't necessarily a bad thing, and the quality of food here is high. Nearby you'll also find a family *trattoria*, gourmet dining with a view, and a relaxed eatery on the road to town that makes a good gastronomic pit stop.

TUSCAN AND ITALIAN
Pizzeria di Fiesole

Piazza Mino 22, tel. 055/599-152, Tues.-Sun.
7pm-11pm, €6-10

Pizzeria di Fiesole opened in 2018 and was an immediate hit. The one-page menu features five cheese and cold cut starters and a dozen pizzas. Toppings are traditional and the crust is light and crunchy. If you still have room after dinner, the *tiramisu* and chocolate *tortina* are superb.

Osteria Il Pentolino

Matteotti 39, tel. 055/012-1125, Wed.-Sun.
12pm-2:30pm and 7pm-10:30pm, €8-12

Osteria Il Pentolino is a family eatery ten minutes east of Piazza Mino. Fabio and Caterina ensure a warm welcome and serve appetizing pasta, meat, and fish dishes. This is a great chance to taste thick *pici* pasta, ravioli stuffed with mushroom and truffles, and *bistecca* Fiorentina. The house wine comes in three sizes and you may not have room for dessert, which is always a surprise. Décor is minimal and doesn't distract from the good food and friendly atmosphere.

✪ La Reggia degli Etruschi

Via San Francesco 18, tel. 055/59385, daily
12:30pm-2pm and 7pm-10pm, €12-14

La Reggia degli Etruschi is an elegant, unpretentious restaurant with great views near Convento San Marco.

a nice lunch spot in Fiesole

There are two bright dining rooms and shaded outdoor tables, popular with couples and families. The kitchen blends traditional recipes with premier ingredients like Roquefort, black truffle, and porcini mushrooms. If you haven't had a three-course meal in Italy yet, this is the place to start a culinary adventure. Reservations are recommended.

Piatti e Fagotti

Via delle Fontanelle 9, tel. 055/527-6764,
Mon.-Sat. 12pm-3pm and 7:30pm-10:30pm,
closed Mon., dinner €7-13

Piatti e Fagotti is on the road to Fiesole from Florence, next to the Dominican monastery. The menu changes daily and is handwritten on a chalkboard. You can order a freshly made *schiacciata* sandwich, or pasta and meat dishes served on colorful plates. It's an appetizing eatery that most travelers stumble upon by accident, and are glad they did.

GELATO

Bar Ferro Battuto

Piazza Mino 8, tel. 328/886-5138, daily
10am-8pm, €5

This small *gelateria* facing the main square serves over 20 ice cream flavors along with fresh juices, smoothies, milk shakes, and coffee. There are a couple of tables under the shade outside and lots of benches in the square.

Bars and Nightlife

Fiesole isn't famous for its nightlife, and there are few bars or clubs in town. Nightlife is focused entirely around Piazza Mino.

JJ Hill

Piazza Mino 40, daily 6pm-2:30am, €5

There is one pub in Fiesole, so if you're craving a pint, head to JJ Hill. They've got Guinness and Harp on tap along with lesser-known brews, and enough bottles to satisfy any thirst. You can hang out in wooden booths or on the terrace outside, eat pub grub, or play darts, but do avoid the bathrooms.

Vinandro

Piazza Mino 33, tel. 055/59121, daily 12pm-12am, €7

This small wine bar with a rustic interior is a good *aperitivo* and late-evening drinking spot. A few outdoor tables and stools face the square, and there's a hearty menu of traditional Tuscan dishes in case you get hungry.

Festivals and Events

Many of Fiesole's events happen in Piazza Mino, including a **fruit, vegetable, and fish market** that takes over the square on Saturdays from 9am-1pm. There's also a popular **arts and crafts fair** dedicated to handmade objects that fills the square on the third Sunday of the month.

Mercatino del Piccolo Antiquariato

Piazza Mino hosts the Mercatino del Piccolo Antiquariato on the first Sunday of the month. With over 20 stalls displaying old radios, military paraphernalia, vinyl records, and 19th-century decorative objects, it attracts collectors from Florence.

Estate Fiesolana

Via Portigiani 3, tel. 055/596-1293, www.estatefiesolana.it, daily 10am-6:30pm

Estate Fiesolana is a music, dance, and theater festival held annually throughout June and July. Events are staged in an ancient Roman amphitheater and performers from around the world demonstrate their takes on classical, jazz, pop, rock, and many other genres. The box office is near the Archeological Area and performances usually take place in the evening.

Recreation and Activities

✪ WALKING AND HIKING

If you like breaking a sweat, lovely views, narrow lanes, and steep climbs, you'll love Fiesole. The town has three walking routes past nature, history, and art. They all start in Piazza Mino, and you can download a map (www.fiesoleforyou.it) or get a hard copy from the tourist office (Via Portigiani 3). Each route takes under an hour to complete, follows mostly paved roads, and passes numerous points of interest.

To find your way, look for the brown *passeggiata panoramica* (panoramic route) signs in Piazza Mino and around town. Unfortunately, they aren't in the most visible locations and are easy to miss. The easiest thing to do if you've lost your way is to ask local residents who have grown accustomed to pointing travelers in the right direction.

Piazza Mino to Convento di San Francesco

Distance: *300 meters*
Duration: *5-10 minutes*
Starting Point: *Piazza Mino*

This uphill walk on Via San Francesco starts in the northwestern corner of the square and is a steep climb all the way to the convent. Views get progressively better and there are two stone benches at the top to catch your breath and look out over Florence.

Via San Francesco

Piazza Mino to Convento San Domenico

Distance: *1.3 km/0.8 mi*
Duration: *15-20 minutes*
Starting Point: *Piazza Mino*

This leisurely downhill stroll passes three fabulous villas, including Villa Medici, on the road that was once the only way into town. The walk ends at Convento San Domenico, which has a checkerboard interior and an altar and several frescoes painted by Beato Angelico. Bus 7 back to Florence stops opposite the convent.

Monte Ceceri

Distance: *2.5 km/1.5 mi*
Duration: *45-60 minutes*
Starting Point: *Piazza Mino*

The third option is an intermediate 2.5 kilometer (1.5mi) route along quiet lanes to Monte Ceceri and the town's ancient quarries. The most secluded section is up a well-marked trail through a pine forest. Comfortable shoes, long socks to protect from stinging nettles, plenty of drinking water, and determination will get you up to Piazzale Leonardo at the summit, where da Vinci is said to have tested his flying machine for the first time.

CYCLING
Fiesolebike

Piazza Mino, tel. 345/335-0926,
www.fiesolebike.it, daily 8am-8pm

Fiesolebike runs half- and full-day tours over quiet lanes and forest trails around Fiesole. Their sunset tour (€56) departs at 5:30pm from their shop in Piazza Mino and a guide leads small groups along the scenic route back to Florence. The ride lasts 3.5 hours with some interesting stops and a great sunset. Experience on a mountain bike is helpful, but most of the journey is downhill and suitable to all. Reservations are recommended in summer when groups fill up fast. You can also rent a mountain bike for €20 per day and explore on your own. Rentals can also be returned in Florence at their Ciclo City (Via G. Orsini 4a) office.

TOURS
Villa Gardens Tours

tel. 055/055, www.museidifiesole.it,
Apr.-June and Sept.-Oct., €5

The town of Fiesole organizes seasonal visits of local gardens. Tours (two hours) begin in Piazza Mino and take place on Thursdays at 4pm. Spots are limited and must be reserved the Monday prior by telephone. A full schedule is available from the website.

Information and Services

TOURIST INFORMATION

To learn more about Fiesole, visit www.museidifiesole.it or www.fiesoleforyou.it.

Tourist Office

Via Portigiani 3, tel. 055/596-1323, Fri.-Sun. 10am-1pm and 2pm-4pm

You can pick up maps and event information from the tourist office just north of the main square near the Archeological Area.

Transportation

GETTING THERE

Fiesole is 15 minutes from Florence by car or taxi, 20 minutes by bus, 45 minutes by bike, and 60-90 minutes on foot depending on your pace. All three options follow **Via San Domenico**, which has sidewalks some of the way up and is relatively safe for cyclists and walkers.

BUS

Number 7 buses leave around every 15 minutes (6am-12am) from Piazza San Marco in Florence. A one-way ticket costs €1.50. Make sure to validate your ticket on board, as checks are frequent and unvalidated tickets result in €50 fines. It's a nice ride that ends in Piazza Mino da Fiesole.

City Sightseeing (tel. 055/265-6764, www.city-sightseeing.com, €23) tour buses also regularly make the journey to Fiesole on Line B. There are dozens of stops on this hop on/hop off service that passes every 30 minutes daily between 10am and 9pm. Note that the route only operates from June 16 until September 16.

TAXI

A taxi from Florence to Fiesole costs €25-35. Prices are higher on weekends, holidays, and after 10pm. Taxis can carry up to four passengers.

GETTING AROUND

It's easy to get around Fiesole on foot. However, the area around town is quite steep, and anyone contemplating cycling there should bring plenty of water. There's a **taxi stand** (tel. 055/4242) in Piazza Mino, which can be useful for getting back to Florence quickly or after buses stop circulating.

PISTOIA

Florence is fantastic, but just 40

kilometers (25mi) away lies a city that's nearly as
beautiful and often overlooked. Pistoia has been
in Florence's shadow since the 14th century, and
its illustrious neighbor has influenced Pistoia's
architecture, culture, and even the character of its
inhabitants. Many of the same Renaissance artists
working in Florence left their mark on Pistoia's
churches and squares. The cities look and feel a lot
alike, from the green shutters and yellow façades
of the palazzi to the dishes served in local trattorias. But there is one big difference. Florence is a

HIGHLIGHTS

✪ **CAMPANILE DELLA CATTEDRALE:** Climb to the top of the city's highest bell tower for a panoramic view of Pistoia (page 144).

✪ **PISTOIA SOTTOTERRANEA:** This subterranean tour along the tunnels where a river once flowed is a fascinating way to discover the city's medieval past (page 144).

✪ **MERCATO SETTIMANALE:** Italy's oldest continuously running market is a spectacle of commerce that transforms Pistoia's main square every Wednesday and Saturday morning (page 148).

magnet for tourists, while the streets of Pistoia are refreshingly free of tour groups and souvenir shops. Here, it's possible to explore the historic center, view monuments, and observe the everyday urban activity of locals in total tranquility.

PLANNING YOUR TIME

Pistoia can be visited in 3-4 hours and is easily combined with a day trip to Lucca or Pisa. Commuter trains from Florence reach the city in a little over 30 minutes and tickets can be purchased on the spot.

Wednesday and Saturday mornings are market days and a chance to see Pistoia at its liveliest. The biweekly event takes over the streets and squares of the historic center and leaves a much different impression than on other days when the historic center is relatively quiet.

ORIENTATION

Pistoia's trapezoid-shaped historic center lies directly north of the train station and was once surrounded by a series of concentric walls that defended **Piazza del Duomo** in the heart of the city. The walls have given way to long avenues off of which smaller side streets lead towards a medieval core. **Via del Lastrone**, one block east of Piazza del Duomo, is full of dining and nightlife options.

Itinerary Idea

ESSENTIAL PISTOIA

1 Arrive in Pistoia midmorning and walk to **Piazza del Duomo.** Pick up a free map from the tourist office located in the square and join one of the group tours if you're interested in history.

2 Buy a ticket and climb to the top of the **Campanile** next to the Duomo to get a 360-degree overview of Pistoia.

3 Stop for a traditional lunch at **Locanda del Capitano del Popolo** and taste medieval flavors that have been prepared the same way for generations.

4 Explore narrow side streets ncarby, like **Via della Torre,** and take an atmospheric stroll through Pistoia's past.

5 At 2pm sharp set off on the 50-minute English-language tour of **Pistoia Sottoterranea** and get an underground perspective on the city.

6 Say goodbye to Pistoia. Return to Florence, or continue on to Lucca or Pisa.

Campanile della Cattedrale, Piazza del Duomo

Pistoia

BISTECCATOSCANA ▼
L'ALBERO VITA ▼

Piazzetta di Sant'Andrea

5 ★ **PISTOIA SOTTOTERRANEA**

Piazzetta San Filippo

Piazza delle Scuole Normali

Piazza Giovanni XXIII

Piazza della Sapienza

PIAZZA DEL DUOMO **1**

CAFFÈ DUOMO ▼

Piazza San Bartolomeo

MERCATI DI PIAZZA DELLO SPIRITO SANTO ■

★ **MERCATO SETTIMANALE**

LOCANDA DEL CAPITANO DEL POPOLO **3**

Piazza del Duomo

2 ★ **CAMPANILE**

SCHIACCIAPENSIERI ▼

CATTEDRALE DI SAN ZENO (DUOMO)

Piazzetta Sozzifanti

★ **4** **VIA DELLA TORRE**

RUST FACTORY ▼
LA DEGNA TANA ▼

i **TOURIST OFFICE**

R. MUTT 1917

RACY MOOD ▼

Piazzetta Romana

FERMENTO BEER HOUSE ▼

Piazzetta dell'Ortaggio

Piazza Gavinana

VALIANI ▼

★

SAN GIOVANNI FUORICIVITAS

MAGICO CHIOSCO ▼

ESSENTIAL PISTOIA
1 Piazza del Duomo
2 Campanile
3 Locanda del Capitano del Popolo
4 Via della Torre
5 Pistoia Sottoterranea

0 ——— 200 yds
0 ——— 200 m

To Train Station

© MOON.COM

Sights

PIAZZA DEL DUOMO

The center of Pistoia has always been Piazza del Duomo and although the fortifications that surrounded the city were torn down in the 19th century to make way for urban expansion, the square has remained unchanged for centuries. It's one of the best looking *piazza* in Tuscany and home to the Duomo, Baptistry, and Campanile.

Half a dozen streets lead into the spacious square, but the most dramatic entrances are from **Via Roma** or **Via degli Orafi**. There are a couple of cafés from which to admire the architecture, but the best seats for observing the comings and goings of locals are on the Baptistery steps.

CATTEDRALE DI SAN ZENO (DUOMO)

Piazza del Duomo, tel. 05/732-5095, daily 8:30am-6pm, free

Pistoia is known as the *città dei pulpiti* (city of pulpits). There certainly are a lot of churches, but the biggest and most revered is the Duomo. It was built in the first millennium on ancient foundations and has been renovated and refurnished countless times since then. What began as a Romanesque church has since been given a black-and-white Renaissance façade, while baroque and 18th-century tastes subsequently altered the insides. On the roof are statues of Saint Zeno (after whom the church was named and who is the patron saint of Pistoia) and Saint Jacob. The three-nave interior contains four chapels, one of which has a silver altar and a monumental sculpture designed by Leonardo da Vinci's teacher.

BAPTISTERY

Piazza del Duomo, daily 10am-6pm, free

Opposite the Duomo is the octagonal 13th-century Baptistery, lined in white Carrara and green Prato marble. The impressive portal leads to a plain brick interior that is in sharp contrast with the elaborate masonry outside. It's worth taking a quick look at the baptismal font inside, but locals prefer to sit on the steps outside.

Piazza del Duomo

❂ CAMPANILE DELLA CATTEDRALE

Piazza del Duomo, daily 10:50am-5:50pm, €7

Pistoia has many bell towers but the Campanile della Cattedrale, which dominates Piazza del Duomo, is the only one that can be visited. It's a steep 200 steps to the top that culminates with a panoramic view of the city, Pistoian plain, and surrounding mountains. On a clear day, it's possible to spot the Duomo of Florence to the southeast. Lines are generally short throughout the day and reservations are not required.

view from the cathedral bell tower

SAN GIOVANNI FUORICIVITAS

Via Francesco Crispi 2, tel. 05/732-4784, free

San Giovanni Fuoricivitas lies a few blocks south of the Duomo and isn't a typical church. It's entered from the side, and the striped marble façade that acts like an optical illusion has little religious iconography. It's called *Fuoricivitas* (outside community) because it once lay beyond Pistoia's ring wall. The exterior is Pisan in style, with layers of dark green and white, which was used in many churches around the city. The interior is notable for its medieval stained glass windows and one of Pistoia's most ornate pulpits.

❂ PISTOIA SOTTOTERRANEA (Pistoia Underground)

Ospedale del Cepo, Piazza Giovanni XXIII 13, tel. 05/7336-8023, tours depart daily at 10:30am, 11:30am, 2pm, 3pm, 4pm, and 5pm, €9, or €6 with bell tower receipt

The Brana River was diverted through Pistoia centuries ago to meet the needs of medieval inhabitants. Today, the underground riverbed is dry, but the ancient passageways, opened in 2010, provide a vivid idea of how the city developed. Guided tours start in the Renaissance hospital above and take visitors on a journey past an anatomical theater, watermills, and the stone embankments where clothes were washed and refuse tossed. Visits last 50 minutes and are led by passionate guides who love answering questions. Some ducking is required, and good shoes, along with a light sweatshirt, are recommended, as temperatures are several degrees lower underground. English-language tours start daily at 2pm.

VIA DELLA TORRE

Pistoia's streets get progressively narrower the closer you get to Piazza del

façade of San Giovanni Fuoricivitas

Duomo and Via della Torre (Street of the Tower) is one of the oldest and most charismatic. It survived urban regeneration through the ages and the name comes from the medieval tower halfway down the street that's barely 150 yards long. Along the way are covered passageways, flying buttresses, and the dusty smell of history. At night a walk here is even more dramatic and feels like entering a portal to the past.

Food

Pistoia isn't anywhere near as touristy as Florence, which means local restaurants can't afford to prepare a bad meal or charge more than what locals are willing to pay. What they do prepare often includes boar, rabbit, and other wild game that's stewed and combined with an assortment of pastas. **Via del Lastrone** is packed with eateries that can satisfy a variety of appetites.

Sandwiches and steaks can also be found in the many eateries clustered in the center. Specialties include *Brigidini*, thin unevenly shaped sugar cookies, and *panforte glacé,* glazed chocolate cakes filled with nuts and candied fruits, which can be found in bakeries and pastry shops throughout Pistoia.

TUSCAN
Schiacciapensieri
Via dei Lastrone 9, tel. 05/7336-4142,
Tues.-Sun. 10am-1am, €5-8
Schiacciapensieri is the fast-casual Tuscan option serving classic *schiaccia* (squeezed) sandwiches and plates piled with aromatic hams and cheeses. There's a row of stools inside but the best seats are outside, facing the pedestrian street. Wine is served by the glass (€2) and good local and foreign beer await on tap.

✪ Locanda del Capitano del Popolo
Via di Stracceria 5/7, tel. 05/732-4785,
daily noon-3pm and 7pm-12am, €8-12
Eating like a Pistoian is easy. Just take a seat at Locanda del Capitano del Popolo and order the daily special that's been cooked the same way for generations. Fusion doesn't exist here and nothing is trendy. The restaurant has been serving *minestrone di fagiole* and *carcerato* soup the same way for over 50 years and no one complains. This is the place to try boar, rabbit, and wild game. Service is friendly and the walls are covered with musical instruments. Weekends get crowded and reservations are required in summer.

Bisteccatoscana
Via Sant'Andrea 30, tel. 05/7318-0175,
Mon.-Fri. 7:30pm-11pm and Sat.-Sun.
12:30pm-2:30pm and 7:30pm-11pm, €35
Bisteccatoscana is all about beef. Cuts of all sizes and kinds are grilled on an open flame and you can watch as meat is cooked. The €35 prix fixe option includes an appetizer, Fiorentina steak, three sides, dessert, and after-dinner liqueur. Wine isn't included, but there are 150 bottles to choose from inside this contemporary restaurant in the northwest corner of the historic center.

L'Albero Vita

Via Sant'Andrea 27, tel. 334/201-9287, Tues.-Sun. 7:30pm-10:30pm and Sat. 12:30pm-2:30pm and 7:30pm-10:30pm, €9-12

There are menus without meat in Tuscany, but that doesn't have to mean boring or bland. L'Albero Vita creates flavorful seasonal dishes and brings out the best in vegetables. The menu is strictly vegan, and the waitstaff is happy to explain ingredients and cooking methods inside this modern one-room restaurant that's popular with local herbivores.

BURGERS

Magico Chiosco

Piazza San Domenico 1, tel. 349/829-6913, Sun.-Thurs. 11am-10pm and Fri.-Sat. 11am-5pm, €4.5-6.50

If you think you can't get a good burger in Tuscany, you haven't been to Magico Chiosco. This informal kiosk between the train station and historic center is an excellent beef stop before or after visiting the city. Its low prices and quality sandwiches attract scooter-riding youth who fill the seats in the outdoor dining area opposite San Domenico church. Burgers are small, so if you're hungry order a few from the blackboard out front.

CAFÉS AND BAKERIES

✪ Valiani

Via Cavour 55, tel. 05/7317-81353, Thurs.-Sat. 7am-11:30pm and Sun.-Wed. 7am-8pm, €5

Valiani is a landmark café that's been serving *pastarelle,* brioches, and *panaforte glacé* pastries since 1831. The magnificent interior inside a former oratory is worth seeing even if you're not into chocolate. But if you are, just point to whatever looks good behind the long glass counter and you'll be served in a snap. Pastries are priced by the kilo, and Brigidini cookies are sold in attractive gift packages. There's a €9 fixed-price buffet lunch every day. Tables out front have a view of the Fuorcivitas church.

Caffè del Duomo

Piazza del Duomo 15, tel. 05/732-4660, Mon.-Sat. 6am-7:30pm, €5

Locals like to debate which coffee bar is the best, and Caffè del Duomo is one of the two or three that are perennially up for the title. It's easy to see why. There's no better location in the city and the espresso is good. You can drink it at the counter next to locals or at the tables set up in Piazza del Duomo. There's a steady stream of regulars who come for focaccia, homemade iced tea, and fresh-squeezed pomegranate juice. Pino behind the bar keeps everyone smiling and knows most of his clients by name.

Bars and Nightlife

There are plenty of places to drink in Pistoia and finding a bar open late isn't a problem. Nightlife is concentrated around **Piazza della Salla** and surrounding streets like **Via del Lastrone**. During the day there's a vegetable market, but at night the area attracts locals who congregate outdoors in summer until the early hours.

COCKTAIL BARS
Racy Mood
Via Castel Cellesi 3, Wed.-Mon. 6pm-2am

This drinking hole opened in 2017 and has quickly become a local favorite. Cocktails are well mixed, bartenders are friendly, and if you're craving a Mojito, you won't be disappointed here.

Rust Factory
Via dei Fabbri 6, tel. 340/086-9582, Sun.-Thurs. 6pm-1am and Fri.-Sat. 6pm-2am

Rust Factory is a windowless industrial-style bar with a concrete interior where cocktails are taken very seriously. The selection of distilled liqueurs runs the gamut from big brands to hard to find, and the barmen are keen to experiment with new flavors and exotic ingredients. Let them know what you're craving and they'll concoct something special.

R. Mutt 1917
Via dei Bacchettoni 10, tel. 327/193-5870, Fri.-Sat. 11pm-4am

R. Mutt 1917 is a 21st-century speakeasy with an anonymous entrance that leads to an unexpected space inside an old palazzo filled with mirrors, columns, and beautiful people. Finding it is a little tricky and no one answers the door until 11pm. After that, just knock and look like you know where you're going. There will be DJs inside spinning dance music and a bar from which to partake in late-night subterfuge.

PUBS
La Degna Tana
Piazza della Sala 1, tel. 05/7399-4117, tdaily 11am-1am

Located in the heart of Pistoia's drinking district, La Degna Tana is a popular Eastern European-style pub with waiters who have nearly as much fun as their patrons. There are half a dozen beers on tap served in pint glasses and immense mugs that can be accompanied by burgers, pretzels, and sausage. Seats outside are good for watching the happenings in the animated square.

Fermento Beer House
Via de Petri 4, tel. 329/899-2946, Tues.-Sun. 6:30pm-1am

If you're intent on a pub crawl, then the next stop should be Fermento Beer House, where you could get turned away for ordering a Corona, Becks, or Tennet. That's not the kind of beer Fermento pours, and it's a good thing. You've probably never heard of the Weisses, pilsners, or IPAs on tap—or many of the craft bottles behind the bar—but discovering new brews is what this place is all about. There's a solid slow-food menu and outdoor seating on a pedestrian street.

Recreation and Activities

CYCLING

Pistoia is flat and therefore a good city to explore on two wheels, with many parks and several bike lanes along the ancient walls.

RENTALS
Cicli Bencini

Corso Antonio Gramsci 98, tel. 05/732-5144, Mon. 3:30pm-7:30pm, Tues.-Fri. 9am-1pm and 3:30pm-7:30pm, and Sat. 9am-1pm

Cicli Bencini rents bikes by the day or hour and is located a few blocks northwest of the train station on a street that leads directly to Piazza del Duomo.

Shopping

Pistoia isn't geared to foreigners on Italian shopping sprees the way Florence is and you won't find many luxury boutiques or souvenir stores. You will find chains and family-owned businesses where locals go for clothing, food, and accessories, which makes shopping here enjoyable.

MARKETS
✪ Mercato Settimanale

Piazza del Duomo, Wed. and Sat. 8am-1pm

Mercato Settimanale has been held in Piazza del Duomo for over 1,000 years, and there were vendors here back before the church was built. It's the oldest continually running market in Italy and takes center stage every Wednesday and Saturday morning. There's nothing touristy about it. This is a real Italian market with scores of kiosks selling fruit, vegetables, meat, fish, shoes, clothes, household goods, books, toys, and everything else a Pistoian needs. It's always animated and the best place to practice your negotiation skills as prices are often flexible.

Mercati di Piazza dello Spirito Santo

Wed. and Sun. 8am-1pm

Mercati di Piazza dello Spirito Santo is also held on Wednesdays and Saturdays. This smaller market of around 20 stands is primarily devoted to shoes. There are stalls selling quality men's, women's, and children's footwear at bargain prices. All the leather shoes are locally made and come in styles that are hard to find anywhere else. If you need help finding a size or want to try on a pair, just ask the attendant.

Tourist Information

Tourist Office

Piazza del Duomo 3, tel. 05/732-1622, daily 9am-1pm and 3pm-5:30pm

The tourist office provides free maps of the city, province, and trekking trails in the area. They don't sell tickets and there is no city card. They do organize **guided group visits** (€10)

that depart daily at 10:30am and on Wednesday and Friday-Sunday at 3:30pm. Tours depart from the office and last two hours. Private tours can be arranged with Laura from the **Pistoia Guide Center** (tel. 335/711-6713, centroguide.pistoia@gmail.com) and personalized according to interest.

Getting There

Pistoia began as an ancient Roman pit stop where travelers heading to or from Florence on the Via Cassia could rest their horses and find sustenance or lodging. It's still a good place for a break and being halfway between Florence and Lucca makes it a convenient day trip addition whatever direction you're headed.

TRAIN

Pistoia is 40 kilometers (25mi) from Florence and easily reached by regional commuter trains that depart hourly from Santa Maria Novella station. The journey takes 30-50 minutes depending on the service and costs €4.60. Pistoia's train station is a short walk south of the historic center. You can also board the numbers 1 or 3 **ATAF Buses** (www.ataf.net, €1.50 for 70 minutes) outside the train station to reach Piazza del Duomo.

Trains from Lucca to Pistoia take 40-60 minutes and cost €5.70. If you are planning multiple stops, you will need separate tickets for each part of the journey.

CAR

The fastest way to Pistoia from Florence is the A11 highway. It's a 25-minute drive with a €2 toll. The SR66 single-lane regional road is another option but takes nearly twice as long. The drive from Lucca is also on the A11, and the 44 kilometers (27mi) can be covered in 30 minutes for a €3.50 toll.

There are several paid parking lots (Misercordia, Cellini, Cavalotti, Pertini) outside the city walls and street parking (€1 per hour) within the historic center. In either case, you'll need to type the number of your license plate at the automated meters and get a receipt, which must be placed on the dashboard.

BIKE

There is no dedicated bike path between Florence and Pistoia, but the SR66 and Via Firenze roads can both be cycled. Neither is particularly scenic and if you want to bring a bike to Pistoia, you're better off taking it on the train.

LUCCA

Lucca's urge to remain indepen-

dent explains the impregnable ramparts built around the city. Inside is a wonderful historic center that's just as pretty as Florence. It's perfect for pedestrians and bike riders, with lively streets, ornate churches, a tree-topped tower, and squares where locals do their socializing. It's all built on Etruscan and Roman foundations and a silk trade that led to steady growth throughout the late Middle Ages and Renaissance. The town is still very animated and there's plenty to see, do, and taste throughout the year.

HIGHLIGHTS

✪ **TORRE DELLE ORE AND TORRE GUINIGI:** Several of the medieval towers that once dotted Lucca's skyline are still standing. You get an equally good view of the entire town, and the Apuan Alps beyond, from either of these towers (pages 155 and 156).

✪ **CYCLING:** Lucca is a cycling town, and there are more rental shops here than pizza parlors. Get a good mountain bike and explore the aqueduct trail or the bike path along the Serchio River (page 160).

✪ **RAMPARTS:** These massive walls ensured Lucca's independence and are the town's biggest attraction. Walk, jog, or cycle around the tree-lined path that loops around town (page 161).

PLANNING YOUR TIME

Lucca is an 80-minute daytrip from Florence and can be combined with a morning or afternoon in Pisa for a 1-2 day trip. Renting a bike here is the best way to see the town and explore riverside cycling trails.

The Mercato dell'Antiquariato antique market attracts over 220 vendors and thousands of collectors to Lucca on the third weekend of every month. Depending on your interest in antiques and tolerance for crowds, it can be either the best or the worst time to visit.

Lucca has two combination ticket offers. The Pinacoteca Nazionale and

Museo Nazionale ticket costs €7, while both towers and the botanical garden can be visited for €9. Both offers are good for two days and can be purchased from any of the participating sights.

ORIENTATION

Lucca's enormous walls have protected and constrained the city at the same time. Large sections of the flat historic center are pedestrianized, and streets intersect more or less perpendicularly, making it easy to get around. **Piazza San Michele** lies in the center and is a popular meeting place with locals, as is **Piazza Napoleone**, the largest square in town, a few blocks south.

Lucca

Map Labels

VIA CATALANI
V. NIERI
V. LUPORINI
VIALE GIOSUE
VIALE EUROPA
V. LAZZARO PAPI
VIA DEL PALLONE
PASSEGGIATA DELLE
VIA CARLO DEL PRETE
VIALE DELLE TAGLIATE TERZA
VIALE CARDUCCI

Piazzale Giuseppe Verdi
Piazzale San Donato
Piazzale Tommaso

PINACOTECA NAZIONALE DI PALAZZO MANSI
VIA TOMMASO
VIA PELLERIA
VIA GALLI TASSI
VIA V. TORO
VIA DELLE STUFA
V. COLOMBARIA
VIA S. GIUSTINA
V. LORETO
VIA SAN

RAMPARTS OF LUCCA
PASSEGGIATA DELLE MURA

MUSEO NAZIONALE DEL FUMETTO E DELL'IMMAGINE
VIA VITTORIO EMANUELE II
VIA DELLA CASERMA
VIA DEL TABACCHI

GELATERIA SANTINI
CASA DI PUCCINI
LA BUCA DI SANT'ANTONIO
Michele
PICCOLO HOTEL PUCCINI
Piazza San Michele
Piazza SAN MICHELE IN FORO
CENAMI

Piazza S. Agostino
Piazza S. Agostino
VIA SAN AGOSTINO
VIA BATTISTI

PRO CLASSIC CYCLE
DARK SIDE
OSTELLO SAN FREDIANO

VIA DELLA
VIA VITTORIO VENETO
VIA FRANCESCO CARRARA
CORSO GARIBALDI
VIA REPUBBLICA
V. CAMILLO CAVOUR

SHAKER
CRONO
Piazza Napoleone
Piazza d. Giglio
San Martino
CATTEDRALE DI SAN MARTINO
VIA DUOMO
VIA SANTA CROCE

PALAZZO TUCCI
VIA FILLUNGO
VIA MORO
VIA ANTONIO

GIGI TRATTORIA
TORRE DELLE ORE
TORRE GUIGI
VIC. ALTOPASCIO
VIA SANTA CROCE
VIC. SAN ANDREA
Piazza dell' Anfiteatro
MERCATO DEL CARMINE
TRATTORIA CANULEIA

Piazza Santa Maria
CICLO DIVINO
DE CERVESIA PUB

CAVALLERIZZA

CAFFETTERIA SAN COLOMBIANO
VIA MARGHERITA
TOURIST CENTER
STAZIONE FERROVIARIA DI LUCCA

VIALE GIUSEPPE GIUSTI
VIA G. MAZZINI
VIA B. CAIROLI

VIA ROSA
V. DELL'ANGELO
VIA CUSTODE
VIA SANTA CROCE

PORTA SAN GERVASIO
Orto Botanico
V. FOSSO
V. GIARDINO BOTANICO
VIA DEL FOSSO
VIA DEL FOSSO

VIA SANTA CHIARA
VIA ELISA
VIA DELLA QUARQUONIA

MUSEO NAZIONALE DI VILLA GUINIGI
VIA BRINERO PAOLI

PASSEGGIATA DELLE MURA
VIALE GIACOMO PACINI
VIA D. PUB MACELLI
VIA CANTORE
VIA PIAVE
VIALE GUGLIELMO MARCONI
VIA DEI BACCHETTONI
VIALE GUGLIELMO

VIA FABIO FILZI

To Busatino and Indian's Cave Ranch
Piazzale Martiri della Libertà
To Ospedale
To Florence
To Florence
Campo di Marte

0 200 yds
0 200 m

© MOON.COM

Itinerary Idea

ESSENTIAL LUCCA

Don't be late to Lucca. Get up early and catch the train from Florence. The historic center is only five minutes from the station. When you arrive, enter Lucca through the San Pietro gate or any of the smaller pedestrian paths.

1 Rent a bike from **Crono**, located close to the walls, for a couple of hours. Ride south and circle the town's ramparts once or twice.

2 When you're ready for a rest, stop at **Caffeteria San Colombo** for fresh-squeezed orange juice and a pastry at the counter.

3 Pedal down any of the ramps into town, and explore streets like **Via del Fosso**, which is divided by a narrow canal.

4 Return the bike, and head down Via Vittoria Veneto on foot towards Piazza San Michele, where you can have a look inside **San Michele in Foro**.

5 Continue walking to **Torre delle Ore**. If the line to climb this tower is too long, head to Torre Guinigi, a few blocks away, for another great view of Lucca.

6 Take a lunch break at **Gigi Trattoria**. Order water, a carafe of house wine, the appetizer plate, and whatever pasta sounds good.

7 If you're leaving for Pisa or ready to head back to Florence, after lunch is a good time to do so. Otherwise, have a look at **Piazza dell'Anfiteatro**, but avoid the bars and cafes lining the square.

8 Leave from the piazza's northern exit and head up Via Fillungo through old Borgo Gate that once marked the town's outer limits. This part of Lucca gets lively in the evening, and **de Cervesia Pub** is perfect for *aperitivo*.

9 Head south and enter **Cattedrale di San Martino** to view the stained-glass interior and Tintoretto's *Last Supper*.

10 Have dinner al fresco at **Trattoria Canuleia.**

Lucca Itinerary

ESSENTIAL LUCCA

1. Crono
2. Caffeteria San Colombiano
3. Via del Fosso
4. San Michele in Foro
5. Torre delle Ore
6. Gigi Trattoria
7. Piazza dell'Anfiteatro
8. de Cervesia Pub
9. Cattedrale di San Martino
10. Trattoria Canuleia

© MOON.COM

Sights

CATTEDRALE DI SAN MARTINO

Piazza San Martino, tel. 058/349-0530, Mon.-Sat. 9:30am-5pm, Sun. 12pm-6pm, free

Lucca is known as the city of 100 churches, and the Cattedrale di San Martino is the biggest of them all. The Gothic cathedral was consecrated in 1070 and the façade completed six centuries later. The stained-glass interior contains important works of art like Tintoretto's colorful *Last Supper*, which is distinctive in that it portrays Jesus at the head of the table rather than the center. The 12th-century bell tower (daily 10am-6pm, €3) was opened to the public in 2016 and provides great views from the top. The **combo ticket** (€9) includes entry to the tower, the nearby

Cattedrale di San Martino

baptistery, and a small museum containing religious relics.

SAN MICHELE IN FORO

Piazza San Michele, 058/358-3150,
Mon.-Sat. 7:40am-noon and 3pm-5:30pm,
free

San Michele in Foro may not be as large as the churches in Florence, but size doesn't matter when the details are this good. Each column in the

San Michele in Foro

triple-tiered façade is different and the inlaid marble fits to perfection. Religious iconography is absent from the exterior except for the winged figure of St. Michael above the pediment. The inside is unusually bare, which makes it a good place to pause and think.

✪ TORRE DELLE ORE

Via Fillungo 20, tel. 058/348-090,
Apr.-Sept. daily 9:30am-6:30pm, Mar. and
Oct. 9:30am-5:30pm, closed Nov.-Feb.,
€4 or €9 combo ticket

Legend has it that the devil was once spotted on Torre delle Ore along Via Fillungo, the main thoroughfare of the city. It's the city's highest tower and so named for the clock that was installed in 1754. If you climb the 207 wooden steps to the top, you'll pass the clock mechanics that require daily winding.

Torre Guinigi

✪ TORRE GUINIGI

Via S. Andrea, tel. 058/348-090, Apr.-Sept.
daily 9:30am-6:30pm, Mar. and Oct.
9:30am-5:30pm, Nov.-Feb. 9:30am-4:30pm,
€4 or €9 combo ticket

The tower was built in the 14th century and distinguishes itself by the holm oaks growing on top. On clear days there are good views of the Historic Center and the Apuan Alps.

PIAZZA DELL'ANFITEATRO

Piazza dell'Anfiteatro has a strange shape to it. The reason lies in the Roman amphitheater that once stood here. In the Middle Ages the stone from the amphitheater was used to build houses, but in 1830 the Bourbons cleared the central area to preserve the original elliptical form. Remains of the two rows of 54 ancient arches can still be seen. Even though it's called Market Square, the stalls once set up here were transferred to the nearby Mercato del Carmine in the 19th century.

CASA DI PUCCINI

Corte San Lorenzo 9, tel. 058/358-4028,
www.puccinimuseum.org, May-Sept.
Wed.-Mon. 10am-7pm, Oct.-Apr. daily
10am-6pm, €7

Around the corner from Chiesa di San Michele in Foro is the house where the great opera conductor Puccini was born in 1858, and where the maestro spent most of his youth. The museum was recently restored, and each of the rooms returned to their 19th-century best. Even if you don't enjoy opera, the house provides insight into Victorian-era tastes and standards of living. A small gift shop (daily 9:30am-6:30pm) is located nearby in Piazza Cittadella 5.

MUSEO NAZIONALE DI VILLA GUINIGI

Via della Quarquonia 4, tel. 058/349-6033,
www.luccamuseinazionali.it, Tues.-Sat.
8:30am-7:30pm, €4 or €7 combo with
Pinacoteca

Museo Nazionale di Villa Guinigi displays cultural artifacts and paintings across three floors of an elegant villa. The archeological section on the ground floor contains many fragments from the past and examples of ancient funerary monuments. The shield once worn by a medieval Lombard warrior is impressive, as are paintings by Fra Bartolomo and his Renaissance contemporaries.

PINACOTECA NAZIONALE DI PALAZZO MANSI

Via Galli Tassi 43, tel. 058/355-570,
Tues.-Sat. 8:30am-7:30pm, €4 or €7 combo
with Villa Guinigi

Pinacoteca Nazionale di Palazzo Mansi was the home of a 16th-century nobleman and has since been transformed into a museum. The luxurious interior includes a hall of mirrors and hall lined with intricate tapestries. The museum has a varied collection donated by Leopold II in 1847. Venetian, Lombard, Roman, and Flemish artists are all present. Tuscan paintings include work by Bronzino, Andrea del Sarto, and Pontormo's *Portrait of a Young Man*.

ORTO BOTANICO

Via del Giardino Botanico 14, tel. 058/395-0596, www.lemuradilucca.it, Nov.-Mar. upon reservation only, Apr.-Oct. daily 10am-6pm, €4 or €9 combo ticket

For a complete change of scenery without having to leave the Historic Center, stroll the Orto Botanico, which was built along the walls and contains hundreds of rare species. It's a quiet place to take a stroll under shaded trees and flowering plants that reach full bloom in late spring.

Orto Botanico

MUSEO NAZIONALE DEL FUMETTO E DELL'IMMAGINE

Piazza San Romano 4, tel. 058/356-326, www.museoitalianodelfumetto.it, Tues.-Fri. 10am-6pm, €4

For serious comic-strip junkies Museo Nazionale del Fumetto e dell'Immagine is a must. The museum demonstrates the techniques used by Italy's premier illustrators, and hands-on exhibits will thrill Disneyphiles whether you speak the language or not. Entry includes a free comic book.

Food

Lucca is full of restaurants, but if you want to eat like the locals, avoid the main streets and major squares. Around the corner from Via del Moro and outside of Piazza dell'Anfiteatro you'll find unadorned *trattorie* and a secret garden where hearty soups, Tardelli pasta, Rovelline Lucchesi, and rabbit stew are served.

TUSCAN AND ITALIAN
✪ Gigi Trattoria

Piazza del Carmine 7, tel. 058/346-7266, daily 12pm-3pm and 7pm-11:30pm, €6-10

The husband and wife who run Gigi Trattoria like talking to strangers and get their kicks from serving great local dishes. You can try them inside the cozy interior with a bike hanging from the ceiling or outside on the little terrace that fills up quickly. Pasta or soups start from €6, and the house wine comes in several sizes.

pasta at Gigi Trattoria

Piazza dell'Anfiteatro

La Buca di Sant'Antonio

Via della Cervia 3, tel. 058/35-5881,
Tues.-Sat. noon-2:30pm and 7:30pm-10pm,
open Sun. lunch, €14-16

What started out as an inn where weary travelers could rest their horses and feed themselves hasn't changed much. Although the horses are gone, the hearty soups at La Buca di Sant'Antonio are pretty much the same. Puccini and Pound were known to dine here, and the candles and white tablecloths make it popular with couples.

Trattoria Canuleia

Via Canuleia 14, tel. 058/346-7470,
Tues.-Sun. 12:30pm-2pm and 7:30pm-10pm,
€10-18

The tranquil garden behind Trattoria Canuleia is the place to leave Lucca behind and get acquainted with ravioli, risotto, and gnocchi. It's relaxing and romantic, with attentive waitstaff who are quick to respond to any request. Pasta is freshly made every day and the tortelli al ragu are delicious.

Buatino

Borgo Giannotti 508, tel. 058/334-3207,
Mon.-Sat. noon-3pm and 7pm-10:30pm,
€10-14

Lunchtime service at Buatino can be hectic—everyone's eager to get their forks into the specials. Dinner is more relaxed and the atmosphere often includes live music. The *tagliatelle al piccione* (pasta with pigeon) makes a good first course and seconds include *bollito misto in salsa verde* (mixed meat stew with green sauce). The wine menu lists over 150 bottles from Tuscany and other Italian regions.

GELATO
Gelateria Santini

Piazza Cittadella 1, tel. 058/355-295,
summer daily 9am-midnight, winter
Tues.-Sun. 9am-9pm, €3-4

Gelateria Santini has been open since 1916 and they've learned a lot about gelato in that time. Besides a dozen homemade flavors they prepare delicious *zuccotti* and *semifreddi* desserts.

COFFEE
Caffetteria San Colombiano
Rampa Baluardo, tel. 058/346-4641, daily 9am-1am, €5

Caffetteria San Colombiano is located along the city ramparts and is a good place to stop for water, juice, or coffee. You can grab it quickly inside or sit at the outdoor tables and watch passing pedestrians. They also serve food and stay open late for cocktails.

Bars and Nightlife

Lucca has a number of bars where you can enjoy beer, wine, and music. Most are located on pedestrian streets or small piazzas that fill up with locals throughout the summer. Drinking is often done outdoors, as many establishments lack seating to accommodate the crowds that animate the city until 2am, when bars close.

TAPROOM
De Cervesia Pub
Via Michele Rosi 20, tel. 058/349-2620, Tues.-Sun. 5pm-10pm, €35

Several microbreweries have opened near Lucca in the last decade, and you can sample beers from them all at De Cervesia Pub. The small pub has only four taps, but there are plenty of cold bottles, too. If you need help selecting a brew, the owner will recommend a beer to suit your palate. Brùton, Forte, and Toptà are the local craft brews. There's not much room inside, so people hang out in the street outside. They also run a **beer shop** (Via Fillungo 92, Wed.-Sat. 12pm-12am and Sun. 5pm-12am).

WINE BAR
Ciclo Divino
Via Michele Rosi 7, tel. 058/347-1869, Mon.-Tues. 5pm-10pm and Wed.-Sun. 11am-10pm, €5-7

Wine is the drink of choice at Ciclo Divino, where you can get a glass or carafe of local vintages and great *crostini* appetizers (€1 each or 10 for €8). The interior is cozy with a bicycle décor, but if you can't find a seat, feel free to drink on the curb outside. To ensure people don't make off with the glasses, they charge a €2 deposit, which you get back when the glass is returned.

BARS
Dark Side
Via S. Frediano 24, daily 6pm-1am, €5-8

If you want to eat while you drink, or sip cocktails past midnight, head to the Dark Side. Their tasty *aperitivo* buffet is free with any drink. The brick walled, wooden ceilinged bar is popular with young locals on the town.

Shaker
Corso Garibaldi 40, tel. 349/724-0051

There are fewer bars south of Piazza San Michele, but Shaker more than compensates. This loud, friendly locale on a pedestrian street attracts foreign and local revelers, who come for the cocktails and a DJ stationed behind the consoles until midnight on weekends.

Festivals and Events

Sagra Musicale Lucchese

Sagra Musicale Lucchese is a series of concerts held throughout May and June and performed within the town's churches. Recent editions were dedicated entirely to the organ. Newly restored ancient instruments often take center stage. The repertoire varies between forgotten classics and new compositions sung by local choirs. Tickets rarely exceed €15 and concerts start at 9pm.

Lucca Summer Festival

Piazza Napoleone is transformed into an outdoor arena in July during the Lucca Summer Festival (www.summer-festival.com). The event, now in its 22nd edition, attracts thousands of fans from across Italy to hear legendary superstars, pop sensations, and major Italian acts. Tickets (€40-80) can be purchased on the day of performances from box offices in Piazza San Michele and Piazza del Giglio. Prices vary depending on who is playing.

Luminara di Santa Croce

Luminara di Santa Croce (Sept. 13) honors the cross that was supposedly brought back from Palestine by a monk and now rests in the Duomo. The nighttime procession is illuminated by thousands of torches that add a surreal effect to the celebration.

Recreation

✪ CYCLING

Cycling is a great way to explore the city, circle the ramparts, and move out into the countryside. There is no shortage of rental shops, prices are fairly standardized, and bike quality is good. Much of the center is off limits to traffic, and streets like **Via del Fosso**, with its canal, are interesting to explore.

RENTALS
Tourist Center Lucca

Piazzale B. Ricasoli 203, www. touristcenterlucca.com, daily 9:30am-7pm

You can rent bicycles from Tourist Center Lucca, near the train station. They provide basic city bikes (€8 for 3 hours or €12 per day) with a front basket and lock, and sturdier all-terrain mountain bikes (€30 per day).

Crono

Corso Garibaldi 93, tel. 058/349-0591, www.chronobikes.com

Crono rents bikes and arranges personalized cycling tours. Olympia hybrid bikes rent for €20 a day, while ultra-light Pinarello bikes with click pedals are €40. Tandems, quads, and rickshaws are also available for slow rides around town.

Pro Classic Cycle

Via Cesare Battisti 60, tel. 058/346-4657, www.proclassiccycle.com, daily 8:30am-7:30pm

If quality matters and you know the

renting a bike in Lucca

difference between a cog set and crank set, head to Pro Classic Cycle. Bicycles are in mint condition and Cesere makes sure every bike he rents matches the journey riders want to take. Prices (€3-15/hour) vary depending on make and model.

BIKE PATHS

Bike lovers have come to the right town! Depending on how much time you have, you can pedal around Lucca's paved ramparts for an hour or head out on longer treks. Terrain is flat and surfaces are mostly hardened dirt that can be walked as well as biked. The city's old aqueduct to the south and the Serchio River to the north are the most popular riding areas, and you won't be alone if you do decide to explore these paths.

✪ Ramparts

Distance: 4 km/2.5 mi
Duration: 20-30 minutes at an easy pace
Starting Points: The ramparts can be

reached from any of the six gates and numerous ramps within town.

The ramparts of Lucca are the symbol of the city and probably have had a lot to do with preserving the beauty inside. They're actually the fourth set of walls; they were transformed into a park during the 20th century before being rediscovered as one of the great attractions of the town. A walk or bicycle ride around the 4-kilometer (2.5 mi), tree-lined perimeter provides wonderful views of Lucca and the surrounding countryside. The walls include 10 heart-shaped bulwarks that stick out from the wall and were built to resist attacks.

Parco del Nottolini

Distance: 4 km (each way)/2.5 mi (each way)
Duration: 60-70 minutes
Starting Point: Behind the train station, across Via Civitali footbridge

To the south, Parco del Nottolini is an easy ride that starts behind the train station and over the Via Civitali footbridge. It extends four kilometers

TUSCANY ON TWO WHEELS

The Tuscan landscape beckons to be explored, so it's no surprise that cycling is extremely popular in this part of Italy. You can pedal around town on urban explorations or set off on longer excursions beyond city limits. Rental shops are often located around train stations and all you'll need is an ID and credit card to get started. Experienced riders will find high-quality road and mountain bikes equipped with locks, helmets, maps, and repair kits. Electric bikes are also common and a good option on the hillside trails of Chianti and Pienza. Most regional trains have dedicated areas for transporting bikes, which can increase riding opportunities and make return trips easier. Many companies specialize in guided bike tours, which is a great way of combining sport and culture. Tours need to be reserved in advance and often require a minimum number of riders.

TOURS

- **Fiesolebike** runs tours in and around Fiesole, including a sunset tour (page 137).

- **Smile and Ride** near the train station in Pisa offer bikes and tours inside and outside the city (page 179).

- **Bike Montalcino** rents a range of bikes and runs tours through the Val d'Orcia, including multiday excursions where you can stay in *agriturismi* along the way (page 272).

- **E-Bike Tuscany** offers tours, including a wine-tasting tour, around Pienza (page 278).

CITY CYCLING

- Florence has a number of bike paths, the longest of which runs **along the Arno** towards Parco delle Cascine (page 107).

- Cycling the 4 kilometers (2.5mi) around **Lucca's ramparts** is a beautiful introduction to the city (page 161).

(2.5 mi) on **Via degli Aquedotti** towards the Pisani Mountains along a 12-meter-high (39-feet-high) **aqueduct** completed by Lorenzo Nottolini in 1851. The 459 arches lead to a spring in **San Quirico di Guamo.** The narrow dirt path crosses several roads, and there are a couple of drinking fountains along the way. Once you get to the end of the aqueduct you can keep going up the hill to the source where locals often picnic.

Parco Fluviale

Distance: *11 km/6.8 mi*

Duration: *1-2 hours*

Starting Point: *Camaiore bridge*

The **Serchio River** passes north of Lucca and forms part of the Parco Fluviale. You can reach it by riding out from the S. Maria entrance of the city and following Via Borgo Gianotti less than a kilometer to the Camaiore bridge. From here, paved and gravel paths run south towards the San Pietro bridge on both sides of the river and north on the southern bank only. Both

LONGER RIDES

- From Pisa, you can cycle 6 kilometers (4mi) to the town of **Asciano**, passing alongside much of the city's ancient walls on the way (page 179).

- **Parco Fluviale** is a pleasant 11-kilometer (7mi) riverside path near Lucca (page 162).

- **Palagione-Ulignano** is an easy 40-kilometer (25mi) loop outside of Volterra, passing tiny villages and panoramic hilltops (page 210).

- The 90-kilometer (55mi) **Palazzo al Piano** loop in Castellina winds through plenty of small towns and vineyards (page 236).

CITY-TO-CITY CYCLING

With branches in Florence, Lucca, Siena, and Pisa, **Smile and Ride** (www. smileandride.com) is a good resource for cyclists. It's possible to rent bikes in one location and drop them off at another branch for free. Some of the more popular rides include:

- Lucca to Pisa

- Siena to San Gimignano

- Montalcino to Montepulciano

VESPA RENTALS

If you've never ridden a scooter, Florence is a good place to start. Drivers don't go very fast and there are fewer cars overall. Scooters are perfect if you have a little experience and want to get outside the city. The best direction is south along the **SR222** state road, which winds its way through Chianti and plenty of picturesque countryside. You can also rent scooters and ride around **San Gimignano** and **Radda in Chianti,** among other towns.

directions are popular with cyclists, joggers, and dog walkers.

Pista Puccini Bike Path

Distance: *17 km/10.5 mi*

Duration: *2-3 hours*

Starting Point: *Camaiore bridge*

The Pista Puccini bike path north of Lucca is great for serious cyclists who want to pedal beyond the city walls. Follow the Parco Fluviale south and keep going once you reach the San Pietro bridge. The trail runs 17 kilometers (10.5 mi) along the Serchio River to the WWF Massaciuccoli Oasis where you can spot rare falcons and ibis fishing in the marshy lake. A raised footpath (daily, dawn to dusk, free) leads to lookout huts that make bird-watching fun, and canoes can be rented from the park office (Via del Parco 6, tel. 058/497-5567, www. oasilipumassaciuccoli.org). It's €8 per adult for 3 hours with a life jacket and a map. Birds are active in the morning and throughout the spring and fall migration seasons.

Cycling to Pisa

Distance: 22 km/14 mi

Duration: 2.5-3 hours

Starting Point: Camaiore bridge

It's possible to ride all the way to Pisa. It's a scenic route southwest along the banks of the Serchio River to the town of Pontasserchio (15km (3 mi) from Lucca) and then on the SP 9 provincial road to Pisa. The final stretch is a bit dangerous with cars and little room on the shoulder for maneuvering. You can carry a bike on the train from Florence or rent one in Lucca for a couple of days. **Smile and Ride** (www.smileandride.com) can organize the opposite journey if you prefer starting out in Pisa and cycling to Lucca.

HORSEBACK RIDING

Indian's Cave Ranch

Via Dorini 318, tel. 338/584-6632, www.indianscaveranch.com

Another fun way to explore the area is on horseback. Indian's Cave Ranch, where a stable holds dozens of horses, is less than a mile from town across the river. You can take an hour-long lesson (€30) if you've never ridden before, or join one of their guided tours (€40-50) along the banks of the Serchio River.

Shopping

There's plenty of shopping to do in Lucca. Shops are usually closed on Sundays and have reduced hours on Mondays.

CLOTHING AND ACCESSORIES

Most clothing and accessories shops are concentrated along **Via Fillungo**, which is lined with Italian clothing stores and boutiques like **Cerri Rossella** (Via Fillungo 164), where local gentlemen go for dress shirts, and **Fillungo 200** (Via Fillungo 202), which sells quality men's and women's shoes at reasonable prices.

MARKETS

Lucca has several vibrant outdoor markets that are fun to browse and good places to find original gifts. A weekly **food and clothing market** is held on Wednesdays and Saturdays from 8am to 1pm in Piazza Varanini. There's also a daily **fruit and vegetable market** in Piazza Santa Maria.

Mercato del Carmine

Piazza del Carmine, Mon.-Fri. 7am-1pm and 4pm-7:30pm

The town's largest market is animated by butchers, fishmongers, and green grocers. Stalls are lined up outside when the weather is good and move indoors in the adjacent covered market whenever it rains.

Mercato dell'Antiquariato

Mercato dell'Antiquariato is the second-oldest **antique fair** in Italy, and fills half a dozen squares and side streets with hundreds of stalls. There's jewelry, maps, oddities, and collectibles of all types. The event happens on the third weekend of every month and takes over much of the city.

Accommodations

Lucca is the perfect day trip from Florence, but if you decide to spend the night there are plenty of inexpensive accommodations. Be careful where you stay, however, as parts of the city—especially the southern part of town near Porta San Pietro—can get very loud during the summer when bars remain open late and dance music fills the streets until early morning. Quieter nights can be assured in the residential areas or outside the city walls where accommodation is generally cheaper and only a short walk away. Prices increase substantially during the Lucca Comics festival in late October and throughout the Summer Festival.

Ostello San Frediano

Via della Cavallerizza 12, tel. 058/349-6976, www.ostellosanfredianolucca.com, €30 pp or €70 d

Ostello San Frediano challenges many of the stereotypes surrounding hostels. First, it's not a large dormitory for backpackers, and second, it's not located far from the city center. Instead rooms are many different sizes and the location between Piazza San Frediano and Piazza Antifiteatro is enviable. What remains true, however, is affordability. Your stay comes with a buffet breakfast, and the €20 all-inclusive lunch and dinner served in the large dining room is one of the best deals in Lucca. Guests do need to register for an AIG hostel card, but that can be done on-site at the front desk.

Piccolo Hotel Puccini

Via di Poggio 9, tel. 058/355-421, www.hotelpuccini.com, €75-100 s/d

It doesn't get more central than Piccolo Hotel Puccini. All of the town's monuments are around one corner or the other of this comfortable hotel. Breakfast is an extra €4 that will seem wisely spent. These are simple, clean accommodations that may not be glamorous but leave a good impression. Windows are double-plated and keep out the noise from the street below.

Palazzo Tucci

Via C. Battisti 13, 058/346-4279, www.palazzotucci.com, €150-€190 d

The entrance is the first clue Palazzo Tucci is not the average B&B. This historic residence provides an idea of how 19th-century nobles once lived. The high frescoed ceilings and six spacious rooms and suites ornately decorated in period furnishings are authentic down to the bedposts. Satellite TV, Wi-Fi, and air-conditioning are the only concessions to modernity of this peaceful accommodation that will satisfy even the lightest of sleepers.

Information and Services

TOURIST OFFICE
Centro di Accoglienza Turistica
Piazzale San Donato 15, tel. 058/358-3150,
www.luccaturismo.it, summer daily
9am-7pm, winter 9am-5pm

Lucca goes a long way to welcome visitors. The main tourist office or Centro di Accoglienza Turistica is located near Porta San Donato near the eastern walls of the city. You can deposit bags, grab a free map, and purchase tickets to museums and concerts here. They'll also help you find a hotel in your price range at no charge if you decide to unexpectedly spend the night in Lucca.

The office organizes group tours of the city on Wednesday and Saturday mornings at 11am and every afternoon at 2pm. These cost €13, last two hours, and can be purchased at the office or with the guide, who switches between Italian and English, waiting near the church in Piazzale San Michele.

HOSPITALS AND PHARMACIES
Ospedale Campo di Marte
Via Ospedale 1, tel. 058/39701

Ospedale Campo di Marte is just outside the walls near Porta San Jacopi. Consultations can be made over the phone and there are several pharmacies in the center for resolving minor mishaps. If you can't find the right words just mime the injury or ailment.

Farmacia Comunale
Piazza Curtatone 7, tel. 058/349-1398

Farmacia Comunale is open 24 hours and located in front of the train station.

Transportation

GETTING THERE
TRAIN
The easiest way to reach Lucca from Florence is by train. There are many hourly departures. The regional service takes 80-100 minutes depending on the train and costs €7.60. The second route requires a transfer in Pisa and takes nearly two hours. Both services depart from Stazione Santa Maria Novella and arrive in Stazione Ferroviaria di Lucca (Viale Camillo Benso Cavour 15, www.trenitalia.it) just outside the city walls and within walking distance of Lucca's Historic Center. The last train back to Florence is at 10:10pm and arrives at 11:30pm. Tickets can be purchased from automated machines in SMN or the ticket booths inside the station. Trains are rarely crowded and there is plenty of scenic countryside to enjoy along the way.

Lucca is only 18km (11mi) from Pisa by train and the two cities can be combined into a one- or two-day trip from Florence. There are dozens of daily departures and the 30-minute journey costs €3.60.

BUS

Flixbus (www.flixbus.it) operates two daily departures (8:55am and 9:10am) from Piazzale Montelugo in Florence. Seats on board modern coaches can be reserved in advance and one-way tickets are €15.99. The return journey leaves at 2:55pm and takes an hour. Travelers are dropped off in Viale Regina Margherita near the train station in Lucca and can reach the center on foot.

CAR

Lucca is located off the A11 highway that links the A1 near Florence with the A12 near Pisa. Drivers can choose from 10 paying parking lots (€1.20 per hour) within the walls or park for free in the neighborhood streets outside and walk the rest of the way. There's a €5.40 toll at the end of the journey.

GETTING AROUND

The best way to get around Lucca is by foot or bike. City Buses aren't that useful for getting around the historic center but if you want to discover what's beyond the walls, such as Parco del Nottolini or the Parco Fluviale, hop on one of the buses that depart from Piazzale Verde. Tickets are €1.50 and good for 70 minutes upon validation.

There's a taxi stand outside the train station as well as in Piazza Santa Maria, Piazzale Verdi, and Piazza Napoleone. To order a cab, call Radio Taxi (tel. 05/8333-3434) or Taxi Lucca (tel. 05/8395-5200).

PISA

It's easy to pigeonhole Pisa as a one-monument town. The city's world-famous tower has been the main attraction since the 16th century, but there's a lot more to Pisa than an engineering oversight. Pisa is an elegant, walkable city that's neither too big nor too small. The historic center is lined with pedestrian streets and lovely squares animated day and night by a vibrant university community. The skyline is low, and façades still show signs of the city's golden age when its fleet vied for control of the Mediterranean. A day or two strolling along the

HIGHLIGHTS

✪ **LEANING TOWER:** No city in the world is as closely associated with a single monument as Pisa, and you can't miss this incredible tower at an incredible angle (page 174).

✪ **MURA DI PISA:** Walking along the ramparts of Pisa's medieval walls provides a unique perspective on the city (page 175).

✪ **PALAZZO BLU:** This exhibition space is a hotbed of culture, mixing temporary exhibitions of world-renowned art with a permanent collection of pieces by homegrown painters (page 176).

Arno, observing the city from medieval walls, pedaling past aqueducts, and toasting with locally brewed beer will help you discover another side to Pisa.

PLANNING YOUR TIME

Pisa is a convenient morning or afternoon day trip within an hour of Florence. There are plenty of activities, though, and enjoying the nearby seaside and San Rossore park could easily take up an entire day.

Don't expect to just show up and enter the famed Leaning Tower: Reserve a ticket in advance online at www.opapisa.it. You will be assigned a 30-minute time slot to climb the tower. If you're late, you'll miss your turn! Tickets must be purchased 1-20 days in advance. Same-day tickets are not available. Reserve an early morning or late afternoon slot, when the tower and the Piazza dei Miracoli on the northern edge of the city are relatively peaceful.

ORIENTATION

The Arno River runs through Pisa, and the northern bank has historically been the more developed side. The Ponte di Mezzo and Solferino bridges are convenient crossing points. Via Roma is the quickest way to Piazza dei Miracoli on the northern edge of the city, where many of the famous sights are concentrated.

Itinerary Idea

ESSENTIAL PISA

1 After you arrive in Pisa, walk north from the train station to Piazza Vittorio Emanuele II and take a short detour left on Via Zandonai to see Keith Haring's Tuttomondo.

2 Check the time and make sure you aren't late for your appointment to the **Leaning Tower.** Arrive a few minutes early and follow your group up the tower. Enjoy the view until your 30 minutes are up.

3 Head to the **Duomo,** located in Piazza dei Miracoli near the Leaning Tower, and admire the restoration work, completed in 2018 to mark the 900th anniversary of the cathedral's existence.

4 Make sure to be inside the **Baptistery** (right by the Duomo in Piazza dei Miracoli) on the hour or half hour, when the acoustics demonstration takes place. Afterward, spend a little time on the lawn admiring all the buildings in Piazza dei Miracoli.

5 When you've had your fill, walk to Porta Santa Maria in the southwestern corner of the square and climb up the **Mura di Pisa** city walls. Follow the ramparts above cemeteries, gateways, and aqueducts all the way to Torre di Legno near the Arno River.

6 On your way back to the train station, walk along the northern banks of the Arno and grab a table under the arches at **Vineria di Piazza.** Order a plate of local cold cuts accompanied by red Tuscan wine in Piazza Dante Alighieri. Afterward cross the Arno and catch a train back to Florence.

the Arno River

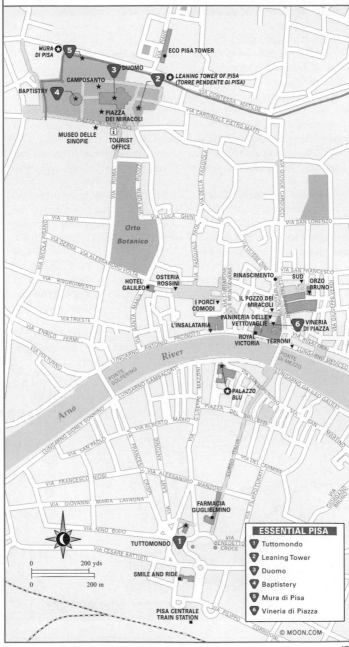

Pisa

MURA DI PISA ⭐ **5**

ECO PISA TOWER ⭐

DUOMO ⭐ **3**

LEANING TOWER OF PISA ⭐ **2**
(TORRE PENDENTE DI PISA)

CAMPOSANTO ★

BAPTISTRY ⭐ **4**

★ **PIAZZA DEI MIRACOLI**

PIAZZA DEI MIRACOLI

★ **MUSEO DELLE SINOPIE**

TOURIST OFFICE 🛈

VIA CONTESSA MATILDE

VIA CARDINALE PIETRO MAFFI

PIAVE

VIA ROMA

VIA PORTA BUOZZI

VIA LUCA GHINI

VIA DELLA FAGGIOLA

VIA PASQUALE PAOLI

VIA GIOSUE CARDUCCI

VIA SAN LORENZO

VIA SAVI

VIA NICOLA PISANO

VIA DERNA

VIA ALESSANDRO VOLTA

VIA RISORGIMENTO

VIA TRIESTE

VIA ENRICO FERMI

VIA VOLTURNO

Orto Botanico

VIA ULISSE DINI

VIA SAN FRANCESCO

VIA SAN LORENZO

RINASCIMENTO ▼

SUD ▼

ORZO BRUNO ▼

OSTERIA ROSSINI ▼

HOTEL GALILEO ●

VIA CURTATONE E MONTANARA

I PORCI COMODI ▼

IL POZZO DEI MIRACOLI ▼

VIA SANTA MARIA

VIA ANTONIO PACINOTTI

L'INSALATARIA ▼

PANINERIA DELLE VETTOVAGLIE ▼

VIA SAN MARTINO

VINERIA DI PIAZZA **6**

ROYAL VICTORIA ▼

TERRONI ▼

LUNGARNO MEDICEO

River

PONTE SOLFERINO

LUNGARNO ANTONIO PACINOTTI

LUNGARNO GAMBACORTI

VIA MAZZINI

VIA SAN FREDIANO

PONTE DI MEZZO

LUNGARNO GALILEO GALILEI

Arno

LUNGARNO SIDNEY SONNINO

VIA SAN PAOLO

VIA FRANCESCO CRISPI

VIA ALESSANDRO MANZONI

⭐ **PALAZZO BLU**

PIAZZA DEL GUELFI

VIA SAN MARTINO

VIA FRANCESCO NIOSI

VIA GIOVANNI MARIA LAVAGNA

VIA GIUSEPPE MAZZINI

VIA ALBERTO MARIO

CORSO ITALIA

VIA DEL CARMINE

VIA FILIPPO TURATI

VIA GIORDANO BRUNO

VIA NINO BIXIO

FARMACIA GUGLIELMINO

VIA CESARE BATTISTI

TUTTOMONDO **1**

VIA BENEDETTO CROCE

SMILE AND RIDE

PISA CENTRALE TRAIN STATION ■

VIA FILIPPO CORRIDONI

| 0 | 200 yds |
| 0 | 200 m |

ESSENTIAL PISA

1	Tuttomondo
2	Leaning Tower
3	Duomo
4	Baptistery
5	Mura di Pisa
6	Vineria di Piazza

© MOON.COM

Sights

PIAZZA DEI MIRACOLI

Piazza dei Miracoli, home to a tower, cathedral, baptistery, and cemetery, is unlike any piazza in Italy: The large, rectangular square is not located in the town center, nor is it surrounded by other buildings. Medieval Pisans chose this site 15 minutes from the city center because there wasn't any space in town and they needed the room to create something that would overshadow their Florentine neighbors.

They began by building the Duomo, then added a baptistery and the famous leaning bell tower, and completed the square with the Camposanto cemetery several centuries later. Bright-white marble from local quarries covers the buildings, all of which have a slight lean due to the softness of the terrain.

Walkways connect the buildings, which are surrounded by perfectly manicured lawns. Piazza dei Miracoli was designated a World Heritage landmark in 1987 by the United Nations Educational, Scientific, and Cultural Organization (UNESCO) and is filled most of the day with travelers, tour groups, and street merchants tempting tourists with selfie sticks and cheap souvenirs. All four monuments are located just minutes from one another. Some parts of the grassy square are open to visitors who would like to sit or lie down, while others are off limits.

Two **ticket offices** are located on either side of the square, along with restrooms and the city's main tourist office. You can visit a single monument (Baptistery, Camposanto, or

Duomo and Leaning Tower of Pisa

Sinopie Museum) in the square for €5, two for €7, or all three for €8. The Leaning Tower requires a separate €18 ticket, which can be reserved in advance. The Duomo is free to enter but does require a pass.

The Duomo requires a free pass to enter. The pass is included with tickets to the other sights and is available online or from either of the ticket offices. Visitors can enter whenever they want and stay as long as they like.

Duomo

Piazza dei Miracoli, www.opapisa.it, Apr.-Sept. daily 10am-8pm and Oct.-Mar. 10am-6pm, weekday mass 8am, 9am, and 9:15am, Sun. 8am, 9:30am, 11am, 12:15pm, and 6pm, free

Construction of the Duomo began in 1063, and the building was consecrated 55 years later in the presence of Pope Gelasius II. Latin inscriptions on the façade recount how victories over Saracen pirates and the sacking of Palermo financed the project. The fact that Pisa's Venetian rivals were building St. Mark's around the same time was an added incentive to make this church the grandest of its kind. The five-nave interior is impressive, although much of the artwork that originally decorated the church was destroyed in a 16th-century fire. That disaster led to the installation of a new roof and the *Christ on His Throne* mosaic behind the altar, which is attributed to Giovanni Cimabue. The colorful floor tiling is original and a good reason to keep your head down. The ornate pulpit by Pisano tells the story of Jesus' life. It was later dismantled and forgotten until 1926, before being returned to its original position. A few pieces were lost at some point, which explains why not all the columns are alike. The Opera del Duomo Museum (Piazza del Duomo 23), next to the Leaning Tower, recounts how the Duomo was built but was closed for restoration at the time of writing.

the Baptistery in Piazza dei Miracoli

Baptistery

Piazza dei Miracoli, www.opapisa.it, Apr.-Sept. daily 8am-8pm and Oct.-Mar. daily 9am-6pm, €5 or €8 combined ticket

This baptistery—the largest in Italy—was the second building added to Piazza dei Miracoli. A succession of architects supervised its construction, but the façade, with its numerous sculptures, is the work of Nicolas Pisano and his son. The four entrances are aligned with the cardinal points and decorated with hundreds of detailed sculptures illustrating stories from the Bible. Inside is rather simple except for the pulpit sculpted by Pisano in 1260 that is a precursor of the Renaissance. The artist broke with traditional design by creating a novel octagonal form, choosing a classical subject matter and representing figures in a realistic way. Another impressive feature is the huge double dome roof with a 100-meter circumference that produces remarkable acoustics. You can test these yourself or wait for the attendant who sings a few reverberating notes on the hour and half hour.

⚙ Leaning Tower of Pisa (Torre Pendente di Pisa)

Piazza dei Miracoli, www.opapisa.it, daily 9am-8pm, €18

Italy is full of leaning towers, but the Torre Pendente di Pisa, or Leaning Tower of Pisa, is the most famous. It's only 5 degrees off-kilter, but that's enough to make it look like a disaster waiting to happen. Construction of the bell tower began in 1173 and took nearly two centuries to complete. Unstable soil caused it to start leaning before it was finished, and the remarkable building has puzzled architects and attracted tourists ever since. Fortunately, structural interventions completed in 2011 have stabilized the 58-meter-high (190ft) monument and made it accessible to the public.

Today visitors can climb the 251 steps to the top via an inner staircase that leads to a circular terrace with good views of the city and seven bells that ring out before mass and at

the Leaning Tower of Pisa

noon. Children under six and people with heart conditions are not allowed to enter. Walking up a leaning tower feels strange and can cause wooziness, but the view at the top and the knowledge that this is one of the man-made wonders of the world make it worthwhile. Don't expect to just show up and enter the Leaning Tower, though. Reserve a ticket in advance online at www.opapisa.it. You will be assigned a 30-minute time slot to climb the tower. Don't be late or you'll miss your turn.

Camposanto

Piazza dei Miracoli, www.opapisa.it, Apr.-Sept. daily 8am-10pm and Oct.-Mar. daily 9am-6pm, €5 or €8 combined ticket

Camposanto (field of saints) is an immense cloistered cemetery on the northern side of Piazza dei Miracoli. According to legend, work on the building began in 1277, after the fourth crusade, when Pisa's archbishop returned with cartloads of earth from the Holy Land. The sacred dirt was intended for the city's most illustrious dead. Another possible reason behind its construction was to reduce the number of graves in and around the Duomo. In either case, it was the first covered cemetery with two long corridors and a grassy inner courtyard reserved for Pisa's most prestigious citizens. The hallways inside are lined with sarcophagi and marble plaques are embedded in the floor where the less well-to-do were laid to rest. During the 14th century, the walls were entirely decorated with frescoes. Many of these were damaged during an air raid at the end of World War II, and reconstruction has been going on ever since. It took 20 years to restore *Triumph of Death*, which was

Camposanto cemetery

returned to its original setting on the western end of the complex known as the Salone degli Affreschi in 2018. The colorful painting depicts the Middle Ages' vision of life and death, with angels and demons fighting over the souls of helpless humans.

Museo delle Sinopie

Piazza dei Miracoli, www.opapisa.it,
Apr.-Sept. daily 8am-8pm and Oct.-Mar.
daily 9am-6pm, €5 or €8 combined ticket
To learn how the frescoes in Camposanto were created, head to the Museo delle Sinopie. The two-story museum is also a nice escape from the crowds outside, with a rare collection of preparatory drawings by medieval artists on paper and parchment that were essential for making frescoes. Unfortunately, most are badly faded and would take a lot of imagination to fully appreciate. A video display on the first floor tells the story of the Leaning Tower, and an interactive exhibit explains the history of frescoes.

✪ Mura di Pisa

Piazza dei Miracoli 9, tel. 050/098-7480,
www.muradipisa.it, Apr.-Sept. daily 9am-7pm
and Oct.-Mar. 10am-3:30pm, €3
Medieval walls are a common feature of Tuscan cities, but what isn't so common is being able to walk along narrow ramparts and view a city from above—which is exactly what the Mura di Pisa allows you to do. This wall was completed in 1284, and the remaining section measures 3 kilometers (1.9mi),

Pisa's medieval walls

with several watchtowers along the way. The meter-wide (3.2ft) walkway was opened in 2018. There are four entrances along the route, but it's best to start at the tower leading to the 11-meter-high (36-ft) wall in the southwestern corner of Piazza dei Miracoli and walk all the way to the end near the Arno. There are only stairs at this location, but the other entry points (at Porta Pacis, Piazza dell Gondole, and Torre di Legno) are equipped with elevators, and tickets are available at each of the entrances. The full walk takes around 30-40 minutes to complete. Comfortable shoes, water, and a hat are recommended. A scenic bike path runs next to the walls much of the way.

✪ PALAZZO BLU

Lungarno Gambacorti 9, tel. 050/220-4650, www.palazzoblu.it, Tues.-Fri. 10am-7pm and Sat.-Sun. 10am-8pm, €12

This former palace is now an art museum and the cultural hub of Pisa that regularly stages world-class temporary exhibitions. Shows dedicated to Pablo Picasso, Salvador Dalí, Andy Warhol, and M. C. Escher have all made stops inside the *palazzo*, which belonged to a succession of powerful families and was converted into its present form over a decade ago. The quality of exhibits is high and there's a permanent collection made up of local painters and 19th-century furnishings. Admission includes an audio guide in English. The large, well-stocked gift shop is a good place to find books and artistic souvenirs.

TUTTOMONDO

Via Riccardo Zandonai, 24/7, free

Keith Haring didn't paint a lot of large-scale murals, but he was invited to create this one during his 1989 stay in Pisa. Tuttomondo (All World) was one of his last works and includes over 30 figures in the artist's trademark energetic style. It took him four days to paint the street-art masterpiece that covers the side of a three-story building where the city's blood donation association is based. There's a café opposite the mural and benches from which to take it all in.

Keith Haring mural

Food

The great concentration of visitors in and around Piazza dei Miracoli has resulted in a large number of restaurants in the direct vicinity of the busy square, but traveler beware: You should avoid these at all costs. Instead, head for the narrow streets and piazze around the colonnaded Borgo Stretto southeast of the square. Here you'll find authentic trattorias with pleasant outdoor seating catering to locals and foreigners with an appetite for Pisan specialties like *zuppa alla pisana* (vegetable soup), *baccalà alla griglia* (grilled cod), and *pasta e ceci* (pasta and beans).

TUSCAN AND ITALIAN
Vineria di Piazza
Piazza delle Vettovaglie 13, tel. 050/520-7846, daily 12:30pm-5:45pm and Thurs.-Sat. 7:45pm-11pm, €8-12
Vineria di Piazza prepares great appetizers, pasta, and steak served in abundant portions at low prices. The wooden decor inside is simple, and outdoor seating is under an archway that circumnavigates a small square. The early evening *aperitivo* option includes one drink and unlimited trips to an extensive buffet.

Osteria Rossini
Piazza Dante Alighieri 4, tel. 333/667-3338, Sun.-Fri. 12-4pm and Fri.-Sat. 7:30pm-10pm, €7-9
The roads leading to the Leaning Tower are full of eateries that haven't seen a local inside for decades. That's not the case at Osteria Rossini, where diners seem oblivious to the tourists just a few blocks away. The lunch menu always includes several daily specials, a variety of local pasta dishes, and a beef tartar made from Tuscan cattle. The wine list is well priced, and the outdoor tables facing the square fill up fast.

L'Insalataria
Lungarno Antonio Pacinotti 40, tel. 050/220-0423, Mon.-Sat. 11:30am-3:30pm and 7pm-10pm, €8
L'Insalataria is a valid vegetarian option with a bohemian interior facing the Arno. The concept is simple: Choose a base of salad, couscous, barley, or rice and then add as many vegetable, cheese, or protein ingredients as you like for a flat fee. Most of the customers are local university students and the menu is in Italian, but staff can help with translation, and pointing works as well as words.

SANDWICHES AND STREET FOOD
Panineria delle Vettovaglie
Piazza delle Vettovaglie 34, €5
Panineria delle Vettovaglie is a hole-in-the-wall sandwich shop selling fresh baguettes stuffed with roast pork and wine for €1.50 a cup. No sandwich here is more than €5, which makes it extremely popular, and lack of seating is a nice excuse to sit down in the little square out front.

I Porci Comodi
Via l'Arancio 4, tel. 392/989-3706, daily 11am-10:30pm, €5-7
For a quick street food option, head to I Porci Comodi on Piazza Dante Alighieri, where sandwiches (€6) and

overflowing trays of cured meat and cheese are served by a friendly crew of enterprising friends. Everything can be accompanied by a glass or bottle of wine and enjoyed inside the tiny eatery or, as usually happens, on the marble benches outside.

PASTRIES
Terroni
Lungarno Mediceo 66, tel. 050/575-191, 7am-2am

Terroni is slang for anyone who works the earth, and it was used by northern Italians as a slur against their southern cousins. It's a good name for a snack bar and pastry shop that specializes in Sicilian pastries like cannoli, *pasticciotti*, profiterole, and many more. Uniformed staff also prepare great coffee and delicious savory options that can be enjoyed at two large sharing tables or wrapped up and taken to go (*per portare via*).

Bars and Nightlife

Pisa is a university town, and on weekends the streets and squares around Borgo Stretto fill up with students. Crowds often end up in the street drinking, which is a summertime ritual for many residents.

BARS
Orzo Bruno
Via delle Case Dipinte 6/8, Mon.-Thurs. 7pm-1am and Fri.-Sun. 7pm-2am
Orzo Bruno serves its own locally brewed beer and appetizers that go perfectly with the pilsner on tap. Prices are reasonable, which is why it's nearly always crowded. There is no table service. During happy hour (daily 7pm-8:30pm), pints cost €3.60.

Sud
Via delle Case Dipinte 21, daily 7pm-1am
Just up the block from Orzo Bruno, Sud is a popular happy-hour bar with live music and an animated staff who make a show of preparing cocktails. Crowds often end up in the street drinking, which is not uncommon in Pisa.

Il Pozzo dei Miracoli
Piazza delle Vettovaglie, daily 6:30pm-3am
If you prefer a shot, head to Il Pozzo dei Miracoli. There are 24 to choose from and none costs more than €3. Bartenders seem to know everyone they're serving, and the mood inside this small bar is always festive.

Recreation and Activities

CYCLING

Pisa has a number of bike paths in the historic center, including a dirt trail that runs along much of the city's ancient walls and many green routes outside of town perfect for exploring local countryside.

BIKE RENTALS
Smile and Ride

Via Pietro Mascagni 13, tel. 375/561-7631, www.smileandride.com, daily 9am-1pm and 2-7pm, €5-15/day

Mario and Elena are passionate riders who opened Smile and Ride to help travelers discover their city. The shop is conveniently located five minutes from the train station and provides colorful city, trekking, and e-bikes by the hour or day. Prices are reasonable, and all bikes are custom-made in Italy. Tandems, kids' bikes, and baby carriers are also available, and rentals include locks and repair kits. Bikes come with loads of friendly advice, and the couple organizes tours of the city and surrounding countryside. Serious cyclists can even rent bikes here and drop them off at partner shops in Lucca, Florence, or Siena for free.

BIKE PATHS
Porta Santa Marta to Asciano Bike Path

Piazza delle Gondole

The Medicean Aqueduct, completed in 1613, starts east of the city walls at Porta Santa Marta gate and extends 6 kilometers (4mi) to the town of Asciano. The dirt path is flat, with arches on one side and fields of wheat, corn, and sunflowers on the other. A round-trip takes about an hour. There are no cars, but there are several street crossings and occasional pedestrians. Once you arrive in Asciano, you can keep going up the hillside to the (now dry) spring that once fed the aqueduct.

the Medicean Aqueduct

PARKS
Parco San Rossore

Tenuta di San Rossore, tel. 050/530-101, www.parcosanrossore.org

Parco San Rossore, Pisa's largest park and natural reserve, lies west of the city and stretches 80 square kilometers (50sq mi) along the Mediterranean coast. It's a mix of forest, dunes, shrub, and farmland that attracts a variety of wildlife. There's a good chance of spotting deer, wild boar, porcupines, and many types of migrating birds. There are a number of scenic paths to follow, along with picnic areas, four visitors centers, and a number of restaurants. To get here, take bus 6 from the train station to the end of the line in Barbaricina and walk from there. Or faster yet, order a cab. The ride to the visitors center (Loc. Cascine Vecchie)

Parco San Rossore

takes 15 minutes and costs €10-12. Cycling to here on the Viale delle Cascine is another good option and the best way of exploring the park.

HORSEBACK RIDING AND BUGGY TOURS
Equitiamo
Viale delle Cascine, tel. 338/366-2431, www.equitiamo.it

This stable in Parco San Rossore organizes 1.5-hour tours (€20) through pine forests for beginning horseback riders and 2.5-hour (€40) outings along the coast for experienced riders. Reservations are required and riders must be 14 years and up.

San Rossore in Carrozza
Casale La Sterpaia, tel. 050/531-910

Horse-drawn buggy tours are available from San Rossore in Carrozza in Parco San Rossore. There are forest (1.5hr/€9.50), river (2hrs/€11.50), and coastal (3hrs/€14) itineraries, all of which must be reserved in advance.

RIVER TOURS
Top 5 Viaggi
Lungarno Mediceo, tel. 050/533-755, staff@ top5viaggi.com, €14 adults, €10 children

Top 5 Viaggi runs river tours up and down the Arno that provide an original perspective on Pisa. A boat leaves every Thursday at 6:30pm from Lungarno Mediceo street, next to the Arno River. Excursions last one hour and operate April 1-October 31. The boat heads upstream, and after a few minutes buildings are replaced by farmland and the Pisan Mountains in the distance. A minimum of 10 passengers is required, and boats hold up to 60.

BEACHES
To get to the beaches below, take the 10-20 bus from Pisa Sesta Porta or

Porta a Mare near the train station and get off in Marina, or further down the coast for the Via Litoranea beaches.

Marina di Pisa

Marina di Pisa is an elegant seaside resort just 12 kilometers (7.5mi) west of Pisa. The beach near town consists of small white rocks rather than sand, which explains why it's not very crowded in August. The advantage of this beach is that it's closer, free, and less crowded than establishments that charge an entry fee or a lounge-chair fee.

Via Litoranea Beaches

In summer, locals flock to the establishments along Via Litoranea, just south of town, where they can lie on sand. Lounge chairs and umbrellas are available to rent, and many clubs have their own restaurant. The water is crystalline wherever you go, and there are gelateria and bars along the street facing the sea.

Accommodations

Eco Pisa Tower

Via Piave 10, tel. 388/861-4442, www.ecopisatower.com, €65-90

It's hard to get any closer to the Leaning Tower than Eco Pisa Tower. Just stick your head out the window of this little guesthouse north of Piazza dei Miracoli and there it is. As the name suggests, the owners are big on sustainability and slow tourism. Rooms are bright Ikea-style affairs in a two-story 1930s building with hardwood floors, a kitchen that's open to guests, and a pleasant garden where turtles roam.

Hotel Galileo

Via Santa Maria 12, tel. 050/40621, www.hotelgalileo.pisa.it, €70-80

Hotel Galileo may be the best one-star hotel in Pisa. The seven doubles and two suites are clean and comfortable, and the hotel is just a five-minute walk down the street to the historic center. Rooms facing the back courtyard are slightly quieter than those in the front, and the price is unbeatable. Breakfast is not included, but there are plenty of bars and cafés in the area.

Royal Victoria

Via Lungarno Pacinotti 12, tel. 05/094-0111, www.royalvictoria.it, €90-120 s/d

The Royal Victoria is a well-worn hotel that has seen better days but whose old-world charm outweighs any inconveniences. Its large rooms overlooking the Arno are breezy and bright, with antique furnishings and few concessions to the 21st century. Foreign and Italian guests gather in the second floor breakfast room, where an Italian-style buffet is served. The small roof terrace is a pleasant place to linger. Charles Dickens, John Ruskin, Alexandre Dumas, and Luigi Pirandello all slept here, and little has changed since they did.

Rinascimento

Piazza Donato Giovan Battista 13, tel. 339/173-9373, www.rinascimentopisa. it, €110-150

Rinascimento is a cozy B&B in the heart of Pisa. There are four spacious rooms with private baths, wood ceilings, terracotta floors, and elegant furnishings. Each is equipped with air-conditioning, a mini bar, and Wi-Fi. A

sweet and savory buffet breakfast is served in a bright communal room, and the proactive staff members go out of their way to satisfy the needs of guests.

Information and Services

Tourist Office

Piazza Duomo 7, tel. 050/550-100,
www.turismo.pisa.it, daily 9:30am-5:30pm

The main tourist office is located opposite the Duomo. You can rent a video guide (€5), augmented reality glasses (€8), and bicycles (€3 per hour/€15 day). The staff also organizes weekend walking tours of the Piazza dei Miracoli (1.5 hours/€16) and historic center (2 hours/€21) in Italian

and English that depart at 11:15am from outside the office. The tourist office does not sell tickets to the Leaning Tower, Baptistery, or Camposanto.

Farmacia Guglielmino

Corso Italia 168, tel. 050/24345, Mon.-Fri.
9am-8pm and Sat. 9am-1pm

There are three pharmacies along Corso Italia, including this one at the beginning of the avenue.

Getting There

TRAIN

The fastest and most convenient way of getting to Pisa from Florence is by train (www.trenitalia.com). There are multiple departures every hour from Santa Maria Novella station to Pisa Centrale 4:30am-12:30am. The journey takes around an hour and costs €8.60. The station is just south of the historic center and within walking distance of all monuments.

BUS

Flixbus (www.flixbus.it) runs three direct morning departures from Florence that cost €12 and take 90 minutes. Buses terminate in the Parcheggio Pietrasantina parking lot northwest of town, 10 minutes by foot from the Piazza dei Miracoli.

CAR

Driving from Florence to Pisa is easy. The SGC Firenze-Pisa freeway, also indicated as the FI-PI-LI (Firenze, Pisa, Livorno) highway connects the two cities. It's an 85-kilometer (53mi) drive that lasts about 80 minutes. There are several parking lots near the Leaning Tower, and the smaller one on Via Vecchia di Barbaricina has an attendant. Parking is €1.50 per hour, or you can hunt for a free space (white line) on the outskirts of the historic center.

BICYCLE

If you've got the legs and the motivation, Smile and Ride (www. smileandride.com) can arrange a bike pickup in Florence. Although it is possible to make it to Pisa in a single day, you're better off breaking it up into a two-day cycling adventure.

GETTING AROUND

Pisa is an easy town to navigate on foot or by bicycle. Buses are useful for reaching the San Rossore Park and the seaside. Tickets (www.pisa.cttnord.it, €1.50) are valid for 70 minutes and can be purchased at the train station, most newsstands, or directly on board (€2.50). About half of the city's 18 lines depart from outside the train station. Taxis are also waiting at the rank out front and can be ordered anytime from Radio Taxi Pisa (www.cotapi.it, tel. 050/541-600).

Ciclopi (www.ciclopi.eu) is Pisa's bike-sharing program, with 14 stations around the city. Users can register online or at the tourist office for a single-day (€6) or weeklong (€12) pass. Once registered, bikes are free the first half hour and €0.90 the second.

SAN GIMIGNANO

San Gimignano is a medieval oasis nestled between olive groves and vineyards that produce the town's trademark Vernaccia wine. It's one of those hill towns that looks stunning both from up close and afar and is as impressive today as it was 800 years ago. The pedestrian streets inside the compact historic center have a long history of welcoming pilgrims, and the town grew rich thanks to its location on the Via Francigena pilgrim route, which stretches from northern France all the way to Rome. Commercial and religious prosperity allowed families to build

HIGHLIGHTS

✪ **DUOMO:** Nearly every square inch of the Duomo is covered in dazzling frescoes designed to make a lasting impression on the medieval pilgrims who passed through town (page 188).

✪ **PALAZZO COMUNALE AND TORRE GROSSA:** One of San Gimignano's historic towers, Torre Grossa is tall and tough to climb, but the view is well worth the effort (page 189).

✪ **PALAGETTO:** San Gimignano is famous for Vernaccia grapes, and this winery, a 10-minute walk south of town, is a great place to taste this refreshing wine (page 191).

ever-higher tower houses that punctuated the town's skyline and remain a distinguishing feature of San Gimignano. There were once scores of these prestigious stone skyscrapers, and competition to build the tallest was fierce. Pilgrims also attracted artists from Florence and Siena who decorated the town's churches and *palazzi* (palaces) with vivid frescoes whose colors haven't faded.

A town this unique attracts a crowd, and San Gimignano's main street and central squares are teeming with visitors throughout the summer. Fortunately there are plenty of quiet side streets, a pleasant shaded path around the town's outer walls, and the beautiful Italian countryside waiting to be explored.

PLANNING YOUR TIME

Getting to San Gimignano from Florence requires a train/bus combination or car. Public transportation takes a couple of hours. Although the town is small, it's worth spending a full day or night during the summer, when concerts are regularly staged. The town can be combined with a trip to Siena.

Depending on what sights you plan to see, you may want to pick up the San Gimignano Pass (€13) at the tourist office. It allows entry to the civic museums and Duomo.

ORIENTATION

San Gimignano lies on a hill and is nearly entirely off-limits to cars. Once you pass through Porta San Giovanni into town, you'll feel immersed in the Middle Ages. The Via San Giovanni main street is an old pilgrim route and still the busiest road in town. It leads to Piazza della Cisterna and Piazza del Duomo, around which all the major monuments are located. A handful of small and medium-sized wineries are located just outside of town in every direction.

Itinerary Idea

San Gimignano is worthy of a full day. If you have a second day in town, rent a Vespa from Bruno Bellini or prepare a picnic and go for a hike on the southern branch of the Via Francigena pilgrim road. In either case you'll be gone most of the day, passing through postcard-perfect Tuscan countryside.

ESSENTIAL SAN GIMIGNANO

1 Get an overview of the town's history as you explore the interior of a tower house at **Casa Campatelli.**

2 Continue to Piazza della Cisterna and enjoy homemade gelato from **Gelateria Dondoli** on the steps of the ancient well in this vibrant square.

3 Pick up a San Gimignano Card at the tourist office and enter the **Duomo** opposite to examine entire walls of detailed frescoes warning sinners of their fate.

4 Climb up **Torre Grossa** next door and visit the grand reception rooms on the first floor of Palazzo Comunale (the building that holds the tower). These historic rooms hosted Dante and other dignitaries.

5 Grab a quick bite of local cheese and cold cuts served on wooden cutting boards at **Da Mariani,** and take the owner's suggestion regarding wine.

6 Walk up to the **Rocca di Montestaffoli** fortress on the western edge of town for a panoramic view, and stroll along the scenic path that follows the city walls.

7 Reserve an original *aperitivo* at the **Palagetto** winery south of town, and sample the local wine, Vernaccia, along with freshly pressed oil and cured ham.

8 Arrive early at **La Vecchia Mura** to get a table on the terrace overlooking the Val d'Esla valley and end the day with a saffron-infused dish.

San Gimignano

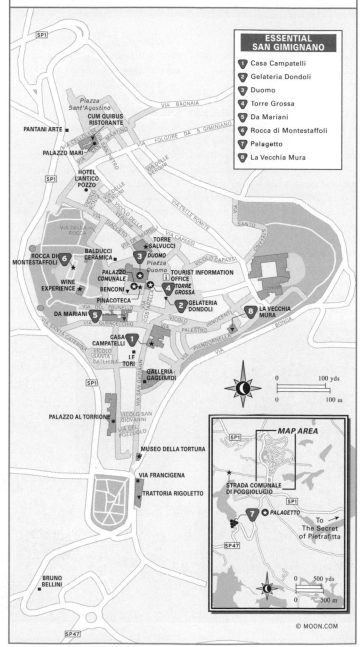

ESSENTIAL SAN GIMIGNANO

1 Casa Campatelli
2 Gelateria Dondoli
3 Duomo
4 Torre Grossa
5 Da Mariani
6 Rocca di Montestaffoli
7 Palagetto
8 La Vecchia Mura

SP1

Piazza Sant'Agostino

CUM QUIBUS RISTORANTE

PANTANI ARTE

VIA BAGNAIA

VIA FOLGORE DA S. GIMINIANO

PALAZZO MARI

VIA CELLOLESE

VIA S. MARTINO

VIA S. PIETRO

HOTEL L'ANTICO POZZO

SP1

VIA DELLE VERGINI

VICOLO FONTI

VIA DELLE VERGINI

VICOLO DELLA VERGINE

VIA DELLE ROMITE

VIA SANTO

VIA DELLA ROCCA

VIA DIACCETO

VIA DE' MARSILI

VIA CAPASSI

TORRE SALVUCCI

BALDUCCI CERAMICA

ROCCA DI MONTESTAFFOLI

6

DUOMO Piazza Duomo

3

VICOLO CAPASSI

WINE EXPERIENCE

PALAZZO COMUNALE

BENCONI

TOURIST INFORMATION OFFICE

TORRE GROSSA

4

VIA SANTO

VIA S. SILVANO

PINACOTECA

GELATERIA DONDOLI

2

8 LA VECCHIA MURA

DA MARIANI

5

VIA DEL PRUNELLO

VIA QUERCECCHIO

VIA COSTARELLA

VICOLO PALESTRO

VIA PIANDORNELLA

VIA INNOCENTI

VIA BONDA

VIA SANTA CATERINA

CASA CAMPATELLI

1

I.F. TORI

VICOLO SANTA CATERINA

VIA PIANDORNELLA

GALLERIA GAGLIARDI

SP1

VIA SAN GIOVANNI

VICOLO SAN GIOVANNI

PALAZZO AL TORRIONE

VIA DEL POZZUOLO

MUSEO DELLA TORTURA

VIA FRANCIGENA

TRATTORIA RIGOLETTO

0   100 yds
0   100 m

BRUNO BELLINI

SP47

MAP AREA

SP1

STRADA COMUNALE DI POGGIOLUGIO

SP1

7 PALAGETTO

To The Secret of Pietrafitta

SP47

0   500 yds
0   500 m

© MOON.COM

187

Sights

CASA CAMPATELLI

Via S. Giovanni 15, tel. 05/7794-1419, www. fondoambiente.it, Apr.-Oct. Thurs.-Tues. 10am-7pm, Nov.-Mar. Thurs.-Tues. 10:30am-5:30pm, €7

Casa Campatelli is one of the last remaining tower houses in San Gimignano and an excellent place to start a visit of town. The same family inhabited the 12th-century home for two centuries and donated it to the Italian Cultural Association (FAI) on the condition it be opened to the public. Visits start with an enlightening 30-minute video that puts the region into geographical, economic, and political perspective. Although the 28-meter (92ft) tower attached to the home cannot be climbed, you can have a look up the empty shaft and explore the other rooms decorated in 19th- and 20th-century furnishings that show how the Campatelli family lived and look as though they never left.

✪ DUOMO

Piazza Duomo 10, tel. 05/7728-6300, www.duomosangimignano.it, Apr.-Oct. Mon.-Fri. 10am-7:30pm, Sat. 10am-5:30pm, Sun. 12:30pm-7:30pm, Nov.-Mar. Mon.-Sat. 10am-5pm and Sun. 12:30pm-5pm, €4, audio guide free

Pilgrims needed a place to pray in San Gimignano, and the Duomo became a regular stop once it was consecrated in 1148. The plain exterior belies a more interesting interior, with a three-nave design and wall-to-wall frescoes illustrating the Old and New Testaments. The most powerful images are of the

Piazza Duomo

Last Judgment and the walls depicting Paradise and Hell. It's very clear which is which, as the latter shows Satan devouring sinners. The **Santa Fini chapel,** along the right nave, contains a cycle of Renaissance frescoes by Domenico Ghirlandaio illustrating the death of Saint Fina, the town's patron saint. The free audio guide is essential for deciphering the magnificent artwork inside.

Duomo

✪ PALAZZO COMUNALE AND TORRE GROSSA

Piazza Duomo 2, tel. 05/7728-6300, daily 10am-7:30pm, €9

Palazzo Comunale was the center of local government in the 13th century and the site of the town's tallest tower, Torre Grossa, which literally means big tower. No building was permitted by medieval law to be higher. It's a steep 54-meter (177ft) climb with a few places to rest along the way and a final ladder up to a small outdoor terrace with a bird's-eye view of all the towers in town and the Val d'Elsa valley. Only 10-12 people are allowed up at a time. A video explains the tower's importance in multiple languages.

On the first floor of Palazzo Comunale, you can visit the Sala del Consiglio communal hall, decorated with frescoes of jousting knights and hunting scenes. A small Pinacoteca art gallery on the upper floors is filled with 12th-14th-century paintings by Florentine and Sienese artists. The small inner courtyard below is lined with the coats of arms of the town's most illustrious families.

In summer, lines for this sight occasionally form but rarely exceed a 15-minute wait. The Rocca is a good alternative since it's free and provides a decent view.

TORRE SALVUCCI

Piazza delle Erbe 12, tel. 320/156-3234, www. torresalvucci.it, €5

Of the 70 towers that once made up San Gimignano's skyline, 14 are still standing, and of those only 2 have access to a roof. Like most of the towers in town, Torre Salvucci is privately owned and isn't always open to the general public. (Call the owners or tourist office to confirm.) When it is open, the 10-story climb up this 50-meter tower provides an idea of what everyday life is like inside a tower, as each floor is dedicated to a specific activity, such as cooking or sleeping. The view at the top is nearly as good as the one from Torre Grossa, and with the benefit of some chairs and an open terrace.

ROCCA DI MONTESTAFFOLI

Via della Rocca, 24/7, free

When the Florentines captured San Gimignano in 1353, they built Rocca di Montestaffoli to make sure they didn't lose hold of this strategic location. The pentagon-shaped fortress housed troops who kept an eye on what was happening inside and outside of town. The walls are still in good shape, and one tower is still accessible.

the towers of San Gimignano

It's a good, free alternative to Torre Grossa and provides a 360-degree view that's best at sunset.

SAN GIMIGNANO WINE EXPERIENCE

tel. 05/7794-1267, www. sangimignanomuseovernaccia.com, daily 11:30am-7:30pm, museum free

Near the entrance to the Rocca di Montestaffoli is this experiential museum operated by the association of local wine growers. Learn about the history of the local wine, Vernaccio, through interactive exhibits that include virtual reality, videos, and holograms. Afterward there's plenty of wine to taste by the glass (€4-7), or you can join a guided mini-master or master tasting (15-60 minutes, €15-30). Tastings must be reserved in advance.

MUSEO DELLA TORTURA

Via San Giovanni 125, tel. 05/7794-0526, Mon.-Fri. 10am-6pm and Sat.-Sun. 10am-7pm, €10

Torture was common in the Middle Ages and anyone accused of a crime was guilty until proven innocent. Many methods were devised for making people talk, and you can see some of the most gruesome at the Museo della Tortura. The three floors display tools used during the inquisition and witchcraft trials, such as the "chair of truth," which was covered in nails and could make prisoners confess just about anything. The ticket also includes entry to the adjacent **Museo della Pena di Morte** (death penalty museum), which has a small collection of modern killing devices that includes an electric chair. There are also branches of this museum in Siena, Volterra, Lucca, and Montepulciano.

Wine Tasting

San Gimignano is surrounded by vineyards, and finding a winery is easy. Pick up a winery map at the tourist office, or just follow the road signs pointing the way to dozens of wineries around town. Most offer guided tastings and tours by enthusiastic multilingual staff that can range from a free glass to a light lunch accompanied by a variety of wines. It's best to reserve in advance as many wineries are small and don't have staff dedicated solely to showing visitors around.

Vernaccia is what's most commonly poured in San Gimignano. This crisp, slightly citrusy white wine was the first to receive a Protected Designation of Origin, or DOP, status and is as important to the local economy as tourism. It has a low alcohol content that makes it a happy hour favorite. The **Association of Vernaccia Producers** (www.vernaccia.it) provides a comprehensive list of all the growers in the area and information for visiting them.

WINERIES
✪ PALAGETTO
Via di Racciano 10, tel. 05/7794-3090, www.palagetto.it

Palagetto is a 10-minute walk south of town on the SP47 provincial road. The family-owned property covering several beautiful acres of hillside grows many types of grapes and is a good place to discover the different stages of wine production. One-hour tours in English start at 4pm and provide a variety of tasting options ranging

vineyards and olive groves below San Gimignano

€10-16. The owners also organize light midday lunches (€27) consisting of four glasses of wine, a platter of Tuscan cold cuts, and a pasta dish. The most interesting months to visit Palagetto are September and October, during the annual grape harvest—it's even possible to participate in the *vendange* (grape harvest) if you fancy getting down and dirty among the vines. Tastings and lunches should be reserved a day or two in advance with Linda.

Panizzi

Loc. Santa Margherita 34, tel. 05/7794-1576, www.panizzi.it

This small cellar produces three Vernaccia, three reds, and a rosé. You can stop by on weekdays and taste four wines of your choosing for €10. Reservations are required and accommodations are available in the vineyard, which is located a five-minute drive west of San Gimignano.

Falchini

Località Casale 40, tel. 05/7794-1305, www.casale-falchini.it

The Falchini family have been in the wine business since the 17th century and once served the Medici in Florence. Their historic estate one kilometer (0.62mi) north of town produces Vernaccia along with Merlot, Cabernet, and Sangiovese. The cellar contains hundreds of oak barrels and even more unlabeled bottles full of aging wine, as well as a tasting room. Reservations required.

Food

San Gimignano has a handful of great trattoria, a Michelin-starred restaurant, and some surprisingly modern variations on local Tuscan culinary traditions that leave a lasting gastronomic impression. Saffron is the star ingredient and its trade was instrumental in the town's medieval prosperity. It's still used in many dishes along with olive oil and the Vernaccia wine that can be found on every menu.

TUSCAN AND ITALIAN

Da Mariani

Via di Quercecchio 19, tel. 338/233-4399, daily 11am-9pm, €6-10

It's all about quality at this little eatery run by a friendly foodie where you can get a delicious plate of mixed cured meats and cheeses with a glass of white wine. Watching Gianfranco prepare *taglieri* platters and panini is half the fun, and you're better off dispensing with the menu and relying on his recommendations. The restaurant is small, with seating for less than a dozen, but the quality is exceptional and worth any wait. Fortunately, it's off the main street and reservations are possible.

Trattoria Rigoletto

Viale Roma 23, tel. 05/7794-0159, Mon.-Sat. 11:45am-2:45pm and 6:45pm-10:15pm, €8-10

There's a chance you'll be the only foreigner at Trattoria Rigoletto, located off the beaten path outside the town walls. This informal restaurant just south of Porta San Giovanni provides a friendly introduction to local pasta dishes like *tagliatelle al tartufo* (pasta with black truffle) and *pici cacio pepe*. You won't get pampered or blown away by the decor, but you will be immersed in authentic Italian atmosphere.

✪ La Vecchia Mura
Via Piandornella 15, tel. 05/7794-0270, Wed.-Mon. 6pm-10pm, €8-11

The food is good at La Vecchia Mura, but the view from the large terrace across the Tuscan countryside is even better. An extensive menu includes dozens of pasta dishes featuring wild boar and truffle and mushroom sauces. Steaks are cooked to medium-rare perfection, and there are plenty of gluten-free options. Unless you plan to come early, make a reservation to ensure a front-row seat to Tuscany.

Cum Quibus Ristorante
Via S. Martino 17, tel. 05/7794-3199, Wed.-Mon. 12:30pm-2:30pm and 7pm-10pm, €25-35

Cum Quibus, San Gimignano's only Michelin-rated restaurant, is elegant without being pretentious, and dishes successfully push culinary boundaries to surprise the palate. Gourmet creativity comes with a price that you probably won't regret paying. Besides an à la carte menu, there are 5- (€85), 7- (€105), and 9-course (€115) tasting menus with flavors and textures that satisfy all the senses. The restaurant has a handful of tables, an intimate hidden terrace, and impeccable service.

GELATO
Gelateria Dondoli
Piazza della Cisterna 4, tel. 05/7794-2244, daily 8am-11:30pm, €3-5

Sergio Dondoli is a master gelato maker. On a good day, he'll prepare 35 original flavors you won't find anywhere else. *Dolceamaro* (sweet and sour) is an award-winner, and Dondoli's version of *cioccolato* (chocolate) remains a well-guarded secret. Flavors vary depending on the season; summer is time for *sorbetto* (sorbet), made with lemons, strawberries, or Sangiovese grapes, which sells out quickly. The steps leading to the old well in the center of the *piazza* is where gelato enthusiasts gather to lick their cones.

Gelateria Dondoli

Festivals

San Gimignano Musica

This classical musical festival (www.
sangimignano.com) runs June-
October. Concerts are staged on
Tuesdays (6:30pm) and Thursdays
(9pm) at five locations around town.
The program, which includes a healthy
dose of Puccini and Verdi operas, is
available from the tourist office in
Piazza del Duomo 1. Tickets cost €12
and concerts last one hour.

Accade'Estate

The Accade'Estate festival is a summer concert series featuring sacred,
Baroque, and orchestral music. It's
held June-October, with weekly concerts performed in Piazza del Duomo
and Rocca di Montestaffoli that usually start at 9pm.

La Ferie delle Messi

La Ferie delle Messi dates from 1258
and is celebrated on the third weekend of June. Groups from all over the
region, as well as the Cavalieri di Santa
Fina association of historic reenactors,
take to the streets in full medieval garb
re-creating life as it once was in San
Gimignano. There is a lively market
in Piazza della Cisterna where craftspeople use ancient skills to turn wood,
stone, and metal into art. Musicians
animate squares, and above town, in
Rocco Montestaffoli, medieval flavors
simmer while a crossbow tournament
takes place. On the second day, participants parade through the streets, and
knights from the town's four *contrade
(neighborhoods)* compete for the *Spada
d'Oro* (golden sword).

Mostra Mercato dello Zafferano di San Gimignano

Saffron is known as yellow gold in
San Gimignano; it helped make the
town wealthy during the Middle Ages
when it was exported to eager clients
in Northern Europe and Asia. It still
holds an important place on people's
plates, and the Mostra Mercato dello
Zafferano di San Gimignano at the
end of October is the chance to learn
more about this versatile spice. There
are tastings, cooking demonstrations,
and a market selling saffron-inspired
products.

Recreation and Activities

WALKING AND HIKING

San Gimignano is surrounded by a medieval ring wall and a foot path that allows visitors to circle the entire town. More strenuous hikes await in every direction and provide wonderful long-distance views of San Gimignano's extraordinary skyline. Guided walks can be arranged through the tourist office and are priced by distance (3km/€15, 6km/€22, and 10km/€25). A minimum of two visitors is required and tours can be arranged whenever you like.

San Gimignano's Ring Walls

Distance: *2km (1.2mi)*
Duration: *30-40 minutes*
Starting Point: *Rocca di Montestaffoli (or any gate in town)*

San Gimignano's second ring walls were built in the 13th century and can be admired close-up along a path that circumnavigates the city. It's a great way to walk off lunch and see the town and the Val d'Esla valley. There's a fortress and a half-dozen historic gates along the way, including Porta delle Fonti, which leads to the medieval well where villagers once washed their clothes. It's a flat, easy walk on paved and wide dirt paths.

Strada Comunale di Poggiolugio

Distance: *3km (1.8mi)*
Duration: *40-50 minutes*
Starting Point: *Piazzale Martiri di Montemaggio*

Strada Comunale di Poggiolugio is a lovely cypress-lined road that begins in Piazzale Martiri di Montemaggio and heads downhill. Grapes grow on both sides and the road winds its way past small farms, forest, and classic Tuscan countryside. It passes the Panizzi winery and ends at Montenidoli winery (tel. 05/7794-1565, www.montenidoli. com), where you can sample homemade olive oil and Vernaccia before heading back.

Via Francigena (Southern Section)

Distance: *6km (4mi)*
Duration: *70-90 minutes*
Starting Point: *Porta San Giovanni or Line 1 City bus to Santa Lucia*

Walking the entire 1,800-kilometer-long (1,100mi) Via Francigena (www. viefrancigene.org) is not an option for most travelers, but you can hike a small section of this ancient pilgrim trail that passes through San Gimignano. It's a challenging route, with significant changes in elevation, that starts out paved and winds its way south towards Monteriggioni past vineyards, olive groves, and sunflower fields. You can turn back when you reach the Vallebuia vineyard 6 kilometers (4mi) outside of town, or keep walking as long as you like. Small red-and-white signs indicate the way,

the walls of San Gimignano

HIKING ITALY'S PILGRIM TRAIL

Christians have been setting off on spiritual journeys since the day after the Last Supper. Their three holiest destinations were and still are Jerusalem, Santiago di Compostela, and Rome. Getting anywhere after the fall of the Roman Empire, however, was tough, and it took centuries for a network of unpaved roads to be reestablished across Europe. Better roads encouraged the faithful from England and France to embark on epic trips that took months—sometimes years—to complete. Over time, a recognized route was created (and documented in the diaries of illustrious pilgrims)

Via Francigena pilgrim route

that stretched from Canterbury, England, through northeastern France, across the Alps and down the western side of the Italian peninsula, ending in Rome. It became known as the **Via Francigena** (www.viefrancigene. org) and was instrumental in the spiritual and commercial growth of many towns through which it passed.

San Gimignano and Siena both benefited from pilgrim traffic and were necessary stops for travelers on their way to or returning from Rome. Both towns grew as pilgrims regularly arrived and merchants thrived by supplying pilgrims with food, lodging, and practical items like shoes and clothing. Local churches also benefited and were expanded and decorated in order to impress passing pilgrims. The Via Francigena became a vital means of communication and cultural unity that helped forge a European identity.

The road never completely vanished. Today, the 1,800 kilometer (1,100 mi) trail is made up of a series of paved and dirt trails that travelers can follow for as long or as little as they like. There are 80 historic rest stops with many offshoots (indicated with brown, yellow, and red markers) that can be walked, cycled, or covered on horseback.

One of the most scenic sections starts a few kilometers south of San Gimignano, and the tourist office in town can supply you with a pilgrim map. There are also dozens of branches and alternative paths that intersect and connect with the Via Francigena, such as **Via Romea del Chianti** (page 236) which links Florence with Siena.

OTHER HIKING TRAILS

There's lots of great hiking in Tuscany outside the famed pilgrim route. Options include:

Taking the backway from Florence to **Basilica San Miniato al Monte** for panoramic views of the city (page 66).

A 60-90-minute trek from Florence to **Fiesole** (page 127). Once you arrive in Fiesole, there are short hikes from Piazza Mino to viewpoints and villas (page 136).

Hiking around **San Gimignano's ring walls** (2km/1.2mi) and down into a valley along cypress-lined roads (page 195).

The **Canali** loop (4.5 km/2.8mi) from Montalcino, which skirts a pine forest and passes several wineries along the way (page 272).

which takes a dramatic right turn just outside of Santa Lucia southeast of San Gimignano. Maps and GPS coordinates are available online.

VESPA
Bruno Bellini
Via Roma 41, tel. 348/412-5488, www.bellinibruno.com, daily 9am-1pm and 3pm-7pm

Riding a scooter in a city is one thing, but driving along the roads leading out of San Gimignano is another. There's far less traffic and much more adventure, with plenty of small villages and endless countryside to explore. Bruno Bellini rents bright-red 125 cc Vespas by the day (€60). He provides maps and helmets, too. A credit card and driver's license are all you need to be on your way. First-time riders should start slowly and practice using the brakes before setting off on a long journey.

TOURS
Stella Soldani
tel. 05/774-3588, www.sienatourguide.it

Stella Soldani is an authorized tour guide for San Gimignano and Siena. Anyone with an abundance of curiosity will appreciate her original itineraries and comprehensive explanations. A three-hour tour is €150 and worth every euro.

Shopping

Via San Giovanni, where pilgrims once shopped, remains one of the busiest streets in San Gimignano. It's lined with souvenir, leather goods, and ceramic stores that do a brisk business and offer mostly locally made products of decent quality.

CERAMICS AND POTTERY
Balducci Ceramica
Piazza delle Erbe 5, tel. 05/7794-3188, daily 10:30am-7pm

Franco Balducci and his wife, Esther, have been making pottery in this shop since 1990. They transform local clay heated to 1,300°C (2,372°F) into decorative and practical pieces. Franco was commissioned to create several sculptures around the city and can usually be found stationed at his pottery wheel, while his wife is happy to answer questions regarding process and technique.

pottery and ceramics shop

Benconi
Piazza Pecori 3, tel. 05/7794-2082,
daily 9:30am-7pm

This little ceramic store just off the main street sells hand-painted plates and mugs. Prices are reasonable: You can pick up a small decorated olive bowl for €16. Many dishes are illustrated with the San Gimignano skyline and make nice souvenirs, which the owners carefully pack in bubble wrap.

SOUVENIRS
Pantani Arte
Via San Matteo, 74, tel. 05/7794-0741,
daily 10:30am-7pm

Forget fridge magnets and head to Pantani Arte for a souvenir that can last a lifetime. The family business has been around for 80 years, and the colorful paintings and wooden sculptures depicting San Gimignano's famous skyline are all handmade in a studio workshop around the corner. Oil, watercolor, and prints come in all sizes and are inspired by local landscapes.

Galleria Gagliardi
Via San Giovanni 57, tel. 05/7794-2196,
www.galleriagagliardi.com, daily
10:30am-7:30am

There must be artists busy at work in the hills around San Gimignano, because Galleria Gagliardi has no shortage of ceramics, paintings, and sculptures. It's an impressive collection that gets creative juices flowing and proves modern art can thrive in a medieval town.

LEATHER
Le Torri
Via San Giovanni 22, tel. 05/7794-3119,
daily 9am-6:30pm

You can smell the quality the moment you walk into Le Torri, where shoes, bags, wallets, belts, and other accessories line the walls of the store's two rooms. Alberto and Roberto can help find whatever you're after and explain how each of their products is made.

Accommodations

HOTELS
Palazzo Mari
Via San Pietro, tel. 340/221-7900,
www.palazzomari.it, €70-85

Palazzo Mari is a small guesthouse on the upper floors of a historic building in the quiet northern part of town. Rooms are distinguished by color (blue, yellow, green, and pink) and nicely decorated by an owner who enjoys interacting with her guests. There's a kitchen, and a comfortable communal area where visitors gather. Wi-Fi and air-conditioning are in good working order, and although breakfast is not included, there are plenty of bars nearby and a coffee machine is available for use.

Palazzo al Torrione
Via Berignano 76, tel. 05/7794-0480,
www.palazzoaltorrione.com, €90-130

If a steep set of stairs doesn't put you off, then Palazzo al Torrione offers stunning views of San Gimignano in each of its rustic antique-furnished rooms. There is a strong sense of cozy, and the woman who manages the B&B is a gracious host. Parking is available nearby, and breakfast features homemade cakes and pastries. If the hotel is full, try Al Torrione II next door.

Hotel l'Antico Pozzo

Via San Matteo 87, tel. 05/7794-2014, www.anticopozzo.com, €120-150

Hotel l'Antico Pozzo is a bright, airy hotel in a charming 17th-century convent overlooking a lively street. Service is the main attraction, along with meticulously refined rooms, many of which have lovely views, four-poster beds, wood-beamed ceilings, and frescoes. There's Wi-Fi, satellite TV, and well-stocked minibars. Bathrooms are large, with powerful showers, and communal areas include a bar and courtyard terrace.

AGRITURISMO

✪ The Secret of Pietrafitta

Località Cortenanno 56/57, tel. 05/7794-0016, www.ilsegretodipietrafitta.com, €110-150

There are dozens of wonderful *agriturismo* (farmhouse) residences outside of San Gimignano, and the sign at The Secret of Pietrafitta welcoming guests to paradise is no exaggeration. It's a great introduction to dolce vita Tuscan style and a difficult place to leave. The renovated farmhouse is a 25-minute walk from Piazza della Cisterna and a convenient option for anyone driving to town. Staff is exceptionally helpful, breakfast is spectacular, and both the pool and restaurant offer stunning panoramic views.

Information and Services

Tourist Information Office

Piazza del Duomo 1, tel. 05/7794-0008, www.sangimignano.com, Mar.-Oct. daily 10am-1pm and 3pm-7pm, Nov.-Feb. daily 10am-1pm and 2pm-6pm

The tourist information office can help book accommodations, restaurants, and bus tickets, and can decipher train schedules. There's an updated list of events, Internet access, and a public payphone. The audio guide (€5) takes visitors on three itineraries of churches, squares, and towers. There's no time limit on the audio guide, though the bureau prefers to have it back at the end of the day so others can use it. This is also the place to pick up the San Gimignano Pass (€13) that allows entry to the civic museums and Duomo. Maps and a guide of the Via Francigena (€8) are also available.

Transportation

GETTING THERE

CAR

From Florence, take the Raccordo Autostradale Firenze-Siena *highway south* to the Poggibonsi Nord exit. Follow Strada Regionale west to the SP1 provincial road that leads to San Gimignano. It's a 62km (38mi) journey from Florence that takes a little over an hour to drive. There are speed cameras along the way, so stick to the 90 kilometers per hour (55mph) speed limit. Once you reach town, there are four large parking lots south, west, and north of the historic center. Parking is €2 per hour or €20 per day.

TRAIN

Trains from Florence to Poggibonsi/San Gimignano run hourly between 5:35am and 12:28am. The journey is a little over an hour, and tickets cost €7.80 each way. Trains from Siena run on the same line and arrive in under 30 minutes (€3.80). The station, however, is a bit of a misnomer and passengers must complete the voyage by bus or taxi. The 130 bus stops every hour between 6:45am to 9:10pm in Piazza Mazzini outside the station and reaches San Gimignano in 25 minutes. Taxis (tel. 05/779-3889) are stationed outside and a lift to San Gimignano requires 15 minutes and €20.

Bus

Sitabus (www.sitabus.com) operates regular service from Florence (bus 131, €8) and Siena (bus 130A, €5) to Poggibonsi, but from there you'll still have to transfer to the 130 to San Gimignano. It's the slowest option, taking several hours to complete.

GETTING AROUND

Most of San Gimignano is pedestrian only, and cars or buses wouldn't be useful even if they were allowed. The town can be easily navigated on foot, but if you need a taxi or want to rent a car or scooter to get back to Poggibonsi or explore the area, call Bruno Bellini (Via Rome 1, tel. 05/7794-0201, www.bellinibruno.com).

VOLTERRA

Volterra isn't an average hill town.

In fact, it's unlike any town in Tuscany, with its own distinct flavors, traditions, and history that dates back thousands of years. There's an extraordinary collection of Etruscan artifacts, a Roman theater, dozens of busy workshops and gorgeous countryside that can be explored on foot, bicycle, scooter, or horseback. The medieval core of the city has remained intact, with towers to climb, palaces to explore, walls to stroll along, and plenty of wine to savor. Discovering it all over a day or two is one of the great pleasures in life.

HIGHLIGHTS

✪ **MUSEO ETRUSCO:** This museum preserves the mysterious remains of the Etruscan civilization that once thrived in Volterra (page 206).

✪ **PALAZZO VITI:** Peek inside a 19th-century home to view a collection of rare objects from across the globe (page 207).

✪ **HORSEBACK RIDING:** Trot up hillsides, through forests, and across ravines as you explore the Tuscan countryside (page 210).

PLANNING YOUR TIME

Volterra is remote and difficult to reach from Florence. It can take 2-5 hours to arrive by bus or train with transfers and is best combined with a visit to nearby San Gimignano, 30 kilometers (18mi) away.

There are a couple of options for sightseeing passes. The Volterra Card, available from participating museums, is good for 72 hours and allows entry to Palazzo dei Priori, Museo Etrusco, Acropolis, Roman Theater, and other sights. It's €16 for one card or €24 for a family (two adults and two children under age 16). There's also an Archeological Card (€5, 24 hours) for Museo Etrusco, the Acropolis, and the Roman Theater that can be picked up on-site.

The Acropolis and Roman Theater close in the event of rain. Museums are free for children under six.

ORIENTATION

Volterra was built around a hill, and roads don't run very straight for long.

Still, it's impossible to get lost here. There are clear signs at nearly every intersection pointing the way to monuments and services. The higher one climbs, the better the view, and the Acropolis overlooks the town's terra-cotta rooftops. It's part of the Archeological Park, on the grassy summit of Volterra, where the town was founded.

a backstreet in Volterra

Itinerary Ideas

You can visit Volterra in less than a day, but you'd be doing yourself a disservice, as the town is best absorbed slowly. More than one day will give you a chance to see some of the countryside outside of town.

DAY 1

Grab the Volterra Card, a map, and the audio guide from the tourist office if you want the lowdown on all the sights.

1 Start in the medieval heart of town, where **Palazzo dei Priori** proudly rises above an imposing square. Step inside the medieval town hall and climb up the tower for a panoramic view.

2 Order a pork or vegetarian *panini* to go from **Al Vicolino.**

3 Enjoy your *panini* at the **Etruscan Acropolis** overlooking town. Imagine how a Bronze Age village might have looked and read the panels describing the ancient temples that once stood on the sight.

4 Walk south through the Archeological Park to **Museo Etrusco.** Pick up the audio guide at the front desk and get a good overview of what Volterra's ancient inhabitants left behind.

5 Head up Via Minzoni and take a right on Via Sotto to see what Silvia is creating out of alabaster inside the **Alabaster Art Studio.**

6 Keep going straight to **Palazzo Viti** and discover the palatial home of a wealthy 19th-century alabaster merchant with an unrivaled collection of artwork and oddities.

7 Follow the walls to the western side of town and sample the nouveau Tuscan menu at **Osteria Fornelli.** Try to score a table on the outdoor terrace and coincide dinner with a spectacular sunset.

DAY 2

1 Mornings are an excellent time to explore and watch Volterra slowly wake. Take a walk along the ancient walls and enter town through the imposing Etruscan-era **Porta all'Arco.**

2 Have an espresso and pastry at **L'Incontro** along Via Matteotti.

3 Climb the **Casa Torre Toscana** house tower to get a different perspective on the town.

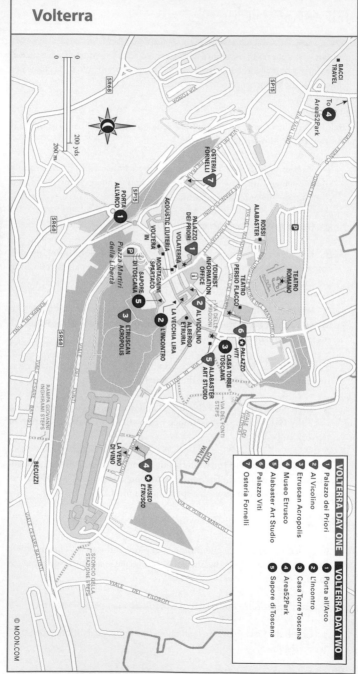

Volterra

BACCI TRAVEL

To Area52Park

SR68

SP15

0

200 yds

0

200 m

OSTERIA FORNELLI 7

PORTA ALL'ARCO 1

SP15

SR68

ACOUSTIC LIUTERIA VOLTERA IN

PALAZZO DEI PRIORI 1

MONTAGNANI SPARTACO

SAPORE DITOSCANA 5

Piazza Martiri della Libertà

ETRUSCAN ACROPOLIS 3

LA VECCHIA LIRA

L'INCONTRO 2

ALBERGO ETRURIA

AL VICOLINO 2

TOURIST INFORMATION OFFICE

ROSSI ALABASTER

TEATRO PERSIO FLACCO

PALAZZO VITI 6

CASA TORRE TOSCANA 3

ALABASTER ART STUDIO 5

TEATRO ROMANO

P

LA VENO DI VINO 4

MUSEO ETRUSCO

RAMPA GIOVANNI INGHIRAMI STEPS

BECUZZI

VIALE DEI FILOSOFI

SCORCIO DELLA STAZIONE STEPS

VIA DEI FONTI

CITY WALLS

VIA DELLE PRIGIONI

DITTA IN VIA

© MOON.COM

4 Take a taxi to the Area52Park stables and head out on one of its equestrian adventures of the Val di Cecina valley.

5 Sapore di Toscana will be open whatever time you get back and can satisfy even the biggest appetites with delicious local ingredients.

Sights

PALAZZO DEI PRIORI
Piazza dei Priori 1, tel. 05/888-6050, daily 9am-7pm, €5 or Volterra Card

This palace has been the seat of local government since 1208 and is where the current mayor and town counselors regularly meet. It's the oldest town hall in Tuscany and was built to withstand sieges. The windows are small, and there's only one door. Visitors can access several frescoed rooms on the first floor, where medieval assemblies were held, and climb the Torre Campanaria upstairs for a panoramic view of town and country.

Florentines eventually subdued Volterra in 1472 and went about imposing their ideals of architecture. At this point, much of the palace's façade was transformed and Florentine conquerors added the statue of a lion on a column to remind locals they were in charge.

Piazza dei Priori

the Roman Amphitheater

⊙ MUSEO ETRUSCO

Via Don Giovanni Minzoni 15, tel.
05/888-6347, daily Apr.-Oct. 9am-7pm and
Oct.-Mar. 10am-4:30pm, €8, Volterra Card
or Archeological Card

The Etruscans were an ancient people who established a loose federation of towns in central Italy 800-500BC. Little is known about them, and their language remains a mystery. The Museo Etrusco houses one of the largest repositories of Etruscan pottery, jewelry, utensils, and funerary urns in the world, displayed over three packed floors. There are more than 500 urns alone. The museum was inaugurated in 1761 and is the oldest of its kind. The lack of explanatory panels makes the audio guide (€3) essential to understanding what you're seeing and how this long gone civilization operated.

ETRUSCAN ACROPOLIS

Viale Wunsiedel, daily 10:30am-5:30pm, €5,
Volterra Card or Archeological Card

The Etruscan Acropolis, located on a grassy hilltop above town, is part of the Archeological Park. This area was sacred to Etruscans, who built several temples here, the stone foundations of which are still visible. (Traces of early Bronze Age tribes dating back 3,000 years were also found here, but you won't see any of that today.) Information panels help visitors imagine how the small site once appeared.

The ruins can be visited in 10 minutes' time. There's also a Roman-era cistern nearby that provided water to inhabitants and was vital for the town's growth. You can climb down into it to get an idea of Roman engineering prowess and the amount of water that was once stored inside.

The park is ideal for picnics and is a popular weekend retreat with locals who lay out on the big lawn nearby during summer.

TEATRO ROMANO

Piazza Caduti nei Lager Nazisti, tel. 05/888-7257, daily 10:30am-5:30pm, €5, Volterra Card or Archeological Card

Locals didn't know this Roman theater existed until it was accidentally discovered underneath a dump in 1951. The 1st-century theater had a capacity of 3,000 and was built next to a bath and a forum with many columns, which have been restored to their original condition. You can get a good view from the town walls directly above the monument for free, or pay €5 and take a closer look at the ancient seats, stage, and backdrop that have survived for centuries. A few plaques (in Italian and English) help explain the Roman presence in Volterra and the entertainment that was once performed inside the theater.

✪ PALAZZO VITI

Via dei Sarti 41, tel. 05/888-4047, www. palazzoviti.it, Mon.-Sat. 10am-5:30pm, Sun. 10am-1pm and 2:30pm-6:30pm, winter by appointment only, €5

Giuseppe Viti (1816-1860) was born into a family of Volterra alabaster merchants and began traveling from an early age. He spent decades in the United States, South America, and Asia growing the family fortune and amassing a unique collection, which is on display today in his palatial former residence. Palazzo Viti is decorated with furniture, paintings, porcelain, and alabaster spanning the 15th-20th centuries. The collection includes silk Chinese fans in the Salotto del Terrazzo and alabaster mosaic-topped tables in the Salotto del Brachettone. Descendants of Viti still own the home but have opened twelve rooms to the public and preserved the palace just as their illustrious ancestor wanted it.

CASA TORRE TOSCANA

Piazzetta S. Michele 6, daily 11am-7pm, €2

Volterra's skyline isn't as dramatic as San Gimignano's, but there are towers here, too, and this 13th-century dwelling is the oldest. On the way to the top, you'll get a sense of the cramped and claustrophobic conditions medieval merchants endured. The wooden stairs are fairly easy to climb, and you can stay as long as you like on the open terrace, which provides wonderful views of town.

Food

Most of Volterra's restaurants are located along **Via Matteotti** or **Via Gramisci**. Wherever you sit down to eat in town, the portions will be large and the menu will include some variety of thick *pici* pasta, often covered with grated Pecorino (sheep) cheese or wild boar ragù. Soups are also common throughout the year, and beans play an integral part in local diets.

TUSCAN AND ITALIAN
Al Vicolino

Via delle Prigione 2, tel. 05/888-6921, daily 10:30am-10pm, €5-7

Panini are an essential part of Italian street food. You can get one of these mouthwatering sandwiches at Al Vicolino, where delicious combinations of bread, ham, cheese, truffle, pesto, olive paste, and many other

GATES OF VOLTERRA

Like most Tuscan cities, Volterra is surrounded by a thick set of walls. These walls were erected by Etruscans around 500BC, reinforced by ancient Romans, and remodeled by Middle Age masons. They were built from white sandstone, quarried nearby, which was later used to pave many of the streets inside the town. The approximate age of a wall can be estimated by the size of the blocks. The Etruscans used the biggest, while medieval builders worked stone nearly the size of modern bricks. Volterra's walls were originally over 7 kilometers (4.3mi) long, but centuries of wear and a population decline eventually reduced them to the 2.6 kilometers (1.6mi) that are visible today.

Porta all'Arco

The walls were punctuated by nine gates. **Porta all'Arco**, the southeastern entrance to town, is the oldest gate, with three very worn heads that date from the 5th century. **Porta San Francesco**, to the north, is the most formidable, with a well-preserved turret and huge wooden doors that remain open. There are traces of a fresco in the vault, a common feature of many medieval gates that welcomed visitors to town. **Porta San Felice** lies between the two and offers a great view along with a fountain where ancient travelers rehydrated themselves (and modern visitors can too, if they like).

Although the walls do not completely circumnavigate Volterra, they can be walked around in long sections. They are best viewed from outside of town, and streets like Lungomuro dei Pratini and Via S. Lino are good places to take a stroll back in time.

accoutrements are prepared while you wait. It's a local institution where regular customers outnumber first-time visitors. Sandwiches are wrapped for easy transport, so you can enjoy them in the square around the corner or carry them to the Archeological Park.

Sapore di Toscana

Via di Castello 5, daily 10am-8pm, €5-8

Bruschetta is made with just a few ingredients: bread, olive oil, and a topping. What makes it so good are authentic local ingredients like the ones used at Sapore di Toscana. This microscopic eatery on a scenic street leading up to the Archeological Park prepares bruschetta topped with tomato, porcini, Pecorino, and honey.

They also prepare panini, crostini, and focaccia, and serve good wine.

La Vecchia Lira

Via Giacomo Matteotti 19, tel. 05/888-6180, Fri.-Wed. 11am-3pm and 7pm-11pm, €8-11

The exterior of La Vecchia Lira doesn't have a lot going for it, but the kitchen certainly does. They run a cafeteria-style option at lunch that instantly satisfies appetites with enticing vegetable, pasta, truffle, and meat dishes. Just grab a tray and the friendly staff behind the counter will serve you. You pay at the cashier at the end, and you can also order from a list of daily dishes written up on the board. Dinner service is traditional, with a menu that includes *pici al ragù* (thick spaghetti-like pasta with meat sauce), wild boar, and *chianina* (regional cattle) steak.

✪ Osteria Fornelli

Piazzetta dei Fornelli 3, tel. 05/888-8641, daily 12pm-3:30pm and 7pm-10:30pm, €10-14

Osteria Fornelli isn't like any restaurant in town. It's a modern osteria with a contemporary approach to food and fabulous views of the Tuscan countryside. Everything looks as good as it tastes, and there's attention to both decor and the dishes, which reinvent local traditions using seasonal ingredients. They prepare a great *pappa al pomodoro* (tomato

stew) and gnocchi with truffles and roasted pork.

ESPRESSO
L'Incontro

Via Giacomo Matteotti 18, tel. 05/888-0500, Thurs.-Tues. 6am-midnight

Incontro means encounter in Italian and this is where old-timers meet up for coffee and conversation most mornings. There's a great selection of pastries that can be eaten directly at the marble counter with a cappuccino, or at the handful of tables. The atmosphere changes in the afternoon when cocktails and light appetizers are served to a bustling crowd of locals and out-of-towners.

Bars and Nightlife

Nightlife in Volterra consists primarily of strolling the atmospheric streets and looking up at the stars. Still, there are a couple of options if you're looking for a bar or *enoteca (wine shop)*.

WINE BARS
VolaTerrA

Via Giusto Turazza 5, tel. 05/888-8765, Thurs.-Sun. 10am-10pm and Mon.-Wed. 10am-8pm

VolaTerrA is a gourmet deli and wine bar that serves local vintages by the glass and sets up a nice buffet every afternoon. There are stools outside along the pedestrian street and plenty of tempting products inside to bring home as souvenirs.

La Veno di Vino

Via Don Giovanni Minzoni 30, tel. 05/888-1491, Wed.-Mon. 11am-1am

If you're intent on staying up past midnight, head to La Veno di Vino. This jovial bar is not refined, nor does it try to be—the large collection of brassieres hanging from the ceiling sets the tone. Wine starts at €2.50 a glass, but the best options are the wine tasting (3 glasses for €10) and *aperitivo* (one glass and one plate of cheese and salami for €8). There's a guitar for impromptu sing-alongs and a small menu of local dishes. If you like what you're drinking, Acca can arrange for a case or two to be shipped home.

Performing Arts

THEATER
Teatro Persio Flacco
Via dei Sarti 37, tel. 05/888-8204,
www.teatropersioflacco.it, €15-22

You wouldn't expect a town this small to have a grand horseshoe-shaped theater with four tiers, an acoustic vault, and 499 red-velvet seats, but it does. The 19th-century theater regularly stages concerts throughout the year. If your visit coincides with a show, get a seat in one of the boxes overlooking the stage. The box office opens 5pm-7pm on the day before performances and at 5pm until showtime on performance nights.

Recreation and Activities

CYCLING

There are more dirt paths around Volterra than paved roads, and if you don't feel like exploring them on foot, rent a bike. There are also easy routes, such as Palagione-Ulignano, that loop around town.

BIKE RENTALS
Becuzzi
Viale Cesare Battisti 14/16,
tel. 05/888-0588, www.becuzzirent.it,
Mon.-Fri. 9am-1pm and 3pm-7pm, Sat.
9am-1pm, Sun 9:30am-12:30pm

Trekking (€15/day), mountain (€25/day), and e-bikes (€30/day) are available from the guys at Becuzzi, who supply the right frame and tires according to where you're headed and how hard you want to pedal. Rentals include helmets, locks, repair kits, and all the advice you need. **Vespa scooters** (€60/day) are also available.

BIKE ROUTES
Palagione-Ulignano Bike Route
Distance: 40km (25mi)
Duration: 2.5-3 hours
Starting Point: Borgo San Lazzaro (SR68)

Palagione-Ulignano is an easy loop outside of town. Riders cycle past tiny villages and panoramic hilltops that are perfect for picnics. The itinerary starts on Borgo San Lazzaro (SR68) and goes over paved roads and dirt trails with little to no traffic. Maps are available from the tourist office and the Becuzzi rental shop.

○ HORSEBACK RIDING
Area52Park
Via di Porta Diana 22, tel. 05/884-2140,
www.area52park.com, €25-53

Volterra is surrounded by beautiful countryside and one of the best ways

Medici fortress in the Archaeological Park

to see it is on horseback. This stable outside Volterra gives anyone who's never ridden an entirely new perspective on these wonderful animals. Area52Park arranges journeys of an hour or longer across rivers, through forests, up hills, and over ancient Roman roads. There's an itinerary for every level of rider, and some wonderful watering holes along the way.

The stable is 4 kilometers (2.5mi) from Volterra, a short taxi ride or long walk away.

Shopping

Every town in Tuscany has some claim to fame, and in Volterra that something is alabaster. The soft marble-like mineral that was discovered by Etruscans over 2,500 years ago has been sculpted by local craftspeople since then. Today, dozens of artisans grind and polish blocks of alabaster into translucent creations whose sale represents an important part of the local economy. (Look for eggs, key chains, and fridge magnets, which are the cheapest objects and sell for around €2-5.) The historic center is full of alabaster shops (all sell locally made products, though quality varies widely), and browsing is a good way to learn about the different variations of the mineral, which can be veined, spotted, or clouded. If you're really interested in alabaster, head to one of the dusty studio workshops that combine craft with commerce.

Besides those who carve alabaster,

Volterra also has plenty of passionate bookbinders, printers, painters, and jewelry makers. A full list of all the artisans working in Volterra is available from the tourist office and www. arteinbottegavolterra.it.

ALABASTER
Alabaster Art Studio
Via di Sotto 2, tel. 05/888-8452, Mon.-Sat. 9am-1pm and 2pm-6pm, Sun. 2pm-6pm
Silvia, who runs the Alabaster Art Studio workshop located down a quiet side street, is less concerned with catering to tourists and more interested in making original objects, such as candleholders, bowls, and vases. She can usually be found sculpting alabaster into all sorts of intriguing forms.

Rossi Alabaster
Piazzetta della Pescheria, tel. 05/888-6133, daily 10am-6pm
Rossi Alabaster is a large enterprise that's been transforming alabaster into chandeliers, chess sets, and statuettes since 1912. The busy workshop above the Roman Theater is covered in white dust and open for visitors to observe the craftsmen behind their machines. Most of the artisans have been doing the same job for decades and everything produced here is on display at the exhibition space area next door.

Via di Castello in Volterra

GIFT AND DESIGN
Montagnini Spartaco
Via Porta all'Arco 6, tel. 05/888-6184

Local craftsperson Montagnini Spartaco prefers manipulating metal rather than stone. His historic one-room bottega is covered with the tools he uses to pound, hammer, and file bronze into delicate statues reminiscent of those of Alberto Giacometti. Entering this workshop is a delight, and it's difficult to leave empty-handed.

GUITARS
Acoustic Liuteria
Via Porta all'Arco 30/a, tel. 342/551-2329

You probably didn't come to Volterra to buy a guitar, but if you're curious to know how they're made check out the Acoustic Liuteria workshop, where Fulvio Cappelli makes his own guitars by hand. The maestro likes to talk, and if you know the difference between a semi-hollow and a solid body, he'll let you strum his acoustic or semi-acoustic creations.

FARMERS MARKET
The local farmers market is held in the parking lot next to the Roman Theater every Saturday morning (8am-1pm). Vendors sell clothes and household items, along with local produce and street food like *porchetta (pork)* sandwiches. During the winter, the market moves to Piazza dei Priori.

Accommodations

Wherever you stay in Volterra, you won't be far from the sights. Hotels are clustered around the compact center and everything can be reached on foot.

HOTELS
Albergo Etruria
Via Giacomo Matteotti 32, tel. 05/888-7377, www.albergoetruria.it, €75-85

Besides being located on Volterra's most animated street, Albergo Etruria also has comfort and friendliness going for it, with amiable staff and a breakfast buffet that leaves nothing to be desired. All rooms are decorated in their own shabby-chic style, and there's a pleasant garden out back. Cyclists can store bikes safely inside, and scooter rentals (€60 per day) are available from the front desk.

Voltera In
Via Porta all'Arco 41, tel. 05/888-6820, www.hotelvolterrain.it, €80-90

The Voltera In is an elegant three star hotel with a spotless, recently refurbished interior. All rooms have air-conditioning, hardwood floors, and wall-mounted televisions. Bathrooms are spacious, but some of the rooms are on the small side. (For more room, upgrade to a suite.) A bar in the lobby is open from 7am until midnight and staff are able to arrange everything you need in town or out. Parking is available nearby and breakfast is served in the communal area on the ground floor.

Tourist Information

Tourist Information Office
Piazza dei Priori 20, tel. 05/888-7257,
www.volterratur.it, daily 9:30am-1pm and
2pm-6pm
The Tourist Information Office is a good place to start a visit and pick up a free map of town. You can also rent an **audio guide** (€5) that comes with a map and covers 15 sites in detail. The tour takes about two hours to complete. There are only six of these, so if you want one, arrive early. The tourist office also arranges walking tours of town with registered English-speaking guides.

Transportation

GETTING THERE
FROM FLORENCE
Train and Bus
There are several options for getting to Volterra from Florence on public transportation. The easiest is by train from SMN station in Florence to Pontedera. There are frequent departures, and the 45-minute journey costs €7 onboard a regional or fast regional (*regionale veloce*) service. From outside the train station in Pontedera, catch **CTT bus 500** (www.pisa.cttnord. it, €3) to Volterra. That trip takes 75 minutes, and the entire journey can be completed in under three hours.

Bus
It's also possible to get to Volterra by bus alone. Take the **Tiemme 131** (www.tiemmespa.it, €4-6) from Stazione Liepoldo in Florence and transfer in Colle V. Elsa to the **CTT 770** (www.pisa.cttnord.it, €3). Note that there are only two departures per day from Florence (12:41pm and 2:45pm). The first requires a one-hour wait in Colle Val Elsa, which is a pretty little town, while the second has only a 15-minute wait and can get you to Volterra in just over two hours. Buses stop in **Piazza Martiri della Libertà** at the entrance to town.

Car
Driving is the most convenient way of getting to Volterra from Florence, and the 81km can be covered in 1.5 hours. Take the autostrade Firenze-Siena highway to the Colle Val d'Elsa Nord exit and the SR68 from there to Volterra. There's a small toll to pay and slightly slower options along single-lane provincial roads.

FROM SAN GIMIGNANO
Bus
From Bivio Santa Chiara in San Gimignano, board the **Tiemme 130** (€2, 25 minutes) to Poggibonsi and the **131** (€1.50, 15 minutes) to Colle Val Elsa, then transfer to the CTT 770 (€3, 50 minutes). There are only four departures per day (6:06am, 8:51am, 11:46am, and 4:56pm) and journey time typically is 2-3 hours.

Car or Taxi

Volterra is 30 kilometers (18mi) southwest of San Gimignano. The drive takes less than 40 minutes on the SP69 and SR68 roads. A taxi between San Gimignano and Volterra costs €75.

Bicycle

You could always pedal from San Gimignano to Volterra and cover the 24 kilometers (15mi) in a couple of hours. It's an uphill and downhill journey on the SP47 provincial road to San Donato and a shortcut through the Castelvecchio Natural Reserve that connects with the SR68 regional road leading to Volterra. There's little traffic, but no bicycle lanes, and roads are narrow in places.

GETTING AROUND

Walking is the best way of exploring Volterra. The town's too small to have a regular taxi service, but there are several NCC (chauffeured car rental) services, including Bacci Travel (Borgo S. Stefano 141, tel. 05/888-1229, www. baccitravel.com), that can get you wherever you need to go in comfortable sedans and minivans. A ride to the Area52Park stables is €20 and the drive to San Gimignano is €75. Prices are higher than taxis and drivers must be reserved a day or two in advance in summer, when demand is high.

CHIANTI

Imagine Tuscany, and Chianti's vineyards and olive groves are what usually come to mind. This iconic territory between Florence and Siena is synonymous with the region itself. There are no cities, major highways, or museums with long lines here. The main attraction is the verdant landscape, tiny hill towns, and red wine.

It may look peaceful now, but for centuries Chianti was a war zone where medieval Tuscan super powers battled for supremacy. Florence eventually gained supremacy in 1555, and fortifications gave way to farming. Grapes and olives

HIGHLIGHTS

✪ **PASTA AL PESTO:** Learn how to prepare a traditional Tuscan meal with the friendly chef at this one-woman cooking school (page 223).

✪ **FATTORIA CASALOSTE:** Discover how Chianti is made and sample the latest vintages at this charming, independent winery outside of Panzano (page 229).

✪ **ROCCA AND ARCHEOLOGICAL MUSEUM:** Castellina's Archeological Museum located within an imposing fortress brings Chianti's medieval and ancient past to life (page 233).

✪ **CASA CHIANTI CLASSICO:** Get to know (and, of course, sample!) wine at this museum, bar, and bistro rolled into one (page 239).

✪ **SCOOTER RENTAL:** The roads that gently wind their way along Chianti's hillsides are idyllic and even better when explored on two wheels (page 241).

are the major crops, and the Chianti Classico wine-growing region covers over 70,000 hectares.

A visit to Chianti is about tasting authentic flavors in family-run *trattorie* and sampling great wine directly from the source. There are hundreds of wineries, and many of them welcome visitors. The *agriturismo* farm stay movement was born here and there are plenty of rustic and luxurious options for anyone who wants to hunker down and explore narrow hillside roads on foot, bicycle, or Vespa.

PLANNING YOUR TIME

Chianti starts on the southern outskirts of Florence and is best explored by car or scooter, as train and bus service is limited. A day is enough time to visit several towns, wineries, and at least one *trattoria*, but two or three days are even better as the area is ideal for lingering. If you're driving, fill up on gas before starting out as service stations can be hard to find. Distance are short, but locals don't drive very fast. Be sure to check ahead of time if you need to make a reservation at the wineries you want to visit.

Agriturismo (farmstays) are a popular alternative to hotels and provide a unique perspective on rural life. They are secluded and surrounded by working fields where guests can learn how local delicacies are produced and participate in various types of cultivation. There are hundreds of *agriturismi* throughout Chianti, many of which operate vineyards. For a relaxing vacation, book a stay of a few nights and limit your exploration to the surrounding area.

The last Sunday in May is the best time for a wine lover to be in Tuscany: This is **Cantina Aperta** (Open Cantina), when wineries open their doors for sampling the wines on offer. In Panzano, **Il Mercato Aprilante** (first Sun. of each month) showcases the creations of local artisans and the

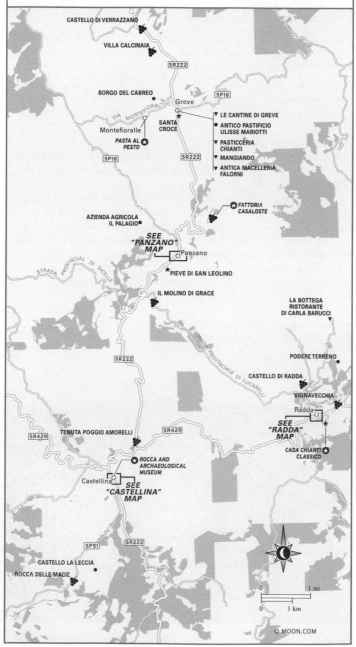

Chianti

CASTELLO DI VERRAZZANO

VILLA CALCINAIA

SR222

BORGO DEL CABREO

Greve

SP16

VIA MONTEFIORALLE

Montefioralle

SANTA CROCE

PASTA AL PESTO

SP18

SR222

▼ LE CANTINE DI GREVE
● ANTICO PASTIFICIO ULISSE MARIOTTI
▼ PASTICCERIA CHIANTI
▼ MANGIANDO
▼ ANTICA MACELLERIA FALORNI

FATTORIA CASALOSTE

AZIENDA AGRICOLA IL PALAGIO

SEE "PANZANO" MAP

Panzano

STRADA PROVINCIALE DI SIECLE

★ PIEVE DI SAN LEOLINO

IL MOLINO DI GRACE

LA BOTTEGA RISTORANTE DI CARLA BARUCCI

STRADA PROVINCIALE DI LUCARELLI

PODERE TERRENO

SR222

CASTELLO DI RADDA

VIGNAVECCHIA

Radda

SEE "RADDA" MAP

TENUTA POGGIO AMORELLI

SR429

SR429

CASA CHIANTI CLASSICO

SR429

ROCCA AND ARCHAEOLOGICAL MUSEUM

Castellina

SEE "CASTELLINA" MAP

SP51

SR222

CASTELLO LA LECCIA

ROCCA DELLE MACIE

0   1 mi
0   1 km

© MOON.COM

WINE TOURS FROM FLORENCE

Heading out on a wine tour with someone who knows the region and has contacts with local wineries saves time and provides a good overview of Chianti. **Chianti Wine Tours** (Via delle Farine 1, tel. 392/633-9101, www.chiantiwinetour.com, €110) offers full-day tours that depart from Florence at 9:30am. The itinerary includes several wineries, lunch, and a visit to San Gimignano. Groups are small and transported by comfortable mini bus. **Grape Tours** (Via dei Renai 19, tel. 333/722-9716, www.tuscan-wine-tours.com) provides group (up to eight participants) and private tours with a range of themes suitable for wine neophytes and experienced palates alike. Passionate and knowledgeable guides are great at explaining the unique history behind each wine. Prices vary according to the wineries visited.

cheese, honey, and oil produced by farmers in the area.

ORIENTATION

The SR222 road that runs south from Florence connects Greve, Panzano, Castellina, and many villages in Chianti. None of these is more than a dozen miles apart, and Radda lies southeast of Panzano on the SP2bis. Towns are small and easily navigated on foot, organized along a single main street leading to a central square, and elevation varies from none to several hundred meters above sea level. Paid parking is located within walking distance outside most towns, and the street parking inside fills up fast in summer. Cyclists are a familiar sight on the SR222, but the shoulder is narrow and riders must be vigilant.

a vineyard in Chianti

Itinerary Ideas

Chianti is the perfect getaway from Florence and a chance to slow down and discover small towns, wineries, and great landscapes. There are museums, old forts, ancient tombs, and many wonderful places to dine. The longer you stay here the better, but you can get a taste of some of the region's best towns on this three-day itinerary.

Be sure to book your tasting tour at **Poggio Amorelli** (recommended here on Day Two) a day or two in advance.

DAY 1

Rent a car in Florence and head out early in the morning towards Chianti. On your first day you'll visit the towns of **Greve** and **Panzano**, where you'll stay for the night.

1 Drive south on the SR222 toward Greve. Stop at **Villa Calcinaia** on the way, and get a taste of Chianti Classico at the source.

2 Explore Greve on foot, and have a coffee and pastry at **Pasticceria Chianti** facing Piazza Giacomo Matteotti.

3 Walk 15 minutes or drive west to the village of Montefioralle, where you can cook a Tuscan lunch with Stefania at **Pasta al Pesto**.

4 Get back on the road, and continue driving to Panzano. Park in the small lot on the hillside and visit **Chiesa di Santa Maria** and the historic center.

5 Have *aperitivo* on the terrace at **Il Vinaio di Panzano,** but resist filling up on appetizers.

6 Walk down Via G. Daverrazzano to **Officina della Bistecca** for Panzano's specialty, *bistecca Panzanese,* and make new friends at the communal table.

7 Enjoy a cocktail or two at **Cocktail Chianti Chiosco** before calling it a night.

DAY 2

Leaving Panzano, you'll visit the towns of **Castellina** and **Radda**, where you'll spend the night.

1 Start the day with a visit of **Pieve di San Leolino,** the hilltop church just south of Panzano. It's a 30-minute walk along the pretty Via San Leolino or a quick drive by car or cab.

Chianti Itineraries

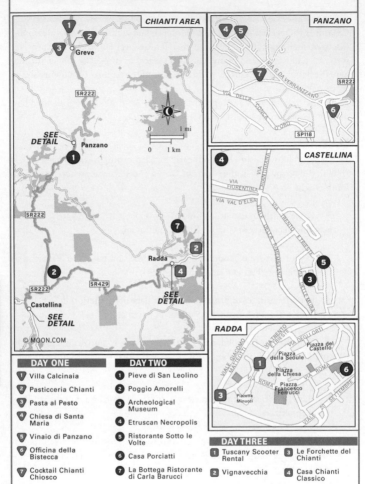

CHIANTI AREA

Greve

SR222

SEE DETAIL
Panzano

SR222

Radda

SR222   SR429

Castellina

SEE DETAIL

SEE DETAIL

0   1 mi
0   1 km

© MOON.COM

PANZANO

VIA G DA VERRAZZANO

SR222

VIA DELLA CONCA D'ORO

SP118

CASTELLINA

VIA FIORENTINA

VIA VAL D'ELSA

VIA CHIANTIGIANA

VIALE DELLE RIMEMBRANZE

VIA TRENTO E TRIESTE

VIA DELLA ROCCA

RADDA

VIA GIACOMO MATTEOTTI

VIA TRENTO E TRIESTE

VIA DEGLI ORTI

Piazza del Castello

Piazza della Seoule

Piazza della Chiesa

VIA ROMA

VIA ROMA

Piazza Francesco Ferrucci

Piazzetta Minucci

VIALE 29 SETTEMBRE

DAY ONE
1. Villa Calcinaia
2. Pasticceria Chianti
3. Pasta al Pesto
4. Chiesa di Santa Maria
5. Vinaio di Panzano
6. Officina della Bistecca
7. Cocktail Chianti Chiosco

DAY TWO
1. Pieve di San Leolino
2. Poggio Amorelli
3. Archeological Museum
4. Etruscan Necropolis
5. Ristorante Sotto le Volte
6. Casa Porciatti
7. La Bottega Ristorante di Carla Barucci

DAY THREE
1. Tuscany Scooter Rental
2. Vignavecchia
3. Le Forchette del Chianti
4. Casa Chianti Classico

2 Drive down the SR222 and stop for a wine tour at the Poggio Amorelli vineyard (reservations required).

3 Continue to Castellina in Chianti, and park in the second lot near the center of town. Explore the Archeological Museum inside the Rocca fortress and climb up the tower for views of the mountains and valleys.

4 Walk uphill to the Etruscan Necropolis, and enter the underground tombs of this ancient civilization.

5 Have lunch at Ristorante Sotto le Volte under the medieval vaulted passageway. Order an espresso, then head east to Radda in Chianti on the SR249.

6 Walk around Radda's old town walls, and order *aperitivo* from Casa Porciatti.

7 Head north on the SP112 to Volpaia and dine on the terrace at La Bottega Ristorante di Carla Barucci.

8 Return to Radda for the night.

DAY 3

Spend your last day in Chianti exploring the area around Radda.

1 Rent a scooter from Tuscany Scooter Rental and drive along the SP72 provincial road.

2 Take a wine and olive oil tour at Vignavecchia on the way back to Radda.

3 Have lunch at Le Forchette del Chianti back in town and ice-cream from Lo Sdrucciolo gelateria next door.

4 Keep exploring southern Chianti and end the afternoon with a visit to the wine museum at Casa Chianti Classico. Stay here for dinner, or return to Radda and dine at your favorite *trattoria*.

Greve in Chianti

Greve, the first historic town on the SR222 road from Florence to Siena, is considered the gateway to Chianti. It's an ancient market town notable for its architecture and gastronomy. The arcades that run along the sides of **Piazza Matteotti** are filled with traditional shops and restaurants. The statue in the middle is Giovanni da Verrazzano, who was born nearby in Castello di Verrazzano and made several journeys to the New World.

There are dozens of wineries outside Greve. Each has its own personality and produces a different variety of Chianti Classico. The first mention of wine growing in the area dates from the 12th century and an export business began soon after. By the 18th century, cultivation was firmly established, and early European visitors were taking note.

Today, vineyard hopping is a popular pastime. Although you can drop in to some unannounced, getting the full tour usually requires reservations, which can be made online or by telephone. A day or two is usually enough warning; however, some wineries get very busy in summer. Most of the larger wineries are used to receiving visitors and staff conduct tours in multiple languages including English.

SIGHTS AND ACTIVITIES
BASILICA DI SANTA CROCE
Piazza Santa Croce, free
This three-nave church lies at the pinnacle of Piazza Matteotti on the site

Greve in Chianti

a wine tasting cellar in Chianti

Chianti Classico is a dry red wine with a fruity flavor that's symbolized by a black rooster. To be labeled Chianti or Chianti Classico, wine must be produced in a designated area just south of Florence and use specific grape varietals, including Sangiovese, which makes up 75-100 percent of the Chianti blend. Limited quantities of Canaiolo, Sauvignon, Merlot, or Syrah can also be used, which means no two Chiantis taste the same. Chianti is aged several months while the minimum for Chianti Classico is one year.

These famous reds aren't the only wines available in the area. Growers seeking to avoid such strict blend restrictions began producing their own original combinations, known as **Super Tuscans,** which are now considered some of the best wines in Italy.

where a medieval chapel once stood. It's not as old as it looks: It was completed in 1835 by Luigi de Cambray-Digny in a neo-Renaissance style. Inside the works of art include a triptych of the *Madonna and Child* by Bicci di Lorenzo.

MONTEFIORALLE

Once the capital of the Lega del Chianti (Chianti League) and heavily fortified, Montefioralle is a small picturesque village on the western outskirts of Greve. It's reputed to be the birthplace of Amerigo Vespucci (look for the house with the 'V' on it), although several towns claim that honor. There's free parking, but it's a nice walk from Greve and

takes less than 15 minutes to reach on foot. The main road is pedestrian only and is lined with a patchwork of stone walls and ivy-clad houses. There are a couple of low-key *trattorie*, an informal bar and a winery down the hill, plus a wonderful cooking school.

✪ PASTA AL PESTO

Via Case Sparse 38, Montefioralle, tel. 340/489-9486, www.pastaalpesto.com, €135pp

You can eat all you want in Chianti and go home with a nostalgic longing for everything you've tasted, or you can learn how to cook a Tuscan meal with Stefania Balducci of Pasta al Pesto. Stefania's passion and

learning to cook at Pasta al Pesto

dedication to ingredients and tradition are contagious, and after a few hours in her kitchen you'll discover that eating well isn't so hard. You'll learn how to make pasta, prepare a four-course lunch or dinner, and have lots of fun. Classes of 2-6 students are conducted in English inside Stefania's home. They last three hours, can be arranged for mornings or afternoons, and always end with a meal.

FESTIVALS AND EVENTS

The market spirit has not faded in Greve, and Piazza Matteotti regularly fills up with farmers and merchants selling locally produced goods. On the last Sunday of each month Il Pagliaio (Piazza Matteotti) is the occasion to sample handmade olive oils and cheeses. Producers are happy to explain the process involved to curious visitors discovering new flavors. Between May and September on the third Thursday of each month, Stelle e Mercanti (Piazza Matteotti, 6pm-11pm) is a nocturnal market where late-night snacks are served in the square.

Cantina Aperta (Open Cantina, www.movimentoturismovino.it, last Sunday in May) is the best time for a wine lover to be in Tuscany. During this annual event, wineries

the village of Montefioralle outside of Greve in Chianti

open up their doors and allow visitors to sample as much wine as they like. Not every vineyard in the region takes part, but there's a high level of participation in Greve. The tourist office provides a list of each year's participants.

WINE BARS
Le Cantine di Greve
Piazza delle Cantine 6, tel. 055/854-6404, Thurs.-Mon. 10am-7pm

For wine within the city limits, visit Le Cantine di Greve. This well-stocked *enoteca* carries 1,200 types of wines, 150 of which can be sampled. There's also a small museum inside.

WINERIES NEAR GREVE

Most vineyards around Greve in Chianti have their own shops where tours and tastings are organized. Vineyard tours often need to be reserved, but tastings are spontaneous and nearly always available. They usually involve several different vintages and may include light snacks or lunch. Whenever something pleases your palate, buy a bottle or have a case shipped directly home. The fun thing about visiting several vineyards in a single day is discovering how much difference a few kilometers make on what's poured into your glass.

Villa Calcinaia
Via Citille 84, tel. 055/853-715, www.villacalcinaia.it, shop daily 9am-1pm and 2pm-6pm

Villa Calcinaia is located on an elegant estate about 1.2 miles (two kilometers) north of town. They produce red, white, and rosé from a number of different grape varieties. Visits can be booked with Vincenzo, who will show you around the vineyard and explain

the production process. Tours last one hour and start on weekdays at 11am and 2:30pm. Afterward you'll sample four recent vintages with cheese and cured meats (€20 per person). Lunch and dinner can also be organized for a minimum of six people, and accommodations in rustic apartments is available in case you want to extend your stay.

Castello di Verrazzano
Via Citille 32a, tel. 055/854-243, www. verrazzano.com, Mon.-Fri. 10am-5pm and weekends 11am-3pm

On a hilltop five minutes north of Villa Calcinaia lies Castello di Verrazzano, where grapes and olives have been grown since 1150. The estate belonged to the Verrazzano family and is the birthplace of the famous explorer. There's a lot of history here and plenty of great stories waiting to be told. Guided visits reveal the vineyards, gardens, and cellars where wine ages in oak casks. The Wine Tour Classico (Mon.-Sat. 10am and 3pm, €21) lasts 90 minutes and includes three glasses of Chianti Classico and a sampling of the family's olive oil, goat cheese, and balsamic vinegar. If you plan on being hungry, book the Wine and Food Experience (Mon.-Fri. noon, €58) and have a three-hour visit of the winery and lunch you'll never forget.

FOOD

Dishes in Greve aren't overly elaborate and rely heavily on local ingredients like olive oil and truffles. Meat is a constant on every menu and wild boar ragu is a favorite along with steaks from Chianina cattle raised nearby. Finding a good wine to accompany a meal is easy, and the house variety is usually an excellent option.

typical wild boar products

TUSCAN AND ITALIAN
Mangiando
Piazza Matteotti 80, tel. 055/854-6372,
Tues.-Sun. noon-3pm and 7pm-11pm, €7-10
Mangiando, a small restaurant from
a husband-and-wife team, doesn't
stray very far from tradition, and the
crostini are a classic Tuscan appetizer.
There are a half-dozen pastas, but if
you've had your fill of carbohydrates,
the steaks are an excellent alternative.
Chianti is the prevalent wine.

Antica Macelleria Falorni
Piazza Matteotti 71, tel. 055/585-3029, daily
10am-7pm
Antica Macelleria Falorni smells like
smoked meat and the historic shop
has been curing its own sausage, salami, and prosciutto since 1806. It's all
hanging from the ceiling and behind
the counter where skilled clerks slice
up *prosciutto crudo, capocollo,* and
soppressata by the gram.

COFFEE
Pasticceria Chianti
Piazza Giacomo Matteotti 26, tel.
055/854-6193, daily 6:30am-7pm, €2-5
There are a number of coffee bars
under the colonnades of the main
square, but Pasticceria Chianti is
the only one that prepares their own

pasticcini (miniature pastries) and
is a good excuse to try local sweets.
You can point to whatever you like
and enjoy them at the counter with a
cappuccino or on the tables outside.
Savory snacks are served from lunch
onwards.

ACCOMMODATIONS
Antico Pastificio Ulisse Mariotti
Via dell'Arco 13, tel. 055/854-7432,
www.anticopastificio.com, €75-90
Whether you need a large apartment,
small apartment, suite, or just a room,
this three-star hotel near Greve's central square is the solution. The third-
generation owners provide a warm
welcome after a day of exploring
Chianti. There's a relaxing garden,
swimming pool, billiard table, and
ping-pong table where guests challenge one another.

Borgo del Cabreo
Via Monte Fioralle Case Sparse 9,
tel. 055/398-5032,
www.borgodelcabreo.it, €150-175
Borgo del Cabreo is a cluster of old
farm buildings outside Greve that
have been given a stylish makeover. If
you want to relax and aren't in a hurry
to get anywhere, this is the place to
stay. All of the 10 superior and deluxe
rooms are beautifully furnished and
have hypnotic views of the surrounding countryside. There's a pool, an
outdoor bar, and extensive grounds
to explore on foot. Guests are given a
complimentary wine tour, and bicycle
hire is available.

INFORMATION AND SERVICES
Tourist Office
Piazza Giacomo Matteotti 10, tel.
055/854-6299, Apr.-Oct. daily 10am-7pm,

Nov.-Mar. Mon.-Fri. 10am-1pm and
3pm-6pm, Sat. 10am-5pm, Sun. 10am-1pm
The tourist office can help find last-minute accommodations and provides a list of monthly events.

KM Zero Tours

Via Luciana 18, Val di Pesa, tel.
349/352-9601, www.kmzerotours.com

KM Zero Tours is a source for gastronomic itineraries and one-day experiences in Chianti.

GETTING THERE

CAR

Car is the most convenient way to arrive and there are two free parking lots near the center of town. Greve is 30 kilometers (18mi) south of Florence on the SR222 and roughly a 45-minute drive.

BUS

Thirty ACVU (www.acvbus.it) buses depart for Greve daily 6:40am-8:15pm from Florence's Autostazione bus terminal (Via Santa Caterina da Siena 15/17), next to Stazione SMN, and take 50 minutes to reach the center of town.

GETTING AROUND

There's a taxi stand in the central *piazza*. Scooter and car rentals are also available at Piazza Matteotti.

Panzano

There's a word for places like Panzano. It's not *paese* (town) or even *villagio* (village). Panzano is a *borgo*, which translates to hamlet, and has a cozy, out-of-the-way feel that makes a big impression. This is the heart of Chianti, halfway between Florence and Siena, with nothing to do except eat, drink, and enjoy the views. There are also dozens of wineries nearby with barrels and barrels of Chianti Classico waiting to be sampled.

Panzano is long and thin. Piazza Gastone Bucciarelli is at the center and where most people start a visit. From there you can walk north on Via G. Daverrazzano uphill towards Chiesa di Santa Maria and a cluster of historic buildings, or in the opposite direction on Via XX Luglio to Officina della Bistecca, which serves some of the best beef in Chianti.

SIGHTS

CHIESA DI SANTA MARIA

Via della Celluzza 2, free

The archway near the northern end of Via G. Daverrazzano marks the entrance to Panzano's medieval core, where Chiesa di Santa Maria rises

Chianti vineyard in autumn, Panzano

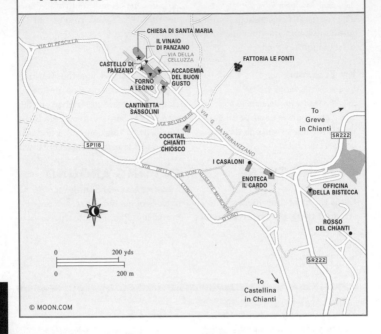

Panzano

above everything. It's a pretty little church with a rough stone façade that was rebuilt in the 19th century to replace a medieval one. The interior is plain but does contain a painting of a 14th-century *Madonna and Baby Jesus* on wood, which was a popular surface for art before cotton was imported from the New World and used to make canvas.

CASTELLO DI PANZANO

Via di Pescille 33

Panzano's castle is now a private resort, but you can get a perfectly good look at the 15th-century outer walls and twin towers from the road outside. Follow Via di Pescille from Chiesa di Santa Maria downhill for about five minutes until you reach a bend in the road with fabulous views on one side and fortifications on the other.

PIEVE DI SAN LEOLINO

Via San Leolino 1, tel. 055/585-2003, free

The parish church of Panzano sits on a lovely hilltop a few kilometers south of town and is one of the best examples of Romanic architecture in Chianti. Like all Tuscan churches, it's been remodeled considerably since the 11th century but still preserves medieval columned arcades, intricate works of art, and a small cloister that's nearly always empty. It's a nice walk up Via XX Luglio, then right on San Leolino all the way to the church. There's little traffic and great views.

EVENTS

Mercato Settimanale

Every Sunday morning the outdoor Mercato Settimanale market (Sun. 8am-1pm) is held in Piazza

Bucciarelli where plants, fruit, cheese, roast chicken, clothes, and housewares are sold. It's the busiest day of the week, and finding parking can be difficult.

Il Mercato Aprilante

Il Mercato Aprilante takes place on the first Sunday of each month to showcase the creations of local artisans and the cheese, honey, and oil produced by farmers in the area. It's a great time to visit and experience Panzano, animated by over 100 tempting stands.

WINE BARS
Accademia del Buon Gusto
Piazza Ricasoli 11, tel. 055/856-0159,
daily 10am-6:30pm

Although driving around small Tuscan roads in search of wineries is fun, you can make life easier by heading directly to Accademia del Buon Gusto. Half wine bar, half wine school, this place is crammed with bottles and animated by a madcap owner who loves sharing his passion for wine. If you want to appreciate the differences between varieties of Chianti Classico and enjoy a glass or two, this is a vital stop. Tastings are free, and there is no pressure to buy.

Il Vinaio di Panzano
Via Santa Maria 22, tel. 055/85-2603,
daily 12-9pm, €7-10

Il Vinaio di Panzano is a good spot to begin educating your wine palate, and to dine on *bruschetta* appetizers and hearty fare. The pergola outside provides welcome shade and a view that's nearly as good as the wine, which can be ordered by the glass, carafe, or bottle. This place makes no attempt at being cool or stylish, but it's charming nonetheless, with excellent prices and a kitchen that remains open all day.

Enoteca Il Cardo
Piazza Gastone Bucciarelli 40/50,
tel. 055/85-2907, www.enotecailcardo.com,
Tues.-Sun. 10am-12am, €8-11

Down in the new part of town, the line between wine bar and restaurant is blurred. You can have a good meal at a wine bar and drink great wine in a restaurant—or do both at Enoteca Il Cardo. They've got dozens of bottles chilling at just the right temperature, the perfect glasses to drink them with, and delicious cheese and cold cut pairings. The contemporary bistro interior is a stylish spot to contemplate Chianti and do a little people-watching. Over 30 local wines are available by the glass, and if you want to learn more about what's inside any bottle, owner Katherine and her enthusiastic team are happy to elucidate.

BARS
Cocktail Chianti Chiosco
Via Giovanni Daverrazzano 55,
tel. 333/924-7541, summer Wed.-Fri.
5pm-12am, Sat.-Sun. 12pm-12am, €5-8

Cocktail Chianti Chiosco isn't a wine bar, but it is the most fun you can have in Panzano. The classy kiosk, near the historic center, comes alive in summer when enterprising bartenders take over the space and mix drinks with panache late into the night. There's a great range of cocktails at low prices, a short snack menu, and a nice view from the terrace where young and old gather.

WINERIES NEAR PANZANO
✪ Fattoria Casaloste
Via Montagliari, 32, tel. 055/85-2725,
www.casaloste.com

Great Chianti Classico can be produced even with limited acreage, and that's exactly what Fattoria Casaloste does. This small, independent winery on the hillsides near Panzano makes a half-dozen reds and isn't afraid to experiment. The Inversus Reserve combines Merlot with Sangiovese grapes and is aged 28 months. It was created in 2003, and only 4,000 bottles are produced per year. It's regularly rated in the 90s (out of a 100) by top wine connoisseurs and sells out fast. Make a reservation to tour the facilities, and sample all the wines along with olive oil and *grappa* liquor. Simple, back-to-basics *agriturismo* accommodation (€90-130) is also available.

Fattoria Le Fonti

Via Case Sparse, tel. 055/85-2194,
www.fattorialefonti.it, Mon.-Fri. 10am-6pm,
Sat. 11am-5pm

A short walk or drive from the center of Panzano, Fattoria Le Fonti produces 40,000-50,000 bottles a year. That's small by Tuscan standards but allows the Italo-Germanic family who operate the winery to follow every aspect of production from pruning the vines to designing the labels. Attention to detail has its advantages, which you can taste in the Sangiovese grapes that make up the majority of the harvest. They also distill some deceptively smooth *grappa* liquor. Tastings are free and don't need to be booked, while tours and an extended sampling of five wines is €10 and must be reserved in advance.

Il Molino di Grace

Localita' Il Volano-Lucarelli,
tel. 055/856-1010, www.ilmolinodigrace.it,
Mon.-Fri. 9am-6pm, Sat. appointment only

Not all wineries go back centuries. Il Molino di Grace was founded in 1997 and is large by Chianti standards. It's also fairly unique in its ambition to combine art with viticulture. Metal

sculptures dot the property and go well with wine. Tastings require no appointment and can be arranged on the spot in the modern cellar overlooking barrels and bottles, but if you want a customized tour, reserve in advance.

FOOD

When visiting a town with a dish named after it, there's only one thing to do: try it. *Bistecca Panzanese* may not be as famous as *bistecca alla Fiorentina* but it's just as good, unless you're a vegetarian, in which case you should avoid this thick cut of beef that's been prepared here since the Middle Ages and is available on nearly every menu in town.

TUSCAN AND ITALIAN
✪ Officina della Bistecca

Via XX Luglio 11, tel. 055/85-2020, www.
dariocecchini.com, daily 1pm and 8pm, €50

Anyone serious about steak needs to head directly to Officina della Bistecca. The Steak Office, as it's called, is as much of a butcher shop as a restaurant. T-bone, rib eye, fillet, tenderloin, Panzanese, and many more cuts are proudly displayed and chopped to size before your eyes. Steaks are enormous and grilled on a charcoal flame to absolute perfection (don't bother asking for well done). Seating inside the cozy eatery is communal, and meals are prepared with great theatrics by Dario Cecchini, who never wastes meat and also carves up locally raised pork. The €50 fixed price menu includes a half-dozen cuts, bean and potato sides, a carafe of red wine, coffee, dessert, and *grappa*. Lunch and dinner start at 1pm and 8pm on the dot. If you can't get in here, try Solociccia (Via XX Luglio 11, €30 fixed price menu) next door.

Whichever restaurant you dine at, make sure to arrive hungry.

Cantinetta Sassolini

Piazza Ricasoli 2, tel. 055/856-0142, Thurs.-Tues. 12:15-2:30pm and 7:15-9:30pm, €9-14

Chianti isn't just about meat, and there are plenty of delicious alternatives. Cantinetta Sassolini prepares an entire menu, including great pasta, risotto, *papa al pomodoro* soup, and fantastic desserts. The family-owned restaurant is slightly more formal, without being stiff, than some of the other restaurants in town, and the young staff is energetic and attentive. Sit outside in the little courtyard if you can.

BAKERY
Forno a Legno

Via Santa Maria 3, tel. 055/85-2740, Tues.-Sat. 8am-1pm and 5-8pm, Sun. 8am-1pm, €5

This bakery is all about bread. Loaves of whole wheat, multigrain, focaccia, and *schiacciata* are pulled out of their wood burning oven all day long and snapped up by locals while still warm. They also prepare traditional sweet breads, like *pan di romerino* with raisins and rosemary and *schiacciata all'uva* during Carnivale season, and make mammoth sandwiches. In the morning, you'll smell this place before you see it.

ACCOMMODATIONS
HOTELS AND BED-AND-BREAKFASTS
Rosso Del Chianti

Via XX Luglio 65, tel. 055/85-2739, www.marinacecchini.info, €85

Getting to know Chianti requires getting to know locals, and the best way to do that is by staying in a B&B like Rosso del Chianti. It's the home of Marina Cecchini, who spoils guests with gracious hospitality and a breakfast of freshly made cakes, bread, jams, and savory options. There's a romantic attic and garden room with private bath both of which are TV free. Marina's brother is Dario, which makes getting a seat at the Officina della Bistecca, down the hill, a breeze.

I Casaloni

Via Giovanni da Verrazzano 11, tel. 335/570-1862, www.casaloni.it, €95-110

I Casaloni offer three spacious self-catering apartments that were recently refurbished and located close to the historic center. Bathrooms and kitchens are brand new, and there are shops nearby for restocking the fridge. It makes an excellent base for exploring Chianti, and the garden with countryside views and pool are a welcome sight after a day on the road. There's parking nearby and a friendly owner on call 24/7.

AGRITURISMO
Azienda Agricola Il Palagio

Via Case Sparse 38, tel. 338/399-7004, www.palagiodipanzano.com, €150-200

If you're trying to get away from it all Azienda Agricola Il Palagio can help. This little corner of paradise on a hillside offers instant serenity. The owner goes above and beyond for guests and treats everyone like a friend. Nothing is rushed or hurried around here, and if you want you can pick your own vegetables, tour the vineyards, or just chill out by the pool. There are only five apartments, all of which seamlessly combine modern with antiquity and look like they belong in an Italian Martha Stewart magazine. Accommodation this nice comes at a price, which might be worth paying for a couple of nights.

CHIANTI
PANZANO

THE AGRITURISMO EXPERIENCE

Tuscan *agriturismi* (farmstays that combine bed-and-breakfast-type accommodations with rural living) provide a unique accommodation experience. Most of these are located in converted farmhouses on land used to grow crops and raise animals. Decor is rustic and the number of rooms is limited. Half- and full-board options are available and meals consist of local ingredients.

Farmstays aren't just about relaxing in secluded countryside locations. They're also a unique opportunity to discover how iconic Italian products are made. If you ever wondered how olive oil is produced, how cheese is aged, or when grapes are ready to harvest for wine, *agriturismi* are the place to stay. You can have a hands-on experience, getting your hands stuck in the vines, for example, or just observe farm life up-close. The people who run these rural establishments generously share their passion for nature and agriculture.

Many *agriturismo* have been upgraded with amazing interiors, spas, and restaurants. Some of the best in Tuscany are listed below. For more selection, www.agriturismo.it lists thousands of such accommodations throughout Italy.

- **The Secret of Pietrafitta,** where you can learn how olive oil is produced, or hang out by the swimming pool with a view of San Gimignano (page 199).

- **Azienda Agricola Il Palagio,** an elegant *agriturismo* located on a working winery outside Panzano (page 231).

- **Podere Terreno,** near Radda, where you can taste the latest Chianti from the casks (page 243).

- **Il Podere Sante Marie,** a small farm on the edge of Montalcino surrounded by vineyards (page 273).

- **Fattoria San Martino,** an eco-friendly option near Montepulciano (page 287).

Selvabella in Chianti

Via di Montagliari 16, tel. 055/852-096,
www.selvabellainchianti.com, €80 d

This enchanting farmhouse nestled on a hillside east of Panzano is ideal for exploring local countryside. Hosts Marta and Bernardo offer Tuscan cooking and pottery lessons and the kind of welcome that feels like being at a friend's home. Their lovely accommodation contains two spacious apartments and plenty of cozy corners on the property. Breakfast is an additional €10 per person, and children under 3 stay for free.

INFORMATION AND SERVICES

Panzano is too small to have a tourist office, but there is a licensed tour guide who can show you around town and take you on unique wine and olive oil tastings: Elena Pietrunti (Via del Mascherone 36, tel. 347/466-7750 www.elenatours.it, €60-80pp) also organizes walking and hiking outings along with weekly cooking classes that start at 4pm and finish with dinner. Elena speaks beautiful English and has a great sense of humor in several languages.

Travelers in search of necessities will find two banks with outdoor

ATMs and a small **supermarket** next to a **pharmacy** on the southern outskirts of town.

GETTING THERE AND AROUND

Panzano is seven kilometers (four miles) south of Greve on the SR222. The stretch between Greve and Panzano is panoramic with lots of distractions on either side of the road. The drive takes about 10 minutes and leads directly to Piazza Gastone Bucciarelli, Panzano's central square. There's a big **parking lot** just outside of town and a smaller one up the hill close to the historic center. Both are free, and once you've parked, there's no need for a car as everything can be reached on foot.

Castellina in Chianti

Castellina in Chianti may be small, but thanks to its strategic location between Florence and Siena, it has always punched above its weight. The town, along with Radda, was a member of the Lega del Chianti and was destroyed and rebuilt a number of times over the centuries. The result was the Rocca fortress with its impressive 14th-century tower that dominates town. Castellina can trace its origins back to shepherds who roamed these parts and Etruscans who were buried in the nearby necropolis. Wine and olive oil aren't a recent phenomenon here: They've been harvested nearby for thousands of years.

SIGHTS

✪ ROCCA AND ARCHEOLOGICAL MUSEUM

Piazza del Comune 17-18, tel. 347/679-0752, www.museoarcheologicochianti.it, June-Aug. daily 11am-7pm, Apr., May, Sept., Oct. daily 10am-6pm, other months by appointment only, €7

Rocca ("Rock") is an aptly named fortress in the center of town built by the Florentines during their centuries-long struggle with Siena. It looks impregnable from the outside and houses the Archeological Museum that contains Bronze Age, Etruscan, and Medieval relics spanning thousands of years. Many precious objects come from the nearby necropolis where ancient Etruscan aristocrats were laid to rest. The fortress also includes an impressive tower that offers a view of the Chianti mountains, Val d'Elsa valley, and San Gimignano.

Tablets with interactive explanations in English are available from the ticket office, or you can download the museum app. Guided tours are also available on Wednesdays at 10am in summer and 6pm the rest of the year. They last 50 minutes and must be reserved in advance (info@ museoarcheologicochianti.it).

VIA DELLE VOLTE

Castellina's fortifications included walls that once surrounded the town. Most of these were destroyed or dismantled long ago, but a half-buried passageway along Via delle Volte delimitates where they once stood. This is a great walk on the northern edge of town. There are regular gaps in the vaulted tunnel where towers

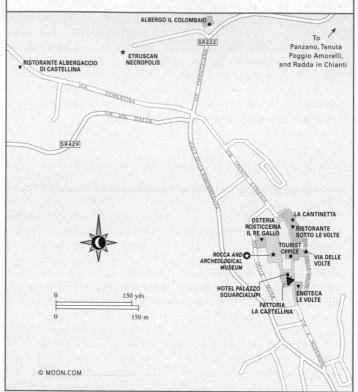

Castellina

ALBERGO IL COLOMBAIO

SR222

★ ETRUSCAN
NECROPOLIS

RISTORANTE ALBERGACCIO
DI CASTELLINA

VIA FIORENTINA

VIA VAL D'ELSA

SR429

To
Panzano, Tenuta
Poggio Amorelli,
and Radda in Chianti

LA CANTINETTA

OSTERIA
ROSTICCERIA
IL RE GALLO

RISTORANTE
SOTTO LE VOLTE

TOURIST
OFFICE

ROCCA AND
ARCHEOLOGICAL
MUSEUM

VIA DELLE
VOLTE

HOTEL PALAZZO
SQUARCIALUPI

ENOTECA
LE VOLTE

FATTORIA
LA CASTELLINA

0   150 yds

0   150 m

© MOON.COM

once stood, and workshops and restaurants now occupy many of the spaces where defenders were once stationed. The passageway runs the length of Via delle Volte to the edge of town.

ETRUSCAN NECROPOLIS

Via Chiantigiana 17, tel. 057/774-2090, www.museoarcheologicochianti.it, free
Etruscans often chose the highest spot for their tombs, which explains the location of this ancient cemetery. The site, situated on the northern end of Castellina with great views of town, contains four well-preserved burial mounds from the 7th century BC a

few yards from one another. It's possible to enter each one, though they are all pretty similar. Each consists of several underground stone chambers facing the cardinal points. Personal items have been removed to local museums, so today the tombs are empty. Still, the quality of the stonework indicates that Etruscans cared a lot about their ancestors. A flashlight will come in handy here. When it rains the earthen floor inside gets muddy.

EVENTS

There's a weekly market (Via IV Novembre 8am-1pm) in town that sells local wine, bread, and cheese.

WINE BARS
Enoteca Le Volte
Via Ferruccio 12, tel. 057/774-0308,
daily 9am-10:30pm

There's a lot of wine to choose from at Enoteca le Volte and taking Aleandro's advice can simplify things. He's funny, friendly, and cordial in a way you only find in these parts, and never too busy to talk wine. Prices are honest, and the plates of local meats and cheeses served on wooden cutting boards disappear quickly. The best seats are outdoors underneath the medieval corridor.

La Cantinetta
Via delle Volte 8, tel. 05/774-0868,
Mon.-Tues., Thurs.-Sat. 3:30-7pm

Any winery with its own wine bar is a good sign, and La Cantinetta doesn't disappoint. There's been a *cantina* here since the 14th century, and the current owners cultivate seven hectares outside of town. You can taste their version of Chianti Classico and some Super Tuscans, which are not restricted to containing 70 percent Sangiovese grapes, along with local snacks while knowledgeable staff recount the area's long history.

WINERIES
Tenuta Poggio Amorelli
Poggio Amorelli, tel. 057/774-1373,
www.famigliamazzarrini.it, daily 11am-3pm,
€25/€50

If you have the inclination to wander through vineyards, visit a cellar, and discover how wine gets made, this is the place to do it. Poggio Amorelli offers wine tastings (10 minutes), guided tours, and lunch tours. The first only scratches the surface; the second provides enological insight into what you're drinking; and the

Castellina in Chianti

third culminates in a meal. Tours (€25) last an hour and end with a sampling of six vintages that include a Vermentino white wine and Super Tuscan. The lunch option (€50) includes oil, cheese, salami, handmade pasta, truffles, and vegetables from an organic garden served on a panoramic terrace. Reservations required.

Fattoria La Castellina
Via Ferruccio 26, tel. 05/774-1882, www.lacastellina.it, Mon.-Fri. 10:30am-12pm and 3-4:30pm, tasting €22

Chianti Classico may be the most famous wine in the area, but it's not the only wine produced here, and the 30 hectares at Fattoria la Castellina grow a mix of red and white grapes. You can visit the 15th-century estate and taste the results or stay for a light lunch (11:30am-12pm, €32) that includes four wines. In either case, you'll need a reservation unless you decide to stay at their *agriturismo* accommodation overlooking the vineyards. They also run a shop with the same name selling their wine in town on Viale della Rimembranza 28.

Rocca delle Macie
Loc. Le Macie 45, tel. 057/77-321, www.roccadellemacie.com, daily 10am-6pm

This relatively new winery has made a name for itself with a Riserva di Fizzano and Tenuta Sant'Alfonso that are fruity with spicy, mineral notes sommeliers rave about. It's located on the SP51 road a mile south of Castellina and is hard to miss. Wines are reasonably priced, and there are four tours (€15-40) to choose from lasting 1.5-2 hours that end with a guided tasting of the latest vintages.

RECREATION
BIKE, VESPA, AND VINTAGE CAR RENTALS
Noleggio 500
Via IV Novembre, 35, tel. 057/714-81001, www.noleggiochianti500.it, daily 9am-1pm and 3-7pm

Gabriele Ciabattini is a Fiat 500 fanatic who started a rental company to share his love of this iconic Italian automobile. He rents vintage and modern cars by the day (€160) along with Vespas and hybrid (€20 per day), mountain (€20), and e-bikes (€35) by Skott. Helmet, lock, and spare tires are included. If you can't make it to him, he'll bring the bikes to you for a small fee.

For a ride with plenty of small towns, vineyards, and roadside curiosities, try the Palazzo al Piano ring route. It starts from Castellina and winds up and down the Val d'Elsa toward Siena and back on the Via Chiantigiana for a total of 90 kilometers (55 miles).

exploring Chianti on a Vespa

HIKING
Via Romea del Chianti
The ancient Via Romea del Chianti pilgrim road, a branch of the 3,045-kilometer Via Francigena (www.viefrancigene.org) that medieval pilgrims took between Canterbury and

Rome, passes through town. The southern section toward Siena was recently rediscovered and is one of the most scenic that takes walkers along dusty roads up and down scenic hillsides far from civilization. You don't have to walk the full 23 kilometers (14 miles) to Siena: Even a couple of kilometers on the ancient route leaves a lasting impression. There are forests, vineyards, and crumbling way stations where pilgrims once rested throughout the journey. The hike isn't steep or strenuous, and the countryside is so seductive it's hard to turn back.

FOOD

TUSCAN AND ITALIAN
Osteria Rosticceria Il Re Gallo
Via Toscana 1, tel. 057/774-2000, Tues.-Sun. 12:30-3pm and 7-10pm, €8-12

This old-fashioned *osteria* in the center of town serves abundant portions of high-quality food at surprisingly low prices. There are daily specials along with classic Tuscan dishes like *bistecca alla Fiorentina* grilled to perfection and wonderful homemade desserts. The best seats are outside on the pedestrian street.

Ristorante Sotto Le Volte
Via delle Volte 14, tel. 057/774-1299, Thurs.-Tues. 12-10pm, €11-13

Ristorante Sotto le Volte has one of the most romantic locations in town, under the medieval vaulted passageways. It's not bad on the stomach, either, with fresh pasta that includes *pici* with rabbit sauce, *tortelloni* with truffle, and *pappardelle* with wild boar. There are plenty of beefsteak seconds and a tiramisu with a caffeine kick. A two-course meal with coffee, water, and wine is about €50.

Ristorante Albergaccio di Castellina
Via Fiorentina 63, tel. 057/774-1042, Mon.-Sat. 12:30-2:30pm and 7:30-9:30pm, €18-25

If you don't get to Chianti every day, it might be worth splurging at a Michelin starred restaurant. This one is a short, uphill walk outside town that will surprise the palate with unexpected flavor combinations and seduce the eyes. The atmosphere is quiet and calm, with an attentive staff that anticipates every need. You can choose between the restaurant or *osteria*, which is the budget option and slightly more casual. There are à la carte and two tasting menus that can be paired with wine at a reasonable price. First courses include risotto, *pici*, gnocchetti, and ravioli while seconds are a chance to taste pigeon, duck, or rabbit steamed, stewed, and grilled.

ACCOMMODATIONS

HOTELS
Albergo Il Colombaio
Via Chiantigiana 29, tel. 057/774-0444, www.albergoilcolombaio.it, €80-90

Albergo il Colombaio is a small three-star hotel at the entrance to town that was once used by sheep herders in the 1900s. Not much has changed since then, and the stone interior provides a marvelous rustic atmosphere. Roberta and her mother supply a warm welcome, and there's a pool out back. Breakfast is served in a vaulted dining room and includes homemade pies and cakes.

Hotel Palazzo Squarcialupi
Via Ferruccio 22, tel. 057/774-1186, www.palazzosquarcialupi.com, €150-165

Hotel Palazzo Squarcialupi is a grand old residence with a split personality. One side of the hotel faces the heart of Castellina while the other looks out onto the green hills of Chianti. The bucolic side also has a lovely garden, small pool, and a terrace from which to enjoy the view. The interior is fit for Tuscan royalty, with high-ceilinged rooms, a spa, and a restaurant that serves wine that the hotel produces nearby.

Castello La Leccia

Località La Leccia, tel. 05/7774-3148, www. castellolaleccia.com, €250-€325

Deciding whether to stay in town or out can be a question, but Castello la Leccia five kilometers (three miles) south of Castellina makes the choice easy. This winery-cum-hotel surrounded by olive groves has an air of exclusivity, which staff quickly dispel with their professional charm. There are 12 designer rooms in 3 different sizes, and children under 14 are discouraged, which leaves plenty of tranquility for couples of all ages. Grounds are finely manicured, and the pool has a panoramic view. An extensive buffet breakfast, canteen visit, and bottle of Chianti Classico are all included in the price.

INFORMATION AND SERVICES

The **tourist office** (Via Ferruccio 40, tel. 05/7774-1392, Tues.-Sat. 10am-1pm) provides information about the frequent wine-related events organized in the area.

GETTING THERE

Castellina is 13 kilometers (8 miles) south of Panzano on the SR222. It's a 20-minute, mostly uphill drive by car and 30 minutes by scooter.

Radda in Chianti

Radda in Chianti is a tiny hill town that was once capital of the Chianti League and heavily fortified. It changed hands many times in the Middle Ages and eventually fell under the influence of Florentines who built the Palazzo del Podesta, the town hall from which the surrounding area was ruled. There was a gradual exodus over the centuries as locals left for larger towns, and it wasn't until the 1970s that Radda experienced a renaissance. Beauty was rediscovered, buildings, squares, and towers slowly restored, and local entrepreneurs began opening the *agriturismi* and wineries that have become the main attraction. The town can be seen and circled in less than an hour, but it's hard to tire of the narrow streets and patchwork of yellowish stone houses or the inviting wine bars.

SIGHTS
Palazzo del Podesta

Piazza F. Ferrucci 1, tel. 057/773-9633, free

It may not look like it today, but Radda was one of the most important towns in southern Chianti, known as Chianti Senese, and a key member of the Chianti League. This town hall, completed in 1489 by Florentine architects, was the symbol of that power and where local leaders met to govern the town. It's been renovated and refurbished over the centuries, and the clock on the façade dates from 1873. The modest building was the seat

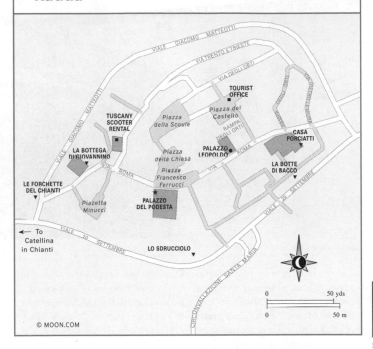

Radda

TOURIST OFFICE
VIALE GIACOMO MATTEOTTI
VIA TRENTO E TRIESTE
VIA DEGLI ORTI
VIA PIETRO LEOPOLDO
Piazza del Castello
RAMPA DEGLI ORTI
CASA PORCIATTI
TUSCANY SCOOTER RENTAL
Piazza della Scoule
VIA ROMA
PALAZZO LEOPOLDO
LA BOTTEGA DI GIOVANNINO
Piazza della Chiesa
LA BOTTE DI BACCO
LE FORCHETTE DEL CHIANTI
Piazza Francesco Ferrucci
VIALE 20 SETTEMBRE
PALAZZO DEL PODESTA
Piazzetta Minucci
← To Catellina in Chianti
VIALE 20 SETTEMBRE
LO SDRUCCIOLO
CIRCONVALLAZIONE SANTA MARIA
VIALE GIACOMO MATTEOTTI

0   50 yds
0   50 m

© MOON.COM

of local government for four centuries and used as a prison until 1944. It sits on the main square facing **San Niccolò church** and today houses the tourist and mayor's office.

Ramparts

The walls that protected Radda during the Middle Ages are still intact around the northern perimeter and testify to the town's importance. They were built by the Florentines, destroyed by the Aragonese, and rebuilt and reinforced many times after that. The best view of the walls is from Viale Giacomo Matteotti, but you might as well walk around the entire town, which only takes 20-30 minutes. The walls can be reached from Via Roma at the eastern or western entrance to town.

✪ Casa Chianti Classico

Circonvallazione Santa Maria 18, tel. 057/773-8187, www.casachianticlassico.it, Tues.-Sun. 11am-7pm

Casa Chianti Classico is a wine museum, bar, and bistro all in one located in an old convent just outside of Radda. It's a good place to get or

Chianti Museum inside Casa Chianti Classico

239

Casa Chianti Classico

continue a wine education. Mini courses (1 hour, €25, must reserve in advance) begin at 11:30am and 4pm and cover terroir, technique, and a sampling of three wines accompanied by locally cured meats. Otherwise, you can just show up and visit the free museum that describes the history of Chianti Classico through an interactive and sensorial tour. Visitors are given a glass of wine, which they slowly discover through touch screens and digital exhibits that engage all the senses. There's also a wine shop that provides tastings (three glasses €5 or €8). Every Thursday night throughout summer, there's a buffet with live jazz in the courtyard that includes two glasses of wine for €15.

WINE BARS
Casa Porciatti
Camminamento Medievale, www. casaporciatti.it, Mon.-Sat. 10:30am-7:30pm and Sunday 10:30-1pm, €5-7

Casa Porciatti serves great wine and food inside a charming 13th-century building. It's the place to sample over 400 different bottles, 20-25 of which are available by the glass every day. If you don't have a clue, staff will guide your palate inside this cozy wine cellar with a *botegga* (deli) next door (Piazza Quattro Novembre 1, Mon.-Sat. 8am-1pm and 4-8pm) full of mouth-watering Tuscan ingredients.

La Bottega di Giovannino
Via Roma 6, tel. 057/773-8599, Wed.-Sun., €7-10

La Bottega di Giovannino is popular with locals who come to this friendly *vineria* for good house wine, wooden trays piled high with appetizers, and daily specials from the kitchen. The sister-brother team behind the bar offer a wide selection of Chianti Classico, *crostini*, and a kids menu, which is rare in Chianti.

WINERIES NEAR RADDA
Vignavecchia

Regionale 429, tel. 057/773-8090,
www.vignavecchia.com, Mon.-Fri. 9am-5pm,
weekends by reservation only

Vignavecchia (which translates to old wine) is one of the 33 wineries that started the Chianti Classico label in 1924 and has been bottling the good stuff since 1840, when owner Odoardo Beccari swapped a career in botany for enology. His descendants still work on the family vineyard and produce small quantities of excellent wine. The winery is a mile east of Radda and easily reached by foot. You can drop by without booking during the week, but reservations are required on weekends.

Castello di Radda

Località Il Becco 101/a, tel. 057/773-8992,
www.castellodiradda.com, Mon.-Sat.
10:30am-5:30pm May.-Oct., Mon.-Fri.
10:30am-5:30pm Nov.-Apr.

Castello di Radda is within sight of Radda. This large, newly built, family-owned winery may not be as charmingly rustic as others, but it does produce five reds and one rosé, all of which have won awards for excellence. Sample wines in their elegant tasting rooms overlooking vineyards, then visit the world-class production and bottling facilities. The winery is 10 minutes (about 4 km/2.5 mi) north by car on the SP114.

RECREATION
☉ SCOOTER RENTALS
Tuscany Scooter Rental

Viale Giacomo Matteotti, 12,
www.tuscanyscooterrental.com, €60 per day

One of the most memorable ways of exploring Chianti is behind the wheel of a scooter. Tuscany Scooter Rental

Radda in Chianti

can set you up with three types of 125cc Vespas that are simple to drive and only require a driver's license and credit card to rent. If you know what you're doing, you can also opt for a Ducati or BMW, but special motorcycle licenses are required. You can pick scooters up from their office in Florence and drive south or at their Radda location in the center of town. They sell useful self-guided maps and provide helmets and locks. Vespas sell out fast in July and August, and if you intend to explore Chianti on two wheels it's never too early to reserve. There are plenty of roads to follow, but if you prefer nature, the SP72 starts less than a mile east of town and heads north through some of the remotest parts of Chianti.

TOURS
Chianti Live
Viale 20 Settembre 17, tel. 057/7 73-5670, daily 9am-7pm, €30-60pp
If you want to hire a tour guide, go winery hopping with an expert, or set off on horseback, head to Chianti Live. This small travel agency does it all at reasonable fees.

EVENTS
The Mercato Sotto le Mure market (Piazza IV Novembre, fourth Monday of the month 3-8pm) is held monthly underneath the town walls. There are vegetable, fruit, cheese, wine, bread, and sausage stands.

FOOD
TUSCAN AND ITALIAN
Le Forchette del Chianti
Viale Giacomo Matteotti 5, tel. 057/773-8923, Fri.-Wed. 12pm-1am, €12-14
Located along the town walls on a street that's often overlooked, Le Forchette del Chianti ("the forks of Chianti") delivers on all counts. Food is good, service is friendly, and prices are reasonable. Ingredients are locally sourced, with no fusion intrusions that get in the way of Tuscan tradition. This simple eatery has been serving the same menu for generations and isn't likely to change. Unlike most restaurants, they don't close between lunch and dinner, which is good news for anyone who arrives in the afternoon with an appetite.

La Botte di Bacco
Via XX Settembre 23, tel. 057/773-9008, daily noon-2:30pm and 7pm-9:30pm, €14-18
La Botte di Bacco is romantic, with white tablecloths and an outdoor terrace. Maybe it's the tomato soup, maybe it's the wine, or possibly it's the outdoor terrace. Prices here are a little higher than average.

La Bottega Ristorante Di Carla Barucci
Piazza della Torre 1, Volpaia, Utel. 057/773-8001, Wed.-Mon. 12:15-2:30pm and 7:15-9:30pm, €7.50-9
The farther you get from Chianti's main attractions, the lower the prices get, but the food remains just as good. Located in the village of Volpaia, just a 15-minute (7.5 km/4.7 mi) drive north from Radda on the SP112 provincial road, La Bottega Ristorante Di Carla is the simplest of several *osteria* in town. Everyone gets a warm welcome here, and the shaded gravel garden in the back is a marvelous retreat in which to enjoy a meal while looking out on beautiful countryside. Owner Carla Barucci has a natural sense of hospitality and has been satisfying diners with *antipasto di crostini, pici con pesto,* and *coniglio al tartufo* for decades.

GELATO
Lo Sdrucciolo

Via XX Settembre 15, tel. 057/773-8720

The gelato and *sorbetto* at Lo Sdrucciolo are made the old-fashioned way, and you can enjoy them (and the view) on the benches across the street. Stick around long enough, and it'll be *aperitivo* time when the town youth show up, and savory snacks and cocktails replace ice-cream cones.

ACCOMMODATIONS
HOTELS
Palazzo Leopoldo

Via Roma 33, tel. 057/773-5605,
www.palazzoleopoldo.it, €110-130

Travelers have been coming to Palazzo Leopoldo since the 14th century, and the building has retained all its Renaissance charm. It feels like a museum with all the comforts of a four-star hotel and staff that aren't afraid to dote. There are modern spa facilities below ground, an excellent restaurant with romantic outdoor seating, and the possibility of taking cooking courses in the hotel kitchen.

La Bottega di Giovannino

Via Roma 6, tel. 057/773-8599, €35 per
person or €60 with dinner

It may be hard to move after a few hours drinking at this wine bar, but if you overdo it, you're in luck: They conveniently rent rooms with bygone décor at affordable prices. Each comes with private bath, nice views, and dinner for only a little extra. It's a great place to stay in the center of town. Rooms are private, though the hotel charges by the person.

AGRITURISMO
Podere Terreno

Località Volpaia, tel. 347/795-3620,
www.podereterreno.it, €80-90

Podere Terreno is a small farm a few minutes north of Radda offering simple *agriturismo* accommodation. Cristina is a wonderful host and goes out of her way to advise on what to do or taste in Chianti. The five bright rooms are named after grapes, and all have private baths and garden views. Televisions are nowhere to be found, and a good night's sleep is almost guaranteed. Days can be spent fishing at the nearby pond, walking along cypress-lined lanes, or learning how a Tuscan farm is run. Breakfast and half-board are available.

INFORMATION AND SERVICES

The **tourist office** (Piazza del Castello 6, tel. 05/777-38494) provides basic information.

GETTING THERE

Radda is 13 kilometers (8mi) from Castellina and a 20-minute drive along the SR429. There are several less direct routes, but these are not well indicated and getting lost is easy. Roads are narrow in this part of Chianti, and lanes are not usually divided with a line. There's plenty of **parking** in Radda along Viale Giacomo Matteotti and Via del Cimitero on the eastern edge of town. Some of it is paid (blue lines) and some is free (white lines) for one hour, although how this is enforced remains an Italian mystery.

SIENA

Siena first rose to prominence under the Lombards in the 6th century AD. It experienced a population influx during the Middle Ages when wealthy families began building their houses along the Via Francigena on the highest part of town. Prosperity brought about conflict with Florence and the numerous battles that ensued are immortalized in Dante's *Divine Comedy.* Beating the Florentines was one thing, but surviving the plague of 1348 was another. The Black Death brought construction to a halt and began a long period of instability, which ended

HIGHLIGHTS

✪ **PIAZZA DEL CAMPO:** This extraordinary shell-shaped square in the heart of the city is active day and night (page 249).

✪ **TORRE DEL MANGIA:** Climb the highest tower in Siena for an unrivaled view of Tuscany (page 250).

✪ **DUOMO:** Siena's cathedral is second to none in terms of craftsmanship and beauty, with paving featuring mythological and biblical tales (page 250).

✪ **MUSEO DELL'ACQUA:** Siena's newest museum offers the unique opportunity to go underground to discover where the city gets its water (page 253).

with Siena's submission to its larger neighbor.

Modern Siena isn't stuck in the past; It's a lively city with a substantial university population that keeps it animated and makes sure there's more to do than admire old buildings. Eating and drinking are the main activities, and the brick-lined streets of the center are packed with inexpensive eateries where meals and conversations are easy to start. The other major pastime is the biannual *Palio* horse race held in Piazza del Campo, which the Sienese obsess about and prepare for all year long.

PLANNING YOUR TIME

Florence and Siena are an hour and a half apart by rail, and there's frequent daily service between the cities. Siena can easily be navigated in an hour or two on foot, but two days is perfect for seeing most of the sights inside the city walls and some outside. Weekdays are less crowded and the city makes a good base from which to explore the surrounding area.

Although Siena does not have city-wide sightseeing passes, municipal museums such as Torre Mangia, Museo Civico, and Santa Maria della Scalla offer a €20 combined ticket that can be used over two days and is available for purchase from each of the sights.

ORIENTATION

Siena, built over a series of low hills, feels more like a small town than a city. Piazza del Campo is the geographical center and largest open space from which a tangle of streets emerge. The Duomo and Torre del Mangia are the most useful landmarks and can facilitate navigation.

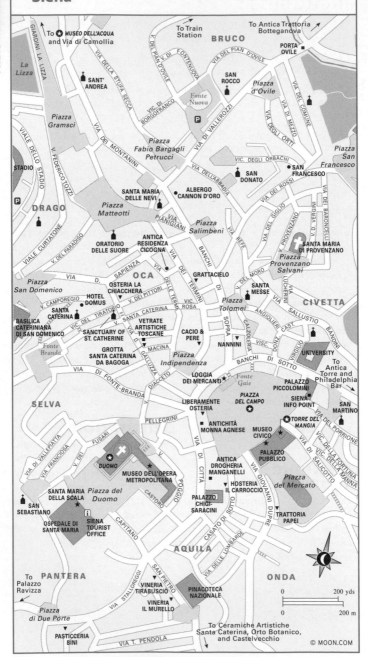

Siena

Itinerary Ideas

For your first day in Siena, make sure you've reserved the full ticket for the Duomo (the Opa Si pass), which includes entry to all the sights. You can buy this at the Duomo ticket office (daily 9am-6pm), but there may be lines in summer, so you might want to purchase it online or over the phone instead (tel. 05/7753-4511, www.operaduomo.siena.it).

DAY 1

1 Piazza del Campo has been the center of Siena's cultural and political life for centuries and is a good place to start a visit of the city. Walk around the herringbone-paved square and throw a coin into the Gaia fountain, which was built in 1346 and is supplied by an underground aqueduct more than 18 miles (30km) long.

2 Enter Palazzo del Pubblico on the southern end of the square and climb Torre del Mangia. Enjoy the view from Siena's slender tower.

3 Head over to Siena Info Point for a one-hour tour (starting at 11am) around the historic center to discover how the tower got its name, what lies underneath the city, and why the Duomo was never completed.

4 Order a three-course meal at Osteria la Chiacchera, just a short walk north of Piazza del Campo. Arrive early to get a seat on the wooden tables outside along the slanted medieval street off Via della Galluzza.

5 Have an afternoon espresso at Osteria la Chiacchera, then head west to the Duomo. Learn about the interior at the listening stations scattered around the church and climb up to see unfinished sections of the building.

6 Explore the narrow streets around the historic center and window-shop along Via di Città. In one shop, Antica Drogheria Manganelli, you'll find great gastronomic souvenirs.

7 Get a head start on aperitivo at Vineria il Murello. Spend the rest of the evening sampling local wine, cheese, and cold cuts at this festive wine bar.

DAY 2

1 Take a walk to the southwestern corner of town and sample traditional pastries pulled fresh from the ovens of Pasticceria Bini.

2 After breakfast, watch ceramics being made by skilled hands at nearby Ceramiche Artistiche Santa Caterina, next to Siena's Porta Tufi gate.

Siena Itineraries

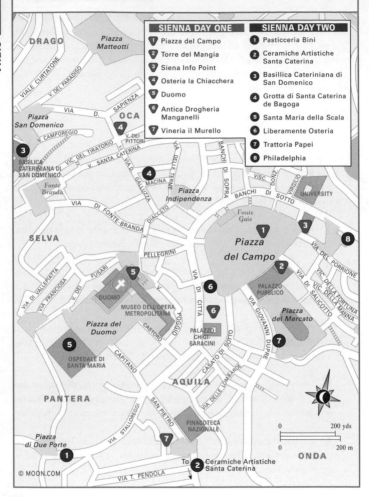

DRAGO

Piazza Matteotti

SIENNA DAY ONE
1 Piazza del Campo
2 Torre del Mangia
3 Siena Info Point
4 Osteria la Chiacchera
5 Duomo
6 Antica Drogheria Manganelli
7 Vineria il Murello

SIENNA DAY TWO
1 Pasticceria Bini
2 Ceramiche Artistiche Santa Caterina
3 Basillica Cateriniana di San Domenico
4 Grotta di Santa Caterina de Bagoga
5 Santa Maria della Scala
6 Liberamente Osteria
7 Trattoria Papei
8 Philadelphia

VIALE CURTATONE

V. DI PARADISO

VIA D. SAPIENZA

OCA

Piazza San Domenico

V. CAMPOREGIO

V. DEI PITTORI

3 BASILICA CATERINIANA DI SAN DOMENICO

VIC. DEL TIRATORIO

V. SANTA CATERINA

VIA D. GALLUZZA

4

4 MACINA

Piazza Indipendenza

VIA DELLE TERME

BANCHI DI SOPRA

VISC. DI DONZ

BANCHI DI SOTTO

VIA VIRGILIO

UNIVERSITY

Fonte Branda

VIA DI FONTE-BRANDA

DIACCETO

3

8

SELVA

PELLEGRINI

Fonte Gaie

1 Piazza del Campo

2

VIA DEL PORRIONE

VIA DI VALLEPIATTA

VIA FRANCIOSA

FUSARI

V. DEI

5

VIA DI CITTÀ

6

PALAZZO PUBBLICO

VIC. DELLA FORTUNA

VIC. DELLA MANNA

VIA DI SALICOTTO

DUOMO

MUSEO DELL'OPERA METROPOLITANA

CASTORO

6

Piazza del Mercato

Piazza del Duomo

POGGIO

PALAZZO CHIGI-SARACINI

CASATO DI SOTTO

VIA GIOVANNI DUPRÈ

7

5

CAPITANO

OSPEDALE DI SANTA MARIA

SAN PIETRO

VIA DELLE LOMBARDE

AQUILA

PANTERA

VIA STALLOREGGI

PINACOTECA NAZIONALE

Piazza di Due Porte

1

7

ONDA

© MOON.COM

To 2 Ceramiche Artistiche Santa Caterina

VIA T. PENDOLA

0   200 yds
0   200 m

3 Zigzag north past fountains and up Via Fontebranda to **Basilica Cateriniana di San Domenico,** Siena's second largest church, where you can see the severed head of the city's patron saint.

4 At **Grotta di Santa Caterina da Bagoga,** five minutes away, have a cozy lunch sampling wild boar pasta and other local specialties.

5 Explore the ancient hospital of **Santa Maria della Scala** opposite the Duomo. Make sure to pick up the audio guide that's included with the ticket and explains each of the exhibits.

6 Enjoy an outdoor aperitivo facing Piazza del Campo at **Liberamente Osteria.** Order a refreshing Apple Mojito or Negroni and enjoy the light snacks that come with your drink.

7 Have your last supper in Siena at **Trattoria Papei,** south of Piazza del Campo and opposite the city's covered market. Feast on one of their Flintstone-size T-bone steaks or a plate of pici pasta.

8 Celebrate the city with the friendly folks at the **Philadelphia** bar until closing time.

Sights

⊙ PIAZZA DEL CAMPO

Wherever you enter Siena, you are inevitably drawn to Piazza del Campo. The main square has inherited its famous seashell shape from the whims and jerks of medieval urbanization. Fonte Gaie fountain at the northern end is a beautiful replacement for the 15th-century original sculpted by Jacopo della Quercia and now kept safe in Santa Maria della Scala. It's also the location of Siena's famous horse race, the *Palio delle Contrade.*

Museo Civico
Piazza del Campo 1, tel. 05/7729-2226,
Mar. 16-Oct. 10am-7pm and Nov.-Mar. 15
10am-6pm, €9, €13 with Santa Maria della
Scalla, €20 with Santa Maria della Scala and
Torre della Mangia

Siena's city history museum is located inside Palazzo Pubblico, the town hall built in the 12th century and still used by local government. The museum consists of a series of elaborately decorated rooms, the most impressive of which is the Sala dei Nove, where the medieval town council met and administrative decisions were made. The walls were painted with an allegory of good versus bad government in order to remind officials how they should govern, and to warn them of the consequences of corruption and greed.

A visit to the museum doesn't take long, but if frescoes and grand interiors aren't your thing, you may want to skip this one. It is, however, a quiet place with good views of the square and the most important *palazzo* in the

city. Tickets are available in the courtyard on the ground floor.

✪ Torre del Mangia

Piazza del Campo 1, summer 10am-7pm daily,
winter 10am-4pm daily, €10

Also within Palazzo Pubblico is the
entrance to the Torre del Mangia
tower, which rises 102 meters (334
feet) and provides great views of
Tuscan countryside. The tower took
23 years to build and was completed
in 1348 by the Rinaldi brothers, who
replaced the initial architect, who was
guilty of *mangia* (eating) the funds set
aside for the project. It's been a symbol
of the city ever since and was a useful
watchtower during the city's centuries-long feud with Florence. All that
separates you from a view reminiscent
of the frescoes in the rooms below is
300 steps. Fifty visitors are allowed up
the tower at a time and you can stay on

Torre del Mangia

the outdoor terrace at the top for up to
15 minutes.

✪ DUOMO

Piazza del Duomo, tel. 05/7728-6300,
www.operaduomo.siena.it, Mon.-Sat.

Piazza del Campo

10:30am-5pm and Sun. 1:30pm-5pm, €5
Duomo only, Opa SI Pass €15

The Duomo is hard to miss: It's the largest edifice in town. Built in Roman-Gothic style, it's one of the great cathedrals of Italy and might have been the biggest in the world had the plague not brought construction to a halt. The alternating white-and-black marble is striking and the vast number of columns inside the colorful interior creates many interesting perspectives. The pavement was laid in the 15th century and consists of 56 immense squares featuring mythological and biblical tales. It's covered much of the year to protect the marble and is exposed from mid-August to the end of October. The pulpit, carved by Nicola Pisano, dramatically illustrates the life of Christ. There's also a panoramic **Porta Cielo** (daily 10:30am-6pm, €20) route up the inside of the cathedral that provides an overhead

view of the central apse and the city outside. It's a guided tour that leaves every 30 minutes and has a maximum of 18 participants.

There's a lot to see inside the Duomo including the **Piccolomini library** with frescoes by Raffaello (he's the one wearing red pants and holding a candle), the **Baptistry** sculpted by Donatello, an ancient underground **Crypt,** and the **Museo dell'Opera** that explains how the cathedral was built. The **Opa Si Pass** (€15) allows you to discover seven sights over three days and is available online, by telephone, or from the **Duomo Ticket Office** (Piazza del Duomo, tel. 05/7753-4511, www.operaduomo. siena.it, daily 9am-6pm) in the square outside. The latter does get crowded in summer. Individual tickets to each sight (€5) are available, but if you want to see it all, the pass is the best option. You can also rent a guide

Duomo di Siena

(info@guidesiena.com, €150 for three hours), obtain interactive touch-screen tablets (€7) that follow three itineraries, or use audio stations (€2) located at different points within the Duomo.

Santa Maria della Scala

Piazza Duomo 1, tel. 05/7728-6300, www. santamariadellascala.com, Mar. 15 -Oct. 15 10am-7pm daily, Oct. 16 - Mar. 14 Mon., Wed., Fri. 10am-5pm, Thurs. 10am-8pm, Sat.-Sun. 10am-7pm, €9, €18 with Duomo, €20 with Museo Civico and Torre Mangia

Santa Maria della Scala, one of the oldest hospitals in Europe, was founded around the turn of the first millennium to care for the city's poor and pilgrims traveling along the Via Francigena road. It continued nursing locals until 20 years ago when it was transformed into a massive museum complex. It's a combination of church, hospital, gallery, and archeological dig that reveals Siena's ancient and medieval past. Three floors contain interactive displays and informative videos. The basement houses the Archeological Museum with Etruscan ceramics and Roman sculptures recovered in and around the city. Upstairs the frescoes lining Sala del Pellegrinaio document the building's history and what life was like in a 13th-century hospital. Along the way are four chapels, remnants of the original Fonte Gaia fountain, and modern art exhibits.

Santa Maria della Scala takes several hours to explore. Special tours of the underground aqueducts below the hospital are arranged on the second and fourth Saturday of each month.

PINACOTECA NAZIONALE

Via San Pietro 29, www.pinacotecanazionale. siena.it, Tues.-Sat. 8:15am-7:15pm, Sun. 9am-1pm, €4

Since the 1920s, Palazzo Buonsignori has housed the Pinacoteca Nazionale and a premier collection of Sienese artwork. Most of the paintings date from the 13th to 17th centuries, and the collection presents a clear picture of how art developed in the city over the years. There is an unrivaled quantity of gold-painted canvases, many of which were donated by local churches and convents. Works by Ambrogio and Pietro Lorenzetti, Sassetta, and Beccafumi are all on display. The sculpture room in the second-story loggia has an excellent view of the city.

TERZO DI CAMOLLIA

The Terzo di Camollia district is on the northern edge of the city; although it was rebuilt in recent centuries, many of its medieval monuments have been preserved. Via di Camollia runs through the center of the neighborhood and is the home of churches San Pietro and Santa Maria, completed in 1484. At the end of the road is Porta Camollia, one of the original medieval entrances to the city. Anyone who understands Latin will be able to read the inscription welcoming visitors to Siena.

BASILICA CATERINIANA DI SAN DOMINICO

Piazza San Domenico 1, tel. 05/7728-6848, www.basilicacateriniana.com, Mar.-Oct. 7am-6:30pm and Nov.-Feb. 9am-6pm, free

Dominican monks founded Basilica di San Dominico in 1226. They chose a simple Gothic style and red bricks that were cheaper than marble and compatible with their vows of poverty. The Cathedral is entered from the side and can be reached from a number of directions, the most impressive of which is Via Fontebranda. Inside, the massive single nave interior is decorated with flags representing the 17 *contrada* neighborhoods of the city and frescoes recounting the life of Saint Catherine, who attended mass here regularly. Her severed head is preserved in the Renaissance chapel on the right wall and is occasionally paraded around the city on special occasions.

TERZO DI SAN MARTINO

East of Piazza del Campo is the Terzo di San Martino neighborhood. Via di Città is the main thoroughfare and is flanked by the city's finest palazzi. Palazzo Piccolomini is distinguished by immense blocks of ashlar Rossellino, used to bring a little Florentine style to Siena. Almost directly opposite is the slightly curved Palazzo Chigi-Saracini that now houses a music academy. Farther down on the right is Loggia dei Mercanti, which marked a transition between Gothic and Renaissance architecture when it was added in the 16th century. The street also passes Piazza Salimbeni, enclosed on three sides by three buildings in three different styles. It's a good test for anyone who gets Gothic, Renaissance, and baroque confused.

Piazza Salimbeni

ORTO BOTANICO

Via P. A. Mattioli 4, tel. 05/7723-2875, daily 10am-6pm, €5

Biagio Bartalini liked plants so much he founded the Orto Botanico in 1784. The 2.5-acre botanical garden situated in a small valley near Porta Tufi is divided into three sections. The first contains the most local Tuscan species you'll see in one spot. They include herbs, aromatics, and medicinal varieties that were used by Ospedale di Santa Maria in the 18th century. Aquatic plants, fruit trees, and cacti grow in the other areas and a tepidarium protects vulnerable leaves. The garden is a favorite destination of birds that serenade visitors with song. Serious horticulturists can reserve a tour of the grounds.

✪ MUSEO DELL'ACQUA

Strada delle Fonti di Pescaia 1, tel. 05/7729-2614, www.museoacqua.comune. siena.it, appointment only, €10

Siena has no river, which meant that getting a drink of water was a big problem during the Middle Ages. The 12th-century solution was a 25km (15mi) network of tunnels that carried running water directly to the city. The Museo dell'Acqua ("water museum"), which opened in 2010, reveals how this ingenious system of medieval engineering worked through multimedia displays and a visit of underground passageways. The museum is run by an association of volunteers who organize guided visits by appointment only. Hour-long tours in Italian and English depart at 10am, 11:15am, 4:30pm, and 5:45pm from Thursday to Sunday. The museum is on the northwestern outskirts of the historic center and a 20-minute walk from Piazza del Campo.

Food

Although it's less than 230 kilometers (140 mi) from Rome, Siena feels a lot farther away in gastronomic terms. Here the most popular pasta is *pici,* which resembles thick spaghetti; hearty vegetable *ribbolita* stews are served; and grilled meats are rarely missing from menus. The best places to try such dishes are the rustic *trattorie* scattered around the city. Don't worry if you have trouble choosing one; it's hard to go wrong. Wherever you eat, portions will be generous, and a complete meal rarely exceeds €20.

TUSCAN AND ITALIAN
Castelvecchio

Via Castelvecchio 65, tel. 05/774-7093, daily noon-2:45pm and 7pm-10:45pm, €7-12

Mass tourism may have lowered the standards of some Siena restaurants, but Castelvecchio is not one of them. Simone Romi is attentive to the quality of food he serves and the service he provides both locals and visitors. The menu changes daily and the prix fixe (€25) is a good option if you want to get a wide sampling of Tuscan flavors. It comes with an antipasto, three different pastas, two seconds, and dessert.

✪ Trattoria Papei

Piazza del Mercato 6, tel. 05/7728-0894, daily noon-10:30pm, €8

Historic may be a strange way to describe a *trattoria*, but it's the best way to summarize the traditional Tuscan food and lively atmosphere at Trattoria Papei. They've been cooking almost continually since 1939 and you can taste their savoir faire in every dish. Prices are extremely reasonable and the selection of grilled meats will satisfy any carnivore. There's plenty of seating outdoors and a great house wine to accompany meals.

Osteria la Chiacchera

Costa di Sant'Antonio 4, tel. 05/7728-0631, Wed.-Mon. noon-3pm and 6:30pm-10:30pm, €6-7

Osteria la Chiacchera is a rustic classic with wooden tables, brick vaulted ceilings, and a handwritten menu. A three-course meal here with dessert costs under €25 and will leave you smiling. It's wise to make a reservation in summer and ensure you get a chance to taste the traditional dishes inside this miniscule *osteria*.

Grattacielo

Via dei Pontani 8, tel. 334/631-1458, daily 11:30am-3pm and 7:30pm-10pm, €10

Cravings for cheese and cured meats can strike at any moment in Siena. When they do, Grattacielo (or skyscraper) has a cutting board ready. The *osteria* also prepares one locally inspired dish each night. But perhaps the best thing about this place is the feeling you get walking in the streets afterward realizing how little you paid for such good food.

Grotta di Santa Caterina da Bagoga

Via della Galluzza 26, tel. 05/7728-2208, Tues.-Sun. noon-3pm and 7pm-11pm, Sun. noon-3pm, €10-12

Getting to Grotta di Santa Caterina da Bagoga is half the fun. The labyrinth-like streets leading to the restaurant are some of the most suggestive in the city. The owner is a former *palio* rider and the tables outside provide a unique environment to have lunch or dinner. The cooking is strictly Sienese and offers a wide choice of seasonal dishes. Wine is mainly from the Rufina and local hillsides.

Hosteria il Carroccio

Via di Casato di Sotto 32, tel. 05/774-1165,
Thurs.-Tues. 12:15pm-2:45pm and
7:15pm-9:45pm, €8

Hosteria il Carroccio remains one of the most affordable options around Piazza del Campo. Service may be a little hurried but it's always efficient. Waitstaff dispense with menus in the evening and you may have to ask them to repeat the offerings. Antipasti includes *salumi* and there is generally some variation of wild boar pasta. Good salads are also served.

Antica Trattoria Botteganova

Via Chiantigiana 29, tel. 05/7728-4230,
Tues.-Sat. noon-2:30pm and 7pm-10pm, Sun
noon-2:30pm, €10-14

Antica Trattoria Botteganova is considered one of the best restaurants in Siena. It's outside the city walls on the SS408 in the direction of Montevarchi, but gourmets won't mind the detour. An elegant, rustic interior and refined table settings complement the elaborate fish and meat dishes chef Michele prepares. The three tasting menus (€37-45) are an introduction

pane rustico

to creative Sienese cuisine and should be approached on an empty stomach. Reservations are almost always required on weekends.

PASTRIES

Nannini

Via Banchi di Sopra 22, tel. 05/7723-6009,
daily 7:30am-10pm

Nannini is a popular bar in Siena where locals go for espresso and pastries. The sweets are memorable and gelato fans may end up adding it to their top-10 list.

Pasticceria Bini

Via Stalloreggi 91, tel. 05/7728-0207,
Tues.-Sun. 8:30am-8pm

Pasticceria Bini is a little outside the center but worthy of a pastry pilgrimage. They've been baking all the town's specialties, from *panforte margherita* to *cannoli alla mandorla,* since 1944. The selection is widest in the morning but there's still plenty to sample later in this elegant shop.

Bars and Nightlife

For a small city, Siena has a high proportion of wine bars that are filled from *aperitivo* onward with locals and visitors out for a good time. Most late-night establishments have outdoor seating that quickly spreads to the stone benches and marble steps where university students gather. Drinking is nearly always combined with food, and even the humblest bar provides delicious Tuscan snacks that go marvelously with wine or beer.

WINE BARS

Siena is a wine town with lots of *vinerie* (wine bars), where you can sample regional vintages accompanied by plates of cheese and cold cuts known as *taglieri*. Two of the best are located on the same street five minutes from Piazza del Campo.

Vineria Tirabusciò

Via San Pietro 16, tel. 05/7760-1324, Fri.-Wed. 12pm-10pm

This one-room eatery has a great selection of natural wines listed on a huge blackboard. It's hard to choose, but fortunately, the owners are patient and enjoy sharing their knowledge of viticulture. Wines are available by the glass, quarter-liter carafe, or half-liter carafe, and are easily matched with generous helpings of cured meats and raw milk cheeses. There's no Wi-Fi here for a reason and conversation is encouraged.

Vineria il Murello

Via San Pietro 48, tel. 05/774-0403, daily 10:30am-11pm

Vineria il Murello is a homey drinking spot serving some of the most appetizing *taglieri* in the city. This small, cozy locale, animated by a friendly owner and regulars who periodically pop in, is hard to leave. It's a great place for an afternoon *aperitivo*, and if you can't find space inside there's a stone bench running along the building opposite that becomes an impromptu living room most nights.

BARS

Liberamente Osteria

Piazza del Campo 27, tel. 05/7727-4733, daily 9am-2am

Venues located on monumental squares aren't usually the best place to eat or drink, but Liberamente Osteria is an exception. The fabulous view hasn't deteriorated the quality of the cocktails or raised prices unreasonably. Drinks are served with light snacks and the barman mixes 10 different types of Negroni. Sit at an outdoor table facing the square.

Philadelphia

Via Pantaneto 18, tel. 05/7716-52544, Sat.-Thurs. 5pm-2am and Fri. 11am-2am

Philadelphia is an American-style bar with an animated owner who puts everyone at ease and dispenses tasty

bars and restaurants in Piazza del Campo

cocktails, shots, and a large selection of beers. It's hard not to make friends here, and strangers at the beginning of a night are cheering to each other's health by the end. There's a short but satisfactory list of *taglieri* (cheese and cold cuts served on a wooden platter), good music, and finding somewhere to sit is never a problem.

LIVE MUSIC

Cacio & Pere

Via dei Termini 70, tel. 05/7715-10727, Tues.-Sun 7pm-1am

Cacio & Pere is one of the few bars in Siena with weekly live music and DJ sets. It's popular and crowded with a mix of locals, exchange students, and travelers who fill the small brick-walled interior. Service at the bar can take a while but staff is friendly and happy to improvise cocktails based on any liquor. There's little to no seating depending on the night and drinking is done standing.

Festivals and Events

Festa di San Giuseppe

Lots of saints are celebrated in Siena but it's Festa di San Giuseppe on March 19 that's the most spirited.

Via Dupre in the city center is lined with stalls displaying arts and crafts and selling toys and sweets. Around Piazza del Campo and the church of

the annual Palio horse race

San Giuseppe the intoxicating smell of *frittelle* (fried rice) is hard to resist and outdoor stands remain open until late.

Palio delle Contrade

Twice a year Siena turns back the clock and transforms the Piazza del Campo into a racetrack where thousands cram to watch the *Palio delle Contrade*. For locals the main event is on July 2, while the second race on August 16 is nicknamed the "*palio* of the tourists." Both days begin with a parade around the outer perimeter of the *piazza*, which is covered in sand to prevent horses from slipping. It's best to arrive several hours before the mid-afternoon start. The best places to stand are on the outer edges to the left or right of the fountain from where nearly the entire course can be observed. The race consists of three laps and an anything-goes approach, with the winner carried back to his *contrade* for a victory dinner where the horse is the guest of honor.

Shopping

Via di Città is the main shopping street in Siena and contains clothing, book, food, and craft shops. Most days it's filled with tourists hunting for souvenirs. Don't let that stop you from taking a look and stopping by some of the more interesting addresses.

ANTIQUES

Antichità Monna Agnese

Via di Città 45, tel. 05/7728-2288, daily 10:30am-12:30pm and 2:30pm-7pm

Antiques aren't hard to find in Siena. What is hard to find is a selection as vast as that at Antichità Monna Agnese. The store is a favorite with collectors who appreciate Italian country furnishings and can date objects down to the decade. Novices who can't distinguish between centuries may still find the collection of antique jewelry interesting. Agnese usually participates in the craft and antiques market held on the third Sunday of each month in Piazza Mercato.

CERAMICS AND STAINED GLASS

Ceramiche Artistiche Santa Caterina

Via P.A. Mattioli 12, tel. 05/774-5006, Mon.-Fri. 9am-11am and 4:30pm-6:30pm

Ceramiche Artistiche Santa Caterina is a dusty ceramics workshop down a narrow alley near the Porta Tufi entrance to the city. Marcello Neri and his wife Franca have been behind the pottery wheel for decades, and have mastered the art of ceramics. The Sienese style is recognizable by its exclusive use of black and white, with designs inspired by the Duomo. This is the place to discover how clay gets transformed into marvelous decorative objects and purchase something unique.

Vetrate Artistiche Toscane

Via della Galluzza 5, tel. 05/774-8033, Mon.-Fri. 10am-6pm

Stained glass may not be high on your souvenir list but the artists at Vetrate Artistiche Toscane may change your mind. Their secular and religious creations come in every size and shape and make a nice addition to nearly any wall. The store doubles as a

storefront with ceramics and souvenirs

workshop where craftsmen can often be observed. They also run glassblowing apprentice workshops during the summer.

MARKET
Antica Drogheria Manganelli
Via di Città 71-73, tel. 05/7728-0002
Antica Drogheria Manganelli is what a supermarket looked like a hundred years ago. This one opened in 1879 and carries everything you need to faithfully recreate a Tuscan dinner when you get back home. The pasta is handmade by small producers in the area and some of the vinegar sold is over 80 years old.

Accommodations

HOTELS AND BED-AND-BREAKFASTS
San Francesco
Vicolo degli Orbachi 2, tel. 05/774-6533,
www.bb-sanfrancesco.com, €75-100 s/d
San Francesco is in the Bruco *contrada*, a working-class neighborhood where support for local *palio* riders is intense. The 16 rooms at the B&B are immaculate and equipped with the essentials. There's something homey about the simplicity and the Tuscan greeting that guests receive from owner Massimo Giuliani. He's the best person to ask for shopping, dining, or sightseeing advice. A 30-percent advance deposit may be required depending on the season.

Albergo Cannon d'Oro
Via Montanini 28, tel. 05/774-4321,
www.cannondoro.com, €80-100 s/d
Dante mentions Albergo Cannon d'Oro in his *Purgatory* poem and

that may have something to do with the old set of stairs guests must climb to reach the rooms. If stairs aren't a problem (there are several rooms on the ground floor), this medium-sized hotel at the intersection of a vibrant neighborhood near Piazza Salimbeni is an excellent, no-frills option. Breakfast is included and the friendly staff can provide assistance 24 hours a day.

Antica Residenza Cicogna
Via dei Termini 76, tel. 05/7728-5613,
www.anticaresidenzacicogna.it, €85-100 s/d
The Cicogna family restored a medieval *palazzo* and turned it into an ideally located B&B minutes from Piazza del Campo and Duomo. Each of the five rooms at Antica Residenza Cicogna is decorated in a unique style and benefits from high frescoed ceilings. Breakfast is an opportunity to taste local biscuits and

breads like *cavallucci, copate,* and *panforte.* Fresh fruit and yogurt are also served.

Antica Torre

Via di Fiera Vecchia 7, tel. 05/7722-2255, www.anticatorresiena.it, €90-120 s/d

Antica Torre has preserved the marble paving and cast-iron beds that might have greeted medieval travelers. There are two rooms per floor at this small hotel 10 minutes from Piazza del Campo. The two on the top floor provide rooftop views and a glimpse of the Tuscan countryside in the distance. Breakfast is an additional €7.

Hotel Domus

Via Camporeggio 37, tel. 05/774-4177, www.hotelalmadomus.it, €90-130 d

Hotel Domus is located inside a former sanctuary and management clearly understands the relation between cleanliness and godliness. The modern rooms, however, have little to do with the past and are all equipped with comforts like air-conditioning and LED TVs. Many have balconies with great views of the city.

✪ Palazzo Ravizza

Pian dei Mantellini 34, tel. 05/7728-0462, www.palazzoravizza.it, €120-180 s/d

Palazzo Ravizza is a vintage 30-room *palazzo* that hasn't lost its Renaissance charm. The hotel dates from the 1920s and has been run by the same family in a peaceful *contrade* within walking distance of everything. Modern comforts have been added without sacrificing the building's character and the shaded garden provides a welcome summertime refuge. Parking is available and the international breakfast is a great way to start the day.

Information and Services

Siena Info Point

Piazza del Campo 69, tel. 05/7728-2384, www.sienainfopoint.com, daily 10am-4pm

The Siena Info Point is a good place to start a visit. Pick up a free map or sign up for their one-hour group tours (€15) led by authorized guides. It's an informative introduction to the city that leaves daily from their office at 11am with additional departures at 1pm and 6pm during the summer. If you prefer something private or gastronomic they offer dozens of interesting themed tours.

Siena Tourist Office

Piazza del Duomo 2, tel. 05/7728-0551, www.terresiena.it Mon.-Fri. 10am-7:30pm and Sat.-Sun. 10:30am-6:30pm

There's an official Siena Tourist Office facing the entrance to the Duomo. They offer free maps, basic information, and bathrooms (€0.50).

Transportation

GETTING THERE

TRAIN

Trenitalia (www.trenitalia.it) regional trains leave daily from Santa Maria Novella Station in Florence to Siena. The journey takes 90 minutes and tickets cost €9.10.

The station in Siena is 1.2 miles (2km) north of the city and a 25-30 minute walk from Piazza del Campo. The 3, 4, 7, 8, 10, 17, and 77 **city buses** (www.tiemmespa.it, €1.50) depart from outside the station and take 10 minutes to reach Piazza del Sale near the historic center. **Taxis** (tel. 05/774-9222, www.taxisiena.it) are also waiting outside the station and a ride to the heart of the city is around €10. Prices are higher on weekends and at night.

BUS

SITA (Piazza Gramsci, tel. 05/7720-4246, www.trainspa.it) buses also leave from Florence's train station (Via Luigi Alamanni) and make a dozen stops along the way. A one-way ticket to Siena costs €7.80 and can be purchased online or at the SITA office in the *piazza* outside the station. Buses arrive in Piazza Antonio Gramisci, a short distance from Piazza del Campo.

CAR

The 78-kilometer (50 mi) **Firenze-Siena highway** links Florence to Siena and takes one hour to drive. When arriving from the **A1 highway,** exit at Chiusi for a scenic drive along the N146 or take the following exit at Valdichiana to reach Siena faster.

GETTING AROUND

The historic center of Siena has been pedestrian-friendly since the 1960s and there's no better way of exploring the narrow streets and alleys than on foot. Public buses run through the modern parts of town and there is extra-urban service to many of the surrounding communities that leaves from Piazza Gramsci. A car is useful for reaching destinations further afield and can be rented from **Hertz** (Via Sardegna 14, tel. 05/774-5085, Mon.-Fri. 9am-12:30pm and 3:30pm-7pm, Sat. 9am-12:30pm).

Siena Rent (Via G. Mazzini 77, tel. 05/7705-1919, www.sienarent.com, daily 9am-1pm and 3pm-7pm) near the train station is a local option that is open on Sundays and rents cars and scooters.

Siena also runs a bike-sharing service with 15 stations around the city. The **Bicincittà** app can be downloaded from the Android or iPhone stores. It costs €10 for a 5-hour rental that can be used within 24 hours, or €15 for 10 hours within 48 hours.

TUSCAN HILL TOWNS

Tuscany is full of beautiful land- scapes, but only one has been declared a World Heritage Site by the United Nations Educational, Scientific, and Cultural Organization (UNESCO). The Val d'Orcia starts south of Siena and looks like nothing else in the region. Here, spaces are wider, medieval towns are spread farther apart, and hills resemble an undulating sea of green.

Montalcino, Pienza, and Montepulciano form an impressive trio filled with architecture inspired by Renaissance ambitions and overlooking vineyards, olive groves, and cypress-lined

HIGHLIGHTS

✪ **FORTEZZA DI MONTALCINO:** There are lots of great views in Tuscany, but the one from this fortress in Montalcino stands out, overlooking the Val d'Orcia valley and a patchwork of colorful countryside (page 268).

✪ **ABBAZIA DI SANT'ANTIMO:** This abbey south of Pienza was a center of Benedictine devotion for nearly 1,000 years. The monks have gone, but their spirit has remained (page 268).

✪ **PIAZZA PIO II:** Pienza's harmonious plaza exemplifies Renaissance ideals of proportion (page 274).

✪ **PALAZZO COMUNALE:** This imposing palazzo has a lofty bell tower with an incredible view (page 281).

✪ **CANTINA CONTUCCI:** Montepulciano's oldest winery is the perfect setting for learning about and tasting the town's famous Vino Nobile wine (page 283).

roads that lead to ancient abbeys and hundreds of small wineries. Wine plays a fundamental role in the local economy and the mineral-rich soil, mild climate, and altitude provide the perfect conditions for growing grapes. A glass of red is always nearby, as are tempting trattorias serving *pici* pasta, fortresses to climb, and trails leading into this incredible corner of Tuscany.

PLANNING YOUR TIME

Towns south of Siena aren't easily accessed by bus, and even with a car they take a couple of hours to reach from Florence. There's a lot to see, do, and taste, and a minimum 1-2 nights is necessary to fully savor the area. Note that advance reservations of a day or two are encouraged at most wineries.

The September-October grape harvest is the most interesting season to visit local wineries. Autumn is also when annual *sagra* festivals are held, celebrating local ingredients like chestnuts, olives, and grapes.

You don't have to visit all three towns—settling down in one for a couple of days can be as rewarding as seeing them all. Pienza's position in the middle makes it a good base from which to explore the area or sit back and relax.

ORIENTATION

Montalcino, Pienza, and Montepulciano lie about 20 kilometers (12.4mi) apart from one another on the **SP146** road. They're roughly all on the same latitude, and each was built along narrow ridge tops that have influenced layout and street design. Getting around each town on foot is easy, and main squares are located at the highest points. Each town has parking near the historical center and at least one gas station.

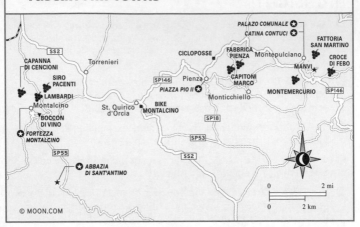

Itinerary Ideas

There's lots to see (and drink) on this itinerary, and you'll pass through some of the most outstanding countryside in Tuscany. Outside of city walls are wineries, convents, and trails ripe for exploring on foot or bike.

Before you take off, make reservations for Tiezzi (covered on Day 1) and an afternoon tour at Montemercurio (covered on Day 2).

DAY 1

Make an early start from Florence to avoid traffic and arrive in Montalcino before lunchtime.

1 When you arrive in Montalcino, settle in for lunch at a simple *osteria,* like Osteria di Porta al Cassero, and pop into the Duomo nearby afterwards.

2 Have an after-lunch espresso, then head south to the Fortezza di Montalcino fortress that once guarded the city and walk along the scenic ramparts.

3 Walk over to Tiezzi winery. Take a tour to get the inside story on Brunello, the local varietal, from a family who has been making it for decades (reservations recommended).

4 Toast good-bye to Montalcino and hit the road to Pienza, 14 miles east along the SP14 and SP146 provincial roads. Follow the pedestrians to Piazza Pio II, and sit down to admire the architectural perfection of this uniquely proportioned square.

Tuscan Hill Towns Itineraries

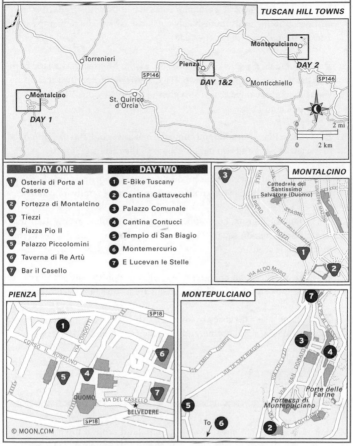

TUSCAN HILL TOWNS

Montepulciano

Torrenieri   Pienza   **DAY 2**

SP146   **DAY 1&2**   Monticchiello   SP146

Montalcino   St. Quirico d'Orcia

DAY 1

0   2 mi

0   2 km

DAY ONE

1. Osteria di Porta al Cassero
2. Fortezza di Montalcino
3. Tiezzi
4. Piazza Pio II
5. Palazzo Piccolomini
6. Taverna di Re Artù
7. Bar il Casello

DAY TWO

1. E-Bike Tuscany
2. Cantina Gattavecchi
3. Palazzo Comunale
4. Cantina Contucci
5. Tempio di San Biagio
6. Montemercurio
7. E Lucevan le Stelle

MONTALCINO

Cattedrale del Santissimo Salvatore (Duomo)

VIALE   SPAGNI   VIALE DELLA LIBERTÀ

STROZZI

VIA ALDO MORO

PIENZA

SP18

CORSO IL ROSELINO   VIA CONDOTTI

DUOMO   VIA DEL CASELLO

★ BELVEDERE

SP18

© MOON.COM

MONTEPULCIANO

VIA DI VOLTAIA NEL CORSO

VIA EMILIO NORD   VIA LE SAN BIAGIO

VIA DELLA ZECCA   VIA SAN DONATO

Porte delle Farine

Fortezza di Montepulciano

To   VIA DEL POLIZIANO

5 When you've had your fill of the buildings surrounding the square, head inside **Palazzo Piccolomini.** Take the audio tour to discover the secrets of this palatial estate and the pope who once lived there.

6 Have a wine-infused meal (or give the local craft beer a try) at the **Taverna di Re Artù**.

7 Make it to the Belvedere lookout before sunset and enjoy an evening cocktail at **Bar il Casello** on the walls overlooking the Val d'Orcia.

DAY 2

1 After waking up in Pienza, join a half-day tour with **E-Bike Tuscany** of the panoramic trails immediately outside of town. The tour stops at an *osteria*, so you've got lunch covered.

2 After lunch, drive 15 kilometers (9mi) east to Montepulciano and park near the southern entrance to town. Have an afternoon *aperitivo* at **Cantina Gattavecchi,** accompanied with a glass of the local wine, Vino Nobile di Montepulciano.

3 Walk to Piazza Grande and climb the bell tower of **Palazzo Comunale** for a view of lakes and two Italian regions in the distance.

4 Visit the oldest wine cellar in town, **Cantina Contucci,** and check out the huge cellars that have been managed by the same family for centuries.

5 Get on the hop-on, hop-off bus run by Montepulciano City Tour that leaves from the main square. Get off at **Tempio di San Biagio,** known for its incredible acoustics.

6 Take an afternoon tour (reserve in advance) at the **Montemercurio** winery south of town. It's a 30-minute walk (or a quick taxi ride) from town.

7 Walk or take a taxi back to town. End the day at **E Lucevan le Stelle** listening to jazz, sipping wine, and enjoying ravioli under the stars.

Montalcino

Montalcino is an enchanting hill town south of Siena surrounded by thick ring walls and protected by a medieval castle. It lies in the stunning Val d'Orcia valley, which is crisscrossed with trails ideal for hikers and cyclists. Unlike most towns, there's no major square or gathering place in Montalcino so socializing takes place along the narrow streets of the center. **Via Guiseppe Mazzino** runs north to south through the center of Montalcino and fills up most afternoons with locals out for a stroll.

The land around town is covered with vines from which the world-famous **Brunello** is produced. Brunello was born in 1888, after Ferruccio Biondi Santi decided to stray from traditional Chianti formulas and exclusively use Sangiovese grapes. Unlike its northern neighbor that's drunk young, Brunello requires a minimum of five years to age, two of which must be in oak casks. Brunello is serious business, and every winery must submit its bottles for inspection before receiving the coveted DOCG (Denomination of

Montalcino

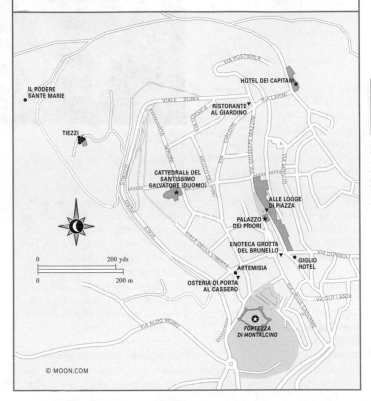

© MOON.COM

Controlled and Guaranteed Origin) label. Rosso di Montalcino is the local alternative to Brunello that can come from different varietals and is only aged one year.

SIGHTS

PALAZZO DEI PRIORI

Costa del Municipio 2, tel. 05/7784-9331, Mon.-Sat. 9am-5:30pm, free

Every medieval Tuscan town was governed by a *priore* (leader) who gathered with local officials and visiting dignitaries in the town's Palazzo dei Priori, which was nearly always located at the center of town. (None was

as grand as the one in Florence, whose name was later changed to Palazzo della Signoria.) Montalcino's version was built in two different eras, which can be distinguished by the color and smoothness of the stone. (Lighter, smoother stone was used during the Renaissance.) It has a small loggia where citizens could meet (and still do), and a bell tower decorated with the coat of arms of Sienese families who once ruled the town. The tower isn't open to the public, but the ground floor of the palazzo, where the tourist office is located, often hosts free exhibitions.

✪ FORTEZZA DI MONTALCINO

Via Ricasoli 54, tel. 05/7784-9211,
daily 9am-8pm, €4

Controlling Montalcino has always been essential for anyone wanting to rule over this part of Tuscany. The town was fortified by Etruscans, Romans, and citizens of the Republic of Siena, who began constructing Fortezza di Montalcino in 1361. They built this pentagonal fortress to last, and it is remarkably well preserved. (The Florentines did eventually succeed to take it, though, with a little help from the House of Hapsburg.) Today, you can walk around the ramparts to get a panoramic view of the Val d'Orcia. Entry is through an *enoteca* (wine bar) in the courtyard that offers tastings and light Tuscan finger food.

CATTEDRALE DEL SANTISSIMO SALVATORE (DUOMO)

Via Spagni 28, free

Cattedrale del Santissimo Salvatore, also known as the **Duomo,** was completed in 1832 to replace an 11th-century church. The atrium, formed by six mammoth columns, is rare in religious architecture and dominates the little square out front. The Latin inscription along the frieze translates to "In nothing else lies salvation." The monumental scale of the church continues inside, with an immense central nave that was large enough to accommodate the entire 19th-century congregation of Montalcino.

✪ ABBAZIA DI SANT'ANTIMO

Localita S. Antimo 222, tel. 075/678-9754,
www.antimo.it, Apr.-Oct., daily, 10am-7pm,
mass 6:30pm and Sun. 11am, Nov.-Mar. daily

Palazzo dei Priori in Montalcino

10:30am-5pm, mass daily 4:30pm and Sun.
11am, €6 with video guide

This medieval abbey is one of the best examples of Romanesque architecture in Tuscany, and although the last Benedictine monks left in 2015, the abbey still has plenty of spirit. You can learn about the medieval chapel, crypt, and monastic pharmacy with the help of a handy video guide. The shop in the former treasury is a useful stop if you want to purchase herbal remedies and beer made according to ancient recipes.

Sant'Antimo is 10 kilometers (6mi) south of Montalcino off the SP55 and takes 15 minutes to reach by car. Paid parking is a short walk away.

WINE BARS

Finding a wine bar in Montalcino is about as hard as locating a slot machine in Vegas: They're everywhere. If

Abbazia di Sant'Antimo

you can't make it to a winery to taste the local wine, Brunello, the best way to understand the difference a year or latitude can make is to visit a wine bar. Personnel are friendly, and generations of tourists have taught them what travelers want. That usually entails a tasting of 3-4 different wines served with a cheese and a cold-cuts platter.

Enoteca Grotta del Brunello

Costa di Piazza Garibaldi 3, tel.
05/7784-7177, daily 9am-7:30pm,
€5-8 tasting fee
Most wine bars in Montalcino are rustic, but if you prefer something cool, head to Grotta del Brunello. The interior is a pleasant mix of old and new, but the most important thing is the wine. There's an exhaustive list of Brunello that's accompanied by salami, cheese, and dips that are as good as those at any restaurant in town. Best of all, the staff takes the time to answer questions and won't get annoyed if you don't know the difference between Brunello and Rosso di Montelcino (it's the aging).

Alle Logge Di Piazza

Piazza del Popolo tel. 05/7784-6186,
daily 7am-12am, €6-9 tasting fee
Alle Logge di Piazza has one of the best locations in town, opposite Palazzo dei Priori and next to the old covered market. It's a favorite *aperitivo* spot with locals, who gather on the outdoor terrace and in the cozy back room. There are dozens of Brunellos to choose from, along with spritz served with light snacks and a menu of more substantial dishes.

WINERIES NEAR MONTALCINO

If you like wine, you've found your heaven in Montalcino. There are dozens of vineyards within sight of

panoramic view of Montalcino

town, many of which are clustered to the north. The tourist office provides useful wine maps that facilitate winery hopping. Most wineries are best reached by car or taxi, but some, like Tiezzi, are a short walk from town. All are within an hour by bike.

Tiezzi

Loc. Soccorso, tel. 05/7784-8187, www.tiezzivini.it, €10 tasting fee

Tiezzi is a hidden gem of a winery located just west of Montalcino (you can walk to it in 10 minutes). It's a family-run business that's been doing things the old-fashioned way since 1870. Enzo Tiezzi is the latest vintner and a wonderful host. He makes Brunello from two separate plots, so you can taste the difference that age and the location of vines make. Tastings should be reserved 1-2 days in advance.

a wine shop in Montalcino

Capanna di Cencioni

Loc. Capanna 333, tel. 05/7784-8298, www.capannamontalcino.com, Mon.-Sat. 9:30am-12:30pm and 2pm-6pm, €15pp

It doesn't get any more picturesque than this medium-size winery on a hillside opposite Montalcino. Davide and Daniele lead informative and fun tours in English from the fermenting room to the cellar, where Brunello is aged in enormous Slovenian oak casks.

Ninety-minute tours starting at 10am and 2pm Monday-Saturday end with a tasting. Reservations are recommended, and accommodations are available (€120-150 d) in their newly built wine *relais* (inn).

Siro Pacenti

Loc. Pelagrilli, tel. 05/7784-8662, www.siropacenti.it, Mon.-Fri. 9am-12pm and 3pm-5pm, €20pp tour and tasting

Soil minerality, altitude, and weather have an effect on wine, and Siro Pacenti seems to have the right combination. It's been making top-10 Brunello lists for decades, and the three labels the winery produces have a flavor profile you won't find anywhere else. A tour helps explain why. It lasts 1.5 hours and ends with a tasting of the latest vintages, served without snacks. Tours are conducted in English weekday mornings and afternoons. You can also show up any time for a glass of wine.

Lambardi

Località Canalicchio di Sotto 8, tel. 05/7784-8476, www.lambardimontalcino.it,

This small winery produced its first 500 bottles of Brunello in 1978, and today it barely gets 12,000 out of the 6.5-hectare vineyard that lies five minutes by car northeast of Montalcino. Grapes are used to make a Brunello, a Rosso di Montalcino, and a refreshing white wine.

FOOD

TUSCAN AND ITALIAN
Ristorante al Giardino

Piazza Cavour 1, tel. 05/7784-8026, Wed.-Mon. noon-3:30pm and 7pm-10:30pm, €9-12

Owner and chef Gianluca Dipirro subscribes to a slow-food philosophy

Sangiovese vineyards outside Montalcino

that he puts into practice every day at Ristorante al Giardino. Pasta and bread are both rigorously made in-house, beef is grass-fed, and traditional recipes are often elaborated with modern cooking techniques. Desserts are a highlight that shouldn't be skipped.

Osteria di Porta al Cassero

Via Ricasoli 32, tel. 05/7784-7196,
Thurs.-Tues. noon-2:30pm and 7pm-9:30pm,
€8-11

This simple, laid-back *osteria,* around the corner from Fortezza di Montalcino, serves large portions of Tuscan comfort food, including rabbit, wild boar (which has a strong meaty flavor and is often stewed or used as the base in ragù), beef tongue, and plenty of pasta. If wild boar doesn't sound appetizing, it's probably because you haven't tried theirs yet. Service is swift and friendly, with lots of chatter among the Italian clientele who make up a healthy majority of the clientele.

Boccon Di Vino

Via Traversa dei Monti 201,
tel. 05/7784-8233, Wed.-Mon. 12:30pm-2pm
and 7:30pm-9:30pm, €13.50-15.50

One of Montalcino's best restaurants, Boccon Di Vino, is located just east of town and comes with an awesome view of the Val d'Orcia valley. Count on traditional Tuscan cuisine and a tasting menu that ensures a memorable meal for €38. Reserve an outdoor table overlooking the valley and let the Brunello do the rest. It's a 20-minute walk on Via Traversa dei Monti or a quick drive.

FESTIVALS AND EVENTS

Visit Tuscany (www.visittuscany.com) provides an updated calendar of wine and food festivals in the area.

WEEKLY MARKET

Every Friday 7am-1pm locals head to Via della Libertà to do their food, clothing, and housewares shopping.

About a dozen vans park along the street a couple of blocks east of the center and set up a great variety of wares. Goods are not always priced, and haggling is common.

Vendemmia

If you really love wine and want to experience how it's made, arrive in Montalcino at the end of September or beginning of October. That's when the grapes are ready and the *vendemmia* (grape harvest) begins. It's the best time to see a winery in action and witness grapes being picked, crushed, and fermented.

RECREATION
CYCLING

There are over 1,000 kilometers (620mi) of off-road trails in the Val d'Orcia that are perfect for mountain biking. This isn't leisurely Sunday cycling, but the sweaty stuff, up and down hills and over gravel and dirt paths, through some of the most scenic countryside in Tuscany. Maps, GPS coordinates, and terrain descriptions can be downloaded from MT Biker (www.themtbbiker.com). You can rent a bike and tackle it yourself or join a tour.

Bike Montalcino

Via Pietro Strozzi, tel. 347/053-5638,
www.bikemontalcino.it, €120 half-day tours
Bike Montalcino leads guided tours past vineyards, hillsides, and castles. Some are half-day trips (€20 per rider, plus bike fee), but many are full-day or multi-day excursions where riders spend the night in *agriturismi* (farmhouses) along the way. Tours never exceed 10 riders and must be reserved in advance. The company also rents mountain bikes (€20 per day) and e-bikes (€40 per day) if you want to head

out on your own. Bike Montalcino provides maps and tips for riders who prefer solo riding.

HIKING
Canali

Distance: *4.5 km (2.8mi)*
Duration: *70-80 minutes*
Starting Point: *Via Lapini*
All roads out of Montalcino lead down and this loop to the west of town has a steady decline of 270 meters (885ft). It starts at the town's northernmost gate and skirts past a pine forest before reaching the valley floor covered in vineyards. There are several wineries along the way that make good impromptu grape stops. Whenever you come to a fork, take the path to the left, which is dusty and half paved with little to no traffic. It eventually leads uphill to the southern entrance of town.

TOURS
Artemisia

Viale della Libertà 12, tel. 05/7784-6021,
www.winetravelsforyou.com, €60-120pp
For wine tours, cooking lessons, or to learn how goat cheese is made, head to Artemisia. The guides here know

exploring the Val d'Orcia by bike

many local winemakers and have access to some of the best cellars in the area. They also organize truffle-hunting tours in nearby forests with specially trained sniffer dogs. Tours are private or small group, and transportation is included.

ACCOMMODATIONS
HOTELS
Hotel dei Capitani
Via Lapini 6, tel. 05/7784-7227,
www.deicapitani.it; €120

A pool with a view and breakfast served on a magnificent terrace are the main draws of Hotel dei Capitani. The building was once used by Sienese patriots fleeing Florentine armies and is decorated with basic utilitarian furniture.

Giglio Hotel
Via Soccorso Saloni 5, tel. 05/7784-6577,
www.gigliohotel.com, €150

Giglio Hotel has re-created a bygone atmosphere in 12 rooms with hand-painted ceramics, cast-iron beds, and pastel-colored walls. The smell of freshly baked bread from the kitchen is the only alarm you'll need and is waiting every morning as soon as you can tear yourself away from the panoramic views out the windows.

AGRITURISMI
✪ Il Podere Sante Marie
Località Santa Maria 298, tel. 05/7784-7081,
www.santemarie.it, €80

A lot of vineyards offer hospitality, but none is as simple and authentic as Il Podere Sante Marie. This little *agriturismo* on the outskirts of town with 2.5 hectares of vines can get you back to nature and give you a hands-on wine experience. There are three rooms, two of which are equipped with kitchenettes and direct access to nature.

The best thing about this place is the owner, Marino, who shares his knowledge of wine with gusto.

INFORMATION AND SERVICES
The tourist office is located inside Palazzo dei Priori and provides free town, regional, and winery maps.

GETTING THERE
CAR
There are several ways to reach Montalcino from Florence by car, but the most direct is the Austostrada Firenze-Siena south to Siena, followed by the SR2 Cassia southeast and Strada Provinciale del Brunello south to Montalcino. The 117-kilometer (73mi) journey takes around two hours on roads that get progressively narrower. Another option is the A1 highway south to the Valdichiana exit and west on the SP63, SP38, and SP14 provincial roads from there. There is a toll on this route.

Paid parking (€1 per hour) is available in two lots on the western side of Montalcino.

PUBLIC TRANSPORTATION
Getting to Montalcino by public transportation is also possible but requires a transfer in either Siena or Buonconvento. Take the train (www.trenitalia.it) from Florence to Siena (€9.30) or Buonconvento (€12.90) and the 114 bus (€3) from either town to Montalcino. The entire journey can take as little as three hours or up to five depending on the train you catch. There are frequent daily departures, and the 114 bus stop is right outside Buonconvento train station. Passengers are dropped off in Via Pietro Strozzi near the entrance to Montalcino's historic center.

GETTING AROUND

Montalcino is small, and some restaurants and nearly all wineries are outside of town. Getting to them is a downhill journey and relatively easy, but returning may require a taxi. You can order one from Taxi Service Montalcino (tel. 347/193-8291, www.taxiservicemontalcino.it). Let them know your destination and ask for the price before agreeing to a pickup.

Pienza

It's always been easy for Italians to be proud of hometowns like Florence, Siena, or Pisa. But if you happened to be from Corsignano (now called Pienza), there wasn't a whole lot to be excited about—until Pope Pio II, that is. In order to provide his birthplace with instant prestige, he commissioned architect Bernardo Rossellino in 1459 to transform a sleepy medieval town into an ideal city. The construction that followed was the first based entirely on the principles of Renaissance urban planning. Piazza Pio II and Palazzo Piccolomini presented a new way of treating public spaces that influenced architects for centuries to come. To complete the transformation, the town was renamed Pienza.

SIGHTS

✪ PIAZZA PIO II

One of architect Rossellino's first alterations to modern-day Pienza was Piazza Pio II. The square gained a new trapezoidal shape covered in a brick herringbone pattern that was divided by marble paving. Proportions are harmonious throughout the plaza, from the height of adjacent buildings to the inlaid marble circle in the middle, which is a good vantage point for observing what modern architecture looked like 500 years ago. Long stone benches along each of the *palazzo* façades are another good spot from which to admire the details of this remarkable square.

PALAZZO PICCOLOMINI

Piazza Pio II, tel. 05/7728-6300, www.palazzopiccolominipienza.it, Tues.-Sun. 10am-6:30 pm; €7 with audio guide

Palazzo Piccolomini, named for Silvio Piccolomini, the pope who financed Pienza's extensive makeover, cost a small fortune to complete. It was built around an internal courtyard and hanging garden that looks out over the Val d'Orcia. This was Pope Pio's summer residence, and he was hosting dinner parties here a mere three years after construction began. Guided audio tours (45 minutes) take visitors through halls that retain their period furnishings and reveal secret passages that facilitated quick getaways. (Most palaces built at the time came equipped with escape routes in case of political upheaval.)

DUOMO

Piazza Pio II, free

Next to the Palazzo Piccolomini stands the Duomo, constructed at the same time and nearly as quickly. The cathedral's façade is divided into three vertical and horizontal sections aligned with the paving in the

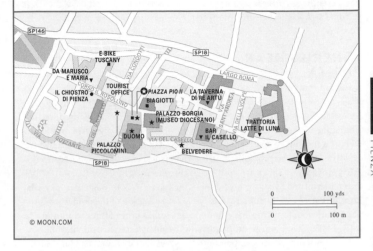

Pienza

piazza. When comparing the medieval church of San Francesco nearby with the Duomo, it becomes clear that times have changed. Inside, the Pope commissioned a post-Gothic style inspired by German trends of the time. The *Assumption* painting by Vecchietta, which depicts the Virgin Mary entering heaven, is the highlight of the interior.

PALAZZO BORGIA
(Museo Diocesano)

Corso Rossellino 30, tel. 05/7874-9905, daily 10:30am-1:30pm and 2:30pm-6pm, €4.50 or €5 ticket with Duomo crypt and labyrinth

Palazzo Borgia, another building that was given a makeover by Rossellino, is more austere than its neighbors facing the square. The building was inhabited by another future pope, and the metal rings along the walls outside are where wealthy medieval visitors parked their horses. Today it houses the Museo Diocesano, which is the best place to see examples of 13th- and 14th-century religious triptych paintings, tapestries, and altar pieces displayed in chronological order.

WINE BAR
La Taverna di Re Artù

Via della Rosa 4, Fri.-Wed. 11:30am-8pm, glasses of wine €5-8

This cozy tavern off Pienza's main street serves a wide selection of local wines by the bottle or glass. Service is informal as are the cheese and charcuterie dishes that come on wooden platters and are accompanied by honey and dipping jams. The bruschetta appetizers are delicious. In addition to wine, the tavern also stocks excellent local craft beer.

BAR
Bar il Casello

Via del Casello 3, tel. 05/7874-9105, Wed.-Mon. 10am-1am, drinks €6

Closing time is early in Pienza and ordering an after-dinner cocktail would be impossible if it weren't for Bar il Casello. During the day, it serves coffee, tea, and iced drinks that taste better when sipped on one of the chairs

275

outside the bar overlooking the valley. Early evening *aperitivo* is a good time to come and watch the sun sink over Tuscany.

WINERIES NEAR PIENZA

Capitoni Marco

Podere Sedime 63, tel. 338/898-1597, www. capitoni.eu, daily 9am-3pm, tastings free

This authentic Tuscan farmstead with 50 hectares of olive groves, vineyards, and woods has been providing hospitality since 1692. Vines are split between Merlot and Sangiovese, and the family that currently runs things is passionate about making wine naturally. Make an appointment to learn what that entails and sample their bottles of Frasi and Capitono whenever you like. Tours (20 minutes, available in English) and tastings are always free at this super-friendly winery.

Fabbrica Pienza

Loc. Borgetto, tel. 05/7881-0030, www.fabbricapienza.com, Mon.-Sat. 10am-5pm, Apr.-Oct., €15-90

Fabbrica Pienza was opened in 2013 by a couple of Swiss expats with a passion for wine. They created a modern winery where attention to design and architecture haven't gotten in the way of making great wine. It's produced organically with Sangiovese and Syrah grapes in a state-of-the-art cellar, where wine lovers are welcome to experience three tours. The Great Classic (€40pp) includes a walk through the vineyards, an explanation of the production process, and a taste of three wines and one olive oil. It lasts 60-70 minutes, must be reserved, and is conducted in Italian, French, or English. Otherwise you can stop by unannounced for the introductory group tour and tasting (€15) that takes 45-50 minutes.

Pienza Duomo

FESTIVAL DELLA VAL D'ORCIA

Every August, Pienza, Montalcino, and several other towns in the region participate in the **Festival della Val d'Orcia** (www.parcodellavaldorcia.com). Depending on the year, themes may focus on theater, music, or dance. What remains constant are the stunning outdoor backdrops. Small stages are set up in each town, allowing for intimate performances that feature opera and classical music. The names of performers aren't well known, but artistic quality is high and the ambiance can't be beat.

FOOD

TUSCAN AND ITALIAN

Trattoria Latte di Luna

Via San Carlo 2, tel. 05/7874-8606,
Wed.-Mon. noon-2pm and 7pm-9pm, €8-12

The two sisters doing the cooking at Trattoria Latte di Luna rely on traditional handmade pasta and ragù that's been simmering since the morning. The wine list includes around 30 labels, and those seated at outdoor tables enjoy the little *piazzetta* all to themselves.

GROCERIES

Da Marusco e Maria

Corso Rossellino 15, tel. 05/7874-8222,
daily 9am-2pm and 2:30pm-8pm, €6-10

It's easy to organize a picnic in Tuscany—Belvedere Walkway is a good place to have one. All the food you need is inside gourmet grocers like Da Marusco e Maria, which has an extensive variety of local pecorino cheeses wrapped in straw and flavored with nuts. They also carry wine, which they'll open for you, and lots of dried sausage. Fresh bread is a few doors down at **Vecchia Dispensa del Corso** (Corso il Rossellino 29).

FESTIVALS AND EVENTS

Mostra Mercato di Piante e Fiori

Pienza is already beautiful, but it becomes enchanting during Mostra Mercato di Piante e Fiori (second weekend in May), when Renaissance designs are re-created with flowers, hedges, and small trees in Piazza Pio II and along Corso il Rossellino.

Gioco del Cacio Fuso

Pienza is famous for its Pecorino cheese. The reputation stems from the aromatic grasses in the area, which produce a uniquely flavored sheep's milk. Gioco del Cacio Fuso occurs on the first Sunday in September and is an opportunity to witness the town celebrate its produce. Craft and culinary stands line the main *piazza* and offer visitors a taste of local gastronomy.

Market

An organic market is held in Piazza Galleti 9am-5pm on the first Sunday of every month March-December. All the products are made within a 50-kilometer (31mi) radius of town. Pecorino cheese, olive oil, and wine are sold, and nearly all the stands provide free samples to tempt buyers.

pecorino goat cheese

RECREATION

WALKING AND HIKING

Belvedere Walkway

Distance: *91 meters (300ft)*

Duration: *10 minutes*

Starting Point: *Piazza Pio II*

Views are a big attraction in Pienza, and one of the best is from the Belvedere walkway on the southern edge of town. There are a few benches, a nice bar (Bar il Casello), and plenty of stunning views of the Val d'Orcia. Sunsets look even better from here. *Belvedere* literally means "beautiful view," and this paved brick pathway is more a place to stop and look out at the countryside than do any serious walking. It's popular with couples and is one of the most romantic spots in town.

CYCLING

A bike is the best way to explore the countryside beyond Pienza. Set off on your own, or hit the trails with an expert guide.

If you prefer to ride solo, take Corso Rossellino east all the way to the end and follow the small red-and-white CAI (Italian Alpine Club) signs down the white dirt trail towards Monticchiello 5.5 kilometers (3.4mi) away. It's an up and down journey with a dislevel of 174 meters suitable for medium and advanced cyclists. You can ride the same way back or take a left at the first farmhouse for a change of scenery.

E-Bike Tuscany

Via della buca 23, tel. 347/881-5780, daily 9am-7:30pm

E-Bike Tuscany rents classic mountain bikes (€25 per day) and e-bikes (€35 per day) with Yamaha and Bosch motors. It also offers tours, which staff can recommend based on your ability. The wine tasting tour starts from

Val d'Orcia outside Pienza

Belvedere panoramic walkway

€85 per person and includes tastings of eight wines, four Pecorino cheeses, and a whole lot of prosciutto. Excursions last 4-5 hours and cover 30-65 kilometers (18.6-37mi). GPS link, safety jacket, helmet, and tool kit are all included.

Cicloposse

Via I Maggio 27, tel. 05/7874-9983,
www.cicloposse.com, Mar.-Oct. daily
8:30 am-1pm and 2:30pm-8pm; €20 for
full day

Hybrid bikes (€30/day), racing bikes (€40/day), and e-bikes (€4/day) are all available at Cicloposse. Whichever you choose, your bike comes equipped with helmet, lock, saddlebag, and mileage counter. Anyone who wants to learn more about the area can join Marco on one of the daylong or weeklong cycling tours the company regularly organizes. Full-day tours to Montalcino and other hill towns range €160-200, including bike rental and van support. A minimum of four riders is required.

SHOPPING
HOME DECOR
Biagiotti

Corso il Rossellino, 67, tel. 05/7874-8478;
www.biagiottipienza.com, Mon.-Sat.
9am-1pm and 3pm-7pm, €30 and up

Hammer, anvil, and fire. That's all they need at Biagiotti to turn out wrought-iron objects of exceptional beauty. There are candelabra, wall-mounted dragons, and beds that recall the town's medieval past and make original souvenirs.

ACCOMMODATIONS
HOTEL
Il Chiostro di Pienza

Corso Rossellino 26, tel. 05/7874-8400,
www.relaisilchiostrodipienza.com,
€150-160 s/d

Il Chiostro di Pienza is a former monastery in the center of town, with large, airy rooms overlooking the valley. Beds are more comfortable than the ones the monks slept in, and the outdoor restaurant is a valid option for lunch or dinner.

BED-AND-BREAKFAST
La Saracina

SS146 km 29,700, tel. 05/7874-8022,
www.lasaracina.it, €230-270 s/d

La Saracina, 8.2 kilometers (5mi) northeast of town off the SS146, is a bed-and-breakfast that feels like an oasis. La Saracina is a restored farmhouse in a picturesque landscape away from anything even remotely stressful. Two rooms and one apartment form the basis of the accommodation that's a favorite with newlyweds. A large swimming pool and a variety of leisure activities help pass the time.

INFORMATION AND SERVICES
Tourist Office

Piazza Pio II; tel. 05/7874-9905;
daily 10am-1pm and 3pm-7pm

The tourist office is located inside Museo Diocesano. It provides maps and a monthly event calendar. Staff also arranges tours and can help visitors find accommodations.

GETTING THERE

CAR

Pienza is 23 kilometers (14mi) east of Montalcino along the SP14 and SP146 provincial roads. Drivers can arrive directly from Florence via the Cassia or A1 highway by exiting at Bettolle or Chiusi. There is one large parking lot (€1/hour) a few hundred meters north of the historic center. Yellow lines indicate resident-only parking, blue is paid parking, and white is free.

PUBLIC TRANSPORTATION

The easiest way to Pienza from Florence is by bus. The **Tiemme** (www.tiemmespa.it) B23 leaves hourly from the *autostazione* (bus station) next to SMN station and arrives in Buonconvento, from where you'll need

to transfer to the 112 to Pienza. The entire journey takes 3 hours and costs €14. Passengers are dropped off within walking distance of the town center. The closest train station to Pienza is Chiusi-Chianciano Terme. The journey from Florence takes 1.75 hours and tickets cost €13.80. Next you'll need to catch a Tiemme bus to Montepulciano and transfer there to Pienza. This part of the journey takes another 2 hours and tickets are €7.

GETTING AROUND

There aren't many taxis in Pienza, and **Il Postalino** (tel. 335/542-4668, www.ilpostalino.com) has a virtual monopoly. If you need a ride to a winery, don't wait until the last minute or taxis will be busy driving someone else around.

Montepulciano

Montepulciano is an enchanting Tuscan town overlooking the Valdichiana and Val d'Orcia valleys. It has Etruscan and Roman roots, and wine has played a vital role in the town's development since the Middle Ages. Florence and Siena fought for control of the area, and when the Medici eventually triumphed in the 16th century, they began an aesthetic overhaul that transformed Piazza Grande into a Renaissance showcase. Today, the imposing ring walls and narrow streets are filled with dozens of wine bars and rustic cantinas where Montepulciano wine in all its variations is aged and served.

Most of the wineries around Montepulciano produce **Vino Nobile di Montepulciano,** a strong, fruity red wine that is strictly regulated and

requires 70 percent Sangiovese grapes. Nobile must also be aged at least two years. Aging may take place entirely in wooden casks or in a combination of wood, glass, and other receptacles. Getting the right profile is an art that has been practiced in these parts for centuries. The tremendous variety of soil types around Montepulciano and the different approaches to winemaking mean that no two wineries will produce a Vino Nobile that tastes exactly the same. Visiting a couple of vineyards is the best way to understand this unique wine.

SIGHTS

Piazza Grande

The town's main square, located at the summit of Montepulciano, was transformed many times over the centuries,

Montepulciano

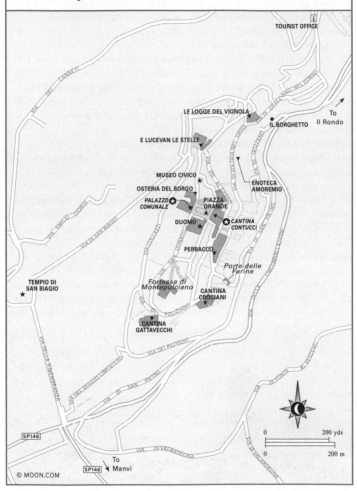

but the size and the buildings facing the large square today would be familiar to 15th- and 16th-century eyes. Nothing is very uniform here, including the stone pavement that varies in color, texture, and shape. Around the square are the most important buildings in town, including the **Duomo**, **Palazzo Comunale**, **Palazzo Contucci**, and Palazzo del Capitano.

The **Pozzo dei Griffi e dei Leoni** well, opposite the Duomo, is one of the oldest parts of the square and decorated with the coat of arms of the Medici, who ruled over Montepulciano.

✪ Palazzo Comunale
Piazza Grande 1, tel. 05/787-121

Palazzo Comunale was built in the 13th century and given a façade lift in the 15th by the pioneer Renaissance architect Michelozzi. If it looks remarkably similar to Palazzo della Signora in Florence, that's because Cosimo de'Medici wanted it that way. The inner courtyard has an elegant double loggia and well, but the most impressive feature is the view from the imposing bell tower. On a clear day, you can see all the way to the Sibillini Mountains in Le Marche and the Gran Sasso in Abruzzo. It costs €5 to climb and is particularly steep, so use the handrails and avoid stopping for selfies until you get to the top.

Duomo

Piazza Grande, tel. 05/787-1951

The Duomo was completed in 1680, although the brick façade looks like someone forgot to finish the job. The modern-looking bell tower to the right was actually built in the 14th century and is the only remaining part of the church that preceded the Duomo. The interior is similar to many Florentine churches in its austerity and understatement. The Latin cross layout is divided into three naves supported by massive columns. There are few artworks other than the triptych painting *Assumption of the Virgin* by Taddeo di Bartolo. If you've had your fill of naves, you can skip this one.

Museo Civico

Via Ricci 10, tel. 05/7871-7300, Apr.-Oct. Wed.-Mon. 10am-7pm, Nov.-Mar. Sat.-Sun. 10am-6pm, €6

There's so much art in Tuscany that even small towns like Montepulciano have collections worthy of much larger institutions. The Museo Civico is a mini-Uffizi both in atmosphere and the quality of its collection, which spans centuries. You can start in the 14th century and gaze all the way through to the 18th

Montepulciano

on masters such as Luca Signorelli, il Sodoma, Domenico Beccafumi, and Michelangelo da Caravaggio. The museum puts on regular temporary exhibitions, and a section is devoted to archaeological and terra-cotta finds. Guided tours in English are available upon request online.

Tempio di San Biagio

Tempio di San Biagio
Via di S. Biagio 14, tel. 05/7875-7290,
€3.50 with audio guide
This magnificent church on the south-western outskirts of town is located on the site where a vision of the Virgin Mary reportedly materialized in 1517. Devout locals laid the foundation the following year. The interior is organized around a Greek cross plan and has an impressive dome that allows for incredible acoustics. (Just try clapping your hands underneath and see what happens.) The audio guide does a good job explaining this masterpiece of religious architecture, which includes a semi-detached bell tower.

Walking to the church from Piazza Grande takes around 10 minutes and there's a little shop, Vino Nobile (Via di San Biagio), selling wine and snacks opposite. If you're in the mood for a picnic, this is a perfect setting, and there's plenty of seating around the church.

WINE CELLARS AND WINE BARS
Montepulciano has one of the highest concentrations of wine bars and cellars in Tuscany, giving you an opportunity to drink the best and get to know first-hand about the town's trademark wine, Vino Nobile di Montepulciano, a dry red wine with an intense aftertaste.

Knowing the difference between a *cantina* and *enoteca*, however, is essential. The first produces a small selection of wine from local vineyards that's stored in a cellar, which can usually be visited. Many offer free tastings and there's often a shop onsite where bottles can be purchased. An *enoteca* is a wine shop/bar that sells many different types of wine primarily from Montepulciano but also Tuscany and other Italian regions. Food is usually available and the shops generally stay open longer than *cantinas* do. There's no shortage of either in Montepulciano, and finding your favorite is what a visit here is all about.

CANTINAS
✪ Cantina Contucci
Piazza Grande 13, tel. 05/7875-7006,
www.contucci.it, daily 10am-6:30pm,
enoteca daily 11am-7pm, free
Cantina Contucci goes back 1,000 years and is the oldest winemaker in Montepulciano. Forty-one generations of the same family have harvested grapes here, and although their *cantina* is now a regular tourist stop, it's no less worth a visit. Inside are three floors devoted to the history of Vino Nobile, the locally produced wine, where you can roam around for free. The *palazzo* is still used to store wine and is filled with giant oak barrels and thousands of bottles aging along brick corridors that remain chilly even in summer.

On the top floor there's also a great view of town. Two glasses of wine are on the house, and you can sample all the labels for free as long as you make a purchase. Most bottles cost €8-15.

Cantina Crociani

Via del Poliziano 15, tel. 05/7875-7919,
www.crociani.it, daily 10am-1pm and
3pm-7pm, free

Something about wine seems to make people in the sector friendly, and Susanna Crociani is no exception. She enjoys sharing the particulars of her ancient *cantina*, which cultivates 16 hectares of vines and olive groves outside of town. The brick vaulted ceilings and long underground corridors make drinking wine here even more enjoyable. You can taste the same wine from different years along with their aromatic oil, which is available at the adjacent shop. Tastings are accompanied by light snacks.

Cantina Gattavecchi

Via di Collazzi, 74, tel. 05/7875-7110, summer
daily 11am-6pm, winter daily 11am-1pm and
3pm-5pm, free cellar visit, €5 tasting

Eat, drink, learn. You can do it all at this quaint *cantina* located in a former monastery on the southern tip of town. The wine is stored downstairs in large oak casts that the owners proudly show off. After viewing, you're likely to be thirsty. Fortunately, there's no shortage of wine, and you can sit at the wooden tables inside or out to enjoy a tasting of three local wines or a full meal (€10-14) of *pici* with ragù, enormous antipasto platters, and rosemary-flavored steaks.

ENOTECHE

Perbacco

Via del Teatro 19, Perbecco,
tel. 05/7871-6743, Wed.-Sun. 11am-8pm,
€4-10 tasting

Perbacco is a modern, informal *enoteca* with an elegant brick and wood-beamed interior. The wine here comes from just about everywhere. The people serving it know their vintages and are a great source of recommendations if you have something particular in mind. Charcuterie, cheeses, and light appetizers are offered with a great selection of daily wine specials served by the glass.

Enoteca Amoremio

Via di Voltaia nel Corso 39,
tel. 05/7879-9337, Tues.-Sun. 11am-7pm

Located along one of Montepulciano's main streets, Amoremio is a modern *enoteca* serving biological wines produced in its nearby winery. You can taste the difference the lack of pesticides makes while you sit out on a lovely back terrace with gorgeous views. The €20 tasting includes three wines, cheese, cold cuts, and lots of viniculture. Visits of the winery are also possible and include a walk through the vineyards led by owner Maurizio Comitini.

Vino Nobile wine

WINERIES NEAR MONTEPULCIANO

Montemercurio

Via di Totona 25, tel. 05/7871-6610, www.montemercurio.com, Mon.-Fri. 9am-6pm, tasting €15

Anyone can drop by this small, family-run vineyard to learn about the sustainable methods they use to produce award-winning wine. Informative and fun tastings are conducted by a sommelier who speaks English. Visits start with a 30-minute tour of the *cantina* and vineyards and end with the sampling of their latest creations, including three reds, two whites, a rosé, a dessert wine, and a *grappa*. Tastings can be reserved with Irene Lesti and are free to anyone who buys over €100 worth of wine.

Manvi

Via Villa Bianca 13, tel. 392/746-4727, Mon.-Sat. 9am-5pm, tasting €15

There are a lot of boutique vineyards scattered around Montepulciano in only a handful of hectares that manage to produce great wine. Manvi is one of them, but it's the husband and wife team from India that makes coming here so special. You get a lot more than a glass of wine. You get a warm welcome, plus the opportunity to see firsthand how their full-bodied Vino Nobile is produced, aged, and bottled.

Croce di Febo

Via di Fontellelera 19/A, tel. 340/2811-972, www.crocedifebo.com, Apr-Oct. Tues.-Sun. 11:30am-7:30pm, tasting €15-35

Visits to Croce di Febo last around two hours and include a walk through the vineyards, a tour of the production facilities, and a taste of the three wines produced by the winery accompanied by locally sourced snacks in their lovely cantina. Reservations

are required for tours conducted in English and the light lunch option, but you can stop by anytime to sample a glass or purchase bottles from this winery 7 kilometers (4mi) outside of Montepulciano. If you can't make it here, the owners also run the **Enoteca Amoremio** (Via di Voltaia nel Corso 39, tel. 05/7879-9337, Tues.-Sun. 11am-7pm) in town.

FOOD

There's no shortage of thick *pici* pasta covered in wild boar ragù, fresh *panzanella* summer salads, locally bred pork, and thick beefsteaks from Tuscan Chianina cattle in Montepulciano. Lots of restaurants have terraces looking out over gorgeous countryside, and they all serve the local wine, Vino Nobile di Montepulciano.

TUSCAN AND ITALIAN

E Lucevan le Stelle

Piazza San Francesco 5; tel. 05/7875-8725, daily noon-11pm, €7-12

If you imagined sunsets overlooking the Val d'Orcia with a glass of Vino Nobile in your hand, you probably already know about E Lucevan le Stelle. The terrace is a pleasant place to relax after a day of Tuscan exploration, and the interior is equally intriguing, with its oversized doors and archway framing a modern lounge where jazz quartets often perform.

Le Logge del Vignola

Via delle Erbe 6, tel. 05/7871-7290, Wed.-Mon. 12:30pm-2:30pm and 7:30pm-10:30 pm, €10-15

Situated in the highest part of town, Le Logge del Vignola provides 10 finely set tables in elegant surroundings. Dishes balance a respect for tradition and innovation that are most notable in the first courses. *Pici* pasta is made fresh and served with tripe and beans. Seconds include thick Fiorentina steaks and glazed lamb chops. The wine list consists primarily of local labels, and different-size carafes are available for anyone intimidated by an entire bottle.

Osteria del Borgo

Via Ricci 5, tel. 05/7871-6799,
daily Apr.-Oct. and Wed.-Mon. Nov.-Mar.,
noon-3:30pm and 7pm-10pm, €8.50-€12

Just off Montepulciano's main square, Osteria del Borgo provides rustic indoor and shaded outdoor seating on a small terrace with countryside views. Traditional Tuscan dishes are a mainstay of the menu, which features delicious cheese appetizers and three versions of *pici* pasta. Desserts are all homemade, and the restaurant's version of cheesecake may be better than the one back home. Reservations are a must during the summer high season.

FESTIVALS AND EVENTS

Cantiere Internazionale d'Arte di Montepulciano

Palazzo del Capitano, Piazza Grande 7,
tel. 05/7875-7089, www.fondazionecantiere.
it, July-Aug.

Cantiere Internazionale d'Arte di Montepulciano was conceived in 1976 as a way for professional musicians, dancers, and actors to interact with students, fans, and anyone who enjoys singing in the shower. The goal is to create a collective performance where everyone takes part. Many locals participate, and the result of this original collaboration is performed throughout July and August. Even passing visitors are encouraged to lend their voices. Events are held in Palazzo Comunale and several other palazzi around town.

Bravio delle Botti

The rolling of the casks, or Bravio delle Botti, is a daylong event on the last Sunday in August. The casks weigh 80 kilograms (176lbs) and are pushed uphill through the streets of Montepulciano by teams representing the neighborhoods in town. A historic parade starts at 4pm and the race itself begins at 7pm from Colonna del Marzocco. The finish line is in Piazza Grande, where the winning team receives a prized banner that's been contested for 600 years.

RECREATION

TOURS

Montepulciano City Tour

www.montepulcianocitytour.it, tel.
329/781-5381, daily Apr.-Nov. 10am-7pm,
€8 per adult or €24 for a family of four

Montepulciano City Tour provides convenient visits to the historic center aboard electric minibuses. Rides last 40 minutes and cover 65 sights that are highlighted by an audio/video guide. It's a pleasant way to get a quick overview of town before or after exploring on foot. Tickets are available online or directly on board. The same company also operates three open-top bus tours of the surrounding region (www.valdichianagrantour.it), with hop-on, hop-off options that make it possible to visit four different towns in a single day. This is a great option for travelers without a car and should be reserved in advance in summer.

ACCOMMODATIONS

HOTELS

Il Borghetto

Via Borgo Buio 7, tel. 05/7875-7535,
www.ilborghetto.it, €105-120 s/d

Elena Trovati knows how to make guests feel at home, and her small hotel on the ramparts of town

the view from Montepulciano

overlooking the lakes of Val di Chiana is a good place to start the day. Il Borghetto is well located for visiting Montepulciano, and adjacent parking makes it easy to head off on excursions. Ask for a room with a view.

Il Rondo

Via di Martiena 9, tel. 05/7871-6899, www.albergoilrondo.com, €125-135 d

The pastel-colored rooms of Il Rondo lie 500 meters (1,640ft) from the entrance to town in a peaceful villa steeped in 18th-century décor. There's plenty of parking out front and a reliable Wi-Fi connection.

AGRITURISMO
✪ Fattoria San Martino

Via Martiena 3, San Martin, tel. 05/7871-7463, www.fattoriasanmartino.it, €180-220 d

Fattoria San Martino takes ecology to the next level. The *bioturismo* (biological accommodation) on the outskirts of Montepulciano has a recharging station for electric vehicles, serves breakfast with ingredients grown on the farm, and runs a charming organic restaurant. Water is heated using solar power and wood, and beds have non-allergenic king-size mattresses. The four suites are large and decorated in a handcrafted, shabby-chic style that goes well with the country surroundings. The chemical-free bio-pond is an innovative compromise between man and nature, and of course the owners encourage use of the bus that stops nearby. Bikes are also available, along with vegetarian cooking and natural-dyeing classes.

INFORMATION AND SERVICES
Tourist Office

Piazza Minzoni, tel. 05/7875-7341, www.prolocomontepulciano.it and www.montepulcianoliving.it, Mon.-Sat. 9am-1pm and 3pm-7pm, Sun. 9am-1pm

The tourist office is located outside the walls in a parking lot near the northern entrance to town. They've got maps, event info, postcards, and

Montepulciano gadgets such as key chains, magnets, and mugs for sale.

Strada del Vino Nobile

Piazza Grande 7, tel. 05/7871-7484, www.stradavinonobile.it, Mon.-Sat. 9:30am-1:30pm and 2:30pm-6pm, Sun. 10am-1pm

Strada del Vino Nobile is a separate association from the tourist office promoting the Valdichiana territory of southern Tuscany. It's the place to sign up for daily guided walks, bike rides, and minibus tours of local towns, spas, and wineries.

GETTING THERE

CAR

The fastest way to Montepulciano from Florence by car is south on the A1 highway. Get off at the Valdichiana exit (€6.20) and continue west along the SP327, SP135, and SP17 provincial roads. The town is well indicated, and the 110-kilometer (68mi) journey can be completed in 90 minutes. Alternatively, you can drive to Siena and follow the Raccordo Siena Bettolle from there. Both options are mostly on two-lane roads, but the latter is free and is just 30 minutes longer. Montepulciano is 14 kilometers (8.7mi) from Pienza and a 20-minute drive on the SP146 provincial road.

There are a dozen paid (blue lines) and free (white lines) parking lots scattered around town, as well as free parking on an unpaved road on the southwestern edge of town. It's a short hike from there to Piazza Grande. Meters are paid at the designated machines using coins or credit cards.

GETTING AROUND

Montepulciano doesn't have a regular taxi service, but rather private chauffeurs who shuttle visitors around wineries and to nearby towns. They get very busy in summer, when finding a last-minute ride is nearly impossible. If you need to get somewhere, reserve in advance with Tuscany Transfer (www.tuscanytransfer.it, 24/7) or Umberto Benigni (tel. 05/783-0427), who operates from the nearby town of Chiancano.

ESSENTIALS

Getting There

Although there is a small airport, Florence is easily accessible by train from other parts of Italy.

AIR

The airport in Florence is small, so travelers from outside Europe may find it easier to fly to Rome (Aeroporto di Roma-Fiumicino, FCO), then taking a train to Florence (90 minutes).

AIRPORTS
Aeroporto di Firenze-Peretola

FLR, Via del Termine 11, tel. 055/30615, www.aeroporto.firenze.it

Florence's Aeroporto di Firenze-Peretola has no direct flights to the United States (although planned renovations may open the airport to intercontinental routes in the future). Delays and cancellations due to inclement weather are common.

Aeroporto di Pisa-San Giusto

Piazzale D'Ascanio 1, tel. 050/849-111, www.pisa-airport.com

Tuscany's busiest airport, Aeroporto di Pisa-San Giusto in Pisa, is less than an hour and a half away from Florence by bus, train, or car. There are direct flights from JFK to Pisa during the summer.

AIRLINES
Flying From North America

There are no direct flights to Florence and only one seasonal flight to Pisa.

Flying from Europe

There are direct flights between London Gatwick and Florence with BA (www.britishairways.com) and many more connecting flights from London, Paris, and Amsterdam with Air France (www.airfrance.com), Lufthansa (www.lufthansa.com), and KLM (www.klm.com). Low-cost airlines like Vueling (www.vueling.com), Ryanair (www.ryanair.com), and EasyJet (www.easyjet.com) also fly to Florence from many European capitals. Aer Lingus (www.aerlingus.com) operates flights from Dublin airport, which is equipped with a U.S. immigration office. Passengers are screened in Ireland and bypass customs when returning to the United States. Alitalia offers three daily departures between Rome and Florence.

Flying from Australia and New Zealand

Getting to Italy from down under is a long journey. Quantas (www.qantas.com), Emirates (www.emirates.com), and Etihad (www.etihad.com) operate daily departures from Sydney, Melbourne, and Perth. Most flights require a transfer in Dubai or Abu Dhabi and total travel time is around 22 hours. China Southern (www.csair.com) is often the cheapest option but requires one or two stops in China and can take up to 40 hours. Travelers from Aukland can transfer in Australia with the above airlines or fly Qatar (www.qatarairways.com), Korean Air (www.koreanair.com), and Emirates on single-stop flights with transfers in Hamad, Seoul, or Dubai.

TRAIN

European train networks are well integrated but getting between countries by rail can still take a long time. Single tickets can be purchased through www.trenitalia.it; if you are on a European vacation and visiting many countries, purchase a rail pass from Eurail (www.eurail.com) or Rail Europe (www.raileurope.com).

Getting to Florence from the other major cities in Italy (Rome and Venice) is fast, easy, and convenient. There are two operators. The state-owned Trenitalia (www.trenitalia.com) and private Italo (www.italo.it) both provide frequent daily departures. The Trenitalia Frecciarossa (red arrow) service is slightly more expensive but operates more trains, making it popular with business travelers; tourists generally prefer Italo, which sends a monthly newsletter with discount codes. Both companies use the same track and leave from the same stations.

Italian high-speed trains are modern, clean, and equipped with Wi-Fi, electrical outlets, leather upholstery, snack machines, and bar cars. Tickets can be purchased online or at train stations from automated machines or service booths. The Italo website is easier to navigate and if you sign up for the newsletter you'll receive advantageous offers every month. There are several levels of comfort on board but even standard seating is adequate.

High-speed trains depart from Santa Maria Novella train station.

CAR

The **Schengen Agreement** removed border controls between members of the European Union and made travel hassle-free. The ongoing immigration crisis, however, has led some governments to reinstate checks. Entering Italy from France, Switzerland, Austria, or Slovenia isn't a problem, but leaving Italy can be trickier as border officials check incoming vehicles.

Getting Around

Depending on the destination, driving or taking a train are generally the best ways to travel between towns in Tuscany. Once you've arrived, most towns are easily navigated on foot or bicycle. Even the smallest towns have paid parking lots located close to the town center.

DRIVING

Italy's **highways** (*autostrade*) are generally very good. Drivers collect tickets at booths as they enter the network and pay tolls in cash or credit, based on distance traveled, upon exiting highways. **Autostrade** (www. autostrade.it) manages highways and provides real-time traffic information in English. Signage should be familiar to drivers from around the world; however, there's a much greater use of **yield**, and **roundabouts** are frequent in urban areas. To review the rules of the Italian road, visit the **Italian Office of Tourism** (www.italia.com).

The **minimum driving age** in Italy is 18. Police and Carabinieri frequently set up control posts along roads and randomly stop cars. The **blood alcohol limit** in Italy is 0.5, which is lower than in the U.S. and U.K. (both 0.8) but on par with most European nations.

Driving in Tuscany isn't as hard as you might imagine. Tuscan drivers generally drive slow and obey the rules of the road, which are more or less the same as they are throughout continental Europe. Still it's wise to get the maximum insurance when renting a car and remain on the defensive. Filling up gas is slightly different than it is back home and the prevalence of diesel can be confusing, but most stations have attendants who can assist drivers.

Car Rentals

You'll need a **passport** and a **driver's license** if you plan on renting a moped or car. (Specify automatic transmission if you're unfamiliar with manual.) An **international driver's permit** is not required but can avoid confusion if you're pulled over. It's available from AAA (www.aaa.com) for $20.

Cars can be rented from Europcar (www.europcar.com), Sixt (www.sixt.com), Maggiore (www.maggiore.com), Hertz (www.hertz.com), and other companies upon arrival at the airport in Florence or from rental offices located near the Santa Maria Novella train station. The latter option is more practical, as parking can be difficult to find and much of the historic center in Florence is a limited traffic zone (ZTL). The ZTL is only accessible to residents, although drivers renting cars within the zone are exempt.

Skyscanner (www.skyscanner) and Kayak (www.kayak.com) can help find the best rental prices. Always get the maximum insurance. Anything can happen on Italian roads, and if you observe cars carefully you'll notice a high percentage of dents. Florence has less traffic and more considerate drivers than, say, Rome. Many streets are partially pedestrianized and it's easy to find a spot on the outskirts and walk or ride a bus to the center.

Car Sharing

Car2Go (www.car2go.com) and Enjoy (www.enjoy.eni.com) are the two largest car-sharing services in Italy. Both are easy to use and provide access to hundreds of vehicles throughout central Florence. Registration is online and requires a passport, driver's license, and international permit. Once the app is downloaded you can locate and use cars for as little or as long as you like. You're also exempt from parking fees and don't pay for gas. It's a practical way of getting around and costs less than a taxi. Car2Go operates a fleet of white two- and four-seat Smart cars while Enjoy uses red FIAT 500s that seat four.

a Tuscan road

The cost of Enjoy is €0.25 per minute up to a maximum of €50 per day while Car2Go is €0.29 per minute and €59 per day. Cars can leave the zones in the city where they are found but must be returned to these zones once you're finished driving them.

You can avoid driving yourself with Bla Bla Car (www.blablacar.it), which connects passengers with drivers traveling throughout Italy. Prices range €15-30 depending on distance. Some Italian is necessary for navigating the website.

TRAIN

Trenitalia (www.trenitalia.it) operates all commuter, regional, and intercity trains throughout Italy. Tickets are inexpensive, and train interiors have a romantic wear and tear about them. Tickets can be reserved in advance, but frequent service makes it as easy to purchase at the time of departure. Stations in Florence, Pistoia, Luca, Pisa, and Siena are equipped with easy-to-use touch-screen kiosks in multiple languages including English.

BUS

Buses are an inexpensive alternative to trains or cars. Flixbus (www.flixbus.com) runs daily service from Florence (Villa Costanza) to Lucca, Pisa, and Siena, while Tiemme (www.tiemmespa.it) serves Siena, Chianti, and many Tuscan hill towns. One-way tickets rarely exceed €15 and depots are located near train stations or the center of town. Most intercity buses leave from Stazione Santa Maria Novella or the Autostazione in Florence. There are stops along the way, and travel is around twice as long as train service.

BICYCLE

Tuscany is one of several bike-friendly regions in Italy, and all the major cities are suitable for cycling. Rental companies usually offer hourly, half-day, and full-day rates, and provide a range of bikes including electric models useful on longer excursions. Most commuter trains have a space dedicated to cyclists and there is a small additional fee for transporting bikes.

The area south of Florence is hilly with many offroad trails that are ideal for mountain bike enthusiasts. Cycling here is one of the best ways to experience nature. A number of companies specialize in cycling tours and many tourist offices provide detailed maps with local bike routes. Riding on backroads is also very common, and although emergency lanes are often nonexistent, Tuscan drivers drive slowly and are generally respectful of cyclists.

HISTORICAL TIMELINE

753 BC: Rome founded by legendary twin brothers Romulus and Remus.

509 BC: Roman Republic established after Etruscan rulers expelled from the city.

146 BC: Rome defeats Carthage in Third Punic War and gains hegemony over the Mediterranean.

44 BC: Julius Caesar assassinated, putting a definitive end to the Republic.

27 BC: Augustus becomes first Roman emperor.

AD 312: Constantine becomes first emperor to convert to Christianity.

410: Visigoths led by King Alaric sack Rome and mark the decline of the Empire.

1320: Dante completes the *Divine Comedy,* which spreads Tuscan Italian and standardizes language around the peninsula.

1397: Medicis open bank in Florence, eventually becoming the largest and most powerful in Europe.

1401: Ghiberti and Brunelleschi compete to build baptistery doors in Florence, marking unofficial start of the Renaissance.

1436: Duomo in Florence is completed.

1504: Michelangelo unveils statue of *David.*

1861: Italian city-states and regions unify into a single nation governed by a constitutional monarchy.

1884: Espresso machine invented in Turin.

1922: Mussolini marches on Rome and takes political control of Italy.

1944: American and Allied troops liberate Rome from German forces.

1946: Italians choose to become a republic in national referendum.

1955: FIAT manufactures the model 600 car and postwar economic recovery accelerates.

1960: Federico Fellini releases *La Dolce Vita.*

1982: Italy wins World Cup.

1994: Berlusconi elected Prime Minister.

2006: Italy wins fourth World Cup in overtime shootout against France.

2018: 5 Star anti-establishment movement gains parliamentary majority.

Visas and Officialdom

PASSPORTS AND VISAS

United States and Canada

Travelers from the United States and Canada do not need a visa to enter Italy for visits of 90 days or less. All that's required is a passport valid at least three months after your intended departure from the European Union.

European Union/Schengen

Citizens from all 28 countries belonging to the European Union can travel visa-free within the European Union. The United Kingdom will remain a full member of the European Union until its exit is officialized. How that will affect travel in the future is unclear at the moment; however, the matter should be resolved in 2019.

Australia and New Zealand

Visas are not required for Australian or New Zealand citizens visiting Italy for 90 days within any 180-day period in the Schengen Area (European Union). New Zealanders between 18-30 can apply for a special working holiday visa at the Italian Embassy in Wellington.

South Africa

Visas are required to visit Italy and can be obtained through Capago (tel. 087/231-0313, www.capago.eu). The application process begins online and requires stopping into one of the visa application centers located in Cape Town, Durban, Sandton, and Pretoria. Getting a visa takes two weeks and there is a fee.

EMBASSIES AND CONSULATES

Lost or stolen passports can be replaced at the consulate (Lungarno A. Vespucci 38, 055/266-951, 9am-12:30pm) in Florence. Proof of citizenship and a photo ID are required. Replacements are issued on the spot and cost €135. Citizens with after-hours problems can contact the embassy at any time by calling 055/266-951. The embassy and consulates are closed during Italian and U.S. holidays. For bureaucratic questions before arriving to Italy call the U.S. Department of State (tel. 1-888/407-4747 from the United States or 1-202/501-4444 from any other country, Mon.-Fri. 8am-8pm EST).

There are no embassies for the UK, Canada, Australia, or South Africa in Florence. The British Embassy (Via XX Settembre 80a, tel. 06/4220-0001, www.gov.uk) in Rome provides consular services by appointment only. Emergency assistance, however, is available by phone 24/7. The British Consulate (Via S. Paolo 7, tel. 02/723-001) in Milan can assist travelers throughout Northern Italy.

The Canadian Embassy (Via Zara 30, 800/2326-6831, Mon.-Fri. 8:30am-noon) handles all citizen services and is located northwest of the historic center in Rome. The Australian (Via Antonio Bosio 5, tel. 06/852-721), New Zealand (Via Clitunno 44, tel. 06/853-7501, www.nzembassy.com), and South African (Via Tanaro 14, tel. 06/852-541, www.lnx.sudafrica.it) embassies are also located in Rome.

CUSTOMS

Travelers entering Italy are expected to declare any cash over €6,000 and are prohibited from importing animal-based food products into the country. Duty-free imports for passengers from outside the European Union are limited to one liter of alcohol, two liters of wine, 200 cigarettes, 50 cigars, and 50 milliliters of perfume.

Bags are more likely to be heavier upon leaving Italy, and U.S. citizens are limited to $800 worth of goods deemed for personal use. Anything over that amount must be declared and will be taxed. Fresh fruit and vegetables, cheese, and animal-based products are not allowed into the United States. Further details regarding what can and cannot be imported into the country are available from the U.S. Department of State (www.state.gov).

Canadian regulations are fairly lenient and allow cheese, herbs, condiments, dried fruits, baked goods, and candies; for a complete list, visit the Canadian Border Services Agency (www.cbsa-asfc.gc.ca). Australian regulations are particularly stringent and customs officers go to great lengths to avoid contamination. All fruit, vegetables, ham, salami, and meat products are forbidden. Fake designer goods will also be confiscated and may lead to a fine. If you're in doubt consult the Australian Department of Immigration and Border Protection (www.border.gov.au).

DINE LIKE A LOCAL

Italians have their own way of doing things—especially when it comes to food. Here's how to blend in with locals:

- **Embrace a light breakfast.** Forget about eggs and bacon: Sidle up to locals at the nearest bar and order a cappuccino and a pastry.

- **Know the coffee culture.** Italians drink coffee at specific times. Cappuccinos are rarely ordered after noon or in restaurants, and should never accompany or immediately precede a meal. Espressos are ordered at the end of lunch and/or dinner, and during midday or midafternoon breaks.

- **Skip the salt and olive oil.** Salt, olive oil, and Parmesan aren't meant to be added to food and won't appear tableside so don't search for them.

- **Forget about eating on the go.** Italians eat standing at bars and sitting at restaurants, but you'll rarely see them eating while they walk. The only exception is gelato, which makes strolling through historic streets even better.

- **Accept the slowness.** Service may be slower than you're used to. It might be hard to get the waiter's attention, or the second bottle of wine may never arrive—just remember the sun is probably shining and you are in Italy. A little patience along with good-natured persistence will ensure a good time. Frustration won't.

Food

There are all sorts of places to eat in Italy, and travelers should attempt to experience as many of these as possible. When choosing where to eat, avoid restaurants where staff actively encourages you to enter and menus are displayed in more than three languages. Authentic establishments attract Italians and are not located next to major monuments. Generally, however, it's hard to have a bad meal in Italy, and if it looks good it usually tastes good as well.

Every Tuscan town has its specialties but one thing you'll find in Florence, Siena, and Montalcino is *pici.* This thick, spaghetti-like pasta is a regional favorite and a fixture of countless menus. It can be topped with hearty wild boar ragu, mushrooms, truffle, or a simple tomato sauce.

Trying all the variations is a gastronomic quest worth embarking on.

ITALIAN EATERIES
RESTAURANTS

The most common sit-down eateries are *trattoria, osteria,* and *ristorante.* The first two have humble origins and are cheaper than *ristorante.* The typical *trattoria* serves local dishes within a rustic atmosphere. The best have been in business for generations and have a devoted local following. Service can be ad hoc and waiters are not overly concerned with formality. *Osteria* are similar, but have fewer items on their menus and rarely stray from tradition. *Ristorante* are more expensive and elegant. They may have uniformed waiters, an extensive wine cellar along with a sommelier, and fine table settings. Menus often diverge from tradition and combine flavors in novel ways. *Trattoria, osteria,* and *ristorante* are open lunch and dinner, and continuous service throughout the day is rare.

Traditional round pies and sit-down service are available at *pizzerias,* which also serve a variety of fried starters such as *suppli* (rice balls stuffed with mozzarella) and *fiore di zucca* (zucchini flowers with anchovies). Pizza is also a staple of many restaurant menus and easy to find. Quality is generally good and it's hard to pay more than €8 for a pie.

STREET FOOD
The most popular street food in Italy is pizza, which is available on demand at *pizza al taglio* (pizza by the cut) shops from mid-morning onward. The pizza inside these standing-room-only shops with little or no seating is baked in large rectangular tins. There are a dozen varieties waiting to be cut, and customers randomly line up to order whatever they like. Slices are weighed and reheated if necessary, and they can be eaten immediately or wrapped up for future consumption. Payment is usually made at a dedicated cashier.

Markets are another good destination for tasty fast food from morning to early afternoon. Stalls in the Mercato Centrale in Florence have been serving the same flavors for generations and here you can sample beef or tripe sandwiches, drink inexpensive local wine, and sample seasonal fruits.

BAKERIES AND *PASTICCERIA*
Fornaio (bakeries) open before dawn and remain busy until mid-afternoon. There's one in every neighborhood and they supply locals with all types of bread, buns, and sweets. You'll also find cakes, cookies, tarts, pastries, white or red pizza, and unique treats served during holidays. Most items are priced by the kilo and purchased for takeaway. *Fornaio* can be crowded in the morning, and some use numbered ticketing systems to avoid confusion. Each city has its own specialties that vary in form and substance.

Pasticceria shops are entirely dedicated to sweets and keep roughly the same hours as bakeries. They prepare cookies, tarts, and cakes along with an array of smaller finger-sized pastries Italians serve as mid-afternoon snacks (*merenda*) or offer to visiting friends. Some *pasticceria* serve coffee and prepare one or two items for which they are famous. There's a tremendous variety from city to city.

COFFEE BARS
Coffee bars and cafés open nearly as early as bakeries and provide different services throughout the day. In the morning they supply locals with espressos or cappuccinos and *cornetti* (breakfast pastries), which are either plain or filled with cream, jelly, or chocolate. *Cornetti* rarely exceed €1 and are a cheap and tasty way to start the day. Most bars are supplied by bakeries, but some have their own ovens.

By mid-morning, coffee bars trade sweets for triangular *tramezzino* and *panini* sandwiches stacked behind glass counters. These cost €2-4 and can be eaten at the counter, table, or taken away. Larger bars provide *tavola calda* (lunchtime buffets) with a selection of first- and second-course dishes. It's hard to spend more than €15 for a complete meal with water and coffee.

Bars usually operate on a "consume now, pay later" policy with a dedicated cashier off to one side who calculates checks. Counter service is slightly cheaper, always faster, and where most locals do their eating and drinking. There's a big difference between neighborhood bars and those overlooking heavily touristed squares. **Cafés** in those squares are far more elegant and some have been around for centuries. Prices are higher although the food is more or less the same. The biggest advantage is the view, and the tables outside are usually filled with tourists.

GELATERIA

Gelateria are nearly as common as bars in Italy and stay open late during the summer. They specialize in gelato and sorbet, which come in countless flavors. The best are made on the spot with seasonal ingredients, while less passionate owners cut corners by using preservatives and compressed air to give gelato bright colors and gravity-defying forms. Gelato is priced by the scoop and served in a cone or cup. Clerks will ask if you want *panna* (whipped cream) at no extra cost.

MENUS

Italian menus are divided into courses with an established order. *Antipasti* (starters) are the first thing you'll see and can be as simple as *bruschette* (toasted bread topped with tomatoes) or *fiori di zucchini* (fried zucchini flowers stuffed with anchovies). The point of *antipasti* is to relieve hunger and prepare stomachs for the meal to come. House starters *(antipasto della casa)* are a safe culinary bet and plates of local cold cuts and cheeses are meant to be shared.

The *primo* (first course) can be pasta, *risotto,* or soup. There are hundreds of traditional pasta shapes, all of which are combined with particular

sauces that include vegetables, meat, or fish. This is a chance to get adventurous. Soups are popular in Florence and fortified with pasta, beans, and barley.

Many people surrender after the first course, and that's a shame for stomachs. If you need help getting through a three-course meal, order a *mezzo porzione* (half portion) and leave room for the *secondo* (second course). It consists of meat or fish and is the gastronomic main event. Let waiters know if you want meat rare *(al sangue),* medium rare *(cotta),* or well done *(ben cotta).* Unless you order a **contorno** (side) your steak will be lonely. These generally consist of grilled vegetables or roasted potatoes and are listed at the end of the menu along with desserts and drinks.

Restaurants often have a separate wine menu and daily specials that waiters will translate when possible. Food is relatively inexpensive in Italy and a satisfying three-course lunch or dinner with dessert and coffee runs around €25-40 per person.

DRINKS

Italy has hundreds of natural springs and Italians drink more **mineral water** per capita than any other country in the world. The first question waiters often ask is the type of *acqua* (water) you want. You can choose between *frizzante* (sparkling) or *naturale* (still). A liter costs around €3 and sometimes there's a choice of brands. That's not to say *acqua del rubinetto* (tap water) is bad. It's regularly tested by authorities and safe to drink.

It's difficult to find a restaurant that doesn't have a decent **wine** list. Many eateries have a separate wine menu that includes local, regional, and international bottles. House wine is also available and generally very drinkable. It can be ordered by the glass or in different-sized carafes. Tuscany is the epicenter of Italian oenology and the place to uncork legendary Chianti and Super Tuscans. A glass of house wine is €3-4, a half carafe €4-6, and a full carafe €8-10. Prices are nearly always indicated on menus, but if they're not—or if a waiter brings you a bottle—ask the price before indulging.

Most Italians end lunches with an espresso and occasionally conclude dinners with a *digestivo* (digestif). The latter are high-grade alcoholic spirits and reputed to help digestion. The most famous of these is *grappa*, which is served in a small glass and sipped. Soft drinks are available but not very common on restaurant tables.

SEASONAL SPECIALTIES

Locals can tell the date by what's on display inside bakeries and *pasticcerie*. Most seasonal specialties revolve around sweets, which are prepared during major holidays.

The weeks preceding Christmas transform grocery and supermarket shelves, with entire aisles devoted to chocolate, nuts, dried fruit, and, especially, *pandoro* cakes made from flour, eggs, butter, and sugar. During *Carnivale*, fried pastries are the gastronomic excess of choice. The most popular are the doughnut-like *castagnole alla romana* and fried dough *frappe* covered with powdered sugar and available in bars and bakeries. Easter wouldn't be the same for Italians without *colomba* (dove) cakes topped with almonds and granulated sugar. All are available in bakeries and supermarkets.

New Year's meals nearly always include lentils, which are eaten for good luck, along with *cotechino* (pig's foot). Christmas lunches involve fish while roast lamb is a feature of Easter menus. Season influences what you'll find on tables the rest of the year. Soups are a mainstay of Florentine menus throughout the winter. Italian diets are regulated by the harvest and the produce available at outdoor markets varies throughout the year.

HOURS

Restaurants are typically open 12:30pm-2:30pm for lunch and 7.30pm-10pm for dinner. Most close one day a week and many take an extended break in August or January. Reservations aren't usually necessary, but to guarantee a seat at popular eateries it's wise to arrive early or late. Bakeries open before sunrise and close in the mid-afternoon, while coffee bars remain open all day long and *pizzeria* and *gelateria* stay open late. Italians tend to eat later in summer, when they wait for the sun to set and temperatures to fall.

TIPPING

Tipping is neither required nor expected in Italy. Most restaurants include a €1-3 surcharge *(coperto)* for bread, utensils, and service per customer. Waiters earn a decent living but no one refuses money, and leaving €3-5 behind after a good meal is one way to show appreciation. The other way to express gastronomic gratitude is with words. Italians are proud of their cusine and compliments are always welcome. Customers at coffee bars often leave a low-denomination coin on the counter.

PRODUCE CALENDAR

Italians eat according to the seasons, which means you won't find cherries in winter or kiwis in summer. What you will find is fresh and grown locally. To get an idea of what's in season visit an open-air market. Consult the list below to make sure what you're ordering is ripe:

Spring	Summer	Fall	Winter	Year-Round
artichokes	eggplant	pumpkin	pumpkin	carrots
asparagus	zucchini	white and black truffles	artichoke	endive
green beans	turnips	cabbage	cauliflower	dried beans
fava beans	radishes	mushrooms	broccoli	lettuce
new potatoes	peas	cauliflower	winter melons	leeks
cauliflower	cucumbers	broccoli	Brussels sprouts	celery
broccoli	fava beans	Roman broccoli	radicchio	spinach
cabbage	green beans	chestnuts	oranges	potatoes
zucchini	peppers	grapes	mandarins	chicory
tomatoes	mushrooms	figs	clementines	apples
kiwi	cherries	oranges	grapefruit	pears
strawberries	prunes	mandarins	kiwi	lemons
medlars	peaches	clementines		
peaches	apricots	grapefruit		
	figs			
	melons			
	wild berries			

Shopping

The majority of family-owned shops are dedicated to one thing and one thing only. This can be a single product like shoes, hats, books, clothing, or furniture, or materials like leather, ceramics, paper, or glass.

Most businesses are small and have few employees. Department and flagship stores exist in the center of Florence but attract as many tourists as locals, who prefer to shop in malls and outlets on the outskirts of cities. Luxury boutiques are concentrated around major monuments. Although you're unlikely to find a discarded Giacometti in Florentine flea markets, collectors with patience will be rewarded. There's a great variety to rummage through and antique markets have something for everyone.

SHOPPING ETIQUETTE

Italians entering a shop (or bar) nearly always greet assistants with *buongiorno* or *buonasera* (good morning/good afternoon). Most shop owners and employees are not overbearing and welcome browsing. They're happy to leave shoppers alone; however, they are professional and helpful once you demonstrate interest in an item and will happily find your size or explain how something is made. When leaving a store say *grazie* (thank you) or *arrivederci* (goodbye) regardless of whether you've made a purchase.

BARGAINING

Shopping in Italy is a chance to practice your negotiating skills and discover the thrill of haggling. Price can be theoretical at souvenir stands, flea markets, antique stalls, and even smaller shops, where no one will be offended if you ask for a *sconto* (discount). If a price sounds too high, it probably is—and can likely be lowered.

SHIPPING ITEMS HOME

Don't worry if something that's larger than your suitcase catches your eye. Stores are accustomed to tourists and can arrange for shipment directly to your door. Expect to pay up to 10 percent of the purchase price for home delivery.

SALES

January and September are the best times to shop in Italy. All stores begin the official sale season in unison during these months and windows are plastered with discounts. Every price tag should contain the original and sale price. Check items carefully before buying and don't hesitate to try clothes on, as Italian sizes generally run smaller and fit slightly differently. The sale season lasts four weeks, but most of the good stuff and sought-after sizes disappear after ten days.

HOURS

Italy has its own unique rhythm, and nowhere is that more evident than in shops. Family-owned stores and smaller businesses nearly always close between 1pm and 3pm. Many also close on Sundays and Monday mornings. Larger stores and those located in heavily trafficked streets have continuous hours.

Accommodations

HOTELS

Italian hotels are graded on a system of stars that ranges from one to five. How many stars an establishment has depends on infrastructure and services. Criteria varies from region to region but most three-star hotels are quite comfortable. Reservations can be made online and most hotels have multilingual websites. A **passport** or ID card is required when checking in and early arrivals can usually leave luggage at the front desk. Many smaller hotels operate a "leave the key" policy in which keys must be left and retrieved whenever entering or leaving the accommodation.

Large international chains like **Hilton** (www3.hilton.com), **Sheraton** (www.starwoodhotels.com), and **Best Western** (www.bestwestern.com) all operate in Italy, along with budget accommodations like **Ibis** (www.ibis.com) and **Mercure** (www.mercure.com). Service may be better and rooms slightly larger in these hotels, but they often lack character and could be located anywhere in the world. Many travelers will find themselves better off staying in smaller boutique or family-operated hotels that have managed to retain their charm.

Valuables are best carried or deposited in a hotel safe if available. In addition to the room rate, expect to be charged a city **hotel tax** of €1-5 per guest/per day depending on the number of stars and accommodation type.

It's a small price to pay for waking up in Florence.

HOSTELS AND PENSIONI

Hostels (*ostelli*) aren't just for young travelers: there's no age limit to staying in them. They provide clean, affordable accommodation and many are less sparse than you might expect. Most include single, double, and quad options in addition to classic dormitory-style rooms. A bed costs around €20 per person and may include breakfast. The best thing about hostels, however, is the ambience. They're filled with travelers from all over at various stages of round-the-world adventures. Bathrooms are often shared although many also have private rooms with en suite baths. Italian hostels are overseen by the Associazione Italiana Alberghi per la Gioventù (tel. 06/487-1152, www.aighostels.it).

Pensioni are small, lower-grade accommodations that are usually family-run. Rooms are clean and functional, although you may be required to share a bathroom. They're often located near train stations or city centers in large buildings that may not have elevators. Some enforce curfews and it's best to check at the front desk (if there is one) before heading out for the night.

AGRITURISMI AND CAMPING

Agriturismi are a wonderful Italian invention that combine B&B-type accommodations with rural living. Owners are happy to show you around and the proximity to countryside provides a relaxing break from the city. Many are located on the hillsides surrounding Florence and have swimming pools. Agriturismo (www.agriturismo.it) lists thousands of such accommodations throughout Italy.

Florence also has campsites that remain open from April to September. Facilities usually include a bar or restaurant, showers, and telephones. Some locations are better than others and there are several grounds in Florence that are within walking distance of the historic center. Equipment can be rented if you've forgotten your tent, and bungalows are sometimes also available. For a full list of sites visit the Italian Campsite Federation (tel. 05/588-2391, www.federcampeggio.it).

B&BS AND APARTMENTS

Italy has experienced a B&B boom over the last decade and the country now offers thousands of options. It allows you to stay with local residents and gain an insider's perspective.

To really do as the Florentines do, rent an apartment and get an instant native feel. Short-term rental is especially convenient for families and groups of traveling friends. Not only are prices lower than many hotels, but staying in an apartment allows you to call the mealtime shots and relax in a home away from home. Airbnb (www.airbnb.com) and VRBO (www.vrbo.com) are good places to start apartment hunting. Hometogo (www.hometogo.com) searches over 250 international and local rental sites.

Conduct and Customs

LOCAL HABITS

Italians are attached to their habits and especially those related to food. Mealtimes are fairly strict and most eating is done sitting down at precise hours. Locals generally have a light breakfast and save themselves for lunch and dinner, which are served at 1pm and 8pm. You won't see many Italians snacking on the subway or bus or walking while they eat. Meals are usually divided *alla Romana* (Dutch) between friends but no one will take offense if you offer to pay. Rounds of drinks are not offered as they are in the United States; groups of colleagues each buy their own. Drinking in general is done over a meal rather than with any intention of getting drunk, and displays of public drunkenness are rare.

Most of the things considered rude in North America are also considered rude in Italy. One exception is cutting in line, which is a frequent offense. Italian lines are undisciplined and can feel like a fumble recovery. If you don't defend your place by saying *scusi* or coughing loudly you may be waiting all day for a cappuccino or slice of pizza. Fortunately, number dispensers are used in post offices, pharmacies, and deli counters. Personal space in general is smaller than in Anglo-Saxon countries, and Italians tend to use their hands as well as words to emphasize ideas.

GREETINGS

Italians are exceptionally sociable and have developed highly ritualized forms of interaction. Daily exchanges with friends and acquaintances often involve physical contact, and kisses on both cheeks are common. Bars and squares are the urban settings for unhurried conversation, which is a normal part of everyday Italian life. The proliferation of the cell phone has fueled the passion to communicate, and in some cases has led to an overreliance that can be witnessed on public transportation and sidewalks of Italian cities.

Kissing is how Italians demonstrate respect, friendship, and love. The practice is as Italian as pizza. The most common form is the double cheek kiss. It can be uncomfortable for the uninitiated but no one will impose it on you, and a handshake is equally acceptable. If you observe carefully you'll see women kissing women, women kissing men, men kissing women, men kissing men, and everyone kissing children.

Kisses are exchanged at the beginning and end of most social encounters. An Italian man introduced to an Italian woman (or vice versa) will exchange kisses. Men will shake hands with each other and women may kiss or shake hands. Non-Italians can greet however they please. While citizens of other countries tend to exchange good-byes quickly, Italians love to linger. The time between verbal indication of departure and actual physical departure can be surprisingly long and is generally spent discussing the next day and making preliminary plans for a future meeting.

ALCOHOL AND SMOKING

Legislation regarding alcohol consumption is more relaxed than in

ITALIAN SURVIVAL PHRASES

- *Ciao* [ch-OW] This world-famous word is an informal greeting that means both hello and good-bye. It's used between friends or once you have gotten acquainted with someone.

- *Buongiorno* [bwon-JUR-no] / *Buonasera* [bwo-na-SEH-ra] The first means hello (or literally, good day) and the latter good afternoon. These are formal variations of *ciao* and the first words to say when entering a restaurant or shop.

- *Scusi* [SKU-zee] is an invaluable word that sounds very much like its English counterpart: excuse me. It can be used whenever you want to get someone's attention, ask for something, or need to excuse yourself.

- *Per Favore* [PEAR fa-VOR-eh] / *Grazie* [GRA-zee-eh] are pillars of Italian politeness. *Per favore* is useful when ordering at a bar or restaurant and can go at the beginning or end of a sentence (*un café per favore* or *per favore un caffè*). Once you've been served something it's always polite to say *grazie*.

- *Dov'è...?* [doe-VAY...?] The Italian phrase for *where* can save you from getting lost. Just add the location to the end and do your best to comprehend the answer. *Scusi, dov'e la Uffizi?*

- *Parli inglese?* [par-LEE in-GLAY-zay?] should only be used as a last resort, but if you must it's more polite than launching directly into English.

North America. Alcohol can be purchased in supermarkets, grocery stores, and specialty shops all week long by anyone over 18 and consumed in public. That's a major draw for North American exchange students, who can be spotted staggering down Florentine streets on weekends. Most locals are not prone to excessive drinking, and public drunkenness is rare.

Smoking has been banned in bars, restaurants, and public spaces since 2005, and if you want to take a puff you'll need to step outside or request an outdoor table. Although there is a high percentage of smokers in Italy, that number is falling, and laws regarding nonsmoking areas are respected. Cigarettes are sold at specialized *tabacchi* shops for around €5 a pack.

DRUGS

Italy's position in the center of the Mediterranean, coupled with the country's 4,971-mile (8,000-kilometer) coastline, makes drug smuggling difficult to eradicate. There are major markets for heroin, cocaine, hashish, and synthetic drugs imported by sea from South America, North Africa, the Balkans, and Afghanistan. That said, it's very rare to be offered drugs in Italy during the day and the hardest drug you're likely to be offered at night is hashish (a substance derived from cannabis and mixed with tobacco). Most dealers aren't threatening and will take no for an answer. Discos and nightclubs are more likely to be the scene of cocaine or amphetamines, which kill their share of Italian teenagers every year. Marijuana and hashish are classified as light drugs and are illegal but have been decriminalized since 1990. Personal use in public will not lead to arrest but may bring about a fine or warning. It's not worth the risk, and there's enough perfectly legal wine to go around. Harder drugs such as cocaine, heroin, ecstasy, LSD, and so on are all illegal.

DRESS

Italians like to look good. Even if the standards of formality have fallen in recent years locals of all ages remain well groomed and careful about appearance. It's not just the clothes that are different but the way Italians wear clothes and the overall homogeneity that exists on city streets. Women are elegant, men well fitted, and even retirees look like they're wearing their Sunday best. It's easy to differentiate locals from tourists, who are blissfully unaware of the fashion faux pas they are committing. Tourists can usually be spotted a kilometer away: They're the ones wearing the baseball caps, white socks with sandals, and khaki shorts. Fitting in means paying a little more attention to how you look and may require some shopping to acquire Italian style.

AT PLACES OF WORSHIP

Most churches have a dress code, which is often posted outside. Revealing too much flesh may result in being denied entry. Lower legs, shoulders, and midriffs should be covered. Do not expect to enter cathedrals wearing flip-flops, miniskirts, above-the-knee shorts, or cut-off T-shirts. The same rules also apply to some museums and monuments.

Entry may be restricted during mass and a certain amount of decorum (maintaining silence, refraining from eating and drinking, and acting in a respectful manner) should be observed at all times. Photography is usually allowed but rules vary. Flash photography is not permitted inside some churches and museums where light can damage delicate frescoes.

Health and Safety

EMERGENCY NUMBERS

In case of a medical emergency, dial 118. Operators are multilingual and will provide immediate assistance. The U.S. Embassy (tel. 06/46741) and British Embassy (tel. 06/4220-0001) offer their citizens phone access any time for matters regarding illness or victimization of any sort. Carabinieri (112), police (113), and the fire department (115) also operate around-the-clock emergency numbers.

CRIME AND THEFT

Italian cities are safe and muggings and violent crime are rare. Still, it's best to travel in pairs late at night and be aware of pickpockets at all times.

Most petty criminals work in teams and can be quite young. Youth often beg for change at traffic intersections or on church steps and supplement that income by playing music on subways, recycling scrap metal, and dumpster diving.

Crowded train stations and subways are ideal places for thieves. It's best to keep wallets and other valuables in a front pocket or locked in a hotel safe. Leave jewelry, smartphones, and cameras out of sight and always count your change before leaving a store. Make a photocopy of your passport and other vital documents and call your credit card company immediately if your wallet is stolen. If you are the victim of a pickpocket or have a bag snatched, report it within 24 hours to the nearest police station. You'll need a copy of the police report (*denuncia*) in order to make an insurance claim.

MEDICAL SERVICES

Italian medical and emergency services are relatively modern and ranked second in the world by the World Health Organization. First aid can be performed by all public hospitals and urgent treatment is entirely free of charge. A symbolic copayment is often required for non-life-threatening treatment but does not exceed €30. The emergency medical service number is 118. If you can't wait, go directly to the *pronto soccorso* (emergency room) located in most hospitals.

Vaccines are not required for entering Italy, but a flu shot can prevent unnecessary time in bed if you're visiting in winter.

PHARMACIES

Pharmacies are recognizable by their green neon signs and very common in city centers. Many operate nonstop hours and remain open during lunch. If a pharmacy is closed, you can always find a list of the closest open ones posted in the window. Pharmacists can be very helpful in Italy and provide advice and nonprescription

medicine for treating minor ailments. You'll also find practical items such as toothbrushes, sunscreen, and baby food along with automated prophylactic vending machines out front.

SECURITY

Security in Italy has tightened considerably since the 2015 Paris attacks and there is a greater police and military presence at airports, train stations, and around major monuments. Some Florentine churches, museums, and other popular destinations have adopted new entry procedures involving metal detectors and the depositing of backpacks and oversize bags in cloakrooms. Security around French and U.S. embassies, schools, and cultural associations has also been bolstered and will remain so for the foreseeable future.

There haven't been any terrorist attacks in Italy since the 1980s, and the country has kept a low profile compared to other allies that have actively intervened in Middle Eastern affairs and become the target of terrorist groups. That could always change, and travelers concerned about security can register with the **Smart Traveler Enrollment Program** (www.step.state.gov) to receive the latest alerts and allow the U.S. embassy to contact them in case of emergency.

Travel Tips

MONEY

CURRENCY

The euro has been Italy's currency since 2000. Banknotes come in denominations of €5, €10, €20, €50, €200, and €500 (which is currently being phased out). Denominations are different colors and sizes to facilitate recognition. Coins come in €0.01, €0.02, €0.05, €0.10, €0.20, €0.50, €1, and €2 denominations; these also vary in color, shape, and size. The euro is used in 19 nations across Europe, and each country decorates and mints its own coins. Take time to familiarize yourself with the different values, and count your change after each purchase for practice.

CURRENCY EXCHANGE

Fluctuation between the dollar and euro can have a major impact on expenditures. Over the last decade exchange rates haven't favored U.S. travelers, but since 2014 the dollar has strengthened considerably, and one dollar is now worth roughly €0.85.

There are several options for obtaining euros. You can exchange at your local bank before departure, use private exchange agencies located in airports and near major monuments, or simply use ATM machines in Italy. Banks generally offer better rates but charge commission, while agencies charge low commission but offer poor rates. Automated exchange machines operate nonstop at the airport and inside many bank branches. Look for the *cambio* (exchange) sign in bank windows. When changing money request different denominations and count bills at the counter before leaving.

ATMS AND BANKS

ATM machines are easy to find and are located inside or outside all Italian banks. They accept foreign debit and credit cards, and exchange rates are set daily. Before withdrawing cash in Italy, ask your bank or credit card company what fees they charge. Most have an international processing fee that can be a fixed amount or a percentage of the total withdrawal. Charles Schwab is one of the few financial institutions that does not charge either. Italian banks also charge a small fee for cardholders of other banks using their ATMs.

The maximum daily withdrawal at most banks is €500. ATMs provide instructions in multiple languages. Be aware of your surroundings when withdrawing cash late at night or on deserted streets. If the card doesn't work, try another bank before contacting your bank back home. Italian banks are generally open weekdays 8:30am-1:30pm and 2:30pm-5:30pm. They often have lockers at the entrance for storing keys, coins, and anything else that might activate the metal detectors at the entrance.

DEBIT AND CREDIT CARDS

Before your departure, inform your bank and/or credit card company of your travel plans, as many will block cards after unexpected foreign activity.

Debit cards are a ubiquitous form of payment in Italy, and recent legislation meant to encourage cashless transactions has removed monetary limits. You can therefore buy a coffee, museum ticket, or a pair of shoes with

Maestro- or Cirrus-equipped cards. Newsstands are about the only place that don't accept plastic, and cash-only restaurants are rare. Most Italian smart cards use a chip-and-PIN system. If your card requires old-fashioned swiping, you may need to alert cashiers.

Credit cards are also widely accepted. Visa (tel. 800/877-232) and MasterCard (tel. 800/870-866) are the most common. American Express (tel. 06/4211-5561) comes a distant third, and Discover is unknown. Cards provide the most advantageous exchange rates and a low 1-3 percent commission fee is usually charged on every transaction.

SALES TAX

The Italian government imposes a value-added tax (IVA) of 22 percent on most goods. Visitors who reside outside the European Union are entitled to tax refunds (www.taxrefund. it) on all purchases over €155 within stores that participate in the tax-back program. Just look for the Euro Tax Free or Tax Free Italy logo, have your passport ready, and fill out the yellow refund form. You'll still have to pay tax at the time of purchase but are entitled to reimbursement at airports and refund offices. Forms must be stamped by customs officials before check-in and brought to the refund desk, where you can choose to receive cash or have funds wired to your credit card. Lines move slowly and it's usually faster to be refunded at private currency exchange agencies such as Forexchange (www.forexchange. it), American Express (www.americanexpress.com), Interchange (www.interchange.eu), or Travelex (www.travelex.com). They facilitate the refund process for a small percentage of

your refund. All claims must be made within three months of purchase.

COMMUNICATIONS
TELEPHONES

To call Italy from outside the country, dial the exit code (011 for the US and Canada) followed by 39 (Italy country code) and the number. All large Italian cities have a 2 or 3-digit area code (055 Florence) and numbers are 6-11 digits long. Landline numbers nearly always start with a zero, which must be dialed when making calls in Italy or calling Italy from abroad. Cell phone numbers have a 3-digit prefix (347, 390, 340, etc.) that varies according to the mobile operator and are 10 digits long total.

To call the United States or Canada from Italy, dial the 001 country code followed by area code and number. For collect calls to the United States dial 172-1011 (AT&T), 172-1022 (MCI), or 172-1877 (Sprint).

Numbers that start with 800 in Italy are toll-free, 170 gets you an English-speaking operator, and 176 is international directory assistance. Local calls cost €0.10 per minute and public phone booths are slowly disappearing. Fees for calling cell phones are higher.

Cell Phones

Your smartphone will work in Italy if it uses the GSM system, which is the mobile standard in Europe. All iPhones, Samsung Galaxy, and Google Nexus devices function, although rates vary widely between operators. Voice calls to the United States can vary from as much as $1.79 (Verizon) to $0.20 (T-Mobile) per minute depending on your plan. Most companies offer international bundles that include a certain amount of text messaging, data transfer, and voice traffic. If you don't want any unexpected bills, compare offers and choose one that meets your expected needs.

You can also purchase a SIM card in Italy at any mobile shop and use it in your phone. **Wind** (www.wind.it), **Tim** (www.tim.it), and **Vodafone** (www.vodafone.it) are the most common operators, with stores in all three cities and at airports. This option will require a passport or photo ID and may take a little longer, but it can be the cheapest and most useful if you plan to make a lot of domestic and international calls.

If your phone doesn't use GSM you can rent or buy one in Italy. Rentals are available at the airport but are expensive. New phones are a cheaper option and available from the European telecom operators mentioned earlier. A basic flip phone can cost as little as €29 and be purchased with prepaid minutes. ID is required and some operators have special deals for foreign travelers.

You can save on telephone charges altogether if you have access to Wi-Fi. Many hotels and bars have hot spots, and using FaceTime, Skype, or other VOIP operators is free.

Pay Phones

The advent of cell phones has led to a steady decline of public pay phones. Those still standing operate with coins or phone cards that can be purchased at *tabacchi* or newsstands. Ask for a *scheda telefonica* (phone card), which can be inserted into a slot in the telephone.

WI-FI

Getting online in Italy is easy. Florence has a Wi-Fi network that makes it simple to stay connected throughout a journey. Access is free; however,

registration is required and there are time and traffic limits. Both Trenitalia and Italo train operators provide onboard Wi-Fi, as do most Italian airports and hotels.

POSTAL SERVICES

Francobolli (stamps) for standard-size postcards and letters can be purchased at *tabacchi* shops. Larger parcels will require a trip to the post office. **Poste Italiane** (tel. 800/160-000, www.poste.it) offices are yellow, and larger branches are usually open weekdays 8:30am-7:30pm and Saturdays 8:15am-12:30pm. Grab a numbered ticket at the entrance and prepare for a short wait. A postcard to the United States costs €0.85 as long as it doesn't exceed 20 grams and remains within standard dimensions. The cost of sending letters and other goods varies according to weight; such items can be sent *posta prioritaria* (express) for a couple of euros extra. Mailboxes are red and have slots for international and local mail. Travel time varies and it can take weeks for a postcard to reach its destination.

Stamp collectors in Florence may be disappointed, as most post office clerks slap computerized stickers onto correspondence.

WEIGHTS AND MEASURES

Italy uses the **metric system.** A few helpful conversions: 5 centimeters is about 3 inches, 1 kilogram is a little over 2 pounds, and 5 kilometers is around 3 miles. **Celsius** is used to measure temperature, and 20°C (68°F) is a good air-conditioning setting inside hotels and cars. Summers often break the 35°C (95°F) barrier, and it's best to stay indoors when that happens.

Italy is on **Central European Time**, six hours ahead of the U.S. East Coast and nine of the West Coast. Military/24-hour time is frequently used. Just subtract 12 from any number after midday so that 1300 becomes 1pm and 2015 is 8:15pm.

Italians use commas where Americans use decimal points, and vice versa. That means €10,50 is 10 euros and 50 cents, while €1.000 is a thousand euros. Italians order dates by day, month, and year—which is something to remember when booking hotels and tours.

ACCESS FOR TRAVELERS WITH DISABILITIES

Special-needs travelers may find life in Florence challenging. Italy is not especially accessible to the blind or wheelchair bound, and sidewalks can be narrow and uneven. One positive is that many museums and monuments are free for special-needs travelers and their companions.

Florence is very accessible. The center is flat, pavements are in good condition, and traffic is limited. Many museums are easily navigated and free for the otherly abled and their companions. There's also no need to wait in line to enter the Uffizi or Accademia as long as you have visible or documented proof of medical conditions. You can rent wheelchairs from the tourist office near the train station. There are 14 fully accessible public bathrooms in the city center, and many museums have created special **tactile tours** (tel. 055/268224) for the visually impaired. A group of specialized guides provide tours and the list is available online or from the **tourist office** (Piazza Stazione 4, tel. 055/212-245, Mon.-Sat. 9am-7pm and Sun. 9am-1pm).

Traveling between cities by train is convenient for anyone with reduced mobility. **Italo** (tel. 892929, www.italo.it) goes to great lengths to accommodate passengers. Seat numbers and other signage are written in braille, and two seats in car 8 are reserved for wheelchairs. These are located next to restrooms and snack machines designed for maximum accessibility. In-station assistance can be arranged up to one hour before departure at Florence SMN daily from 8am to 10pm. **Trenitalia** (tel. 800/906-060) provides similar services and assistance.

TRAVELING WITH CHILDREN

Italians go crazy for kids, and if you're traveling with a baby or toddler expect people to sneak peaks inside the stroller or ask for the name, age, and vital statistics of your child. Restaurants and hotels generally welcome young travelers, and some high-end accommodations offer babysitting services for parents who want to sightsee on their own. Many restaurants have children's menus, and most have high chairs. Half-size portions (*mezza porzione*) can also be requested for small appetites.

Tickets to museums, amusement parks, and public transportation are discounted for children under 12, and free for kids under 6. **Trenitalia** has several offers geared toward families, who can save up to 20 percent on high-speed rail tickets. **Italo** has similar deals and toddlers sit on laps unless an extra seat is reserved. Trains are roomy and give kids plenty of space to roam or be entertained by the landscape outside. There are diaper-changing facilities, and Italo has a cinema car with eight high-definition screens playing family-friendly movies.

Italian tots are used to taking naps, and a mid-afternoon break back at the hotel can prevent evening tantrums. Parents may want to intersperse fun and high-octane activities with visits to monuments and museums. Most parks are equipped with playgrounds. It's hard for kids not to love Italy, and involving them as much as possible in the journey will help leave an impression they'll never forget.

FEMALE AND SOLO TRAVELERS

Women attract the curiosity of Italian men whether traveling alone or in groups. For the most part advances are good-natured and can simply be ignored. If you do feel threatened, enter a shop, bar, or public space. Should harassment persist, call the police (113) and remain in a crowded area. At night, it's best to avoid unlit streets and train stations. If you must pass through these areas walk quickly and keep your guard up. Having a cell phone handy is a wise precaution, and periodically keeping in touch with family back home never hurts. Hotels often go out of their way to assist single travelers and will be happy to order a cab or make reservations whenever necessary.

SENIOR TRAVELERS

Italy has a high life expectancy (83) and median age (46), which makes gray hair a common sight and visiting seniors feel young again. There's also a general respect for older people, who are an integral part of economic and social life.

Seniority has benefits. Anyone over age 65 is entitled to discounts at museums, theaters, and sporting events as well as on public transportation and for many other services. A passport or valid ID is enough to prove age, even if these are rarely checked. Carta Argento (Silver Card) is available from Trenitalia for over-60s traveling by train and provides a 15-percent discount on first- and second-class seating. The card costs €30 but is free for those over 75. It's valid for one year and can be purchased at any train station. Italo offers anyone over 60 a 40-percent discount on all first-class train tickets.

Italy gets very hot in the summer so it's important to remain hydrated and avoid peak temperature times. You'll also walk a lot so take frequent breaks and join bus or ferry tours whenever you need a rest. If you take medication, bring as much as you need as prescriptions can be hard to fill.

LGBT TRAVELERS

Italians in general are accepting and take a live-and-let-live approach. It's not uncommon to see same-sex couples holding hands today and the sexual preferences of emperors and Renaissance artists are all well known. Violence against LGBTs is rare, although cases of physical and verbal harassment do occasionally make headlines. Florence is LGBT friendly.

Italian homosexual couples have benefited from the same civil union status as heterosexuals since 2016. Italy was one of the last European countries to enact such legislation, doing so more than 20 years after Denmark. Still, it was a big step, and a sign Italian society (or Italian politicians) is open to change.

TRAVELERS OF COLOR

The face of Italy has been changing since the 1980s, and the country has become increasingly diversified with communities of Eastern Europeans, Asians, South Americans, and Africans contributing to the cultural mix. Ethnic minorities no longer turn heads, and if any Italians are surprised to find you in their bar, hotel, or restaurant they certainly won't show it. Blatant discrimination is rare, but if you think you've been refused service based on race, report the incident to local police or caribinieri, who treat all acts of racism seriously.

Tourist Information

TOURIST OFFICES

Florence has tourist offices where city travel cards, maps, and event information can be obtained. Hours vary but most are open nonstop from 9:30am until 6pm. Staff are multilingual and can help reserve local guides, order tickets, or get directions. Offices are located in airports, train stations, and near major sights such as the Uffizi.

LOST AND FOUND

Hopefully you'll never need an *oggetti smarriti* (lost and found), but they do exist in Italy. All airports have dedicated offices at baggage claim. If you forget something on board a Trenitalia train, contact the passenger assistance office located inside Santa Maria Novella (Florence, 7am-10:30am). Italo has fewer staff inside stations but you can call Italo Assistance (tel. 892/020, daily 6am-11pm) for help finding things. Fortunately, objects lost on high-speed trains have a high recovery rate. Objects lost in the historic centers may wind up at central lost-and-found offices.

MAPS

Maps are available at tourist offices for free in Florence. They are also sold at newsstands and bookstores. Examine the selection carefully and choose a map that's easy to read, easy to fold, and small enough to store conveniently. Paper quality varies, and some maps are laminated and come with sight descriptions on the back. Once you have a map, try to orient yourself and memorize major landmarks and rivers. Studying maps and memorizing the layout of each city beforehand will make getting around easier once you arrive.

Finding the name of a street you're standing on is simple, but finding that same street on a map can be tricky. Often, it's quicker to locate a *piazza* or a nearby cathedral, museum, or monument. Also, asking for directions is the best way to start a conversation with a stranger and learn something new. Sometimes it's best to put a map away and rely on your senses to navigate around.

Italian Phrasebook

Most Italians have some knowledge of English, and whatever vocabulary they lack is compensated for with gesticulation. It can, however, be more rewarding to attempt expression in the melodic vowels of Dante rather than succumb to the ease and familiarity of your own language.

Fortunately, Italian pronunciation is straightforward. There are 7 vowel sounds (one for *a, i,* and *u* and two each for *e* and *o*) compared to 15 in English, and letters are nearly always pronounced the same way. Consonants will be familiar although the Italian alphabet has fewer letters (no j, k, w, x, or y). If you have any experience with French, Spanish, Portuguese, or Latin you have an advantage, but even if you don't, learning a few phrases is simple and will prepare you for a linguistic dive into Italian culture. Inquiring how much something costs or asking for directions in Italian can be a little daunting but it's also exciting and much more gratifying than relying on English.

PRONUNCIATION
VOWELS
a   like *a* in *father*
e   short like *e* in *set*
é   long like *a* in *way*
i   like *ee* in *feet*
o   short like *o* in *often* or long like *o* in *rope*
u   like *oo* in *foot* or *w* in *well*

CONSONANTS
b   like *b* in *boy,* but softer
c   before e or i like *ch* in *chin*
ch like *c* in *cat*
d   like *d* in *dog*
f   like *f* in *fish*
g   before e or i like *g* in *gymnastics* or like *g* in *go*
gh like *g* in *go*
gl like *ll* in *million*
gn like *ni* in *onion*
gu like *gu* in *anguish*
h   always silent
l   like *l* in *lime*
m   like *m* in *me*
n   like *n* in *nice*
p   like *p* in *pit*
qu like *qu* in *quick*
r   rolled/trilled similar to *r* in Spanish or Scottish
s   between vowels like *s* in *nose* or *s* in *sit*
sc before e or i like *sh* in *shut* or *sk* in *skip*
t   like *t* in *tape*
v   like *v* in *vase*
z   either like *ts* in *spits* or *ds* in *pads*

ACCENTS
Accents are used to indicate which vowel should be stressed and to differentiate between words that are spelled the same.

ESSENTIAL PHRASES
Hi Ciao
Good morning Buongiorno
Good evening Buonasera
Good night Buonanotte
Good-bye Arrivederci
Nice to meet you Piacere
Thank you Grazie
You're welcome Prego
Please Per favore
Do you speak English? Parla inglese?
I don't understand Non capisco
Have a nice day Buona giornata
Restrooms Bagni
Yes Si
No No

TRANSPORTATION

Where is...? Dov'è...?

How far is...? Quanto è distante...?

Is there a bus to...? C'è un autobus per…?

Does this bus go to...? Quest'autobus va a...?

Where do I get off? Dove devo scendere?

What time does the bus/train leave/ arrive? A che ora parte/arriva l'autobus/treno?

Where is the nearest subway station? Dov'è la stazione metro più vicina?

Where can I buy a ticket? Dove posso comprare un biglietto?

A round-trip ticket/a single ticket to... Un biglietto di andata e ritorno/ andata per...

FOOD

A table for two/three/four... Un tavolo per due/tre/quattro…

Do you have a menu in English? Avete un menu in inglese?

What is the dish of the day? Qual è il piatto del giorno?

We're ready to order. Siamo pronti per ordinare.

I'm a vegetarian. Sono vegetariano

May I have... Posso avere…

The check please? Il conto per favore?

beer birra

bread pane

breakfast colazione

cash contante

check conto

coffee caffè

dinner cena

glass bicchiere

hors d'oeuvre antipasto

ice ghiaccio

ice cream gelato

lunch pranzo

restaurant ristorante

sandwich(es) panino(i)

snack spuntino

waiter cameriere

water acqua

wine vino

SHOPPING

money soldi

shop negozio

What time do the shops close? A che ora chiudono i negozi?

How much is it? Quanto costa?

I'm just looking. Sto guardando solamente.

What is the local specialty? Quali sono le specialità locali?

HEALTH

drugstore farmacia

pain dolore

fever febbre

headache mal di testa

stomachache mal di stomaco

toothache mal di denti

burn bruciatura

cramp crampo

nausea nausea

vomiting vomitare

medicine medicina

antibiotic antibiotico

pill/tablet pillola/pasticca

aspirin aspirina

I need to see a doctor. Ho bisogno di un medico.

I need to go to the hospital. Devo andare in ospedale.

I have a pain here... Ho un dolore qui...

She/he has been stung/bitten. È stata punta/morsa.

I am diabetic/pregnant. Sono diabetico/incinta.

I am allergic to penicillin/ cortisone. Sono allergico alla penicillina/cortisone.

My blood group is...positive/

negative. Il mio gruppo sanguigno
è... positivo/negative.

NUMBERS

0 zero
1 uno
2 due
3 tre
4 quattro
5 cinque
6 sei
7 sette
8 otto
9 nove
10 dieci
11 undici
12 dodici
13 tredici
14 quattordici
15 quindici
16 sedici
17 diciassette
18 diciotto
19 diciannove
20 venti
21 ventuno
30 trenta
40 quaranta
50 cinquanta
60 sessanta
70 settanta
80 ottanta
90 novanta
100 cento
101 centouno
200 duecento
500 cinquecento
1,000 mille
10,000 diecimila
100,000 centomila
1,000,000 un milione

TIME

What time is it? Che ora è?
It's one/three o'clock. E l'una/sono
le tre.

midday mezzogiorno
midnight mezzanotte
morning mattino
afternoon pomeriggio
evening sera
night notte
yesterday ieri
today oggi
tomorrow domani

DAYS AND MONTHS

week settimana
month mese
Monday lunedi
Tuesday martedi
Wednesday mercoledi
Thursday giovedi
Friday venerdi
Saturday sabato
Sunday domenica
January gennaio
February febbraio
March marzo
April aprile
May maggio
June giugno
July luglio
August agosto
September settembre
October ottobre
November novembre
December dicembre

VERBS

to have avere
to be essere
to go andare
to come venire
to want volere
to eat mangiare
to drink bere
to buy comprare
to need necessitare
to read leggere
to write scrivere
to stop fermare

to get off scendere
to arrive arrivare
to return ritornare
to stay restare
to leave partire

to look at guardare
to look for cercare
to give dare
to take prendere

Index

INDEX

List of Maps

Photo Credits

MAP SYMBOLS

═══ Expressway	○ City/Town	ⓘ Information Center	♠ Park	
═══ Primary Road	◉ State Capital	🅿 Parking Area	⚑ Golf Course	
∿∿∿ Secondary Road	◉ National Capital	♦ Church	✚ Unique Feature	
⋯ Unpaved Road	◎ Highlight	🍇 Winery	✎ Waterfall	
⋯⋯ Trail	★ Point of Interest	🚩 Trailhead	▲ Camping	
⋯⋯ Ferry	• Accommodation	🚇 Train Station	▲ Mountain	
━━ Railroad	▼ Restaurant/Bar	✈ Airport	⛷ Ski Area	
═══ Pedestrian Walkway	■ Other Location	✈ Airfield	🗺 Glacier	
━━ Stairs				

CONVERSION TABLES

$°C = (°F - 32) / 1.8$
$°F = (°C \times 1.8) + 32$
1 inch = 2.54 centimeters (cm)
1 foot = 0.304 meters (m)
1 yard = 0.914 meters
1 mile = 1.6093 kilometers (km)
1 km = 0.6214 miles
1 fathom = 1.8288 m
1 chain = 20.1168 m
1 furlong = 201.168 m
1 acre = 0.4047 hectares
1 sq km = 100 hectares
1 sq mile = 2.59 square km
1 ounce = 28.35 grams
1 pound = 0.4536 kilograms
1 short ton = 0.90718 metric ton
1 short ton = 2,000 pounds
1 long ton = 1.016 metric tons
1 long ton = 2,240 pounds
1 metric ton = 1,000 kilograms
1 quart = 0.94635 liters
1 US gallon = 3.7854 liters
1 Imperial gallon = 4.5459 liters
1 nautical mile = 1.852 km

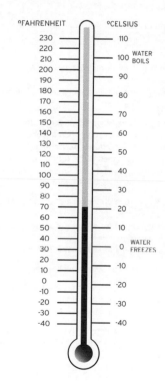

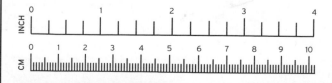

MOON FLORENCE & BEYOND
Avalon Travel
Hachette Book Group
1700 Fourth Street
Berkeley, CA 94710, USA
www.moon.com

Editor: Nikki Ioakimedes
Graphics and Production Coordinator: Lucie Ericksen
Cover Design: Faceout Studios / Derek Thornton
Interior Design: Domini Dragoone
Moon Logo: Tim McGrath
Map Editor: Kat Bennett
Cartographers: Karin Dahl and Kat Bennett
Proofreader: Elina Carmona

ISBN-13: 978-1-64049-067-3

Printing History
1st Edition — May 2019
5 4 3 2 1